An Introduction to Eighteenth-Century Fiction

Raising the Novel

John Skinner

palgrave

First published 2001 by
PALGRAVE
Houndmills, Basingstoke, Hampshire RG21 6XS and
175 Fifth Avenue, New York, N.Y. 10010
Companies and representatives throughout the world

PALGRAVE is the new global academic imprint of
St. Martin's Press LLC Scholarly and Reference Division and
Palgrave Publishers Ltd (formerly Macmillan Press Ltd).

ISBN 0–333–77624–0 hardback
ISBN 0–333–77625–9 paperback

This book is printed on paper suitable for recycling and
made from fully managed and sustained forest sources.

A catalogue record for this book is available
from the British Library.

Library of Congress Cataloging-in-Publication Data
Skinner, John, 1945–
   An introduction to eighteenth-century fiction: raising the novel /
John Skinner.
      p. cm.
   Includes bibliographical references and index.
   ISBN 0–333–77624–0
   1. English fiction—18th century—History and criticism.   I. Title.

PR851 .S52 2001
823'.509—dc21   00–048342

10 9 8 7 6 5 4 3 2 1
10 09 08 07 06 05 04 03 02 01

Printed in China

For Ledger and Mary

Contents

Preface

If asked what I personally regarded as the most significant feature of English eighteenth-century fiction, I would sidestep a wide range of pressing historical, political and ideological issues, to note frankly that – inside or outside the academy – ever fewer people actually read it. It is a suggestion which will upset teachers and scholars considerably, and publishers even more; rather than ignore such uncomfortable truths, however, one might briefly consider possible explanations for this trend.

One reason surely is an increasing sense of distance from the subject. This distance is less linguistic than cultural. There is little reason to assume that an Australian or an Indian student – let alone an Italian or German one – will be interested in the kinds of cultural continuities traditionally peddled by teachers of English literature: that the novel was invented in eighteenth-century England, eventually producing Jane Austen, who is in turn the fountain-head of a classic realist tradition. One can hardly even expect students in a post-industrial, multi-ethnic Britain or the United States to feel much affinity with small privileged sectors of *English* society almost three hundred years ago.

There are also aesthetic barriers. It is a critical cliché to note the formal and expressive range of the canonic eighteenth-century fiction: between them, Defoe, Richardson, Fielding, Smollett and Sterne seem to have anticipated just about every question confronting the modern novelist; and Aphra Behn even raises a number of issues overlooked by her male successors. But one might also reverse the coin: much of what is present in these writers will today seem remote and bizarre. There is, in fact, only one novelist from the 'long' eighteenth century who is not an endangered species outside the protectorates of university English departments: Jane Austen. Plenty of people read her, moreover, without the need of secondary literature. With the other five, however, one often suspects that critical and theoretical studies are an end in themselves: the primary text can occasionally disappear.

At a more banal level, the fiction of the period presents logistic problems. Richardson's *Clarissa* runs to a million words. For the same investment in time spent and pages read, the modern reader could cover many of the key works of, say, Caribbean or African literature in

English. And when one has solved the problem of fitting Richardson into a university syllabus, there remains the question of availability. Thanks to such collections as the Oxford *World's Classics* series, a core of eighteenth-century novels are now available in inexpensive editions; it may be some time, however, before such novels are on sale in supermarkets or on airport bookstalls.

All of the above reservations were taken into account in the writing of this book, which aims at both comprehensiveness and accessibility. There are no tactfully veiled summaries of Austen novels, but other works are discussed in a way intended to help students who have not yet read them, and even to stimulate some who never will. I personally consume eighteenth-century fiction avidly, but have tried to write as reader-friendly a survey as possible for those who don't. The two parts of the book, and even the individual chapters, may thus be read independently and in any order.

An Introduction to Eighteenth-Century Fiction is neither traditionally historical nor fashionably historicist. It provides a selective review of novel criticism, followed by discussions of canon formation and genre; there is then comprehensive treatment of Richardson and Fielding, followed by readings of major eighteenth-century novels with attempts to cross-reference their authors. There is little historical background in the sense of the Jacobite rebellions or the anti-Napoleonic backlash; there is, on the other hand, a consistent attempt to gender eighteenth-century fiction, and readers inherently hostile to such an approach would be advised to try for a refund at once. A more detailed conceptual model for the study is introduced at the end of the opening chapter.

During the completion of this book, there were no fellowships or endowments, no Fulbright scholarships or Guggenheim grants, no assistants to do my legwork or grade my students' papers, no Gatsby's guest-list of distinguished scholars on whom to inflict work in progress. An introductory survey like the present one is naturally indebted to earlier critics, so it is generally distinguished scholars who have unwittingly 'inflicted' their work on me. Needless to say, no study literally experienced as an 'infliction' makes it into the introductory chapter or concluding bibliography; the range and quality of previous scholars, in fact, is often inspiring and occasionally daunting.

Almost all research for this study was carried out in the Cambridge University Library, which copes reasonably well with the vast numbers of articles and monographs generated by Anglo-American academic overkill. The library staff were as courteous and helpful as I could have wished; but then I made no special demands. This particular institution also has the most pleasant working environment of any major library that I know.

Thanks are due once again to my department Chair, Risto Hiltunen, for his support and encouragement during the writing of this book. I am also grateful to my anonymous reader at Palgrave for detailed and constructive criticism; I was given the reader's complete annotated typescript, which – after the initial shock – proved extremely helpful. If the final result is any better than the original version, much of the credit should go to this reader. I am also grateful to my editor Margaret Bartley, who has the gift of suggesting very radical (and necessary) changes in the most tactful of ways; she has also waged a steady war on my excessive use of the parenthesis, one example of which she just missed.

There are no other people who helped substantially in the completion of this book. There are even two or three who, in the short term, may have hindered me, in the sense that the pleasure of their company was usually greater than anything offered by the more tedious stages of producing a study of eighteenth-century fiction. During the more enjoyable moments, on the other hand, I doubtless neglected the same individuals. I mention no names, but will now try to make amends.

Finally, besides my formal dedication, I would like to make a less conventional one to my readers. I had a book to write rather than an ideological axe to grind, and I hope that the results will prove both useful and entertaining to all.

Naantali, Nådendal   JOHN SKINNER
Valles Gratiae, Finland
john.skinner@utu.fi

Part I

Novel Departures

1
Critics and Theorists

Outside conventional literary histories, the vast secondary bibliography for eighteenth-century fiction can be broadly divided into two kinds of study. One typically provides a series of elaborate readings of canonical texts, together with a conceptual model that often seems tacked on as an afterthought. The other begins with a sophisticated hypothesis, which is then applied to a select group of writers – generally some permutation of Defoe, Richardson and Fielding.[1] The two approaches have accounted for much academic work over the last half-century. Within the first category, Dorothy Van Ghent's classic study of the English novel offered valuable insights into *Moll Flanders* and *Tom Jones*, whilst its hard-nosed reading of *Clarissa* shocks even yet;[2] Van Ghent's interpretations are still found recycled today, although few now remember her overall thesis.[3] In the second group, Nancy Armstrong's more recent *Desire and Domestic Fiction* has a well-articulated thesis for her 'political history of the novel', although it hardly refers to any actual eighteenth-century fiction beyond the first part of *Pamela*.[4]

The above examples reflect a perennial divide between critics and theorists. The ascendancy of theorists at the end of the twentieth century was underlined by Armstrong's next book, in collaboration with Leonard Tennenhouse, *The Imaginary Puritan*.[5] This inquiry into 'Literature, Intellectual Labor, and the Origins of Personal Life' located the origins of the eighteenth-century British novel in puritan New England: a thesis with at least superficial parallels to those legendary Cold War claims that jazz was invented in the Soviet Union. Such a comparison clearly travesties a fine study, based on the importance of the new 'print capitalism' in the American colonies, and later in Britain, too. The main intertextual link between New England and the emergent novel, however, seems to be the captivity narratives of Englishwomen held by Native Americans and the imprisonment of Richardson's Pamela in Mr B.'s house in Lincolnshire: the textual base for the theoretical model is now largely reduced to a single section of the first volume of *Pamela*.

3

Raising the Novel tries to bridge the gap between critics and theorists in two ways. First, it provides the present brief review of some major approaches to eighteenth-century fiction over the last half-century; it attempts to offer insights into the ideological preferences (or intellectual biases) of individual scholars, and orientate the reader approaching the secondary (or even the primary) literature for the first time. It is a highly selective, and inevitably personal, account, beginning with the opening of the fictional canon by feminist critics in the 1980s, before turning to the seminal studies of Ian Watt and Michael McKeon. It then considers a number of other studies that have complemented, without ever replacing, the work of these two scholars. This leads to a discussion – with examples – of 'universalist' *versus* 'historicist' approaches to eighteenth-century fiction, useful perhaps in view of the present virtual eclipse of the former method. The chapter then concludes with a brief exposition of the modestly innovatory parameters on which this study is based.

The other attempt to mediate between critics and theorists is evident in Chapter 2, which introduces an explicit pool of novelists, or corpus of novels, from Aphra Behn to Jane Austen; for eighteenth-century fiction did not dry up in the 1760s. The conceptual model of the study is then tested against *all* of these writers; if the conclusions are not sensational, they will at least be applicable to more than *Moll Flanders* or *Tom Jones*.

Finding a new critical base for eighteenth-century fiction is a daunting task. Even among the five writers complacently regarded as the 'great' early novelists – Defoe, Richardson, Fielding, Smollett and Sterne – there is an extraordinary range. If one then abandons the five 'monuments' for the often more rewarding sights around them, such diversity merely increases – together with the problems of the critic or theorist aiming at comprehensiveness. A case in point is the term 'novel' itself. The combined prefaces of *Robinson Crusoe*, *Moll Flanders*, *Pamela*, *Joseph Andrews* and *Roderick Random* (to cite only the most famous examples) do not mention the word; it was a concept with which most serious writers would not have chosen to be linked anyway. This significant omission hints at ambiguities lying in wait: for rather than charting the 'rise', 'emergence' or 'development' of a genre, some modern studies seem anachronistic back-projections of a classic realist novel that really emerged in the nineteenth century and still remains an important literary yardstick today. Contemporary critics themselves were unsure about the new literary form. There is a fine collection of early critical comments in Ioan Williams's *Novel and Romance, 1700–1800*; many will feel, however, that Williams's editorial lucidity is only matched by the extent of eighteenth-century literary confusion.[6]

And yet the writers of these prefaces (together with Sterne) are usually lumped together and touted – in the notorious metaphor – as the *fathers* of the novel. In a less overtly gendered trope, by analogy with the tradition of scriptural authority, the 'big five' are also traditionally identified as the *canonic* novelists. The third chapter examines this process of literary institutionalization more fully, beginning with the respectable and easily available early nineteenth-century editions of novels, assembled by such pioneers as Anna Laetitia Barbauld, William Mudford and Sir Walter Scott. One may combine the two concepts at once, however, and suggest that, if the Church *fathers* established *holy writ*, then novelistic *writ* (in the sense of what was published and propagated) retrospectively established the five fictional *holy fathers*.

Disputes over canonicity notwithstanding, the five eighteenth-century novelists cited undoubtedly form a remarkable group, for their lives no less than their writings. In either context, Defoe is exemplary: out in the politically premature Monmouth Rebellion against Catholic James II in 1685, and subsequently indicted but pardoned; unsuccessful in such varied activities as civet cat farming, brick and tile manufacture, marine insurance, oyster breeding, or the wool and linen trades (with spells in prison for business debts); more successful as first modern journalist, pamphleteer and government agent (possibly double agent as well); surviving the pillory unscathed and even profitably, by the distribution of a topical tract; turning at the age of fifty-nine to fiction and producing *Robinson Crusoe* almost incidentally among a dozen or so publications for the year 1719.[7]

Completing all his major narratives within five years, Defoe was then – if we are to accept conventional literary history – irresponsible enough to stop 'inventing the novel' and turn to such utterly dissimilar and time-consuming projects as the *Tour thro the Whole Island of Great Britain* (three volumes, 1724–7), the *Atlas Maritimus & Commercialis* (1728), or *The Compleat English Gentleman* (first published 1890). An English Flaubert would not have been so capricious. There is also a good case for regarding Samuel Richardson, rather than Defoe, as the 'father' of the modern English novel; and a possibly even better one for regarding Aphra Behn as its 'mother'. Both claims resurface in the course of this study. It is worth noting here, however, that the idea of Defoe as any kind of novelist at all may have originated with a canny bookseller towards the end of the century. The 1787 catalogue for Francis Noble's circulating library thus lists:

De Foe's Adventures of a Cavalier
                    of Roxana
                    of Moll Flanders
                    of Captain Singleton
De Foe's History of the Great Plague in London
De Foe's Voyage Round the World by a Course Never
    sailed before.[8]

Here is an early example of fiction as commodity. Such astute pack-
aging of a promising literary product would certainly have pleased
Defoe.

The careers of the other proto-canonic novelists are also strangely
haphazard. Individual precursors are sometimes acknowledged, but
none of the five could draw on a respectable and established novelistic
tradition. Fielding gravitated to fiction *via* journalism and the theatre,
while Richardson stumbled on it through his involvement with a letter-
writing guide. And yet, the relevance of all five to subsequent literary
history cannot be overemphasized; there is hardly an aspect of modern
fiction which is not anticipated by at least one of the group.

Here, then, is a drama with five principal *actors*, but not a single *actress*;
and in a period when most fiction was written by and for women, such
an anomaly requires comment. Enshrined within the *canon*, the five
stars generated a long-accepted literary orthodoxy. The canon may
have remained stable for so long because its components – according to
vague and rarely formulated criteria – were the 'best' of their kind, or
simply because it was perpetuated by men. These twin aspects of the
canon's easy informality and its apparent gender bias were neatly
conflated in a classic essay by Lillian Robinson, who once referred
wittily to a 'gentleman's agreement'.[9] If *canon formation* is always open
to attempts at *canon reformation*, then the first major efforts in this
direction were made by feminist critics in the 1980s. Three studies, in
particular, are worth closer attention.

Jane Spencer's *The Rise of the Woman Novelist*[10] divides neatly into
two halves, under the respective headings of 'The Woman Novelist as
Heroine' and 'Heroines by Women Novelists'. The first of these
sections deals with such political questions as the ideology of femininity, and such economic ones as women novelists and the literary
market; its centrepiece is a discussion of self-portraiture in the fiction of
Aphra Behn, Delarivier Manley and Jane Barker. The second section
discusses a number of individual novels, dividing the protagonists along
broad thematic lines: 'Seduced Heroines: The Tradition of Protest';

'Reformed Heroines: The Didactic Tradition'; and 'Romance Heroines: The Tradition of Escape'.

Dale Spender's *Mothers of the Novel*[11] also stresses the purely quantitative achievement of female novelists. It begins at an earlier point than Spencer and continues well into the nineteenth century. The central section of the study includes a list of over a hundred women writers before Jane Austen, together with some seven hundred works of fiction. Spender also criticizes such male-oriented accounts as Ian Watt's classic *The Rise of the Novel*. The latter's claims for Defoe, Richardson and Fielding as 'fathers of the novel' are the immediate stimulus for Spender's own title. Pointing out that about half of the two thousand novels produced in the eighteenth century were written by women, but that not *one* of these subsequently passed the test of greatness, Spender adds ironically that 'either the laws of probability are in need of revision or there are good grounds for hypothesizing that some other law is operating in the selection process' (p. 119). Her logic seems unassailable.

The third section includes brief essays on the neglect or belittlement of such individual authors as Sarah Fielding (overshadowed by her brother), Ann Radcliffe (*only* an author of Gothic sensationalism), Frances Burney (diminished to the scale of the 'tea-party'), or Maria Edgeworth (a *mere* exponent of regionalism and local colour). Broader in range than Spencer, Spender nevertheless invites reservations over her general approach. This may be fairly described as a massive exercise in affirmative action, and therefore risks becoming transformed into a simple inversion of the original male chauvinism. *Mothers of the Novel* is nevertheless a useful corrective to the kind of literary guide exemplified by Clive Probyn's *English Fiction of the Eighteenth Century*, from which one might assume that Frances Burney was the only significant female novelist of the period.[12]

Janet Todd's *The Sign of Angellica*[13] is arguably the most sophisticated of the three feminist attempts at canon *reformation*. The title refers to a painted sign displayed provocatively by the prostitute Angellica Bianca in Aphra Behn's play *The Rover* (1677). The first woman in England known to have made a decent living by selling her own (literary) wares, Behn may well have associated herself with the prostitute, whose initials she incidentally shares. In the context of the play, Angellica's gesture was regarded by prospective clients as blatant, unfeminine, but highly professional; the same attributes could equally well apply to Behn's own literary activities. Todd regards female fiction as beginning with an analysis of women's many social masks (she refers elsewhere to the 'constructed nature of female consciousness') and explores fluctuations in the female sign throughout the period. She then complements these speculations with a solid blend of literary history and close reading.

Spencer, Spender and Todd anticipate a wave of significant feminist studies in the 1990s. Ros Ballaster's *Seductive Forms*,[14] concentrating on the triumvirate of Behn, Manley and Eliza Haywood, was important both for its revisionary account of precursors of the modern novel and for its comparative study of French and English women writers. The French connection is further emphasized in April Alliston's *Virtue's Faults*,[15] which argues that, during the period from Behn to Austen, fictional boundaries were being drawn up and a literary canon established – in the form of a national *patrimony*. The very etymology suggests a connection with the father, as in *patrilinear* plots and *patrilinear* transmission. For as Claudia Johnson points out in her *Equivocal Beings*:

> The basic strategies of literary history – with its patrilinear models of influence and succession – are indeed inappropriate when applied to an author marginalized from the outset.[16]

Such writers, of course, are predominantly female; they also frequently use epistolary form. But letter-writing for Alliston refers both to 'a correspondence that crosses the boundaries of national tradition' and to 'a literary correspondence among French and English women authors'. The cultivation of this private sphere in both France and England, she suggests, effectively plots a '*mother* country' as a 'state of exile within the empire of the *father*land' [my emphasis]. Such techniques of exploring concealed tropes or springing hidden metaphors are an integral part of revisionist studies of eighteenth-century fiction.

The female tradition is also emphasized in Mary Anne Schofield's *Masking and Unmasking the Female Mind*.[17] This argues for the presence of a 'two-level rhetorical structure' in eighteenth-century fiction, in the sense that feminine stories are pitted against masculine plots. A paradigmatic example here would be Richardson's *Clarissa*, where the heroine's dramatic quest for self-realization clashes with the villain's manic campaign of sexual predation. Stronger as critic than as theorist, Schofield is particularly useful for her individual readings of a dozen women writers from Behn to Inchbald.

There is further historicization of female novelists, together with broad speculation on the economics and sociology of their fiction, in Catherine Gallagher's *Nobody's Story*,[18] a study of market performance among women writers throughout the long eighteenth century. Gallagher's title refers to the famous dedication in the private diary begun by a shy and diffident fifteen-year-old Frances Burney; the study itself deals with a number of literary and superliterary factors in eighteenth-century literary history: 'authorial personae, printed books, scandalous allegories, intellectual property rights, literary reputations, incomes, debts, and fictional characters' (p. xiii). All of these elements are seen as the exchangeable tokens of modern authorship, bringing economic prosperity to the increasing number of women writers who handled them successfully over the course of the century.

The groundbreaking feminist studies of the 1980s and 1990s are often written expressly against more traditional accounts of eighteenth-century fiction. Ian Watt's *The Rise of the Novel*[19] still remains the single most influential example of these, the yardstick by which all subsequent accounts are measured. A frequently neglected aspect of Watt's study is the timespan of its composition. First published in 1957, *The Rise of the Novel* was born – according to its preface – as a Cambridge fellowship dissertation in 1947, although its period of gestation actually began as early as 1938: details which make its continued currency all the more remarkable. F. R. Leavis's once even more influential *The Great Tradition* (revisited briefly in Chapter 2) shares exactly the same timespan, but now seems antediluvian by comparison.

Watt's argument has been neatly, if a little simplistically, described as the 'triple-rise theory': the rise of the middle class, leading to the rise of a new reading public, leading in turn to the rise of the novel. Watt's key concepts are *formal realism* and *individualism*. The former draws convincing analogies between the degree of credibility offered by the new fiction and that required by evidence in a court of law. In both *cases*, it might be added, authenticity is much concerned with gaining *conviction(s)*. Detail of this kind is so widespread in eighteenth-century fiction and so exceptional in earlier literary discourse, Watt argues, that it can be seen as a defining characteristic of the newly emerging novel. *Individualism*, on the other hand, refers to the powerful complex of capitalist enterprise, secularized Protestantism, and bourgeois–mercantile spirit which characterized eighteenth-century England. Defoe's heroes and heroines are the perfect embodiment of these qualities, and *Robinson Crusoe* is analysed in quasi-mythical terms, with its protagonist regarded as a kind of archetypal 'economic man'.

The Rise of the Novel has been criticized from various perspectives. First, it is charged with insularity and ethnocentricity, for its disregard of earlier Spanish and contemporary French fiction. For a period in which cultural and literary links between England and France were so strong, the second omission is particularly unfortunate. A second kind of criticism may be more significant. Examples of *formal realism*, the argument runs, occur in many earlier sources, from Elizabethan rogue literature back to Chaucer. Such claims rest in part on qualitative (and even quantitative) definitions of *formal realism*, and lead inevitably to a third critical objection. This suggests that the level of *formal realism* is not uniform in Defoe, Richardson and Fielding, the three· novelists on whom Watt's model is based. One may point to the persistent 'fairy-tale' and *romance* elements in *Pamela* or even to the almost mythical *cornu-copia* of useful remnants from *Robinson Crusoe*'s wreck, although the most problematic author is generally felt to be Fielding. The latter's fondness for classical imitation and the mock epic may be dismissed as mere functions of discourse rather than fundamentals of story, but the plausibility in a law court of a Thwackum or a Square (*Tom Jones*), not to mention a Beau Didapper or a Mrs Slipslop (*Joseph Andrews*), is open to question.

In addition to such traditional counter-arguments, however, there are also objections based on more recent historical research: the Cambridge Group for the History of Population and Social Structure has argued, for example, that the great increase in literacy occurred during the middle of the *seventeenth* century and not in the *eighteenth*; thus opening the prospect of three generations of readers sitting around idly, waiting for Watt's novel to 'rise'. What they might have read in the meantime can be gathered from such fascinatingly comprehensive surveys as Percy G. Adams's *Travel Literature and the Evolution of the Novel* and J. Paul Hunter's *Before Novels*.[20] And against Watt's casual admission that the majority of mid-eighteenth-century novelists were women, on the other hand, together with the more detailed argument that most readers were too, there remains Lawrence Stone's thesis in *Family, Sex, and Marriage in England, 1500–1800* that female literacy actually *declined* during the period Watt studies.[21]

The Rise of the Novel nevertheless remains the single work which most literary historians of the period (male ones at least) would be proudest to have written; it certainly deserves more credit for its achievements than criticism for its limitations. The latter, incidentally, are tactfully addressed in the title adopted for the book's Italian trans-lation: *Il romanzo borghese in Inghilterra* ('The Bourgeois Novel in England'): Watt is still invaluable, then, if one only remembers that there are other novels, other social classes and other countries.

There was no serious challenge to Watt until Michael McKeon's *The Origins of the English Novel, 1600–1740* thirty years later.[22] Besides its obvious shift in time scale and controlling metaphor (from 'rise' to 'origins'), together with a broader definition of the novel, McKeon's study is also more densely theoretical and correspondingly harder to summarize than Watt's. Its sophisticated dialectic draws on an impressive range of material, from the anthropology of Lévi-Strauss to the socio-political theory of Marx. At the heart of the book, however, is McKeon's own concept of the *instability of categories*, which he sees as characterizing the seventeenth century in both epistemology (or structures of knowledge) and ideology (or forms of belief). These two categories then form the basis for an extended discussion of what he defines, respectively, as 'Questions of Truth' and 'Questions of Virtue'.

As regards 'Questions of Truth', McKeon sees the 'narrative epistemology' of the seventeenth century as dominated by received authorities and earlier, or *a priori*, traditions, a tendency which he calls *romance idealism*. During the course of the century, however, the attitudes generated by this formation came under increasing attack, and were eventually supplanted by a radical new discourse, defined as *naive empiricism*. This process of negation was nevertheless something of a 'journey without maps', and the counter-critique loses its way through excessive enthusiasm and naivety, at which point it sheds its radical dimension and seems paradoxically closer to the original idealism: this third stage of a dialectic process is labelled *extreme scepticism*.

The abstract model, inevitably schematic in such a brief paraphrase, benefits by translation into concrete terms: one may thus begin by recalling the world of French romances, or other 'wonderful journeys' and 'tall stories' (*romance idealism*); and then imagine the relation of these to a *Robinson Crusoe* (1719) or *Moll Flanders* (1722) saturated in Watt's 'formal realism' (*naive empiricism*); and finally consider the thrust of a work such as *Gulliver's Travels* (1726) with its satire on the new knowledge and its exhaustive detail (*extreme scepticism*). It is not McKeon's intention to divide two centuries of fiction into three mutually exclusive categories: the examples offered here are relatively clear-cut for argument's sake, but the dialectic process they represent may often be observed in one and the same work.

With regard to 'Questions of Virtue', the pattern is identical; only the terms are different. The rigidly stratified social order of the seventeenth century (historically associated with the Stuarts), with its attendant hierarchy and privilege, reflects a dominant world view which may be described as *aristocratic ideology*; the social change and constitutional upheavals of the seventeenth century lead, in turn, to the increased power and influence of the mercantile classes, promoting a discourse of *progressive ideology*. But this tendency (like its epistemological counterpart of *naive empiricism*) also generates a counter-critique – more radical, but also similar in some respects to the original aristocratic enemy; McKeon refers to this as *conservative ideology*.

To translate abstract into concrete terms once more, one need look no further than Richardson's *Pamela*. On initial publication, the novel was criticized less for its socially subversive potential than for its sheer incredibility: if a country gentleman was really so desperate to sleep with a servant, he would have done so without any fuss (according to preval-ent *aristocratic ideology*); *Pamela* itself, with an insistence on individual dignity and the inviolability of the heroine, would thus exemplify the new *progressive ideology*; and finally, *Shamela* (and even *Joseph Andrews*), with their attacks on *Pamela* inspired by Fielding's personal scepticism, would exemplify the *conservative ideology* envisaged by McKeon's thesis. It should again be emphasized that the examples chosen are fairly explicit, whereas the three ideologies may also operate in a dialectic relationship within a single work.

The flexibility of McKeon's model is particularly helpful in explaining the case of Fielding, who seems both the innovator of a radical counter-critique and the guardian of an authoritarian neo-classical tradition. The fact that only the last third of McKeon's study applies his theoretical model to specific texts has disappointed some more literary-minded readers: these extended readings comprise six essays, neatly arranged in three thematically related pairs under the headings of 'Romance Transformations' (*Don Quixote* and *Pilgrim's Progress*); 'Parables of the Younger Son' (contrasting the protagonists of *Robinson Crusoe* and *Gulliver's Travels*); and 'The Institutionalization of Conflict' (readings of *Pamela* and *Jonathan Wild* – with extended references to *Joseph Andrews*).

One possible limitation to McKeon's study is that it provides no extended analysis of any individual text by a female writer. Even more significant, however, is a simple semantic point. It makes careful divisions between 'novel' and 'romance', whereas, for the many major theorists writing in French, German or Russian etc., the distinction is not normally available: the word *roman*, or its cognates, in these languages covers both English terms. On the other hand, English-speaking academics widely use the word 'novel' both as the broad equivalent of French, German or Russian *roman*, and in contradistinction to 'romance'. Even the great genre critic Northrop Frye divides prose narrative into the four elements of novel, romance, confession, and anatomy – where 'novel' clearly repres-ents one kind of prose narrative – but elsewhere uses the term 'novel' as synonymous with the higher category.[23] McKeon, too, is prone to such confusion of what semantics would call *hyponimic* and *hypernimic* relations. Readers can hardly be cautious enough in their use of the word 'novel' in eighteenth-century contexts.

Generally speaking, McKeon's dense account requires a great readerly investment for admittedly substantial intellectual returns. A lengthy detour through the literary 'precursor revolutions' of third-century Greece and twelfth-century Europe to culminate in a reading of *Jonathan Wild* nevertheless seems a massive theoretical base – to borrow the author's favourite Marxist terminology – for a modest fictional superstructure: the academic equivalent, perhaps, of using a steamroller to crack a nut. On the other hand, it is certainly more helpful to understand Fielding's first narrative as the working-out of a dialectic process (McKeon) rather than an early reject from a great novelistic tradition (Leavis).

It should also be remembered that McKeon, in relation to Watt, had the benefit of thirty years of hindsight. When *The Rise of the Novel* was published, approaches to fiction seemed to divide fairly evenly between Watt's 'historicism' and the 'universalism' of Frye. The universalist sense that the eighteenth-century novel did not differ essentially from earlier or later fiction obviously precludes discussion of the 'rise' or 'origins' of anything called the 'novel'. Ahistorical approaches are now unfashionable, although two such studies deserve mention here.

The most striking feature of the first example, Scholes and Kellogg's *The Nature of Narrative*, is thus its range.[24] In their attempt to *decentre* the classic realist novel, the authors return to the earliest recorded narrative, the *Epic of Gilgamesh*. Appearing some twenty-six centuries before the beginning of our own era, the latter certainly adds a new perspective to the chronology of Western literature, placing Aristotle (currently) at an approximate half-way point, and the Latin classics well within the latter half of the tradition. Lively, original, and clearly *universalist* in tendency, Scholes and Kellogg say predictably little about the 'novel' as such, and even less about its alleged emergence in the course of the eighteenth century. Even today, however, these writers still provide a healthy corrective to more narrowly specialized views.

A more influential example of the ahistorical approach is Northrop Frye's *The Secular Scripture*,[25] which – indirectly at least – has a great deal to say about novels. Some idea of Frye's own form of universalism (with its unique blend of myth and archetype) can be gathered from the following characteristic passage:

There are therefore four primary narrative movements in literature. These are, first, the descent from a higher world; second, the descent to a lower world; third, the ascent from a lower world; and fourth, the ascent to a higher world. All stories in literature are complications of, or metaphorical derivations from, these four radical narratives.　(p. 97)

The six sections of Frye's study are distinctively entitled: 'The World of Man'; 'The Context of Romance'; 'Our Lady of Pain: Heroes and Heroines of Romance'; 'The Bottomless Dream: Themes of Descent'; '*Quis Hic Locus?* Themes of Ascent'; and 'The Recovery of Myth'. Frye's central thesis is that the plot movements of 'classic realist novels' are in fact transformations (he uses the psychoanalytical term *displacement*) of romance motifs. Frye's sparkling erudition seems less dated than the persistent trendiness of Scholes and Kellogg. Ultimately, the difference may simply be that between two modish academics who dismiss adherents to the realist tradition as 'headless chickens unaware of the decapitating axe', and a critic of genius sometimes regarded as the most profoundly original in the English language.

Of the two studies, Frye's clearly has the most to offer for fiction of a period often unable to distinguish conceptually – or even nominally – between 'novel' and 'romance'. One of Watt's criteria for the new *formal realism* was the abandonment of fantastic romance plots; but in spite of Richardson's introduction of an authenticating editorial apparatus or Fielding's repeated reservations about the 'marvellous', it is doubtful whether this aim is entirely achieved, even in such canonic texts as *Pamela, Joseph Andrews,* or *Tom Jones.* Frye's theory of *displacement* seems increasingly attractive here; and in the case of Smollett, who actually described his highly realistic first novel, *Roderick Random* (1748), as 'a Romance in two small volumes', it may well be indispensable.

At the end of the twentieth century, however, it was historicist rather than universalist approaches that dominated. The major intellectual influences here were the French cultural historian Michel Foucault, and the Russian literary theorist Mikhail Bakhtin.

Foucault's highly personal and iconoclastic *History of Sexuality* is thus the major inspiration of Nancy Armstrong's previously mentioned *Desire and Domestic Fiction.*[26] Armstrong's 'political history of the novel' develops a simple but radical three-part thesis (the word *agenda* is hardly out of place here): *first,* sexuality is not a biological constant, but a cultural construct, and therefore possesses a history; *second,* rather than fiction imitating life, it was written representations of the self (predominantly in the novel) which allowed the modern individual to become an economic and psychological reality – or, more reductively, life presumably imitates fiction; and *third*, this modern individual was first and foremost a *woman*.

The first suggestion reflects Foucault's claim that the presumed objective constants of sex are in fact merely a *discourse of sexuality* – or, expressed more crudely, just *talk* about sex (rather as the so-called facts of history are in reality *historiography*: i.e. *writing* about history). The second point alludes to the epistemological chicken-and-egg debate at the heart of Foucault's thought: whether 'discourse' precedes or predicates 'reality' rather than succeeding and reflecting it. The third point returns indirectly to the influential arguments of Watt and McKeon: for Armstrong has effectively combined an emphatic gendering of Watt's 'individualism' with McKeon's argument for the subversion of *aristocratic ideology*. In the eighteenth century, according to Armstrong, then, specific female ideals were formulated and the virtues of the new woman were prescribed, predominantly, in conduct guides, educational treatises, and *domestic fiction*. This generated an anti-aristocratic ideology which located women's desirability, as opposed to that of men, in elements other than rank or family name. Or, in the author's own words: 'the female relinquishes political control to the male in order to acquire exclusive authority over domestic life, emotions, taste, and morality' (p. 41).

Later sections of Armstrong's study examine such topics as eighteenth-century courtesy literature ('The Rise of the Domestic Woman'); aristocratic ideals under threat from a new, urbanized gentry ('A Country House That is Not a Country House'); and the careful regulation of the woman's sphere ('Economy That is Not Money'). Armstrong also discusses the exclusion of eighteenth-century women writers (and readers) from the classical tradition, and the subsequent legitimation of the new fiction by conduct books or courtesy literature. She concludes with readings of *Pamela*, that archetypal synthesis of fiction and conduct book, and *Emma*, in some ways the culmination of a tradition.

Although its direct engagement with fictional texts is fairly sporadic, *Desire and Domestic Fiction* is suggestive in several ways. Most obviously, the argument for a cultural divide produced by women's exclusion from the classical tradition correlates closely with my own attempts, below, to group eighteenth-century novels around 'literary' (elitist male) and 'non-literary' or 'documentary' (female or *demotic*) poles. There is, in fact, a whole series of broadly analogous divisions in eighteenth-century letters, including Ancients *versus* Moderns, Augustanism *versus* sensibility and 'public' *versus* 'private'. A useful umbrella pairing, also elaborated below, might be a contrast of the *hieratic* (or esoteric and also, by association, elitist) with the *demotic* (or popular); and here it is amusing to note the semantic quirk by which the word *demotic* – once the *s*-for-sex letter has been removed – is a perfect anagram of *domestic*.

Another major insight of *Desire and Domestic Fiction* is the recognition of Jane Austen's access to a 'massively stable framework of domestic relations'; to a vast degree, these elements had also been fictionally processed. Ian Watt referred famously to Austen's synthesis of Fielding's realism of judgement and Richardson's realism of presentation, as if there was nothing else of value for the next sixty years. Armstrong, like several revisionist feminist critics, has done much to counter this view by emphasizing women writers in the second half of the eighteenth century.

In contrast to Armstrong's study, Lennard J. Davis's *Factual Fictions*[27] is concerned less with ideology (or systems of beliefs) than with epistemology (or theories of knowledge). His historicist approach explores 'taxonomies' and 'categories' used consciously or unconsciously, in the seventeenth and eighteenth centuries, to *divide* what we today call narrative. He argues that such distinctions as fact/fiction, history/fabrication, fantasy/representation are not self-evident divisions, but *subjective* and *contextualized*. He also suggests that *fact* and *fiction* were not significant generic distinctions at the end of the seventeenth century, and writes perceptively of the relation between *newes* or 'new things' and the modern concept of *news*, stressing the etymological link both share with the word *novel*. The 'factual fictions' of the eighteenth-century English novel, Davis concludes, thus denote a kind of *fiction* which imitates or impersonates the *factual* or 'documentary'. In spite of its original elements, however, there is one sense in which *Factual Fictions* merely reformulates Watt's classic argument for the new importance of *formal realism*. After the elegance of Davis's arguments, moreover, it is slightly disappointing to find his thesis illustrated by straight readings of the old firm (Defoe, Richardson and Fielding), long established, in a rather tired metaphor, as the 'fathers of the novel'.

But if these and other metaphors, concealed or revealed, are part of any critical or theoretical discourse, they also permeate the novels themselves. Some of the most sophisticated work on eighteenth-century fiction analyses what may be described as dominant or characteristic 'narrative tropes'; it includes studies by Terry Castle, John Bender and James Thomson.

Castle's *Masquerade and Civilization* transfers the theoretical emphasis from Foucault to Bakhtin. The key work here is Bakhtin's

Rabelais and his World, reflecting this critic's lifelong interest in folklore and carnival; a spectacular manifestation of the latter is the *masquerade* in eighteenth-century England.[28] Castle's privileged trope is an evocative image (more strictly, a *metonym*; or 'part for the whole') with which to convey the protean nature of London itself. The contemporary essayist Joseph Addison thus talked of the city's 'promiscuous Multitude'; and the epithet is particularly apt, since – as Castle points out – much opposition to masquerades was grounded in a belief that they encouraged female sexual freedom, and even female emancipation in general. From such a premise, it is only a short step to comparable literary upheavals, and Castle proposes the masquerade as the 'master trope of destabilization' – i.e. the great plot loosener – in the eighteenth-century English novel. Both fictional and real-life masquerades, with their related happenings, provided a great erotic charge; even in Austen, who is rarely so unbuttoned, the ball without the masquerade is a catalyst in *Pride and Prejudice*, as is the masquerade without the ball (for such, effectively, are the amateur theatricals) in *Mansfield Park*.

In view of its announced intention of examining one particularly fertile trope in eighteenth-century fiction, *Masquerade and Civilization* should not be judged as a comprehensive model for the 'rise' or 'origins' of the novel. But Castle's self-imposed restrictions are more than compensated by her important contribution to cultural history. The argument that the masquerade threatened patriarchal structures was admittedly questioned in Catherine Craft-Fairchild's revisionist *Masquerade and Gender*.[29] According to this study, women writers showed that the apparent freedoms of the masquerade were in fact 'nothing more than sophisticated forms of oppression'. Despite this brush with a more sceptical feminist orthodoxy, however, Castle's *Masquerade and Civilization* will provide an important critical stimulus for years to come.

John Bender's *Imagining the Penitentiary* also pursues a single trope or metaphor in eighteenth-century fiction.[30] This study, too, is less a comprehensive theoretical model for the novel than a contribution to cultural studies, with its analysis of the role of fiction in the development of penal institutions. Bender's conceptual frame is a brilliant synthesis of Foucault and Bakhtin: reduced to its simplest terms, his argument is that the 'rise' of the modern novel is analogous to, and contemporary with, the 'rise' of the modern prison.[31] The transition from the traditional, open and promiscuous prison to the modern organized penitentiary thus parallels the movement from traditional, open and promiscuous fiction to the modern organized novel. Key

terms in both processes are Foucault's concepts of *discipline* and *control* –
in the case of Richardson, one might want to add *punish*! Bender notes
that 'sentences' and 'sentencing' are common to both 'processes'; he
might also have revisited Watt's analogy between legal and narrative
process in the context of 'formal realism': for both court evidence (at
least in the prosecution's view) and the new narrative are similarly
intent on gaining *conviction(s)*.

But prisons were also traditionally a *microcosm* or miniature version
of the great outside world, whose social institutions they often parodied
(Smollett's novels, with their many prison scenes, are unsurpassed in
this respect). The potential for anarchy or misrule in this little world-
turned-upside-down therefore has an obvious relation to Bakhtin's own
scenarios of carnivalization.

The central chapters of Bender's study develop a number of striking
literary and legal parallels in the lives and works of Defoe, Fielding,
Hogarth and John Gay, author of the sensationally successful proto-
musical *The Beggar's Opera*, set in London's criminal underworld.
Defoe is obviously relevant here, with his pseudo-autobiographical
'ghost-writing' from the same environment; Fielding, as this study later
argues, may be even more significant, with his simultaneous founding of
a 'new province of writing' and initiation of a new era in judicial reform.

A more recent exploration of a single strategic trope, that of money,
is James Thompson's *Models of Value*.[32] In eighteenth-century England,
Thompson argues, 'both political economy and the novel grew out of
concerns with values and variables'. The age was an important transitional period for monetary reform; it was characterized by a change in
emphasis between intrinsic and extrinsic value, or what coins weigh
versus what they say (stamped on their surface, that is): as the currency
was repeatedly clipped or otherwise debased, the gap between these two
concepts increasingly diverged. The failure to restore and preserve the
coinage led to the emergence of a nominalist conception of currency
(i.e., one unrelated to the real value of the material it contained), culminating in the introduction of Bank of England notes towards the end
of the period. Political economists, Thompson notes, were gradually
forced to acknowledge that, in effect, 'silver was not always silver',
although many novelists continued to insist that 'love was always love'.

According to economic historian Joyce Appleby, however, eighteenth-century England moved towards 'an abstract and consistent and
therefore predictable model of exchange' (p. 128). Novels came to follow the same kind of internal consistency; or, in Thompson's suggestive
comment on the didactic tendencies of eighteenth-century fiction:

While individual novels do not answer individual questions of choice –
this potential mate versus that one – they do offer up a general model
of mating, against which the individual can measure and judge her
own circumstances. In my view, this claim, whereby novels insist that
they describe things as they really are, is the singular, most distinctive, and most powerful feature of novels en masse. Individually, they
are all plainly fictions or fantasies, but collectively they can be trusted
to tell the whole truth.   (Thompson, p. 12)

Or, to complete the analogy, a single example of the new banknotes
perhaps seemed unimpressive, but their sum total constituted a sophisticated new monetary system. Erotic psychology and sexual ethics, then,
adopted new literary conventions, rather as economic exchange
accepted new, if intrinsically almost worthless, currency. It is predictably difficult for a literary study to maintain such levels of abstraction
throughout, and Thompson's later chapters are exhaustive applications
of his own model in close readings of Defoe, Fielding, Burney and
Austen.

The paradigms of Castle, Bender and Thompson represent some of
the most sophisticated and original work in the field of eighteenth-
century scholarship. These subtle readings of tropes and metaphors are
also combined with a profound awareness of contemporary cultural
factors; they thus remain historicist rather than universalist in outlook.

For an example of the universalist approach which is equally sensitive
to cultural context, one may turn to Margaret Anne Doody's *The True
Story of the Novel*.[33] A clear indication of what the reader may expect
from this massive comparative study emerges from Doody's polemical
introduction: it is *contra* Watt and McKeon (for their cultural isolation-
ism); *contra* Bakhtin (for his reliance on a nineteenth-century evolutionary paradigm); *contra* the great Hungarian critic Georg Lukacs (for
his ideological bias towards Marxism) and the equally famous German
scholar Erich Auerbach (for a similar bias towards 'realism'); *contra* the
English historian Lawrence Stone – and all the literary critics who
accept him unquestioningly – for the dubious thesis that 'affectional
individualism' and the 'companionate marriage' were invented in the
eighteenth century.

After such a spectacular opening, Doody goes on to offer what is
virtually three books in one: a new mapping of Greek and Latin prose
fiction;[34] a more innovatory account of the reception and influence of
this body of writing in western Europe into the nineteenth century and
beyond; and a detailed analysis of certain literary tropes, recalling

Northrop Frye's *The Secular Scripture* and displaying traces of Jungian archetypal criticism.

Doody is particularly scathing in her attack on what she regards as the provincial character of most Anglo-American novel criticism, with its theories of the 'rise', 'origin' or 'development' of a narrative form unique to eighteenth-century England: she characterizes this approach, which ignores most prose fiction written outside England, or before the eighteenth century, as having 'taken place by and large within [the] sound of the parish pump'. Her scholarly range is impressive, although, in her zeal to see various Greek novelists as racially aware, multi-cultural proto-feminists, she occasionally risks a parochialism of her own: the more modish politically correct variety peddled by the late twentieth-century American academy.

Such moments are nevertheless eclipsed by the range of insights available to a scholar of Doody's ability. To choose an example from each section of her study: the debate on whether French, German and Russian really 'lack' a distinction between 'novel' and 'romance', or whether English simply makes a spurious one; the extensive finds in eighteenth-century fiction of echoes, analogues and even direct imitation of classical prose models; and the sensitive discussion of the 'labyrinth' trope, a metaphor not only for the intricacies of prose narrative, but even for the complexities of life itself.

Doing justice to Margaret Doody, or even Michael McKeon and Janet Todd, in a couple of paragraphs is a daunting enterprise. Equally troubling, however, is the gap between criticism and theory, on the one hand, and the literary-historical or merely encyclopaedic. At this point, therefore, a dose of pure reductivism may be a useful corrective. Perhaps the most striking characteristic of eighteenth-century novels, let it be said then, is not some technical or ideological common denominator, but the point noted earlier that nobody – outside the academy – actually reads them. In his novel, *I Like It Here*, Kingsley Amis has his protagonist visit the grave of Henry Fielding in Lisbon and remark that it was perhaps worth dying so young if one was to become the only novelist of the period whom the modern reader could still enjoy without making special allowances. It is a fair comment – from Amis's characteristically truculent, no-nonsense protagonist – although it is tempting to add that, if an equivalent reader existed two centuries on, he would probably only find pleasure in Kingsley Amis.

Much scholarly energy is invested in attempts to raise novels and novelists to canonic status. This is a generally harmless exercise: were it not for the fact that the battles for Frances Burney are largely fought and won, one might thus argue that *Evelina* is a 'greater' novel than three or four of Smollett's, or anything produced by Richardson (bar *Clarissa*) and Fielding (with the possible exception of *Tom Jones*). The activity is also fairly pointless, however, and one could just as well move in the opposite direction to take a new hard look at some hallowed classics: why will no scholar admit that *Joseph Andrews* is tedious and Smollett's *Sir Launcelot Greaves* excruciating, whilst *Pamela* rarely rises above the unintentionally comic?

A number of these revaluations are gender related, and the issue of the apparent superiority in traditional canons of male *authors* over female *novelists* may be illuminated by a slightly facetious parallel from the world of the automobile. Well-disseminated, presumably male-inspired, folklore has it that women are generally worse drivers than men. The claim seems equally difficult to prove or refute, although the practice among insurance companies of setting lower premiums for female drivers should give men, at least, pause for thought. In defiance of political correctness and all those hard-nosed actuaries, however, let us claim for the sake of argument that men *are* better drivers – although not by much; for by prevalent social patterns, according to which the male in any household normally has a monopolistic (if not fetishistic) relation to the car, they should be *much* better drivers.

The comparison may be whimsical, but hopefully not irrelevant, and writers are arguably harder to assess than drivers. Where the all-male *proto*-canon is concerned, then, one might not even have expected female writers – with their social, economic, and cultural disadvantages – to have made the first fifty, let alone the first five. Aphra Behn, the first English modern novelist, was scathing about male exclusionary policies in the realm of learning:

> Permitting not the Female Sex to tread
> The Mighty Paths of Learned *Heroes* Dead.
> The Godlike *Vergil* and Great *Homers* Muse
> Like Divine Mysteries are conceal'd from us. . . . [35]

A better analogy than female drivers here might be drawn from those countries where women are still not allowed to drive at all. In equivalent literary terms, in fact, this may bring fortune in misfortune; for only Fielding and a few acolytes apparently needed a grounding in Homer or Virgil in order to do us a novel. For the latter, it should be repeated, is essentially a demotic genre; women were obviously attracted to it precisely because it did not require a classical education; and as female novelists from Behn to Austen helped to perpetuate the form, they in turn consolidated this popular or vernacular element.

The implication of this kind of argument is surely that eighteenth-century fiction must be read in new ways. It hardly matters if Aphra Behn's *Love-Letters Between a Nobleman and His Sister* is the first modern English novel; on *first* encounter, some may still find it unreadable, although *Oronooko* is mercifully shorter and thematically suited to current academic preoccupations with race and gender. When Behn or Manley are revisited by such able revisionist scholars as Janet Todd or Ros Ballaster, however, sparks fly again much as they did three centuries ago. Even the tired sentimental motif of the lover's broken vow acquires a fresh significance in an age when political allegiances could similarly crumble, with literally fatal consequences, overnight; and this kind of allegory is even clearer in Behn's politically, no less than sexually, treacherous aristocratic rakes: for, as a helpful English collo-quialism might have it, they screw the country as cynically as they screw their women.

A judicious combination of historicist and revisionist readings, then, is the key to appreciating much eighteenth-century fiction. This applies not only to the early amatory fiction discussed by Ballaster and Todd, but to the polite romance, the novel of sensibility or Gothic fiction from the end of the period. In this way, even an (anti)-romance such as Charlotte Lennox's *The Female Quixote*, dismissed by short-sighted contemporaries as fifty years out of date, acquires a new urgency; the effect of rereading *Evelina*, on the other hand, is electric. Where senti-mental fiction is concerned, critics such as Nicola Watson show how epistolary form and sentimental content were by no means as anodyne as they often seem today.[36] Both elements contained strong ideological ballast, and Watson draws suggestive analogies between sensibility and political radicalism, or seduction and revolution: all four elements represented subversion and a threat to the patriarchal order of the day. The recuperation of Gothic as female protest writing, finally, is – since studies like Mary Poovey's *The Proper Lady and the Woman Writer* – perhaps the best-known and most developed example of critical revisionism in the context of eighteenth-century fiction.[37]

The most interesting recent studies of the period, as this introduc-tion suggests, have come from feminist scholars. There are certain limitations, however, in reducing academic work to a kind of affirmat-ive action: all significant eighteenth-century novelists are not women any more than all significant jazz musicians are black; admittedly, though, just as the immediate musical associations in this context are

African American, so the immediate literary ones should probably be female.

The idea that there were no significant novels between Burney's *Evelina* (1778) – or even Smollett's *Humphry Clinker* (1771) – and Austen is overturned by the so-called Jacobin or radical novel: its major exponents included three men, William Godwin, Thomas Holcroft and Robert Bage. Scholarly interest in this group effectively dates from Gary Kelly's *The English Jacobin Novel, 1780–1805* and Marilyn Butler's *Jane Austen and the War of Ideas*; the emphasis on women writers was nevertheless restored by Eleanor Ty's *Unsex'd Revolutionaries* and Kelly's own fine follow-up study, *Women, Writing and Revolution, 1790–1827*.[38]

My own interest in the present field dates from a doctoral dissertation on Cervantes's *Don Quixote* and the eighteenth-century English novel, where three of the canonic figures haunting this introduction required separate chapters: Fielding, above all, for *Joseph Andrews* – explicitly 'written in the manner of Cervantes'; Smollett, both for his translation of *Don Quixote* and his reworking of the novel in *Sir Launcelot Greaves*; Sterne, for his elaboration of such quixotic avatars as the Shandy brothers and Yorick. Other more obvious fictional borrowings – *The Spiritual Quixote, The Female Quixote* etc. – became prominent landmarks along the way. Defoe and Richardson, predictably, were unpromising subjects, either for their interpretive insights into Cervantes's characters, or for what I then ingenuously regarded as 'literary influences'. This comparative approach has been continued by several scholars, but now seems to have received its definitive exposition in Ronald Paulson's *Don Quixote in England*.[39]

Even beyond the context of Cervantes, however, there is a fairly obvious division among the five traditionally canonic novelists, ranging Fielding, Smollett and Sterne against Defoe and Richardson. Other writers could then be similarly polarized according to the relative prominence of 'literary' *versus* 'documentary' (or 'pseudo-documentary') elements in their works: say the classical or continental literary sources of *Joseph Andrews, Tristram Shandy* or *The Female Quixote versus* the homegrown domestic letters and journals of *Pamela, A Journal of the Plague Year*, or *Evelina*. It is a complex issue. There are no pure examples of what (in the terminology of linguistics) might be called 'prescriptive' (i.e. literary) or 'descriptive' (i.e. documentary) narratives – one need look no further than Sterne's unashamed *literary* borrowing of *documentary* sources – although the fiction of Fielding, generally, and Smollett, in particular, clearly tends strongly towards the first category. The preface to *Joseph Andrews* seeks a repectable pedigree for the novel in Cervantes and classical epic; that of *Roderick Random* offers distinguished precedents (Cervantes once again and Lesage) for using romance in the service of satire.

Here one may briefly leave one broad distinction for another, which initially – but only initially – seems unrelated. By a curious semantic twist, most of the Latin languages, unlike English, express literary *genre* and sexual *gender* by a single word: cf. Latin *genus*, Spanish *género*, Italian *genere* etc.; the exception is French, with *gendre* and *genre*, although even here the etymological link is obvious. In English, without grammatical *gender* in the language and dependent on the French loan *genre* in literary contexts, the two terms seem both distinct and diffuse. The sexual connotations of *genre* seem to have been removed or, perhaps more accurately, repressed. What is repressed characteristically returns, however, and the ambivalence surrounding (English) 'genre' and 'gender' can hardly be ignored.

The precise link between the ambiguities of *genre* and the predominance of *literary* or *non-literary* elements in individual eighteenth-century novels is easily illustrated. All of the feminist scholars discussed in this chapter argue, in various ways, for the centrality of women writers from Behn to Austen. Nancy Armstrong goes beyond simple canon (re)formation to trace the emergence of a domestic fiction where the individual is no longer represented by title or status but by 'more subtle nuances of behaviour' (p. 4). This process of feminization was mainly implemented by female *novelists*. The latter term is significant, since it invites another piece of semantic sleight, now contrasting male *authors* (suggesting *authority* – explicitly *classical* in many cases) with female *novelists* (and the promise of something *new*).

This is not to equate feminocentric novels naively with the biological *sex* of the writer; but the autocratic cast of Fielding's or Smollett's narrators (with reservations only for the multi-focal *Humphry Clinker*) is striking. It suggests a fictional equivalent to the historians that Armstrong wittily describes as representing the history of male institutions – *to a man*. In the long run, it was the 'documentary' or 'feminizing' tendencies which prevailed in English fiction, at least until Sir Walter Scott: in pure *novel* terms, the burlesque of Fielding's mock-epics-in-prose and the misogyny of Smollett's Juvenalian satire came to seem outmoded male aberrations.

The division between 'literary' and 'non-literary' or 'documentary' is admittedly crude; the deconstruction of *genre* and *gender*, contrasting male *authors* with female *novelists*, is tendentious. The attempt to synthesize the two paradigms then creates fresh problems: Sarah Fielding was, after all, a considerable classical scholar; Samuel Richardson was a man of very modest learning. One way of neutralizing the opposition (in both senses) would be to use some less explicitly gendered pairing for the proposed distinction, such as *patrician* and *popular*, or *esoteric* and *exoteric*, to define the gap between two kinds of writing. The word "patrician" – defined by the *Oxford English Dictionary* (*OED*) as 'belonging to the rank of the *patres*, "fathers"' and 'person of noble birth or rank' – might almost do for Fielding. Problems immediately emerge, however, since the eighteenth-century novel does not begin or end with *Joseph Andrews*, whilst the modern associations of the counter term, *popular*, make it as anachronistic in this context as similarly modern terms like 'enthusiasm' or 'democracy'.

The other pairing – *esoteric* and *exoteric* – is first used by the Greek satirist, Lucian, who ascribes to Aristotle a classification of his own works into precisely these categories. The *OED* defines 'esoteric' as 'designed for, or appropriate to, an inner circle of advanced or privileged disciples'; and 'exoteric' as 'designed for or suitable to the generality of disciples; communicated to outsiders, intelligible to the public'. In the context of the male–female or (virtually equivalent) 'learned–unlearned' divide in eighteenth-century letters, Lucian's contrast is suggestive. Against this proposal, on the other hand, it should be noted that the original usage implied contrasting elements within a *single* writer; whilst a subsidiary gloss for 'esoteric' ('pertaining to a select circle; private, confidential') seems as appropriate to the female *côterie* with which Richardson surrounds himself as it does to the original male preserve of the Scriblerus Club (including Swift, Pope and Gay) so admired by Fielding.

The most suitable pairing, then, might be *hieratic* and *demotic*. The basic definition of the latter ('popular, plebeian, common, democratic') is unexceptionable: it seems made for that 'scurrilous party hack' Defoe, or the 'vulgar, canting' Richardson. *Hieratic*, on the other hand, is glossed as 'pertaining to or used by the priestly class; used in connection with sacred subjects'; whilst the adjective also referred more specifically to a style of ancient Egyptian writing featuring '*abridged forms of hiero-glyphics*'. This distinct combination of formal economy and intellectual exclusivity – a *word to the wise* as it were – characterizes a certain kind of eighteenth-century fiction, more easily identified with Fielding than with Richardson. And finally, *hieratic* also applies to 'a style of art (esp. Egyptian or Greek), in which earlier types or methods, fixed by religious tradition, are conventionally adhered to': here is the rather ponderous and self-serving preface to *Joseph Andrews* in a nutshell.

There is, however, one more example of polarization, a broad formal or technical division which correlates very highly with the various binary positions already suggested. It would contrast the *third-person*, traditionally styled 'omniscient', narrator of *Tom Jones* or Charlotte Lennox's *The Female Quixote* to the *first-person* internal or 'intradi-egetic' central voices of *Pamela* or *Evelina*. Armed with these several pairs of related co-ordinates, one might actually propose literary *identi-kits* for two ideal writers at either end of this long narrative continuum: a patrician or hieratic, highly imitative, classically inspired male *author* with a fondness for third-person narrators; and a popular or demotic, strikingly innovative, topically motivated female *novelist* favouring first-person narrators. Readers may provide their own candidates for either post, although the obvious contenders are once again Fielding and – after a suitable sex-change – Richardson.

This basic contrast is nevertheless tempered by a tendency in each of these writers to gravitate towards the opposite pole. Between *Jonathan Wild* and *Amelia*, for example, Fielding abandons his facetious narrators – if not actually his third-person narrative – as he moves from mock-heroic satirical squib to an ostensibly feminocentric novel. Richardson, on the other hand, gradually rejects his role as mere editor of other people's letters to become – when he published the collective *Maxims* from his three novels – an authoritative source in his own right. Chapters 4 and 5, therefore, discuss the complete fictional output of Richardson and Fielding, seeing their respective literary careers as great trajectories moving in opposite directions from each other.

Not all divisions in eighteenth-century fiction are so clear. The readings of paired texts which constitute the second half of this study thus represent interactions and contradictions, as much as demonstra-tions or affirmations, of the binary distinctions outlined here. Behn's *Oroonoko* and Defoe's *Moll Flanders* (Chapter 6) are a case in point. In spite of her sex and relatively modest social origins, Behn was a High Tory Catholic royalist, whose penchant for heroics was closely related to her sympathies for the old Stuart absolutism; Defoe, on the other hand, received a dissenting education arguably superior to anything Oxford or Cambridge could offer at the time, although his first-person ghosting of a humble female protagonist gave him little chance to display any learning.

Sterne's *Tristram Shandy* and Smollett's *Humphry Clinker* (Chapter 7) are similarly ambivalent. A humble, if Cambridge-educated, country parson before becoming a literary lion in his fifties, Sterne writes the most intimate and circumstantial of first-person narratives, whilst yet revelling in satire and learned wit. Smollett, on the other hand, for whom the scholarly Dr Johnson thought only a Latin epitaph was good enough, produced one of the great epistolary novels of the century. His earliest novel, *Roderick Random* (1748), comes as close as anything in English to classic French or Spanish picaresque but, like most writing in this genre, is a first-person narrative.

Lennox's *The Female Quixote* and Burney's *Evelina* (Chapter 8) produce further discrepancies. As a penurious, modestly educated woman gravitating to the novel from a stage career, Lennox might seem the epitome of female demotic; as its title suggests, however, *The Female Quixote* represents parody and satire, with psychological motivation hardly stronger than that in Swift's patrician *Gulliver's Travels*. Burney, on the other hand, had both paternal repression and personal reticence to thank for her own relative ignorance, whilst the epistolary *Evelina* – at least to those who have never read it – sometimes passes as the epitome of quivering femininity. But the novel is in fact violent, grotesque and satirical to a degree that quite justifies the double acknowledgement to Smollett in its highly articulate Preface.

Radcliffe's *The Mysteries of Udolpho* and Godwin's *Caleb Williams* (Chapter 9), the most celebrated examples of Gothic and Jacobin fiction, respectively – even appearing in the same year – are an irresistible combination; they also take their own toll on my overall conceptual model. Another unlearned female novelist with few demonstrable formal literary influences, Radcliffe nevertheless retains firm authorial control of her third-person narratives; the intellectual Godwin is not quite so consistent, whilst this most radical of English writers (at least, at the time of *Caleb Williams*) also has surprising intertextual affinities with the solidly conservative Fielding.

Austen (Chapter 10) seems to subvert the present model entirely, although her fiction undergoes an evolution quite as interesting as that of Richardson or Fielding. This is underlined in the present study by the emphasis on an early novel, *Northanger Abbey*, and a late one, *Mansfield Park*. In terms of the distinction between 'literary' and 'non-literary' or 'documentary', Austen effectively makes literary borrowings from *within* a documentary (or *pseudo*-documentary) realistic tradition established by Richardson and his female followers. A female novelist – if hardly a demotic one – she also has increasing recourse, ironically, to the kind of third-person omniscience associated with Fielding.

Neither tendency was so clear, however, in Austen's *Juvenilia*, pieces written largely in her teens and not intended for publication. Together with *Northanger Abbey*, these are often mere parodies of eighteenth-century fictional modes; in addition, the three longest pieces in this collection, as well as *Lady Susan* and early versions of *Pride and Prejudice* and *Sense and Sensibility*, are letter fictions and therefore first-person narratives. Although she did abandon epistolary conventions, Austen's ultimate solution to the great internal–external divide of first- and third-person narration was the genial stylistic compromise of free indirect discourse. This technique, found sporadically in earlier writers, is discussed in full in the context of its first great exponent in English fiction.

In spite of – or perhaps because of – its many exceptions and anomalies, then, the present model certainly does more than simply offer another reading of *Pamela*, or even unilaterally advocate a band of neglected women novelists; it may even do greater justice to a Smollett or a Lennox, as well as actually *account for* the exhilarating variety provided by an entire corpus of writers from the long eighteenth century.

2
Sounding the Canon

Watching a movie (and particularly the 'film of the book') rather than reading a novel was once widely regarded by university English departments as a soft option, a kind of mental slumming. Eighteenth-century *gentlemen*, at least, might have had similar reservations about reading anything as trivial as a novel rather than a more mentally exacting philosophical treatise, or culturally significant essay in natural history. Their choice was perhaps made simpler, however, by the fact that most current scientific knowledge was still comprehensible to the layman, while fiction did not yet have such literary heavyweights as Proust or late James. Today, the same English departments may be teaching cultural theory or women's studies and will certainly no longer be questioning the legitimacy of different narrative media. Urban *graffiti*, if politically correct, may rate higher than an ideologically reactionary epic. Similarly, the children (and above all the grandchildren) of those eighteenth-century gentlemen probably possessed handsome bound sets of the same lowly novels, as fiction became increasingly respectable and institutionalized.

These examples reflect the changing status of fiction – and, consequently, of individual writers – in the eighteenth and twentieth centuries, respectively. The process through which certain novels came to be considered 'great', by analogy with the way in which certain books of the Bible came to be seen as authentic, is called canon formation; literary canons are notoriously less stable than biblical ones, however, and have come strongly under attack in recent decades. These issues, at least with reference to the literary half of the comparison, are the concern of the present chapter.[1]

The expression 'raising the novel' can refer amongst other things, then, to the gradual rise in status of a literary genre over the course of three centuries. Expressed only a little reductively: in the eighteenth century, the novel was generally *below* the consideration of a small educated public; in the nineteenth century it was typically in concert with a much larger population group; in the twentieth century it was often *above* the literate masses. Such broad claims naturally require a number of qualifications. The concept of an educated public in the eighteenth century, for example, is remote from anything it might suggest today. The political philosopher Edmund Burke is credited with saying that, in 1790, England had 80,000 readers (in a population of about 6 million). The estimate seems unreasonably low, and may be a more accurate figure for those able to read Burke, a writer more demanding than most eighteenth-century novelists. Some historical estimates of literacy among adult males in England and Wales, while lower than those for Scotland or New England, are nevertheless still as high as 70 per cent.[2] The size of an 'educated public', however defined, is presumably somewhere between these extremes; it is not clear where, so historical comparisons are difficult.

With the nineteenth century, on the other hand, judgements about the status of the novel are easier to make. In the golden age of serialized Victorian fiction, there were close links between writers and a broad reading public. Social questions were valid topics of discussion, and novelists from Dickens to Eliot were able to use their fiction as a forum for public debate. Our best cultural equivalent today may be the more sophisticated American television shows, which introduce controversial issues to a broad and basically receptive audience.

For the twentieth century, finally, reservations are again necessary. The existence of novels *above* the cultural level of a general educated public is largely a legacy of High Modernism from the early decades of the century; its great representatives – such as Joyce, Woolf, Conrad or Faulkner – were aesthetically uncompromising and implicitly elitist. Other kinds of writing emerged to cater for mass demand. The post-modernism of recent decades then increasingly eroded such qualitative distinctions between 'highbrow' and 'lowbrow', the elite and the popular. A novel such as Umberto Eco's *The Name of the Rose*, to choose an example that suitably reflects the internationalism of the modern market, could be received both as an intellectual *tour de force* and – with possible help from the film adaptation – as a popular best-seller.[3]

In a related trend, the rise in the status of the novel, finally, seems to go hand in hand with a decline in the purely utilitarian value of the form. Eighteenth-century fiction is thus normally highly didactic, to a degree that often irritates the modern reader; and the claim holds good for the puritan Richardson as much as for the more unbuttoned Fielding: only the final message is different. In the nineteenth century, subsequently, pure didacticism was generally transformed into less insistent forms of moral awareness, although George Eliot's tendency to preach can still test the modern reader. And for good or bad, finally, the (late) twentieth century generally had a low tolerance threshold for didacticism and little interest in social morality in a fictional context. Clearer distinctions were now made, furthermore, between the writer's literary persona and the actual man or – less consistently – the woman.

Low opinions of eighteenth-century fiction were not automatically removed by the respectable collections of novels appearing at the beginning of the nineteenth, and discussed later in this chapter: the whole field was still contemptuously dismissed, for example, by F. R. Leavis, possibly the most influential British literary critic of the twentieth century. Leavis's own fictional canon, enshrined in his classic study *The Great Tradition*, initially consisted of George Eliot, Henry James and Joseph Conrad.[4] It contained no eighteenth-century writer, and was particularly scathing about Henry Fielding, long considered the most rewarding novelist of the period:

> [W]e haven't to read a very large proportion of *Tom Jones* in order to discover the limits of the essential interests it has to offer us. Fielding's attitudes, and his concern with human nature, are simple, and not such as to produce an effect of anything but monotony (on a mind, that is, demanding more than external action) when exhibited at the length of an 'epic in prose'.   (p. 12)

Joseph Andrews, the original example of the 'comic epic in prose', earns qualified approval, but *Jonathan Wild* (Fielding's first novel in terms of composition) is 'mere hobbledehoydom', whereas by the time of *Amelia* (his last) the author has 'gone soft'; in short, 'life isn't long enough to permit one's giving much time to Fielding' (p. 11). Richardson, Fielding's great rival and contemporary, fares little better:

> The substance of interest that he has to offer is in its own way extremely limited in range and variety, and the demand he makes on the reader's time is in proportion – and absolutely – so immense as to be found, in general, prohibitive.   (p. 13)

And as the final insult, the regrettably insular Leavis hardly rates poor Richardson higher than – dare one say it – *foreign* writers such as Proust. Sterne's fiction is described as 'irresponsible (and nasty), trifling' (p. 11), while Smollett is not even mentioned. Eighteenth-century novels apparently scored low on Leavis's all-important scale of 'moral seriousness', and even for 'entertainment' value of the kind provided by Dickens.

It is hard to believe that this blanket dismissal of eighteenth-century fiction was exactly contemporary with Ian Watt's pioneering *The Rise of the Novel*, discussed in the previous chapter. But Leavis's example also usefully highlights a significant academic tendency. This most colourful of critics presumably did not even read the fiction of Mary Collyer or Samuel Pratt, although there are now those in any large graduate school who do. The result is a rather comic kind of academic inflation, which has surreptitiously affected criticism and theory for over two hundred years.

The trend is well illustrated by James Beattie, the eminent Professor of Moral Philosophy and Logic at Marischal College, Aberdeen. This leading figure of the Scottish enlightenment is generally recognized as the first person to have lectured on English literature in a British university. He constructed a personal taxonomy of romance, although this account ends with a solemn warning against judging the seriousness of the subject by the excessive amount of space devoted to it.[5] At some point, a slightly disconcerted Beattie seems to realize the attraction of the subject, so that his dissertation rapidly becomes more critical than moral.

Some hundred years later, the Scottish-American dilettante William Forsyth could now devote a complete monograph to prose fiction of the eighteenth century.[6] Having begun with the intention of filling the 'idleness of a Long Vacation', Forsyth seems then to have regretted his initiative; he states flatly that 'the novels of the last [i.e. eighteenth] century, with the exception of some well-known names, are deploringly dull. Their plots are contemptible, and the style is detestable' (p. 3). The author's value judgements are equally candid: it is unsafe 'to trust the fidelity of any character drawn by such a democrat as [William] Godwin' (p. 113), whilst *Clarissa* is 'an unpleasant, not to say odious book' (p. 215) written by a 'sentimental little prig' (doubtless another democrat). Forsyth, it transpires, is a fan of Oliver Goldsmith, and turns with relief to *The Vicar of Wakefield* after 'the maudlin sentimentality of Richardson and the coarseness of Fielding and Smollett' (p. 305). A similar admiration for the still little-known Susan Ferrier's *Marriage* (1818) and *Inheritance* (1824), described as 'among the best in the English language', may be conditioned by the common Scottish origins of critic and novelist.

Scholarly inhibitions are still present, but apparently diminishing fast, among more professional twentieth-century academics. J. M. S. Tomkins in his seminal study, *The Popular Novel in England, 1700–1800* (1961), thus worries about writing 'A Book devoted to the display of *tenth-rate* fiction' (p. v); and eight years later, John Richetti's equally important *Popular Fiction before Richardson* (1969) regrets afternoons spent in the British Library consuming what have now advanced to become *third-rate* novels. Richetti is a sensitive critic and perhaps felt his time could have been better spent reading the *Mahabharata* or (presumably) *re*reading the *Divina Commedia*. After the opening of the canon in recent decades, however, Patricia Meyer Spacks can now begin her *Desire and Truth: Functions of Plot in Eighteenth-Century English Novels* (1990) with a reading of what she recognizes as that 'minor classic', Charlotte Lennox's *The Female Quixote*.

Joking apart, even such a breakneck survey raises serious academic issues. In the field of eighteenth-century fiction, a reading of the old *proto*-canon alone (thanks largely to Richardson) is a lengthy process. A first-hand knowledge of all the other novelists between Aphra Behn and Jane Austen requires a further investment of time and energy. To this, one must then add the vast bulk of criticism and traditional literary history. And finally, with the new significance of literary theory, a new and more intellectually challenging range of secondary literature has emerged. With such increased academic specialization, the *Mahabharata* and the *Divina Commedia* may have to be sacrificed entirely.

And the modern reader who finds a workable compromise between reading texts and reading about texts, still risks the kind of cultural insularity and parochialism deplored in Margaret Doody's *A True History of the Novel*. Robert Adams Day argued that, until Richardson, nothing was done in England in the way of letter fiction that was not already done better in France; Ros Ballaster emphasizes the enormous influence of French novelists and memoirists on early women novelists of the period; Ronald Paulson stresses the classical and continental sources for the widespread satirical element in eighteenth-century fiction. These three scholars, at least, are hardly touched by Margaret Doody's criticism of the Anglo-American academy.[7]

The question of fiction written in other languages than English is a significant one. The better educated eighteenth-century women novel-ists and their female readers would have had a reading knowledge of French and Italian; to this stock, more enlightened brothers or husbands might have helped them add some Latin. The resulting linguistic competence would generally have compared favourably with that of more liberated (and mobile) twentieth-century female (or even male) counterparts. It is notable, too, how many eighteenth-century novelists, of either sex, were prolific and proficient translators, or were themselves translated. In a pre-copyright era, when reverence towards original texts was largely limited to the case of the Bible, moreover, these englishings were often considerably freer than equivalent versions would be today, thus tending to blur distinctions between free translations and more conventionally 'creative' writing. From Aphra Behn onwards, there was thus a kind of literary continuum running from original works through adaptations to free and more faithful translations. If the novel itself, then, enjoyed rather lower prestige in the eighteenth century, its most sophisticated consumers were often less insular than their modern academic counterparts.

Some early collections of fiction even suggest that the concept of an 'English novel' is something of an anachronism. Both elements of the term are questionable. As will emerge in this study, it might be safer in the first instance to speak simply of fiction in English. There was no discrimination, and sometimes little distinction, between original English fiction and the often freely creative translations of European (predominantly French) authors. It is true that the percentage of literate or travelled individuals was far smaller in the eighteenth century than it is today; but this group largely coincided with an educated reading public not yet conditioned by a Victorian cultural insularity still present in Britain, or the arrogant new cultural hegemony of the United States. The most famous, if not the most comprehensive, collection of eighteenth-century novels was thus edited by a non-Englishman (Sir Walter Scott) and promised translations of French, Spanish, German and Italian writers together with their English counterparts.

And as for the second term of the rubric, a glance at mid-eighteenth-century terminology suggests that, whatever they called them and however they wrote them, the likes of Fielding, Smollett and Sterne were little interested in (English) *novels*; Defoe was largely invisible (beyond *Robinson Crusoe*) and even Richardson often seemed more concerned with the English than the novelistic element of his writing: his division of the *dramatis personae* at the beginning of *Grandison* into 'ladies', 'gentlemen' and 'Italians' would surely have pleased Leavis.

A relaxed attitude towards translations and translating is one obvious indicator of the kind of status enjoyed by novels and novelists in the eighteenth century: no fiction had yet acquired sacrosanct status. Authors, on the other hand, could be worth much more than the mere sum total of their fictional output, a point that emerges most clearly in a brief anecdote about Smollett. In the course of his walking tour to the West of Scotland with his disciple and future biographer, James Boswell, in 1773, Samuel Johnson visited the Smollett family home at Bonhill, where he was asked whether the monument erected by the writer's cousin should have an English or a Latin text. According to Boswell, Johnson thought an English inscription would be a disgrace to a man of Smollett's learning, whilst Boswell suggested (with his usual complaisance) that 'all to whom Dr Smollett's merit could be an object of respect and imitation could understand it as well in Latin'.[8] And yet neither Johnson nor Boswell had much time for novels.

Several comments spring to mind. First, Smollett's subsequent reputation, still high at the beginning of the nineteenth century, was not as a scholar or man of letters, but as a novelist. Today he is largely neglected in this context, too, and it is a sobering thought that a writer once deemed worthy of the classical scholar is now largely beneath the consideration of the common English reader. Untranslated Latin quotations, on the other hand, abound in his novels (even more so in those of his great rival, Fielding), providing a minor source of irritation to modern readers as they turn to the editorial notes for enlightenment. It is equally sobering, however, that today's learned editor will generally have no more Latin than his reader. The chief interest of the scholar is now the vernacular text, and not the classical models behind it.

The shift in cultural assumptions is so enormous as to bear repetition in fairly drastic terms. The British professor lecturing on Fielding will probably have as much Latin as his least gifted freshman; the American scholar, in turn, will have no more Greek than Navajo or – assuming she has made token gestures to the new multi-ethnicity – perhaps even less. And yet both academics are specialists in a period when Lord Chesterfield defined an illiterate *man* [sic] as one who knew no Greek or Latin, and Gay could sneer at Defoe for wanting 'a small amount of learning'. The latter, incidentally, whilst lacking Fielding's or Smollett's experience of Latin as a *medium* of instruction, nevertheless presumably worked on it solidly as what educators now call a 'target language' for four years at the redoubtable Stoke Newington Academy; a modern British university graduate in Classics, on the other hand, will have probably studied the language for only three.[9]

All of these details reflect the changing literary status of the novel (and the cultural status of its readers) in the course of the eighteenth century. It is thus noticeable that novels enjoyed little prestige in the 1740s, the very term – as noted in the previous chapter – being excluded from the prefaces of *Pamela*, *Joseph Andrews*, and *Roderick Random*. Fielding goes to great lengths to find a pedigree for what he is doing in *Joseph Andrews*, presenting his fiction in terms of a 'comic epic in prose'. His great rival, Smollett, actually gives a rather vague definition of the term:

> A Novel is a large diffused picture, comprehending the characters of life, disposed in different groupes [sic], and exhibited in various attitudes, for the purposes of an uniform plan, and general occurrence, to which every figure is subservient.

But even this does not appear until the dedication of his third novel, *Ferdinand Count Fathom*, in 1753.

The first half of the eighteenth century also normally made a purely quantitative distinction: the novel often corresponded roughly to what the modern reader understands by a *novella*. Qualitatively speaking, on the other hand, learned readers (almost by definition male) identified the form with the writing of Behn, Manley and Haywood.[10] Here, at least, there were no Latin tags, suggesting what is perhaps the one great constant between the eighteenth and twentieth centuries: whereas cultural assumptions about *male* readers may have changed, neither *female* writers nor readers were ever expected to possess such refinements.

In the second half of the eighteenth century, however, there is a marked change in the status of the novel, culminating in a series of collected editions which finally establish and confirm the 'institutionalisation' of the genre: the term is borrowed from Frank Kermode's suggestive study of the literary classic.[11] The latter is much concerned with Virgil, Dante and the 'imperial theme', but also traces the decline of such absolute classics and the emergence of the 'new model' – a text that is simply still being read several generations after it was written. Before reviewing some of the collected editions appearing at the turn of the eighteenth-century, however, it is worth recording the increasing exposure that fiction received in contemporary magazines.

The indispensable aid here is Robert Mayo's *The English Novel in the Magazines, 1740–1815*.[12] Beginning with late seventeenth-century journals, and defining a novel liberally as a story of over 12,000 words, Mayo provides an exhaustive account of the many links between magazines and novels during the period. His survey of the relative importance of various elements of prose fiction, both in single-essay periodicals like the *Tatler* (1709–11) or *Spectator* (1711–14), and in newspapers like the *London Daily Advertiser* or *Public Ledger*, is of immense value for the present study. Literary journalism was a major concern of exactly half of the writers (Fielding, Defoe, Lennox, Smollett and Godwin) considered in Chapters 6 to 10 – and if Burney had yielded to Frances Brooke's urge to collaborate on a new periodical, journalist-novelists would have formed a fine majority.

The relevant issues at this point, however, are the extent to which the better-known novelists were serialized and the nature of public attitudes towards their work. Smollett's *Sir Launcelot Greaves* is often held to be the first English novel published in parts, although this is not entirely accurate, since *Robinson Crusoe* and *Captain Singleton* (to give only two examples) were serialized almost as soon as they were published.[13] In the period from 1740 to 1815, roughly two-thirds of the male authors selected by Mrs Barbauld or the modern *Dictionary of Literary Bibliography* were subject to a total of seventy-five instances of magazine publication. The most frequently featured were Smollett (with ten examples, including three translations and the instalments of *Greaves*), Henry Mackenzie (with eight), and Fielding (with six). John Hawkesworth (nine) and Samuel Johnson (seven) may represent special cases in view of their emphasis on short fiction, sometimes publishable whole or otherwise easier to edit. This last group is closely followed by Smollett's friend John Moore (five examples) and the radical novelist Thomas Holcroft (four). There is no conspicuous gender differential here, moreover, as proportions are roughly the same among female novelists, with twenty writers and sixty-eight examples. Eliza Haywood (nineteen) is easily the most frequent name, followed by Charlotte Lennox (eight), Ann Radcliffe (seven), Charlotte Smith (six), and Elizabeth Griffith (five).

Such data is not in itself very significant, however, and the raw statistics require considerable interpretation. Most obviously, all of the men cited (except Moore), and two of the women (Haywood and Lennox), edited journals or magazines themselves, and thus had a ready outlet for their own writing; and four of Johnson's seven listings concerned the serialization of the same short philosophical romance (and his only fiction), *Rasselas*. Much magazine publication of eight-eenth-century fiction, on the other hand, was in the form of drastic abridgements or so-called *epitomes*; in either case, there was little to distinguish it from the lengthy summaries or extended quotations that accounted for the lion's share of most early book reviews. The accumulation of these points, together with Mayo's comprehensive concluding *Catalogue of Magazine Novels and Novelettes* (with 1375 examples), does however suggest that contemporary readers went for quantity rather than quality, or – more accurately – for quantity, without realizing that they often *got* quality, too. And where production methods, if not actual literary pretentions, are concerned, one might even see a forerunner of the modern concept of 'pulp fiction'.

But Mayo has also shown how magazine editors in the latter decades of the century favoured the 'detached episode', featuring such writers as Johnson, Goldsmith, Henry Brooke and Mackenzie – and later, Charlotte Smith and John Moore. These pieces harmonized well with the shorter fiction, which generally enjoyed greater favour than it does anywhere today outside the convenient undergraduate anthology. It is towards the end of the century, furthermore, that the concept of the novel as a piece of fiction – in the classic definition – 'of a certain length' fully emerges. Short stories come to be seen as a thing apart, and Leigh Hunt's *Classic Tales* anthology (1806–7) is a pioneering example of the consolidation of another literary form;[14] it bears comparison with Elizabeth Inchbald's groundbreaking twenty-five-volume collection, *The British Theatre* (1806–8). The most significant genre-based collection in the present context is nevertheless Anna Laetitia Barbauld's fifty-volume *The British Novelists* (1820), discussed more fully below.

In the preceding decades, however, the eighteenth-century magazines seemed merely to satisfy an almost insatiable public demand for entertainment, and are generally quite remote from any concept of literary canonization. And yet Mayo does find an increased prestige and interest for novels and novelists, reflected in the proliferation of memoirs, characters and anecdotes dedicated to novelists over the final decades of the century. One commercial venture, above all, in the prolific 1780s nevertheless seems to mark the beginnings of a more institutionalized approach: this is Harrison's *Novelist's Magazine* (1780–8).[15]

Harrison's initiative is an important event in the publishing history of eighteenth-century fiction. If it lacked the discrimination of Barbauld's collection or Sir Walter Scott's more famous *Ballantyne's Novelist's Library*, it was nevertheless a considerable advance on the rather arbitrary and haphazard kinds of magazine coverage described by Mayo. Harrison's weekly numbers, when complete, were reissued as a *Magazine of Fiction* in twenty-three volumes; here, then, is an important forerunner of Victorian serialization methods. The result, however, was by no means the repository of *national* literary treasures normally associated with a canon, and the sixty works included are more notable for their large percentage of continental fiction (fourteen French items, two Spanish ones, and even an Italian novel). The concept of a 'national *patrimony*', with all its patriarchal connotations, cleverly traced by April Alliston and discussed in the previous chapter, was not strongly developed.[16]

Of Harrison's English authors also featured by either Barbauld or the modern *Dictionary of Literary Biography*, there are thirteen men and five women, with twenty-five and ten titles, respectively. In the former category are the three major texts of Richardson, five of Fielding (including the *Journey from This World to the Next*), six of Smollett (with the *History and Adventures of an Atom*), and two of Sterne. The other items seem a rather arbitrary miscellany of single works by nine authors: Defoe's *Robinson Crusoe*, Hawkesworth's *Almoran and Hamet*, Sir John Hill's *The Adventures of Mr George Edwards, A Creole*, John Shebbeare's *Lydia*, Francis Coventry's *Pompey the Little* and Robert Paltock's *Peter Wilkins*, as well as predictable contributions from Goldsmith, Johnson and Swift. The sample of women novelists is far less representative, being limited to three of Haywood's late novels (*Betsy Thoughtless*, *Jemmy and Jenny Jessamy*, and *The Invisible Spy*), but only one work published before 1750 (Mary Collyer's *Letters from Felicity to Charlotte*), and two novels each from Sarah Fielding, Charlotte Lennox, and Frances Sheridan.

Significantly, there is nothing by Behn, Manley, or the early Haywood, and (with the exception of *Robinson Crusoe*) no fiction at all written before *Pamela*. Notable omissions among later women writers include Burney, Frances Brooke and Sarah Scott. More positively, novels and novelists are not disqualified by length any more than by nationality. The *Magazine of Fiction* thus reflects the contemporary popularity of collections of tales, often translated from the French.[17] Particularly prominent is the sub-genre of the oriental tale, with the collection including such staples as *Almoran and Hamet*, Sheridan's *Nourjahad*, and Voltaire's *Zadig*; there is also what must presumably, by analogy, be called an 'occidental tale' in Voltaire's *Sincere Huron*.

One may argue that the groups of tales and longer individual pieces broadly correspond to the modern formal categories of *short story* and *novella*, although – in an eighteenth-century context – all of the second category, and even some of the first, would have fitted comfortably within the quantitative parameters of the 'novel'. In the first half of the century, however, the latter was normally low in prestige and short in length; it was a novel of Aphra Behn's, in fact, that Fielding ironically had the ingenuous Mr Mclachlan in *Tom Jones* read for 'improving his understanding and filling his mind with good literature'. The apotheosis of the 'novel' may be traced in any account of Victorian fiction, whereas the modern re-emergence of the term *novella* owes much to nineteenth-century German usage. Feminist revisionary criticism often refers to the 'novels' of Behn and Haywood, and the term is well justified by etymological links with the *novelle* of Boccaccio, *novelas* of Cervantes, and *nouvelles* of various French writers, which provided inspiration for much early English fiction. The suspicion remains, however, that feminist practice more often reflects an exercise in simple affirmative action, identifying *Oroonoko* with the modern prestige term 'novel' rather than the minor form of *novella*.

A new shift of emphasis to a specifically national narrative tradition is only the most obvious feature of Anna Laetitia Barbauld's *The British Novelists*.[18] Conversely, this editor is more flexible than many modern comparativists on issues of length, and her twenty-eight 'novels' range from *Rasselas* to *Clarissa* and *Grandison*. *Pamela* is significantly omitted, on the other hand, although the novel's initial seduction narrative is all that most modern students know of Richardson (with the general reader rarely having time even for this). Philip Larkin once drew an amusing parallel between medieval monasteries, where monks were paid to offer prayers which others could not be bothered to formulate, and English departments, which we pay to 'praise authors... whom personally we find unreadable'. Richardson, quite unjustly, has often been included in this category.

Barbauld could certainly not be accused of such over-reverential attitudes, and sometimes even feels constrained to defend her lighter selections. The Preface to the second edition of her *British Novelists* (1821) thus admits that the collection 'has a better chance of giving pleasure than of commanding respect', although the novel is 'entitled to a higher rank than has been generally assigned it'. Her anthology may be seen as an important step in gaining this status. But although the *British Novelists* marks a significant advance in the institutionalization of the form, the exclusion of *Pamela* suggests that the collection is no mere slave to orthodoxy, or prisoner of cultural piety.

According to a simple gender division, Barbauld's anthology includes thirteen male writers and eight female, responsible for sixteen novels (or thirty-one and a half volumes) and twelve novels (or eighteen and a half volumes), respectively. Among the five traditional 'monuments' of eighteenth-century fiction, Richardson fills fifteen volumes (with *Pamela* excluded), Fielding four (by virtue of *Joseph Andrews* and *Tom Jones*), Defoe (*Robinson Crusoe*) and Smollett (*Humphry Clinker*) two each. Sterne (and the rest of Smollett) is excluded on moral grounds; Defoe is identified exclusively with *Robinson Crusoe*, and even the latter – assumed to be 'a mere schoolboy acquaintance' for many readers – requires special pleading. Double volumes for Richard Graves (*The Spiritual Quixote*) and John Moore (*Zeluco*), single volumes for Henry Mackenzie and Robert Bage (*Hermsprong*), and half-volumes for Walpole, Goldsmith, Coventry (*Pompey the Little*), Johnson, and Hawkesworth account for the remaining eight and a half volumes. The coupling of *Rasselas* with Hawkesworth's *Almoran and Hamet* confirms a taste for the oriental tale. Hawkesworth and Moore, incidentally, are the only two of Barbauld's male authors not included in the *Dictionary of Literary Biography* (hereafter *DLB*).

Among the eight women novelists, just Lennox (*The Female Quixote*, 1752) and Brooke (*The History of Julia Mandeville*, 1763) pre-date the last quarter of the eighteenth century. Burney (*Evelina* and *Cecilia*) and Radcliffe (*The Romance of the Forest* and *The Mysteries of Udolpho*) get five volumes apiece; Lennox, Charlotte Smith (*The Old Manor House*), and Maria Edgeworth (*Belinda* and *The Modern Griselda*), at two volumes each, account for six more. Inchbald receives one and a half volumes (*Nature and Art* and *A Simple Story*), whilst the remaining half-volume goes to Clara Reeve's *The Old English Baron*. The earlier and more sexually explicit fiction of Behn, Manley and Haywood is predictably omitted. All of these writers are included in the *DLB* selection for eighteenth-century fiction, except Maria Edgeworth, who appears in a later volume on Romantic novelists.

Barbauld's accompanying essay, 'The Origin and Progress of Novel Writing', is a learned if unoriginal account of the subject;[19] the 'Prefaces Biographical and Critical', on the other hand, reveal a shrewd and independent mind, and are every bit as interesting as the actual choice of texts. Barbauld's value judgements are disarmingly evident from the mere size of these essays: Richardson gets sixty-six pages, Fielding half of that, and Smollett barely half again. Of other male authors, only Goldsmith (twelve) merits double figures, although this is still a page more than the provision for the most highly rated women novelists, Burney and Edgeworth.

The treatment of Richardson and Fielding transcends mere panegyric, however, for even here Barbauld never pulls her critical punches. She thus regards *Pamela* as 'tarnished by time', and possessing little more than historical interest, being produced when 'a *novel* written on the side of virtue was considered as a new experiment' (vol. I, p. xi). Richardson's subsequent novels are also censured: the first volumes of *Clarissa* are 'somewhat tedious, for the prolixity incident to letter-writing, and require a persevering reader to get through them' (p. xvi), whilst *Grandison* 'would be improved by merely striking out the last volume, and, indeed, a good part of the sixth', with its descriptions of 'dress, and parade, and furniture' (p. xliv).

More ideologically subversive is an amusing comment on Mr B., hero–villain of *Pamela*: 'his ideas of the authority of a husband are so high, that it is not easy to conceive of Pamela's being rewarded by marrying him' (p. xiii). In this embryonically feminist perspective, Fielding predictably fares even worse: 'It is observable that Fielding uniformly keeps down the characters of his women, as much as Richardson elevates his. A yielding easiness of disposition is what he seems to lay the greatest stress upon' (vol. XVIII, p. xxv); or more pertinently still: 'Any portion of learning in women is constantly united in this author with something disagreeable' (p. xxv). One warms easily to Mrs Barbauld.

Another characteristic trait of this early novel critic is a strong romantic sensibility, which nevertheless always remains within the strictest bounds of decorum. Barbauld thus praises *Tom Jones* for 'scenes that interest the heart' and incidents that are 'highly affecting, and calculated to awaken our best feelings' (p. xix); and is similarly indulgent to *The Vicar of Wakefield*: 'Whatever be its faults, we easily forgive the author, who has made us laugh, and has made us cry' (vol. XXIII, pp. xi–xii). Such comments suggest that the exclusion of the frequently bawdy Sterne may have caused a genuine sense of deprivation. *Tristram Shandy* and *A Sentimental Journey* receive judicious praise in Barbauld's introductory 'Essay', even as they are criticized for indelicacies. In *The British Novelists*, Mackenzie – one of the 'more respectable imitators of Sterne' – may therefore be something of a surrogate.

Of the other two proto-canonic eighteenth-century novelists, Smollett's literary stock is seen by implication to be falling: his *Roderick Random* and other novels are 'still' favourites with 'those who can overlook their grossness, vulgarity, and licentious morals'. Despite the length of the relevant essay, however, Barbauld's attitude to Smollett is less than adulatory; her inclusion of *Humphry Clinker* is facetiously (and erroneously) justified by its being the only Smollett novel without a sailor.[20] She is similarly underwhelmed by Defoe, although she apparently anticipates the concept of journalistic 'ghost-writing' in shrewdly defining these narratives as 'rather deceptions than imitations' (vol. XVI, p. i). Defoe is far from surpassing even Smollett, however, and Mrs Barbauld's dismissal of the novelist does not anticipate his rise in stature later in the nineteenth century and throughout the twentieth: 'his education was a common one, and none of his works bear any marks of that polish and elegance of style which is the mingled result of a classical education, and of associating with the more cultivated orders of society'. It is a remarkable comment from the pen of a *woman* hailing from the intellectual equivalent of Defoe's dissenting background and the same 'middle state' as his most famous protagonist. She also naturally fails to distinguish between the education and intellectual capacity of Defoe himself, and those of his protagonists. Mrs Barbauld's judgement on Defoe may be her greatest blindspot for the modern reader.

The early triumvirate of Manley, Behn and Haywood get short shrift. Comment on Manley barely goes beyond a famous reference by Pope;[21] Behn's fiction is dismissed as 'licentious'; Haywood's earlier novels are 'in the style of Mrs Behn's' although her later works are 'by no means devoid of merit'. Among the eight novelists who do feature, on the other hand, the inclusion of Clara Reeve seems more a pious gesture: her proto-Gothic novel, *The Old English Baron* has 'but a moderate degree of merit', although it 'inspires none but noble and proper sentiments'. Lennox's *The Female Quixote* is 'rather spun out too much' and marred by its overt didacticism. Frances Brooke, on the other hand, is 'perhaps the first female novel-writer who attained a perfect purity and polish of style'. Charlotte Smith is treated with respect, but Mrs Barbauld's greatest praise is reserved for Inchbald, Burney, Radcliffe and Edgeworth, each of whom is represented by two works. In addition to individual tributes, she refers to precisely these four in glowing terms:

> we have more good writers living at the present time, than at any other period since the days of Richardson and Fielding. A very great proportion of these are ladies.[22]

And in fact, all but one of Barbauld's last fifteen volumes in her basically chronological selection are by female writers.

In general, however, she offers useful insights on all twenty-one of her writers (with the curious exception of Francis Coventry, who, for reasons unknown, receives no preface, biographical or critical). The introductory essay also comments on eleven other novelists included in the *DLB*, from Behn, Manley and Haywood, through Sterne, Amory, Pratt, Henry Brooke and Day, to Godwin, Holcroft and Opie.

The British Novelists is in many respects a well-conceived collection, although the forthright comments on, for example, Richardson's prolixity emphasize that the editor is far from overwhelmed by her task, or overawed by her subjects. Only in the most transparently figurative sense, then, can the modern reader think in terms of a genuine novelistic 'canon'. The latter term originally had scriptural origins, and it is difficult to imagine the devoutly religious Mrs Barbauld criticizing with equal candour, say, the exhaustive genealogies of the Old Testament or the narrative inconsistencies of the gospels. The sense of a fictional canon, then, happily lacks its mid-twentieth-century rigour – *rigor mortis* might not, in fact, be too strong a term before recent revisions and expansions. On the road to institutionalization, Barbauld's eighteenth-century fictional classics have acquired roughly the same status, say, as Shakespeare in the age of Pope.

Historically, *The British Novelists* never enjoyed the contemporary fame of Bentley's *Standard Novels* or the more lasting reputation of Scott's *Ballantyne's Novelist's Library*. This is unjust, since it is an impressive achievement, and marks Mrs Barbauld as more than a literary-historical footnote – the minor didactic writer whose *Hymns in Prose for Children* (1781) may have influenced Blake's *Songs*. Daughter of the distinguished scholar and Nonconformist minister John Aiken, she received an early grounding in both classical and modern languages. After marrying another Nonconformist minister (and successfully running a school in Suffolk), she later travelled with her husband for a year on the continent. In both respects, she enjoyed educational advantages denied to most women of her day. To this profile, one may add a distinguished record as political radical and pro-abolitionist. Barbauld suggests an intellectual legacy substantially comparable (if hardly compatible) with that of Sir Walter Scott.

Roughly contemporary with Mrs Barbauld's series was William Mudford's abortive *British Novelists* (5 volumes, 1810–17). In purely physical terms, Mudford's collection might seem a poor imitation of Harrison's *Novelist's Magazine*, although its very title suggests more obvious associations with Barbauld. Since it only featured fourteen novels, however – five each by Smollett and Fielding (including *A Journey from This World to the Next*), the other four by Sterne, Swift and Goldsmith – it clearly lacked either the scope or the originality of Mrs Barbauld. Or, stated more bluntly, Mudford's enterprise hardly got off the ground. Worthier competition was provided by Scott.

Ballantyne's Novelist's Library (10 volumes, 1821–4) may have set out to supplement Barbauld's *British Novelists*, which preceded it by some ten years. Whether or not it actually achieved this aim, Scott does seem to have surrendered much of the ground between Gothic romance and satire-*cum*-picaresque, between the *frisson* and the belly-laugh. The 'Advertisement' to the collection had nevertheless promised rather more:

the works of the best of the English Novelists, together with selections from the German, French, and Italian (some of which are already translated, and others in the course of translation), with Memoirs of the Authors' Lives and Criticisms of their Writings, prefixed.

It is interesting to note that Scott, anglophone but not English, reverts to the ethnic diversity of Harrison's *Novelist's Magazine*, even as his publisher perhaps tries to evoke its name. The German and Italian novelists never materialized, however, whilst the French were limited to three translations of Lesage: *Gil Blas*, *The Devil on Two Sticks* and the now almost forgotten *Vanillo Gonzalez*.[23] That Scott's initial emphasis was certainly different from that of Mrs Barbauld may be gauged from the three volumes appearing in 1821: the first collected the four major narratives of Fielding; the second featured the three best-known novels of Smollett; and the third contained his *Ferdinand Count Fathom* and *Sir Launcelot Greaves*, together with the same author's translation of *Don Quixote*. Volume 4 (the sole offering of 1822) combined Lesage with Johnstone's *The Adventures of a Guinea*; volume 5 (1823) provided a miscellany of Sterne (two texts), Goldsmith, Johnson, Mackenzie (three texts), Walpole and Reeve. The year 1824 brought a final flurry of activity with three volumes of Richardson at last (including *Pamela*), and a new miscellany of Swift, Bage (three texts), and Richard Cumberland's *Henry*, before terminating with the five published novels of Radcliffe.

Scott enjoyed immense personal prestige, and certain of his essays on the eighteenth-century novelists (that on Smollett, for example) may be rated above anything produced by Mrs Barbauld. On the other hand, his collection as a whole has neither the balance or comprehensiveness of *The British Novelists*. Uninhibited by modern taboos on essentialism in gender constructions, moreover, Mrs Barbauld could refer to Smollett's 'strong masculine humour' and 'knowledge of the world'; in a collection containing all of Smollett's novels, as well as Lesage, Coventry, Swift and Cumberland, she might have considered that Scott provided quite enough of both. Politically, no less than temperamentally, there is also a wide gap between the two editors: a suggestive point here is that the conservative Scott features three politically moderate early novels by the Jacobin novelist Robert Bage (*Mount Henneth*, *Barham Downs* and *James Wallace*), whilst the radical Mrs Barbauld includes the more controversial *Hermsprong*.

Choosing no novel after Radcliffe's *The Italian* (1797), Scott was also clearly more interested in emerging classics than in contemporaries;

by contrast, *The British Novelists* – although appearing a decade before the first volumes of *Ballantyne's Novelist's Library* – included half-a-dozen texts from the 1790s and even two by Maria Edgeworth from the following decade: *Belinda* (1801) and *The Modern Griselda* (1805). Mrs Barbauld was in fact a keen advocate of contemporary fiction, and her motives seem clear: she surely wished to do justice to contemporary women's writing. Scott has reservations about novels of sensibility by female writers; but, to judge from the selection policy, his 'whole tribe of Jemmys and Jessamys'[24] – in the notorious phrase – also seems to have included such substantial figures as Sarah Fielding, Lennox, Brooke, and Burney. Of his sixteen authors (including Cervantes), only two are women. Scott, then, the more conservative editor, may be seen in some ways as trying to consolidate an already embryonic canon; the more representative Barbauld may actually be pre-empting a new one. She has an important further role in this chapter.

Two more collections may be dealt with more briefly, since their publishing dates lie outside the parameters of this study. One of them, Roscoe's *Novelist's Library* (1831–3, two series), represents an even more conservative selection than Scott's. The first series was limited to a two-volume edition of *Robinson Crusoe*; the new series added sixteen more volumes, with four texts of Smollett, three of Fielding, two of Sterne, plus *The Vicar of Wakefield*, *Don Quixote*, and *Gil Blas*. The *Novelist's Library* does not have an inspiring range, although it is significant for being the first collection to include all five authors who came to form the eighteenth-century proto-canon, and virtually nobody else: its additional works include one other native minor classic and the two continental texts most influential on the novelistic canon as defined here. More interesting still, the new series was illustrated by George Cruikshank, representing another step forwards in the institutionalization of the text as it emerges in the nineteenth century. The association of fictional characters with specific images by a famous artist is an important occurrence. It will acquire its greatest significance with the Victorian novel in the person of Dickens.[25]

Judging from its contents, the next significant collection, Roscoe's *Novelist's Library*, seems to be of simultaneous inspiration with Mudford's *British Novelists*, although its exact contemporary is in fact Bentley's celebrated *Standard Novels* series (1831–5), once described as 'the most famous series of cheap novels ever published'. In the present context, only Bentley's first series of 126 volumes requires brief mention; it includes twelve novelists (and twenty-two novels) featured by Mrs Barbauld and/or the *DLB*.[26]

By their dates of publication, both Bentley's *Standard Novels* (1831–5) and Scott's *Ballantyne's Novelist's Library* (1821–4) are also marginal to the present study, whereas Barbauld's *British Novelists* (1810) is obviously quite central. In terms of literary sociology and publishing economics, however, all three collections are interesting in their anticipation of modern bookselling trends. Scott unites great personal authority with considerable critical acumen to produce an emergent canon of literary classics; its large-scale natural descendants are perhaps (in terms of universality) the Oxford World's Classics series, or (for prestige) the French Pléiade editions.

Bentley's *Standard Novels*, on the other hand, was a more speculative venture. Whilst some of its items (Austen's novels are the prime examples) enjoy genuine classic status today, the original selection was often determined primarily by economic factors and eventually (with publication of the third series) undone by them, too. Its modern equivalents might be the (once) inexpensive Penguin or Viking paperback imprints. The most obvious difference between the Scott and Bentley collections, then, is that, whereas the former generally *confirms* already established classic status, the latter may often *confer* it. For wide availability, good marketing, and cultural topicality produce that virtual oxymoron, the 'Modern Classic' – early nineteenth-century equivalents, say, of Alice Walker's *The Color Purple*.

The British Novelists, then, occupies a unique position between Scott and Bentley. Its long introductory essay and critical prefaces, like Scott's own, reflect the conscious process of institutionalizing a literary genre (much as Inchbald had done for the theatre); the very late cut-off point, on the other hand, suggests that Mrs Barbauld (like Bentley's editor) was also chancing her critical arm and trying to create some modern classics, too. Barbauld's series seems initially to have sold well, although it was later partly eclipsed (quite undeservedly) by the more prestigious *Ballantyne's Novelist's Library*. In the meantime, it was also probably the stimulus for a naive but widespread modern assumption that classics are simply what is available in an inexpensive modern edition. Whether or not this is the case, the scope and originality of Anna Laetitia Barbauld's *British Novelists* make the collection an ideal initial corpus for the study of eighteenth-century fiction.

Mrs Barbauld's critical prefaces indicate that she set a high premium on moral 'purity' and elegance of style, neither of which concepts seems particularly central to modern critical perceptions. The generally excellent *Dictionary of Literary Biography* (*DLB*), on the other hand, does not offer even such vague criteria as these to justify inclusion in its double volume of essays on eighteenth-century novelists.[27] In his introductory essay to the collection, Martin Battestin mentions fourteen male authors by name. In addition to the 'five great masters', there are ten 'single classic men': Cleland, Walpole, Goldsmith, Mackenzie, Godwin and Lewis, with four more – Bunyan, Swift, Johnson and Beckford – who help to define the 'elusive norm', a norm which, it must be added, remains elusive even after Battestin's introduction. Hawkesworth and Moore are notable absences, although other omissions seem generally more arbitrary than sensational.

As a series of bio-critical essays rather than a collection of texts, the *DLB* is obviously different in scope from *The British Novelists* or any of the other early series. Of its forty-nine separate entries (Harriet and Sophie Lee are considered under the same heading), twenty-eight are men and twenty-one women (or twenty-two, if the Lee sisters are restored to independent status). The selection of certain male writers may surprise the modern reader: Congreve is thus included, presumably on the sole basis of *Incognita* (and thus, in fictional terms, another 'single classic' man); Swift appears on the strength of his satires; Johnson qualifies by virtue of *Rasselas*, although John Hawkesworth, author of *Almoran and Hamet* (and several other oriental tales), does not. Hawkesworth and Smollett's medical friend John Moore are incidentally the only two authors selected by Barbauld but omitted from the *DLB*. Some of the male writers covered by the *DLB*, such as Bunyan, Swift or Johnson, require a fairly elastic concept of the novel as literary genre in order to justify their inclusion: but, to view the issue more reductively, where else *could* one place two such 'big' authors?

With regard to female writers, the question of selection is more complex, raising broader issues of feminist revision of the eighteenth-century canon. At this point, one may briefly compare the *DLB* list with the more specialized studies of Janet Todd and Jane Spencer discussed in the previous chapter. Todd's *The Sign of Angellica* (subtitled 'Women, Writing and Fiction, 1660–1800') offers, for example, a lengthy discussion of the popular sentimental novelist Susannah Gunning, as well as the radical Mary Hays, neither of whom are included in the *DLB*; Spencer's *The Rise of the Woman Novelist* ('From Aphra Behn to Jane Austen') also considers Hays, in addition to Catherine Trotter, youthful author of a regrettably little-known epistolary novel, *Olinda's Adventures*, published in 1693. It is only fair to point out, however, that later volumes of the *DLB* also contain entries for Susan Ferrier and the once immensely popular Jane Porter. The former is just outside the period of

Todd and Spencer, but the latter appears to elude both critics, and even the indefatigable Dale Spender.

Spender's *Mothers of the Novel*, subtitled '100 good women writers before Jane Austen', is clearly different in scale (or scope) from the *DLB* or even Mrs Barbauld's *British Novelists*. Some of its major figures – Brunton, Edgeworth, Amelia Opie, and Sydney Owenson (Lady Morgan) – are included in the later *DLB* volume on Romantic novelists, but nearly eighty others are still unaccounted for.

Omissions aside, however, the *DLB* volumes on the eighteenth-century novel also raise other problems with respect to writers included. This emerges most clearly in Battestin's editorial Preface. Of the twenty-nine male authors in the collection, fifteen are recalled favourably in the Preface (the *five* 'great masters' and *ten* 'single classic' men). Of the twenty-two female novelists, however, just *four* are mentioned by name, although this particular imbalance may be less disturbing than the nature of the comments themselves. There is, for example, a guarded reference to 'three of the most interesting women of the period', including the 'prolific and irrepressible *Aphra Behn*'. The subtext of such a back-handed compliment tends to suggest that Behn is an assertive female who talks too much. It is hard, in fact, not to compare Battestin's attitude with those expressed by his own favourite author, and shrewdly noted by Mrs Barbauld:

> It is observable that Fielding uniformly keeps down the characters of his women. . . . A yielding disposition is what he seems to lay the greatest stress upon.[28]

The identification of Sarah Fielding merely as 'Henry's wise and gifted sister' is a classic put-down; the reference to 'the celebrated Gothicist Ann Radcliffe' is patronizing; an allusion to 'Mrs Manley and her tribe' approaches invective. There are no other direct references to women. A concluding comment on the thirty lesser-known novelists (male and female) in the *DLB* selection nevertheless has a rather condescending ring:

> Many of these writers were women who felt only too keenly the unjust social and political restraints that have caused their twentieth-century sisters to protest.

Fortunately, however, Battestin's Preface is ultimately less relevant than the sum of his individual entries, which represent a virtual roll-call of the most distinguished North American scholars of the period; even by the high standards of the *DLB*, the overall level is remarkable.

A brief recapitulation is due, then, on the concept of a corpus of novels or a pool of novelists. The review of scholarly approaches in the first chapter emphasized a gap between critics and theorists. If the former, it was suggested, typically provide a series of readings to which some kind of conceptual model is attached, then the latter elaborate an ingenious theory which is then applied to an ever-diminishing number of carefully selected texts. One possible way of avoiding both processes was to choose a *corpus* of novels for study. An ideal basis for such a body thus seemed the combined resources of the first major collection of English novels (Mrs Barbauld's *British Novelists*) and the most widely regarded modern reference work (the requisite volumes of the *Dictionary of Literary Biography*, edited by Martin Battestin). There was an added appeal here in that Mrs Barbauld edited a six-volume collection, still not superseded, of the correspondence of Richardson; whereas Battestin is both the definitive biographer and an authoritative editor of Fielding. And these two novelists are, by any reckoning, the major players in the story of eighteenth-century fiction.

Chronological constraints imposed by a literal application of the term 'eighteenth century' have been ignored, to allow the inclusion of both Behn and Austen. Accusations of gender imbalance might similarly have been pre-empted by matching the thirty-one male writers featured by Mrs Barbauld and the *DLB* with an equal number of female ones. Since the *terminus ad quem* of the study was Austen, moreover, this aim could have been easily achieved by the addition of four writers mentioned above (Brunton, Edgeworth, Opie and Owenson), together with Austen herself and four more novelists featured in detail by Spencer, Spender, or Todd: Susannah Gunning (*née* Minifie), Mary Hays, and the once celebrated Porter sisters, Anna Maria and Jane.

The result would have been an uncomfortably large group of thirty-one writers of each sex, active between the Restoration of Charles II and the death of Jane Austen. An alternative method would have been to cull the male writers to twenty-one, thus matching the number of female novelists featured in *The British Novelists* and the *DLB* combined. Either solution would have nevertheless eliminated the attractive idea of a ready-made corpus, thus losing one kind of objectivity. The solution finally adopted was to keep the original inequality (in slightly attenuated form) and list both groups of writers in an appendix, letting readers themselves decide what new balances could be obtained by eliminating such historically obscure figures as Arthur

Blackamore or 'Sir' John Hill, not to mention a few of Battestin's 'single classic men'.

Split along gender lines, then, a roll-call of writers would run as follows:

> Penelope Aubin, Jane Barker, Aphra Behn, Frances Brooke, Frances Burney, Mary Collyer, Mary Davys, Maria Edgeworth, Sarah Fielding, Elizabeth Griffith, Eliza Haywood, Elizabeth Inchbald, Harriet Lee, Sophia Lee, Charlotte Lennox, Delarivier Manley, Ann Radcliffe, Clara Reeve, Elizabeth Rowe, Sarah Scott, Frances Sheridan, Charlotte Smith, Mary Wollstonecraft. (A total of 23)

> Thomas Amory, Robert Bage, William Beckford, Henry Brooke, John Cleland, Francis Coventry, Thomas Day, Daniel Defoe, Henry Fielding, William Godwin, Oliver Goldsmith, Richard Graves, John Hawkesworth, Thomas Holcroft, Samuel Johnson, Charles Johnstone, Matthew Lewis, Henry Mackenzie, John Moore, Robert Paltock, Samuel Jackson Pratt, Samuel Richardson, John Shebbeare, Tobias Smollett, Laurence Sterne, Jonathan Swift, Horace Walpole. (A total of 27)

Among the women writers, the only truly significant omission – in a survey from Behn to Austen – may be Mary Brunton, whose *Self-Control* (warmly praised by Austen) actually dates from 1811.[29] Among the men, such unlikely 'novelists' as Bunyan and Congreve can also perhaps be excluded: Bunyan is even chronologically marginal, whereas Congreve's *Incognita* is the only work of this author remotely approaching a modern novel in form or scope.[30]

The exclusion of Congreve and Bunyan, along with Hill and Blackmore, would produce a corpus identical to the *DLB*'s round *fifty*. The addition of Austen as the fifty-first name then eliminates the risk of round-number fetishism. References to other writers are not excluded in this study, but the group provides the basis for the discussion of genre and gender, for example, in the following chapter: none of the arguments advanced there conveniently 'dump' less tractable figures. The second part of the study then concentrates on a smaller number of paired novelists (with the exception of Austen, who is treated separately) and offers detailed readings of key novels. Even here, however, *all* the other writers are kept in sight, and linked where possible to one or more of the specially profiled texts.

3
Genre and Gender

The Russian theorist Mikhail Bakhtin claimed that, whereas epic and tragedy had long reached their final stage of evolution, the novel was the one literary genre still in the process of development. Or, expressed from a slightly different perspective, most readers have a clear concept of what an epic or tragedy involves, and might be expected to recognize one fairly easily when they met it; the case of the novel is hardly so simple. And if, on yet another tack, the epic or tragedy in question were anonymous, the sex of the poet would likewise arouse little debate, so widespread would be the assumption of male authorship for that kind of writing; but an anonymous novel, as literary history repeatedly shows, would again prove a greater challenge. Such issues of genre and gender, admittedly framed rather simplistically here, are the overall subject of the present chapter.

If *gender* has become a minefield in recent decades, then *genre* has been a labyrinth for over two thousand years: reason enough, perhaps, for beginning with the latter, although this chapter will argue that the two concepts are ultimately difficult to separate. From a traditional tripartite division into the epic, dramatic and lyric, definitions of genre became so numerous as to make the term virtually useless for some modern critics; and in a Romantic Age which prized 'originality' and 'spontaneity', theories of genre were even suspect, as mere restatements of outmoded conventions. In the traditional division, moreover, the upstart novel had as yet no place; in modern definitions it is everywhere. The *novel* is thus sometimes regarded as a *genre*, or 'kind', but so is the 'picaresque novel' or the 'novel of manners'; the latter, then, might perhaps be described as *sub-genres*. Most literary works, on the other hand, manage to display features of several genres, however the latter are defined; finding a pure example may therefore be difficult, inviting the conclusion that genres may only exist as unhelpful theoretical abstractions. There is, in fact, a strong temptation to abandon the whole discussion, were it not for the obvious fact that many eighteenth-century writers were strongly influenced by a prescriptive poetics with

52

its concept of clear rules to follow. Classically educated writers such as Fielding or Smollett took these precepts seriously. A definitive modern discussion of genre theory may therefore be helpful.[1]

In his classic survey, Paul Hernadi argues against monolithic approaches, and lists four types of similarity between literary works on which a theory of genre can be constructed. These may be *expressive* (reflecting the mental attitudes of authors in the process of writing); *pragmatic* (based on the effects of literary works on readers' minds); *structural* (viewing literary works as verbal constructs); and *mimetic* (derived from likenesses perceived between the respective imagined worlds of different authors). Curiously enough, however, Hernadi nowhere attempts to link literary forms with the sex of the writer. It is a significant omission for several reasons: a number of languages actually express genre and gender by a single word; the period from Behn to Austen is remarkable for the quantity and quality of its women writers; and scholars now regularly refer to the 'feminization' of the key new literary form in the second half of the eighteenth century. The genre and gender of the novel, then, are a more specific concern in what follows below.

One obvious way of pursuing this argument is to examine the various narrative forms which contributed to the development of the eighteenth-century novel, and decide, in turn, whether these may be specifically linked with male or female writers. Obvious examples here are *epic* (including *mock-epic* or *comic epic*) and epistolary fiction, as representing male and female tendencies, respectively: safe enough hypotheses in the light of *Tom Jones* and *Evelina*, but also plausible on the basis of wider reading. Another more questionable pair of contenders for the same kind of generic division might be satire (predominantly male) and the intimate journal (generally female). One may then attempt to assess the relative significance of other genres or modes (narrative, dramatic, or purely didactic) in the formation of eighteenth-century fiction, together with further possible gender differentials. These aims are reflected in the arrangement of the present chapter under four headings – 'Epic and Satire', 'Letters and Journals', 'Stage and Closet' and 'Instruction and Delight'.

The first two sections are those related most directly to issues of *genre* and *gender*. 'Epic and Satire' thus considers a group of discursive practices and ideological assumptions which can be convincingly associated with the male author; 'Letters and Journals' pursues a similar approach for the female novelist. The remaining sections then abandon these more explicit gender differences to concentrate on two contrasting *non*-narrative modes that are also major formative elements in eighteenth-century fiction: the drama and the conduct book. 'Stage and Closet', as its title suggests, introduces more practical aspects of dramatic performance (or *non*-performance) and publication, as well as related social and economic issues. 'Instruction and Delight', finally, discusses conduct books and the didactic tradition in general. The chapter concludes with brief comment on what 'women's writing' might mean in purely linguistic terms.

Epic and Satire

The issue of 'epic' or 'satire' in the context of eighteenth-century fiction is a clear example of the problems raised by monolithic, or inflexible, theories of genre. In *expressive* terms (i.e. authors' mental attitudes), the two forms are opposed, with epic denoting what Kenneth Burke called a 'frame of acceptance' towards human existence in general, and satire (together with burlesque) embodying a form of rejection;[2] in *pragmatic* terms (effect on the reader), however, epic and satire are the generic forms closest to a classical legacy with which the reader was presumed to be familiar. In purely *structural* terms, on the other hand, *epic* merges into 'mock-epic' (or the 'comic epic in prose') – as in the novels of Fielding – but may also be regarded as a forerunner of heroic *romance*; satire, at least from the time of *Don Quixote*, blends well with mock-epic, but is generally too earthy for romance. In *mimetic terms*, finally, the world actually represented must reflect the vision of the writer; but as Horace Walpole noted, 'the world is a comedy to those that think, a tragedy to those that feel', at which point, generic theory has returned to the original expressive impulse. In the face of such contradictory tendencies, it seems an increasingly attractive alternative to set aside such abstractions and begin instead with a simple attempt to put the gender back into genre.

The gendering of the epic reflects the fact that classical education in the eighteenth century was a male preserve. The point seems almost too obvious to labour, and it is only unfortunate for the critic with a lot to say about it that the genre itself (in its purest form) has fairly limited direct relevance to eighteenth-century fiction. The epic was traditionally a poetic form, and its material was heroic, whether the Trojan Wars (Homer) or the founding of Rome (Virgil); the great English model was Milton, whose revised *Paradise Lost* was published in 1674, the decade in which Aphra Behn began her successful career as a playwright.

The eighteenth century spawned many Miltonic imitations, all largely forgotten.[3] In an age of neo-classic aesthetics but a non-heroic society, however, the two greatest epic perfomances were translations: Dryden's *Works of Virgil* (1697) and Pope's fabulously successful *Iliad* (1715–20) and *Odyssey* (1725–6).

The greatest English poets of the Restoration and Augustan periods, respectively, were also – and one chooses the word advisedly – *masters* of satire. Dryden's speciality was political and religious allegory, such as *Absalom and Achitophel* (1681); Pope's forte was the mock-epic, whether grounded in burlesque as in *The Rape of the Lock* (1712/1714), or in full-blooded satire as in *The Dunciad* (1728/1743). The 'mock-epic', or comic aggrandizement of trivial material (traditional burlesque being the inverse process, or a diminution of the grandiose), thus constitutes a link between epic and satire. It is the 'comic' or 'mock' epic variant that is important in eighteenth-century fiction, beginning with Fielding's *Joseph Andrews* (1742). Even before this, however, Fielding had written the more consistently mock-epic *Jonathan Wild* (not published, however, until 1743), a possible model for Smollett's *Ferdinand Count Fathom* (1753). Predictably, this mode of writing is fairly alien to most eighteenth-century female novelists, although Fielding's Preface to his half-sister Sarah's *David Simple* unhelpfully describes her book as a 'comic epic in prose'. Mock-epic mannerisms have a long tradition, however, becoming virtually a default-mode among classically educated, or simply Fielding-inspired, male authors. They still flourish in Joyce's *Ulysses*.

Satire is another complex issue. Originally a classical genre, and often regarded as the only originally Roman one, it was thus also initially asociated with male authors. The great Latin models were the harshly censorious Juvenal and the mildly urbane Horace. Technically, too, there are two major forms of satire: *formal* (or direct) and *indirect*. In the first type, the satirist speaks – normally in the first person – to the reader, or to another character known as the *adversarius*, in the second type, characters or groups ridicule themselves indirectly by what they say or do. Like epic, satire is also originally associated with literary contexts other than prose fiction: above all, poetry and the stage. Where the novel was concerned, one critic has even suggested that 'satire was poured into an essentially nonsatiric genre'.[4]

Like epic, satire also has many intermediaries on its way to the eighteenth-century English novel. In the context of fiction alone, one major element is the tradition of anti-romance, most famously embodied by Cervantes's *Don Quixote* (1605/1615). Other important continental masters of mock-heroic are Charles Sorel and Paul Scarron; and yet another kind of satirical voice is the sometimes ingenuous, and at other times worldly, protagonist of continental picaresque, from the anonymous *Lazarillo de Tormes* (1554) to Lesage's *Gil Blas* (1715/1724/1735).[5]

A number of qualifications must be made, however, against attempts to gender satire as exclusively male: in their own ways, Behn, Manley and Haywood at the beginning of the period, Burney and Austen at the end, with numbers of female novelists between them, all show a talent for satire. Behn nevertheless had to claim the *male* satirist's prerogative of outspokenness when she begged recognition for her own 'masculine part' in the manifesto to *The Lucky Chance* (1686). Haywood published a satirical attack on prime minister Walpole before the appearance of Fielding's more famous *Jonathan Wild*.[6] Her *Anti-Pamela* collection (1741), with its various spoofs of Richardson, represents the more specialized satirical sub-genre of literary parody.

The clearest challenge to the idea of satire as an all-male preserve, however, is provided by Manley. Her powerful synthesis of satire, scandal and eros – as exemplified by *The Secret History of Queen Zara* (1705) or *The New Atalantis* (1709) – questions all simplistic gender divisions. As the eighteenth century advances, however, and Augustan neo-classical values recede, there is a widespread ideological tendency to see a masculine sphere of satire in opposition to a feminine one of sentiment. The Preface to *Evelina* twice acknowledges Smollett, most acerbic of eighteenth-century novelist–satirists; but Burney's own propensity for satire is subject to self-censorship in her first novel, and to paternal restraint with her unpublished play 'The Witlings'.[7] Austen's satire, although comparisons between two such diverse writers may seem incongruous, actually follows Haywood in its early emphasis on literary parody. After the *Juvenilia* and *Northanger Abbey*, on the other hand, there is increasingly subtle irony – and even humour – in Austen's novels of manners, but correspondingly little satire.

The predominance of male authors in the context of satire is nevertheless borne out by numbers. Just over half of the men in the corpus produced one or more predominantly satirical works by any definition of the term, although satire for this group may be less a natural male proclivity than a simple corollary of reading the classics: well educated young gentlemen cut their teeth on such Latin authors as Juvenal.[8] The satirical models adopted by these and other writers in eighteenth-century fiction are many and varied. A number of novels overturn classificatory schemes, whilst a complex work like *Tristram Shandy* virtually annihilates them. But one may still abstract various smaller groupings: Francis Coventry's *Pompey the Little* (1751), Charles Johnstone's *Chrysal; or, The Adventures of a Guinea* (1760–5), and Smollett's *History and Adventures of an Atom* (1769) are thus narratives where the protagonist is non-human.[9] The first of these works inspired some revealing comments by John Cleland, author of *Fanny Hill*:

> [H]e every where displays a perfect knowledge of the world, through all its ranks and follies. These he ridicules, with a fineness of edge, unknown to the sour satyrist, or the recluse philosopher. Even his negligencies are pleasing. The GENTLEMAN, in short, breathes through the whole performance, and the vein of pleasantry is every where evenly upheld, from the beginning to the end.[10]

No doubt unwittingly, Cleland goes far towards providing both a gender and a genealogy for satire. The satirist is effectively a *man* of the *world* (thus excluding women novelists by sex, and Richardson by education). He holds the opinions of a *gentleman*, and can presumably express these wittily even without benefit of speech: for Coventry's lap-dog protagonist later soils the *Memoirs* of the 'underbred' preacher Whitefield in a company of Methodists, a group regularly targeted by other gentlemen authors, including Fielding himself.

There is more consistent religious satire in the *Spiritual Quixote* (1773) of Richard Graves, whose attacks on Methodism are entirely appropriate for an Anglican vicar. The effect may be less interesting today, however, than Charlotte Lennox's at first sight more restricted parody of seventeenth-century French romances in *The Female Quixote* (1752) a generation earlier: for Lennox (as argued in Chapter 8) also provides a secondary veiled satire of patriarchal order, which must be extrapolated by the attentive reader. Other literary parodies on the same Quixotic model include Smollett's *Sir Launcelot Greaves*, much concerned with legal malpractice; William Beckford's *Modern Novel Readers* (1796) and *Azemia* (1797), with their burlesques of sentimental novels; Thomas Holcroft's *The History of Manthorn, the Enthusiast* (1778–9), one more exposure of religious fanaticism, particularly Methodism; and perhaps even Samuel Pratt's *Shenstone-Green; or, The New Paradise Lost* (1779), satirizing the contemporary fashion for utopian fiction exemplified in turn by Sarah Scott's *Millennium Hall* (1779).

Another critical perspective links satire with a tradition of learned wit, running from Swift through Fielding to Sterne. The resemblances of Swift and Sterne to Thomas Amory and Robert Paltock were also apparent to that pioneer critic, Clara Reeve, whose *Progress of Romance* (1785) collected Paltock's *Peter Wilkins* (1750), Amory's *John Buncle* (1756, 1766) and *Tristram Shandy* (1760–8) together with Swift's satires under the rubric of 'Novels and Stories Original and Uncommon'. A contemporary reviewer described *Peter Wilkins* as 'the illegitimate offspring of no very natural conjunction betwixt *Gulliver's Travels* and *Robinson Crusoe*',[11] although the novel's consistently fantastic element suggests that Swift's genes were stronger. The esoterically learned *John Buncle*, on the other hand, seems closer to Sterne. Northrop Frye's catch-all fictional category of the '*Menippean* satire'[12] (later modified to 'Anatomy') even suggests a suitable *classical* model for Sterne, although due emphasis should also be given to the continental tradition of Rabelais or the indigenous one of Swift.

Two otherwise totally dissimilar novelists such as Goldsmith and Walpole are linked by their common use of the alien protagonist, in *The Citizen of the World* (1762) and the *Letter from Xo Ho* (1757), respectively. Letters from a fictional foreign observer were a favourite vehicle for satire, and Goldsmith's longer work is the best-known English imitation of Montesquieu's *Lettres persanes* (1721), the most celebrated example of this particular literary model. The same outsider status, if at closer remove, also characterizes such 'foreigners' as the Welshman Matthew Bramble in England (and later Scotland) in Smollett's *Humphry Clinker* (1771).[13]

Also relevant here are translations of satire. Goldsmith himself produced a long series, including Paul Scarron's major mock-heroic narrative *Le Roman comique* (1775). The key translator of satirical narratives, however, is undoubtedly Smollett, with his versions of Lesage's picaresque classic *Gil Blas* (1748), and of *Don Quixote* (1755), as well as his extensive collaboration on an edition of Voltaire.[14] As argued in Chapter 7, Smollett and not Sterne (far less Fielding) is the major satirical novelist; he is also the point of reference for the remaining satirical writers in this group, including Shebbeare and Moore.[15]

In conclusion, it may be suggested that, if epic (or *mock*-epic) is fairly straightforward in eighteenth-century fiction, then satire is more complex. Direct or indirect, it may also be mediated by the fictional traveller, foreign correspondent, spy, picareqsque anti-hero or simply some authorial *alter ego*. Typically, however, satirists are *formally educated males* – or, in the proto-canon of eighteenth-century fiction, Fielding and Smollett. Four seminal examples of the tendency are therefore *Joseph Andrews* (1742), *Jonathan Wild* (1743), *Roderick*

Random (1748), and *Humphry Clinker* (1771), all of which are discussed at length in later chapters.

Letters and Journals

The literary mode most closely associated with eighteenth-century female *novelists* is that of letter fiction or the epistolary novel. And here, one should abandon modern preconceptions of the form as antiquated, cumbersome, or simply marginal to the narrative tradition. In her lengthy introduction to *The British Novelists* (1810), for example, Mrs Barbauld regarded it as a technique as valid as any other:

> There are three modes of carrying on a story: the narrative or epic as it may be called; in this the author relates himself the whole adventure; this is the manner of Cervantes in his *Don Quixote*, and of Fielding in his *Tom Jones....* Another mode is that of memoirs; where the subject of the adventures relates his own story. Smollett, in his *Roderick Random*, and Goldsmith in his *Vicar of Wakefield*, have adopted this mode.... A third way remains, that of epistolary *correspondence*, carried on between the characters of the novel.[16]

Playwright Richard Cumberland, in a speculative passage from his novel *Henry* (1795), even reduced the question to one of simple alternatives ('A novel may be carried on in a series of letters, or in regular detail'), and concluded: 'For myself, having now made experiments of both methods, I can only say, that, were I to consult my own amusement solely, I should prefer the vehicle of letters.'[17]

In terms of gender, the case for regarding letter fiction as a 'woman's form' looks strong, but not unassailable. That a number of English writers of *both* sexes actually published epistolary novels well before the appearance of *Pamela* is clearly established. The prototype here is the first volume (at least) of Behn's *roman à clef, Love-Letters Between a Nobleman and His Sister* (1683–7), followed by works from – among others – Manley, Mary Davys and Haywood.[18]

Robert Adams Day's account of European and classical precursors of the English epistolary novel makes the bold claim that 'between 1660 and 1740 little was done in English fiction which the French had not done before and done better' (p. 27). English writers were thus drawing heavily on continental *literary* sources: the letters of Eloisa and Abelard and the *Lettres portugaises* were particularly well known in

England. In the case of Behn and Manley, the travel writing and *chroniques scandaleuses* of Marie D'Aulnoy were also formative. Mme D'Aulnoy's *Travels in Spain* and her more suggestive *Memoirs of the Court of England* (1693) both used epistolary form.[19] Even the letter fiction itself, of course, had classical precedents.[20] Of the classical and continental precursors Day quotes, however, only *Eloisa and Abelard* offers – in embryonic form – the genuine *exchange* of letters that appears in that paragon of English epistolary novels, *Clarissa*.

Among the writers discussed in this survey, twenty of the women wrote epistolary novels (some using no other form), as opposed to barely half-a-dozen among the men. In the first decades of the eighteenth century, it is true, this contrast between the sexes is not so clear, but by the end of the century female pre-eminence is obvious.[21] By and large, moreover, gender distinctions can be usefully related to Robert Adams Day's division of letter fiction before *Pamela* into four different types: love story, scandalous chronicle, letters relating a journey or similar adventure, and 'spy' letters. In the early letter fiction based on the scandalous chronicle, as well as in the more central tradition of the love story, women writers predominate. Letters relating a journey or similar adventure, on the other hand, show a noticeable male bias, with 'spy' letters providing an even clearer example of this.

Richardson's entire fictional output and Smollett's *Humphry Clinker* (1771) are obviously male-authored works which run counter to this trend; Smollett's last novel is nevertheless constructed round a journey, unlike the more stationary love story of *Pamela* (1740). For several other male writers in the second half of the century, moreover, the epistolary precedents are clearer.[22] Even John Cleland's *Memoirs of a Woman of Pleasure* ['Fanny Hill'] (1748–9) – for all its insistent priapism – is ultimately an extended male projection of a feminocentric narrative, just like *Pamela*; but Cleland's 'memoir' itself, two lengthy letters to an anonymous female addressee, is incidentally as remote from the polyvocal tendencies of more complex letter fiction as is the 'journal' that actually constitutes most of Richardson's first novel.[23]

Epistolary narratives with a more satirical turn include Charles Johnstone's highly derivative *The Pilgrim* (1775), where the letters of Choang, the Chinese pilgrim, explain such phenomena as highwaymen, rakes and gamblers to the 'Supreme Mandarin of the Province of Quang-Tong'. The clear model here is Goldsmith's *Citizen of the World*.[24] In both cases, one could argue, the satirical content associated with male authors is more significant than the epistolary form typical of female novelists. Letter fiction describing a journey or similar adventure is also fairly gender specific: the most famous case once again is *Humphry Clinker*, where the male author gives 85 per cent of the material to two male correspondents. One would perhaps expect the vast majority of travel literature at the time (in any form) to be produced by more geographically and socially mobile male writers, and Percy Adams's monumental *Travel Literature and the Evolution of the Novel* confirms this hypothesis.

Among men writing after Richardson, however, only Robert Bage could be regarded as a *predominantly* (four out of six) epistolary novelist. His letter fiction also covers a considerable dramatic range, from utopian fantasy (*Mount Henneth*, 1782) and sentimental odyssey (*Barham Downs*, 1784), to Eastern exoticism and American topicality (*The Fair Syrian*, 1787), and incipient *Bildungsroman* (*James Wallace*, 1788). Another interesting anomaly is Thomas Holcroft, whose two epistolary novels actually suggest something of the contrasting perspectives of Richardson and Smollett: the apparently autobiographical *Alwyn; or, The Gentleman Comedian* (1780) thus describes the hero's experiences with a group of strolling players in rapidly shifting comic scenes reminiscent of *Humphry Clinker*; the 130 letters of *Anna St Ives* (1792), on the other hand, where the heroine aspires to reform the rakish Coke Clifton without being seduced in the process, have obvious echoes of *Clarissa*.

With male authors in general, there is a significant correlation between degree of formal education and certain types of letter fiction. If the satirical protagonists of the university-educated Walpole, Goldsmith, and Johnstone are (in the works cited) quite literally *men* of the *world* like their creators, then the more sentimental Richardsonian letter fiction is characteristically produced by women without benefit of such exposure.[25] The obvious context for pursuing this argument is the juxtaposition, in Chapters 4 and 5, of Richardson (an exclusively epistolary novelist) with Fielding (whose occasional interpolated letters are often mere comic impersonations of sub-literacy). The reverse side is that, for female novelists from Behn to early Austen – among whom a strong formal education is exceptional – letter fiction is almost the rule.

Day's other two categories, the love story and the scandalous chronicle, seem to be predominantly female sub-genres. He describes Mary Davys's *Familiar Letters Betwixt a Gentleman and a Lady* (1725) as 'the most realistic letters in early English fiction' and identifies Haywood's *Irish Artifice; or, The History of Clarina* (1728) as the first work to bring 'sordid and realistic matter' to the form. Manley's semi-fictional second collection, *The Lady's Pacquet Broke Open* (1707), as its title suggests, is closer to scandalous chronicle than to love story.

If *Pamela* was not the original epistolary novel, then it certainly proved a watershed, since after Richardson, English letter fiction generally abandoned satire and scandal to concentrate on sentiment, and thus predictably came from female pens. In spite of these restrictions, however, it still covered a remarkable thematic and technical range. Mary Collyer's *Felicia to Charlotte* (1744) and its sequel, *Letters from Felicia to Charlotte* (1749), have a curiously ambivalent attitude towards love, in their mingling of sentimentalism and virtual self-parody; Sarah Fielding's *Familiar Letters between the Principal Characters in David Simple* normally avoids erotic psychology entirely for a characteristic moral allegory; Elizabeth Griffith, besides more conventional letter fiction, produced the curious quasi-documentary record of her own courtship and marriage in the *Letters between Henry and Frances* (1757, 1767, 1770). Frances Sheridan's *Memoirs of Miss Sidney Biddulph* (1761), in terms of its tragic theme and its publishing history, is the novel most closely associated with Richardson. Frances Brooke has three letter fictions to her name, including the tragic *History of Julia Mandeville* (1763) – praised by Voltaire as the best English novel since *Clarissa*.[26]

Burney's *Evelina* (1775), the major epistolary novel of the last three decades of the century, is discussed in greater detail in Chapter 8, where it is juxtaposed with Charlotte Lennox's *The Female Quixote*. But even Lennox uncharacteristically produced an epistolary novel, entitled *Ephemia* (1790), with an American setting and presumably autobiographical basis. On the other hand, Austen's only exclusively epistolary work (apart from such juvenilia as *Love and Freindship* and *Lesley Castle*) is *Lady Susan*. Often heavily satirical in tone (Terry Castle even draws analogies with *Shamela*), the latter thus almost moves full circle, by returning to an older tradition of letter fiction represented by Manley and D'Aulnoy.

The *Journal* in eighteenth-century fiction is in some respects a kind of appendix to the epistolary novel. Of the narratives discussed in Part II, for example, *Pamela* is as much *journal* as *letter fiction* in simple structural terms; whilst *Evelina* – with its intimate relationship to Burney's diaries – approaches the journal in a purely autobiographical context.

The ideological or aesthetic commitment of a writer to letter fiction is another significant factor: Behn, Burney, and Austen later abandoned or transcended the form, Smollett graduated to it, Lennox finally succumbed; only for Richardson was epistolarity a constant. Smollett's *Humphry Clinker* is a critical anomaly: together with *Clarissa* and *Evelina*, it is the most brilliant letter fiction of the period, although its epistolarity is in some ways almost incidental. Smollett's final narrative provides neither *lettres-confidence* or *lettres-drame*;[27] it may be most usefully seen as travelogue or satire (even if its two male correspondents allow contrasting satirical perspectives).

Virginia Woolf, a novelist who thought at length a century and a half later about most women's issues, has interesting insights on the letter-writing situation. Far from the energetic movement of *Humphry Clinker*, however, she envisaged the archetypal correspondence as involving two individuals, isolated and immobile, surmounting obstacles in order to communicate; by the very terms of the definition, such individuals were normally women, and it is in the context of such social conditioning, finally, that classic letter fiction may be regarded as a potentially female genre.

Stage and Closet

Attempts were made above to isolate certain generic forms – satire, epic, or the picaresque – which, for various social or cultural reasons, could be associated with male (or *hieratic*) authors in eighteenth-century English fiction. These forms were then contrasted with the one narrative mode, epistolarity, which can most plausibly be identified with the female (or at least *demotic*) novelist. In other literary forms, however, such simple gender divisions are less helpful, one obvious case being the drama.

Well over half of the women writers mentioned in this survey wrote for the theatre, with varying degrees of commercial success. To this number, one might add such works as Burney's entertaining comedy 'The Witlings' (suppressed after family concern over its satirical content) or Austen's brief adaptation of *Grandison* (obviously never intended for the public stage). The most successful female dramatist of the entire period was clearly Behn, and seventeen of her plays are extant today; *The Rover* (1677), best known of her characteristic comedies of intrigue, remained popular throughout the eighteenth century.

In the first decades of the eighteenth century, Manley's four plays reflect a whole range of literary impulses typical of the seventeenth century; the periodically prolific Haywood also wrote at least four plays. During the final decades, eight more women among the corpus of novelists wrote substantially for the theatre, whether comedies (both originals and highly professional adaptations), tragedies, or romantic and sensational drama.[28] The most significant female dramatist after Behn, however, was undoubtedly Elizabeth Inchbald. For over twenty years, she remained supreme in both English farce and French comedy. She also played a central part in introducing the German sentimental drama to the late eighteenth-century English public; it is her adaptation of Kotzebue's *Lovers' Vows* which wreaks such physical and emotional havoc in *Mansfield Park*.

The proportion of men who wrote for the theatre is just under half, although several of these – most notably, Congreve – are better known as dramatists. Fielding was perhaps the most versatile and successful playwright of the 1720s and 1730s, writing eight classic five-act comedies, as well as the numerous farces and burlesques for which he is better remembered. Henry Brooke has interesting politico-historical links with the Fielding silenced by the Licensing Act of 1737, since his own tragedy *Gustavus Vasa* (1739) was also banned for veiled attacks on Walpole and his government; Smollett, who waged an unsuccessful campaign for the performance of his blank-verse Scottish tragedy *The Regicide* (written in 1739 and not published until ten years later) might have been happy even for this attention, although his farce, *The Reprisal* (1757), was a highly successful afterpiece.[29]

A writer of Goldsmith's versatility is difficult to place, but the two classic comedies, *The Good Natur'd Man* (1768) and *She Stoops to Conquer* (1773) – together with a seminal 'Essay on the Theatre' – may suggest (as with Congreve) a greater eminence as dramatist than novelist.[30] Of the better-known male authors from the end of the century, William Godwin produced two tragedies,[31] while both Matthew Lewis and Thomas Holcroft were successful and versatile dramatists. Lewis wrote at least a dozen plays, comprising comedy, farce, satire, two tragedies (including *The Harper's Daughter* after Schiller, in 1813), and the melodramas that were the obvious theatrical equivalent of the Gothic novel. Holcroft, whose output was twice even that of Lewis, was equally broad in range, although his most celebrated piece was possibly *The Follies of the Day* (1784), a version of Beaumarchais's highly subversive *The Marriage of Figaro*.

From such a mass of raw data, certain inferences may be made. The marginally greater percentage of women writing for the theatre is probably insignificant, but it is interesting to note that none of these managed to produce a marketable tragedy after Haywood's *The Fair Captive* (1721). Most of the men wrote at least one, however, although none of these could match Joseph Addison's highly regarded (but now almost forgotten) *Cato* (1713). The stock neo-classical tragedy drew on the heroics of Dryden and the subjects of antiquity, and few women writers would have been at home with either element. One may conversely note the relative failure (between Congreve and Richard Sheridan, that is) of male authors in the area of social comedies. Fielding could never produce one to rival his farces in popularity, and, judging by remarks to his cousin Lady Mary Wortley Montagu, remained acutely aware of this failing.[32]

Genealogies of eighteenth-century theatre are commonplace, and Dryden's drama is one obvious influence. But if the latter's heroic tragedies soon proved difficult for even male authors to emulate, the 'laughing comedy' of the Restoration offered greater inspiration: Goldsmith's *She Stoops to Conquer* is a fine example. In his essay 'On the Theatre' (1773), Goldsmith mourned a vanishing tradition and defended the 'laughing comedy' against the currently fashionable 'weeping' one, noting disparagingly that 'those abilities that can hammer out a novel are fully sufficient for the production of a sentimental comedy'.[33]

The cultivation (or rejection) of sensibility is an important cross-fertilizing element between drama and novel in the final decades of the century. If Richard Cumberland's sentimental touchstone comedy *The West Indian* is exactly contemporary with Mackenzie's *Man of Feeling* (1771), then the quite diverse belly laughs of Goldsmith's *She Stoops to Conquer* and Graves's *Spiritual Quixote* also coincided two years later. Attempts to 'gender' sentimental drama are risky; and yet, the strong literary tradition derived from Richardson's *Grandison* and developed by the female novelists through Burney and Austen is known precisely as the *comedy of manners*. Of the novelists considered more fully in Part II, several had major dramatic careers (Behn and Fielding as playwrights, Lennox primarily as an actress). Defoe seems largely indifferent to the stage, Richardson generally disapproving, and Austen at best ambivalent, although Smollett and Burney – in their different ways – were both frustrated dramatists.

More concrete differentials between the sexes appear in other theatrical contexts, and the pioneering Aphra Behn refers explicitly to two of these. If the female dramatist was condemned by society's double standards for writing bawdy or portraying morally dubious actions, she could at least write a good play without benefit of formal classical education. For the Augustan *man* of letters, incidentally, it took a remarkably long time to realize that the female novelist could write a good novel under similar conditions. Behn's argument is developed in her *Epistle to the Reader*, added to the published version of *The Dutch Lover* (1673). There is an ironic postscript to the question more than a century later, moreover, when Inchbald embarked on the 125 prefatory essays for her momentous twenty-five volumes of *The British Theatre*. When she expressed misgivings to Longman about her own ignorance, the publishers assured her that no learning was expected of a woman!

Another socio-cultural dimension rarely acknowledged is the high incidence of women who not only *wrote* for the stage, but *acted* on it, too. Haywood seems to have performed a large number of roles in both London and Dublin; and Behn may have done the same a generation earlier, although this would have been a highly compromising activity. Even Penelope Aubin appeared at the Haymarket to speak the Prologue of *The Merry Masqueraders*. Lennox and Griffith at mid-century had considerable acting careers, whilst the latter – like Frances Sheridan – belonged to a great theatrical family. Inchbald herself acted in London, Dublin, and the provinces for nearly twenty years (1772 to 1789). The only full-time actors in the corpus, on the other hand, were Pratt and Holcroft;[34] in this, as in other matters, both clearly gravitate – like most of their female colleagues – to what was earlier defined as the demotic pole in English fiction.

Among other aspects of female involvement with the theatre, one should not forget economic or even existential factors. Haywood was paid 600 guineas by Sir Richard Steele at the Theatre Royal for her historical drama *Lucius, The First Christian King of Britain*, and it was not until Radcliffe or the later works of Burney that any female *novelist* could command a comparable sum for a piece of fiction. For Mary Davys, eking out a precarious widowhood, or Aubin, described by one modern critic as 'the complete Grub Street hack', writing was a necessity. Certainly, no female playwright ever intentionally wrote 'closet drama' in the manner of Walpole's *The Mysterious Mother*.

On the other hand, for a social group generally denied a decent education and opportunities for foreign travel, the theatrical world could provide important surrogate experiences. Thus by her mid-twenties, after a variegated existence in London and Dublin, Elizabeth Griffith had played Shakespeare's Juliet and Cordelia, Calista (in Nicholas Rowe's *The Fair Penitent*) and Lucinda (in Steele's *The Conscious Lovers*). Still more impressive, Inchbald had left her country home, gone on the London stage, and married a fellow actor – all by the age of eighteen. Just before her death, the Catholic Inchbald followed her confessor's advice and burned her unfinished memoirs; the loss is certainly ours.

The above considerations suggest ways in which women's experience of the theatre may have differed from that of men. To suggest, however, that any dramatic form (even heroic tragedy) might have been an exclusively or essentially 'female genre' is a more hazardous enterprise.

Instruction and Delight

Significant formative elements of mainstream fiction not yet considered include conduct literature and the magazines, the traditional romance and the oriental tale. And here, a clear division emerges: for, rather than suggesting common aims, the didacticism of the conduct book and the escapism of romance might sound mutually exclusive – a case of instruction *or* delight, not both. But after the virtual eclipse of conduct books by more sophisticated magazines, featuring oriental tales and every other kind of fiction (complete or abridged), instruction *and* delight is again a plausible combination.

Now a common denominator of even the strictest conduct book or most frivolous romance is courtship, whether regulated by male presumption or fictionalized through a feminized genre. This shared interest of conduct book and romance, then, is a useful starting-point. The close relation of eighteenth-century fiction to the conduct book tradition is strongly argued in Nancy Armstrong's *Desire and Domestic Fiction*, subtitled 'A Political History of the Novel', although often more a political history of the conduct book. Armstrong argues for a new female focus and a new female role model in eighteenth-century fiction; this so-called *feminization* of fiction is illustrated by readings of *Pamela* and *Emma*. There also emerges a new *male* literary type – to counterbalance the new female – beginning with Richardson's 'good man' and running from Sheridan's Faulkland, Burney's Orville and Inchbald's Dorriforth to Austen's D'Arcy.

The courtship novel itself has also been regarded as clearly gendered in its rejection of 'masculine plots of pursuit, seduction, and betrayal' for 'feminine ones of courtship and marriage'.[35] Eliza Haywood, a prolific writer of erotic fiction who was then silent for many years before producing more soberly didactic novels, would neatly exemplify the transition from the first to the second type. Other courtship novels, according to the above definition, would include works by Mary Collyer, Haywood, Lennox, Frances Brooke, Sarah Scott, Burney, Wollstonecraft, Smith, Inchbald and Edgeworth – or approximately half of the female novelists under consideration. Among male authors after Richardson, on the other hand, only Mackenzie's *Julia de Roubigné* and Holcroft's *Anna St Ives* are unambiguously courtship novels.

The gendering of the *oriental tale* is far more problematic, as may be seen from the various precursors of the mode. In 1716, Fielding's cousin Lady Mary Wortley Montagu thus left England for a two-year residence with her ambassador husband at the Ottoman Court, and her fifty-two Turkish Embassy letters (often strongly anecdotal) were widely read. Antoine Galland's translation of Near Eastern tales had begun appearing in French as the *Mille et Une Nuit* in 1704, with an English version appearing almost concurrently; the interest provoked by the collection could hardly be exaggerated.

It is possible to see the *Arabian Nights* (to adopt their common English title) as a 'counterpart of sorts to the great male tradition' of the eighteenth century; by extension, then, the oriental tale might have been thought to appeal to 'female novelists'.[36] Among oriental tales by male authors, Johnson's *Rasselas* is presumably the best known. There are also a number of tales in periodicals such as Johnson's *Rambler* and Hawkesworth's *Adventurer*. The list would also include the many famous redactions of tales from the *Arabian Nights* found in Addison's *Spectator* and Steele's *Guardian*. It is incidentally a tale from the latter that provides the source for Lewis's sensational Gothic novel, *The Monk* (1796).[37]

The oriental tale also seems to show a clearly gendered division in the context of *satire*, a distinction which may be seen in terms of subversion *versus* restraint. By a rule of thumb, the narratives of the oriental in Europe (such as Goldsmith's or Walpole's reworkings of the *Lettres persanes* or 'spy' motif) are predominantly satirical, and feature male protagonists. The narratives of the oriental (and even the European) in the east, on the other hand, may often be read in a feminist perspective as the 'rejection of divinely and *patriarchally* sanctioned singularity of purpose' [my emphasis].[38] The only incidental reservation here might be one of labels: the term 'oriental' covers such a diffuse, catch-all range of narratives, as to lose much of its usefulness.[39]

The non-satirical oriental tale, with its rich dose of exoticism and escapist fantasy, also has obvious generic and thematic links with the similarly diffuse category of *romance*. Regarding the origins of the latter, Gillian Beer notes helpfully that, in the early Middle Ages, the term 'romance' referred to the new vernacular languages derived from Latin, and only subsequently to aspects of the literature written in these tongues. The old French *romant* or *roman* thus came to mean both 'courtly romance in verse', as well as 'popular book'; or, as Beer neatly concludes:

> The 'popular' and the 'aristocratic' strains in the romance are already suggested in the term; though the subject-matter of the romances was courtly, its language could be understood by all.[40]

The *demotic* and the *hieratic* (the humble Richardson and the aristocratic Fielding, as it were) are thus inscribed within a single text.

Several of the novels discussed at length below have regularly been defined as romances, whether by their authors or by their critics: they include such utterly disparate productions as *Oroonoko*, *Pamela*, and *Roderick Random*. Two more texts, *The Female Quixote* and *Northanger Abbey*, are moreover classic examples of *anti-* or *parody*-romance; it will later be necessary to consider both eighteenth-century perspectives on the form (culminating in Clara Reeve's admirable *Progress of Romance*) and more sophisticated twentieth-century theories (particularly Northrop Frye's famous thesis of the novel as a *displacement* of romance). The immediate issue, however, is a possible gender differential among romance writers, a case that might be argued as follows.

Although *Don Quixote* is a kind of watershed in the history of the romance, it also concludes a cycle, according to a pattern for which English fiction between Behn and Austen provides a number of analogues. The most obvious example is that of *Pamela*, inspiring *Shamela* and a host of other lesser known anti-Pamelas. The criminal romances popular in the first decades of the eighteenth century are similarly a target of Fielding's parody in *Jonathan Wild*. A more widespread sub-species at the beginning of the century was the long French romance exemplified by Honoré d'Urfée's *L'Astrée* or Madeleine de Scudéry's *Le Grand Cyrus*.[41] Charlotte Lennox's *Female Quixote* is the anti-romance intended, rather belatedly, to parody the form. And, perhaps most famously, the Gothic Romances of Radcliffe, anticipated by Walpole's *Castle of Otranto* (1765), Reeve's *Old English Baron* (1777), and Sophia Lee's *The Recess* (1783–5), were the immediate stimulus for *Northanger Abbey*. Beckford's *Modern Novel Readers* (1796) and *Azemia* (1797) later took a similar impetus from sentimental fiction, and so the pattern continues. At this point, it is worth remembering Gillian Beer's useful reminder that 'the realistic novels of one age or audience have an uncanny way of becoming "romances" in another setting' (p. 5).

But this account is over-simplified: Austen clearly admires Radcliffe, and perhaps other Gothic novelists, too; as far as novels of chivalry are concerned, moreover, Cervantes's *Don Quixote* is at once the *negation* and the *apotheosis* of romance – the ultimate parody and the sublime celebration. In either case, attempts to gender such a profoundly ambivalent genre might be hazardous. If one exchanges literal gender distinctions for largely co-terminous cultural or educational ones, however, a broad hypothesis emerges. According to this, the formally educated male author, *hieratic* (to resume the religious metaphor) and moving generically 'down-market' (to co-opt an economic one), maintains an essentially detached, even ironically subversive, attitude towards romance; Smollett's *Roderick Random* is a good example. The less culturally privileged *demotic* novelist, moving 'up-market' from even more ephemeral forms, is better equipped – in a serious and constructive spirit – to adopt and adapt the genre to contemporary ideological debates; this is noticeable in the context of Lennox and Radcliffe. In this sense, too, female novelists seem to correlate highly with romance, and male authors with parodies or inversions of the genre.

It is interesting to note finally that in formulations of this kind, the woman writer represents the norm, and the male author a kind of supplement, suggesting one possible sense in which *romance* (and/or the *novel*) might truly be a female genre. Combining this argument with the later readings of individual novels, a sceptical reader might again deduce that Richardson was a woman and Lennox a man, whilst Austen underwent a sex change. And perhaps, in some figurative sense, these claims are true.

The linking of various literary genres with gender will remain contentious. When gender is combined with social class, however, and both categories are then viewed in the light of totally segregated eighteenth-century educational practices, the new complementary binary of *hieratic* and *demotic* is a more feasible concept. It also recalls distinctions made in one of the most celebrated comparative studies in European literary history: Erich Auerbach's *Mimesis*.[42] Central to Auerbach's study of the 'representation of reality in Western literature' was his hypothesis of *Stiltrennung*, or 'separation of styles': at its simplest, a higher style grounded in the classical languages and their formal rhetoric *versus* a lower style drawing on the Bible and Christian tradition. There is also a related division of subject matter: Auerbach thus comments on an account by the Greek historian Thucydides, of an impending military expedition:

> the movement is characterized as a whole . . . just as the observer sees it, looking, as it were, from above; but it could not possibly occur

that reactions so various among so many individuals of the common people should be made a major subject of literary treatment.   (p. 44)

There is even a fundamental syntactic distinction, denoted in traditional grammar by the terms *hypotaxis* and *parataxis*. The *hypotactic* sentence is characterized by the use of subordinate constructions joined by conjunctions; the *paratactic* sentence prefers phrases linked through juxtaposition (and . . . but) or punctuation. Virtually any sentence from classical prose will exemplify hypotaxis; scholars from late antiquity to the Renaissance, on the other hand, regularly criticized the Bible for its crudely paratactic style.[43] And since a classical education in eighteenth-century England was a virtual monopoly of the male sex, Auerbach's stylistic distinctions should correlate quite highly with the gender-based ones argued in this study.

Fielding predictably fulfils critical expectations, as in the opening lines of *Amelia*:

The various accidents which befel a very worthy couple after their uniting in the state of matrimony will be the subject of the following history. The distresses which they waded through were some of them so exquisite, and the incidents which produced these so extra-ordinary, that they seemed to require not only the utmost malice, but the utmost invention, which superstition hath ever attributed to Fortune: though whether any such being interfered in the case, or, indeed, whether there be any such being in the universe, is a matter which I by no means presume to determine in the affirmative.

Readers may count for themselves, but the second sentence seems to contain eight subordinate clauses. There is a popular, if vanishing, con-cept of something known as the 'Latin period' (i.e. sentence); Fielding – with his classical education and neo-classical aesthetics (further discussed in Chapter 5) – is one of its finest exponents.

Smollett can be stylistically the most Latinate of all eighteenth-century novelists, as a random passage from *Ferdinand Count Fathom* illustrates:

In this manner did the crafty Fathom turn to account those ingratiat-ing qualifications he inherited from nature; and maintain with incredible assiduity and circumspection, an amorous correspondence with two domestic rivals, who watched the conduct of each other, with the most indefatigable virulence of envious suspicion, until an accident happened, which had well-nigh overturned the bark of his policy, and induced him to alter the course, that he might not be shipwrecked on the rocks that began to multiply in the prosecution of his present voyage.   (pp. 106–7)

Surely, no eighteenth-century female novelist could ever have written that! The Latinate element is both syntactic and lexic, although Smollett is also master of other styles, as may be seen from the first letter of the hypochondriac Bramble in *Humphry Clinker*:

Doctor,
    The pills are good for nothing – I might as well swallow snowballs to cool my reins – I have told you over and over, how hard I am to move; and at this time of day, I ought to know something of my own constitution. Why will you be so positive? Prithee send me another subscription –   (p. 5)

Comparisons are not entirely valid, of course, since the first passage is third-person narration, whilst the second is first-person self-characterization, recalling the colloquialism of Sterne. It may be significant, too, that *Fathom* (1753) was published seven years before the first volume of *Tristram Shandy*, and *Humphry Clinker* (1771) four years after the last.

A more relevant comparison with the beginning of *Amelia* might be the opening lines of Charlotte Lennox's *The Female Quixote*:

The Marquis of —— for a long Series of Years, was the first and most distinguished Favourite at Court: He held the most honourable Employments under the Crown, disposed of all Places of Profit as he pleased, presided at the Council, and in a manner governed the whole Kingdom.
    This extensive Authority could not fail of making him many Enemies: He fell at last a Sacrifice to the Plots they were continually forming against him; and was not only removed from all his Employments, but banished the Court for ever.

Here, in spite of authoritative aspirations (i.e. as both omniscient narrator and didactic satirist), Lennox's style is still paratactic – that is demotic.

For the paratactic style in full flow, on the other hand, one may turn to virtually any page in the pseudo-autobiographies of Defoe, although the opening lines of Godwin's *Caleb Williams* offer an even more extreme example:

> My life has for several years been a theatre of calamity. I have been a mark for the vigilance of tyranny, and I could not escape. My fairest prospects have been blasted. My enemy has shown himself inaccessible to entreaties, and untired in persecution. My fame, as well as my happiness, has become his victim. Every one, as far as my story has been known, has refused to assist me in my distress, and has execrated my name. I have not deserved this treatment.

Godwin's almost staccato narrative seems to anticipate quite literally the breathless pursuit which forms the subject of the novel. He also understands how someone from Caleb's cultural background (comparable to that of Moll Flanders or Pamela) might be expected to write; or perhaps he merely draws on his own demotic and Christian fundamentalist origins.

With the support of Auerbach, then, it may be possible to transcend mere gender divisions and list a number of overlapping stylistic, aesthetic or ideological tendencies, which may be arranged on opposite sides of an eighteenth-century narrative divide. These might be tabulated in diagrammatic form as follows:

male author (authority)	female novelist (novelty)
epic/mock-epic	letter fiction/journal
hieratic	demotic
hypotaxis	parataxis

This may be crudely schematic, but such binaries are certainly suggestive in the context of Fielding's histories or Richardson's feminocentric fictions. The paired texts of the final five chapters, on the other hand, are chosen for their widely acknowledged significance in the development of eighteenth-century fiction, rather than their reinforcement of the above arguments. They may thus contradict, as often as they confirm, the ideas developed here. Hopefully, however, these encounters will still prove fruitful.

4

Two Literary Parabolas (i): Richardson from *Familiar Letters* to *Grandison*

After the remarks on critics and theorists in the first chapter, it will be useful to consider Richardson's entire prose output rather than one specific text. For it is striking how often an exceptionally large chunk of this writer's work serves rather modest critical aims (say *Grandison* considered solely as a kind of men's 'conduct book'), or a comparably small chunk inspires such bold theoretical ones (say the role of *Pamela I* in the feminization of the novel). And since Richardson is so central to this study, there had best be as much of him as possible.[1]

His output is admittedly large, far in excess of the three substantial letter fictions which – by themselves – defeat most readers today. The ultimate reason for a broader textual base, however, derives from a sense that Richardson's total prose production inscribes a kind of *parabola*. More subtle than anything that can be defined in terms of mere technical refinement, this movement illustrates a shifting relation between homiletics and poetics, between the position of moral preceptor and that of original novelist. Or, expressed in more practical terms: having once accepted the implicitly humbler role of 'editor', Richardson – as a consistently didactic writer – is then confronted by various problems of authority and legitimization. These problems exist at the simple level of narrative organization, even without the rhetorical ambiguities of epistolary form. Or, expressed even more crudely: for all his dedication to *showing*, a writer of Richardson's moral intensity cannot but hanker after a few more opportunities for plain *telling*. *Pamela I* thus uses an occasional editorial link, whilst *Clarissa* resorts to explanatory footnotes in later editions, before the extraordinary baroque complexity of *Grandison* allows Richardson any number of conduits – male or female – for the views he wants to express. And in his last published work, the *Maxims* (1755), containing reflections from the mouths of characters in the three novels, the balance shifts even further: no longer *author* posing as *editor*, Richardson is now (for the reader who may have previously accepted the autonomy of his characters) the *editor im*posing as *author*.

The obvious solution to the question of textual authority is to legitimize one's *own* narrative, or simply to tell the whole story oneself: a philosophy perhaps of 'I say what I mean, and I mean what I say', favoured by narrators as diverse as Fielding's anonymous males and Lewis Carroll's Humpty Dumpty.[2] Or, seen in another perspective, the choice often corresponds to one of *first-* or *third-*person narrators. There is no doubt that Richardson is increasingly drawn towards the latter. Whilst he never formally abandons letter fiction, the ever lengthier accounts of external events by ever more sensitive and intelligent correspondents effectively generate extended sections of *third-*person narrative. In *Grandison*, the resulting synthesis has a remarkable subtlety and comprehensiveness; it is easy to understand why this work, rather than *Clarissa*, is the true progenitor of the English novel of manners.[3]

It nevertheless seems that after *Grandison*, Richardson was overcome by mental and physical exhaustion; the intellectual effort of saying everything one had to say, whilst effectively excluding oneself from saying it, doubtless took its toll. As a result, the very *Index* to *Grandison* (assembled well after the novel's completion), together with the *Maxims*, initiates a process well defined by critic Jocelyn Harris as the 'compiling moralist' repudiating the 'flexible creations of the novelist'.[4] These processes are further discussed below. It is enough here to reiterate the trope of the *parabola* to characterize Richardson's writing. Fielding's fiction, it will be argued later, inscribes a similar kind of arc, although – with an increasing reliance on *first-*person digressions and interpolations – it should be clear that its trajectory moves in precisely the opposite direction to Richardson's. But that is another story.

Pamela *and Non-literary Models*

Richardson's first known publication is *The Apprentice's Vade Mecum; or, Young Man's Pocket-Companion* (1733), falling squarely within a contemporary didactic tradition: it might have been written by Defoe. Despite its unappealing title, this long pamphlet is not without interest. With a puritan mistrust of the stage, Richardson is also sensitive to aristocratic snobbery about trade, while his subversive view of classical mythology and the ancients is certainly remote from anything recorded by Fielding.[5] This early work has occasional flashes of brilliance, but the overall impression is that of a solemn tract, squarely located in a tradition of popular homiletics.[6]

Between the appearance of the *Vade Mecum* and initial work on the *Familiar Letters* (finally published in 1741) Richardson edited and revised a number of books, including Defoe's *Complete English Tradesman* and *Tour thro the Whole Island of Great Britain*, together with a version of *Aesop's Fables*.[7] The *Letters* themselves are at once more ambitious than their modern short title suggests, and certainly more entertaining than the conventional letter-writing manuals of Richardson's day.[8] They provide both formal models and extensive practical advice.

The most celebrated examples in the collection are understandably numbers CXXXVIII ('A Father to a Daughter in Service, on hearing of her Master's attempting her Virtue') and CXXXVIX ('The Daughter's Answer') for their anticipation of *Pamela*, although the collection contains a number of extended sequences with narrative potential. These include the three-way exchange between father, daughter, and the latter's suitor in Letters XIII–XXI. Rather more mundane is the correspondence over a loan and delays in its repayment (CXVI–CXXIII), although the lively eleven-letter series from 'a young Lady in Town to her Aunt in the Country' (CXLIX–CLIX) stands comparison with the efforts of Smollett's Lydia Bramble in *Humphry Clinker*. The sequence on second marriages (CXL–CXLIII) may reflect personal experience; an earlier letter ('From a Father to a Daughter, against a frothy French Lover') reinforces national stereotypes. The theme of the highly graphic Letter LXII ('A young Woman in Town to her Sister in the Country, recounting her narrow Escape from a Snare laid for her, on her first Arrival, by a wicked Procuress') seems well in character; the extraordinary exercise in grotesque of Letter LXXVI ('A humourous Epistle of neighbourly Occurrences and News, to a Bottle-Companion abroad') is less typical.

Richardson then set aside his model letters to produce an epistolary novel proper; his enthusiasm for the new enterprise is clear from the fact that the first two volumes of *Pamela* were completed, by the author's own reckoning, in exactly two months – despite the demands of a full-time printer's job. Even more striking than this redirection of creative energy, however, is the literary relationship between the two projects. In its clear evolutionary link with the *Familiar Letters* (and the unpretentious didactic works that preceded them), *Pamela* seems a classic example of the fiction derived from 'non-literary', rather than 'literary' models. But *Pamela* even has other claims to such status, according to Richardson's correspondence with his Dutch translator, Johannes Stinstra, and his long-standing friend, Aaron Hill. Writing to Hill in 1741, Richardson recalls in some detail the story surrounding a country house, heard at third hand some twenty-five years previously:

> The owner was Mr B. a gentleman of a large estate in more counties than one.... The lady...was one of the greatest beauties in England; but the qualities of her mind had no equal: beneficent, prudent, and equally beloved and admired by high and low. That she had been taken at twelve years of age for the sweetness of her manners and modesty, and for an understanding above her years, by Mr B—'s mother, a truly worthy lady to wait on her person. Her parents ruined by suretiships, were remarkably honest and pious, and had instilled in their daughter's mind the best principles. When their misfortunes happened first, they attempted a little school, in their village, where they were much beloved; he teached writing and the first rules of arithmetic to boys; his wife plain needle-works to girls, and to knit and spin; but that it answered not: and when the lady took their child, the industrious man earned his bread by day labour, and the lowest kinds of husbandry.[9]

Only the comprehensiveness of the account suggests that Richardson could actually be expanding the original anecdote from invented material fresh in his mind; and the same hypothesis might also apply to the sequel of the story, as retailed to Hill:

> That the girl, improving daily in beauty, modesty, and genteel and good behaviour, by the time she was fifteen, engaged the attention of her lady's son, a young gentleman of free principles, who, on her lady's death, attempted, by all manner of temptations and devices, to seduce her. That she had recourse to as many innocent stratagems to escape the snares laid for her virtue; once, however, in despair, having been near drowning; that, at last, her noble resistance, watchfulness, and excellent qualities, subdued him, and he thought fit to make her his wife. That she behaved herself with so much dignity, sweetness, and humility, that she made herself beloved of every body, and even by his relations, who, at first despised her; and now had the blessings both of rich and poor, and the love of her husband.[10]

Here, the age of the original protagonist (identical with Pamela's), the reference to family persecution (reminiscent of Mr. B.'s sister, Lady Davers), and – above all – the near drowning (recalling Pamela's brief suicide fantasy), again suggest that Richardson could be elaborating the original anecdote. We will presumably never know, although, in the 1753 letter to Stinstra, Richardson is more guarded about the factual basis of the novel ('The Story of Pamela had some slight Foundation in Truth'), and now claims to have heard the tale only fifteen years before beginning *Pamela*, although the source (a gentleman, *via* the local innkeeper) remains the same. But whether *Pamela* is expanded anecdote or not, it surely suggests the non-literary origins appropriate to a novelist whose lack of formal education, like his moral zeal, was only exceeded by Bunyan's.

Links have long been proposed between *Pamela* and the *Familiar Letters*,[11] thus providing a useful corrective to modern novel-centred readings of Richardson. It is worth remembering that in the 1740's, conduct books were an integral part of middle-class experience, whilst the untrue events of 'novels' were, at best, ethically ambivalent; Richardson's contemporaries would have understood and applied – without much prompting – such Pauline misogyny as I Timothy 4: 7 ('But refuse profane and old wives' fables'), quoted in *The Apprentice's Vade Mecum*.

The strongest case for a 'literary' impulse in Richardson is the *theatre*: numerous sources for the importunate rake and hard-pressed maiden have been found in Restoration and early eighteenth-century drama. The very universality of such seduction plots may suggest, however, that the novelist had no need to enter a theatre to find them: far from being influenced by any specific literary motif, then, *Pamela* would correspond to a 'general literary drift' of the period.

Another possible literary model for *Pamela* is the *romance* tradition. Hubert McDermott makes a strong case for identifying Richardson's narratives quite literally with the *genre* of romance: *Pamela* would thus typify a sub-genre of the 'Religious Romance', while *Clarissa* would represent a parody or inversion of the 'Passionate Romance' – a kind of passionate romance gone wrong, as it were, since all of Richardson's readers and doubtless Lovelace himself (it is argued) had assumed that Clarissa would eventually succumb.[12] *Pamela* has also been linked to pastoral romance, particularly Sir Philip Sidney's *Arcadia* (1590). Richardson printed the works of Sidney during the years 1724 and 1725, and it is widely assumed that he borrowed the name of Pamela from this source.[13]

A third and more remote literary model could be the popular fable. Richardson produced his own compilation of Aesop's animal fables in 1739, and there are borrowings from the Greek author throughout his fiction.[14] The distinction between 'literary' and 'non-literary' models becomes increasingly tenuous in the case of Aesop, a *classical* author peddling what is often patently *folk*-lore. It is none the less fair to conclude that Richardson relies predominantly on non-literary (or documentary) sources, and even deviations from these norms owe little or nothing to higher classical genres or the continental romance tradition.

The capacity of *Pamela* to transcend the purely didactic in order to become a *literary* model in its own right is another story. Traditionally, if wrongly, acclaimed as the first epistolary novel in English (or even as the first modern novel, *all categories*), Richardson's fictional debut poses problems on both accounts. If the 'epistolary' concept becomes increasingly marginal (*Pamela* is, after all, mostly journal or memoir), then one may also question the implications of the word 'novel', for in mere formal terms, *Pamela* is a poor fictional prototype: the occasional tedium of the second volume of *Pamela I* (not to mention *Pamela II*) sometimes suggests plain homiletics without much novelistic invention.

Certain elements of the narrative were nevertheless emphasized by twentieth-century critics as anticipating the concerns of the modern psychological novel. The most celebrated of these is the recurrent clothes motif, whether it concerns the embroidered waistcoat which Pamela insists on staying to finish for Mr B. (p. 72), or the three bundles of clothes for the three possible spheres of the heroine's future life (pp. 110–11).[15] Equally 'novelistic' in this sense are those rudimentary flashes of psychological insight, still perhaps in search of adequate literary presentation: the rough depiction of Pamela's nascent love ('why can't I hate him'), or Mr B.'s gnawing jealousy of Parson Williams, at least motivating – if by no means excusing – his treatment of his future wife.[16] But *Pamela* does not rely for very long on narrative suspense. It is by no means the erotic 'cliffhanger' sometimes assumed, for the seduction-*cum*-courtship plot is resolved at a very early stage: marriage is agreed on at the opening of the second volume, although Richardson then manages to sustain almost as much narrative again in *Pamela I*, not to mention the two-volume sequel of the following year.

Despite its remarkable transformation of non-literary material and its subsequent status in traditional histories of the *novel*, however, the main interest of *Pamela* transcends the purely generic connotations of that term. For Richardson's fictional debut raises the broader issues suggested by the concept of the female – or more properly, in Richardson's case, *demotic* – *novelist* with the promise of something *new*.[17]

Pamela's veiled social critique thus illustrates perfectly the powerful theoretical model developed by McKeon, particularly his 'Questions of Truth', according to which a new radical ideology questions a traditional aristocratic one. This process may be followed as early as the tenth letter, when Pamela writes: 'This very gentleman (yes, I *must* call him gentleman, though he has fallen from the merit of that title) has degraded himself to offer freedoms to his poor servant' (pp. 53–4). Such relatively mild comment on the idea of *noblesse oblige* is later reinforced by a severer gloss, after a visit from the local gentry, on family pedigree, with the conclusion that 'Virtue is the only nobility':

> But indeed, even we inferiors, when we get into genteel families, are infected with this vanity; and though we cannot brag of our *own*, we will sometimes pride ourselves in that of our principals. But for my part, I cannot forbear smiling at the absurdity of persons even of the first quality, who value themselves upon their *ancestors* merits, rather than *their own*. For is it not as much as to say, they are conscious they have *no other*. (p. 84)

Imprisoned on Mr B.'s Lincolnshire estate, however, Pamela grows increasingly bitter, as shown by her harsh comment on the abduction ('And pray . . . how came I to be his property? What right has he in me, but such as a thief may plead to stolen goods?'). The scandalized Mrs Jewkes murmurs of 'downright rebellion' (p. 163), although the heroine's indignation hardly seems excessive in the light of Sir Simon's complacent comment:

> Why, what is all this, my dear, but that our neighbour has a mind to his mother's waiting-maid! And if he takes care she wants for nothing, I don't see any great injury will be done her. He hurts no *family* by this. (p. 172)

As Pamela justifiably remarks to her parents, 'it seems, that *poor* people's virtue is to go for nothing'. Mr B.'s claims of omnipotence after the final seduction attempt – 'you now see that you are in my power! You cannot get from me, nor help yourself' (p. 242) – are more disturbing to the modern reader than the rather farcical attempt itself. For Pamela has no form of legal recourse, since Mr B. (local Justice of the Peace in both Bedfordshire and Lincolnshire) effectively *is* the law.

The implied critique of aristocratic authority in these comments is difficult to miss. In this context, the heroine can be seen both as tough defender of her own moral and physical integrity, and even as representative of a new socio-political radicalism. Such approaches nevertheless tend to ignore the fact that the spirited censure of the first two volumes is largely absent from the sequel. Pamela's new sub-missiveness is actually anticipated in the first journal entry of volume two, when, on the way home to her parents at last, she is overtaken by Mr B.'s hard-riding groom with new instructions. Behind the humble plea for Pamela's return, however, lies the spectre of a new submission, another set of standards to which she must conform, whilst Mr B. vets her as a suitable wife: 'let me see, by your compliance, the further excellency of your disposition' (p. 286). After Pamela's spirited resistance in the first volume, the final stages of courtship are far more conventional, as the relationship between the young couple assumes clearly gendered roles, reflecting Richardson's unusually firm commitment to the mutually reinforcing institutions of patriarchy and Christian marriage.

Pamela's self-effacement thus sounds ominous as she anticipates her likely programme as a married woman, divided between family accounts and management, or visits to the deserving poor and any of the local gentry who will receive her. Essentially, however, she will live for and through her husband, as she plainly admits:

> Then, sir, if you will indulge me with your company, I will take an airing in your chariot now-and-then: and when you return from your diversions, I shall have the pleasure of receiving you with chearful [sic] duty; as I shall have counted the moments of your absence. (p. 299)

Such sentiments are predictably mannah to Mr B. ("'Proceed, my dear girl," said he, "I love to hear you talk"'), who completes these predictions with the one topic that Pamela's modesty forbids her to raise:

> I hope you will have, superadded to all these, such an employment, as will give me a view of perpetuating my happy prospects, and my family at the same time; of which I am almost the only one, in a direct line. (p. 301)

In retrospect, then, for all her shrewd anticipation of conjugal life, Pamela is not as radical on gender roles as one might wish to believe. She listens respectfully as Mr B. entertains her with reminiscences of his

Grand Tour, and reciprocates with a few pieces on the harpsichord: gender stereotypes could hardly be clearer.

Furthermore, Pamela has no intellectual pretensions. Mr B. certainly does, however, and later intends to offer his bride a copy of his occasional essays. Despite a certain courage in facing down criticism of his marriage, Mr B. does not strike the reader as a powerful mind, and one shudders at the banalities this collection might contain. Pamela also runs rings round Mr B. in the sexual contest (which is *not* to accuse her of calculation or hypocrisy), and, judging by her synthesis and counter-critique of his written proposals, she is a match for him intellectually as well. There is much irony (whether Richardson wanted it or not) in the fact that such a remarkably articulate young woman will dedicate her life to anticipating her husband's every wish, at the price of silencing her own voice. The abiding impression is of talent wasted: she will be allowed to keep up her 'scribbling', but the vision of Pamela helping to make 'jellies, comfits, sweetmeats, marmalades, cordials' has an uncanny resemblance to the early domesticated George Eliot.

Clarissa *and the Promise of Something New*

The weaknesses of *Pamela* are not limited to the technical ingenuousness and moral ambivalence parodied by Fielding's *Shamela* (1741). There is also the limitation imposed by the single correspondent, requiring the mediation of all external views by the same pen, as a result of which the supposedly modest Pamela must regularly sing her own praises. Also restrictive, but not fatally so, is Pamela's lack of sophistication, apparently precluding any deeper insights: much of the novel's social critique thus emerges indirectly, as it does with the naive young protagonists of classic picaresque or the *ingénus* of Voltairean satire. The discrepancies between *Pamela I* and *II* could be explained rather reductively by suggesting that, whilst the first part represented an imaginative re-creation of the heroine's sensibility, the second was pure, unadulterated Richardson. And here it is fair to remember the crude unauthorized sequels of the novel, which compelled the author to embark on a continuation for which he was ill-prepared.[18]

Clarissa avoided the above issues by introducing two pairs of highly articulate correspondents, and raising the social status of both central characters with respect to *Pamela*. The present discussion of Richardson's second novel revolves round the idea of the female (or demotic) *novelist* literally offering something *new*. It will concentrate on two textual elements: the extreme sensitivity of all the correspondents to different contemporary constructions of gender; and the striking literateness, and even literariness, of the correspondents themselves.

At its simplest, *Clarissa* is a war of the sexes, although the conflict is naturally highly uneven in social, economic and legal terms. Virtually every aspect of human behaviour recorded in the novel is reduced to an issue of *gender*. There is thus an almost constant confrontation between the conventional female stereotypes embraced by Lovelace, Belford, the Harlowe men, and Colonel Morden, and the more subversive critique of men proceeding from Anna Howe and even (on occasion) the heroine herself. The most disparaging male is Clarissa's brother James: 'daughters are chickens brought up for the tables of other men' (L 13). The most misogynistic is Uncle Antony: 'The devil's in your sex!...The nicest of them will prefer a vile rake and wh—' (L 32.4).[19]

The main source of female stereotypes, however, is Lovelace. Occasionally capable of the kind of invective associated with Uncle Antony, he more typically represents a patronizing form of hackneyed male wisdom: 'The sex! the sex, all over! – charming contradiction!' (L 99); 'that sweet cowardice which is so amiable in the sex' (L 103); or more cynically, 'sweet dears, half the female world ready to run away with a rake, *because* he is a rake' (L 219). He is also full of male clichés about female capriciousness: 'If you would have a woman do one thing, you must always propose another!' (L 127); 'what business have the sex, whose principal glory is meekness, and patience, and resignation, to be in a passion' (L 202); 'curiosity, damned curiosity, is the itch of the sex' (L 323). The construction of femininity in terms of fickleness and instability reflects a predictable pattern in a young aristocratic libertine.[20]

In certain cases, however, Lovelace's judgements have a grim irony. The declamatory 'Knowest thou not moreover, that man is the woman's sun; woman is the man's earth?' (L 203.1) is at least valid in the sense that he treats Clarissa like *dirt*; whilst certain other comments from the arch intriguer himself – 'show me a woman, and I'll show thee a plotter!' (L 228), or 'Plot, contrivance, intrigue, strategem! – Underground moles these ladies' (L 248), *etc.* – might, under happier circumstances, register their full comic irony. And Lovelace's celebration of Clarissa as divine has a particularly hollow ring when the same letter celebrates her captivity ('And is she not IN MY POWER?', L99). The paradox of treating woman simultaneously as goddess and prisoner is further explored in the context of Lennox and Burnley in Chapter 8.

The cruder stereotyping of women by Lovelace and Belford comes to an end when one rake is thwarted and the other reformed, and it is now Colonel Morden who assumes something of Lovelace's oracular pseudo-authority on female behaviour. He thus regards the relationship of Clarissa and Anna as an exception to the general rule that '*Friendship* ... is too fervent a flame for female minds to manage', although he regards Anna's behaviour towards Hickman as demonstrating that 'even women of sense are not to be trusted with power' (L 520). Against such indiscriminate constructions of femininity, Clarissa and Anna react with sensitivity and occasional indignation. Both women thus query conventional male dimensions of the gender equation; as Clarissa writes in an early letter to Anna, 'Say what they will of generosity being a *manly* virtue; but upon my word, my dear, I have ever yet observed that it is not to be met with in that sex one time in ten that it is to be found in ours' (L 5). In simple structural terms, moreover, Anna functions as a vent for stronger reactions than those Richardson will allow Clarissa. She is contemptuous, for example, of Colonel Morden's indelicacy on the subject of Clarissa's rape: 'Upon my word, my dear, I who have been accustomed to the most delicate conversation ever since I had the honour to know you, despise this sex from the gentleman to the peasant' (L 456). Anna is generally more frustrated than Clarissa by gender restraints, a point made symbolically in her comment on female hoops: 'All they're good for, that I know, is to clean dirty shoes and to keep ill-mannered friends at a distance' (L 74).

Anna's views on men become increasingly hostile. In an early letter, she suggests humorously: 'all men are monkeys more or less ... that you and I should have such buffoons as these to choose out of is a mortifying thing, my dear' (L 46), and half-seriously offers Clarissa a means of escape from both Lovelace and the Harlowe men: 'A woman going off with a woman is not so discreditable a thing, surely!' (L 87). She later seriously proposes the rejection of all male suitors in favour of some kind of female cohabitation. Anna's suggestions, together with her increasing virulence ('these men are a vile race of *reptiles* in *our day*, and mere *bears* in *their own*', L 455), have led some readers to see a covert lesbian plot. Even the normally milder Clarissa can thus ask ambivalently whether the love of David and Jonathan really surpassed this particular love of women (L 359); whilst she only surrenders the miniature picture of Anna after a moving apostrophe: '*Sweet and ever-amiable friend – companion – sister – lover*!' (L 476).[21]

However literally such comments are read, the subversion of entrenched patriarchal attitudes forms an important part of what is 'new' in the female (or demotic) *novelist* of the period. But *Clarissa* is also remarkable for the high degree of literariness exhibited by the four major correspondents. The most conspicuous gender marker in eighteenth-century culture, as shown in Chapter 3, was a knowledge of the ancient languages. Women might speak French and even Italian, but, according to an almost universal rule, study of the classical languages was a man's preserve. A knowledge of Latin (however rudimentary) was above a certain social level, effectively a badge of maleness, hardly less exclusive than the wearing of a sword in an earlier age; men guarded the privilege jealously, parading it self-consciously on suitable occasions, as in Mr Walden's debate with Harriet Byron in *Grandison*.[22] In this light, it becomes easier to understand the distinction made in this study between 'male' *authors* (with their suggestion of *authority*, often classical) and 'female' *novelists* (with their promise of something *new*). New vistas open here, leading to literary patterns where *genre* and *gender* often conflate.

Clarissa herself is made highly sensitive to the abuses of a classical education, and even to certain classical literary genres. She thus criticizes her brother for having '[l]earning enough . . . to make him vain of it among us women' but being unable to 'make his learning valuable either to himself or to anybody else' (L 91); and elsewhere, she credits her servant Betty with more sense than she herself has heard at table from her brother's college companions (L 63). She also quotes without censure Betty's presumably ironic comment:

> I cannot indeed but say . . . that I have heard famous scholars often and often say very silly things: things I should be ashamed myself to say – but I thought they did it out of humility, and in condescension to those who had not their learning.

Betty's 'famous scholars' doubtless include the Reverend Elias Brand, whose underhand report of Clarissa's behaviour (L 444) – with no less than *five* untranslated Latin tags – marks the novel's high point in classical pedantry.

Details of this kind inevitably evoke the one classical genre most suspect to Richardson's female correspondents, that of satire. The text expresses various reservations about the utility and moral justification of the form, with Clarissa eventually allowing that '*permitted* or *desired* satire may be apt, in a generous satirist, mending as it rallies' (L 91); whilst her mentor, Mrs Norton, insists that 'the end of satire is not to exasperate, but amend' (L 308). Elsewhere, in various *female* comments (from both Clarissa and Anna) on famous *scholars* and arrogant young *gentlemen*, it is natural enough to see Richardson, the self-made man, settling scores with those who despised his humble background and lack of classical learning.

Lovelace himself, incidentally, is never guilty of pedantry and appreciates Clarissa's literary attainments, including her knowledge of Shakespeare; Clarissa is also later revealed by Anna as having possessed exceptional, if partly unexploited, linguistic ability:

> You may take notice of the admirable facility she had in learning languages; that she read with great ease both Italian and French, and could hold a conversation in either, though she was not fond of doing so (and that she was *not*, be pleased to call it a fault): that she had begun to apply herself to Latin.   (L 529)

The socio-cultural significance of the last detail now requires no further emphasis. Clarissa's twentieth-century counterpart might have aspired to become a general.

In turning to the erudition of Richardson's main correspondents, one feels reluctance at using the supreme achievement of eighteenth-century English fiction as a mere quarry for literary references: *Clarissa* is far more than a confrontation of classical and demotic elements. On the other hand, a glance beyond the sexual pathologies and ideological minefields which dominate most critical discussion of *Clarissa* also suggests how Richardson – in *Grandison* – could later produce the paradigm of the late eighteenth-century novel of manners.

Within the rich intertextuality of the novel, however, the four main writers all reflect significant gender-based cultural alignments. In his opening letter, Lovelace thus recalls his first disappointment in love, even as he deprecates the florid, classicizing rhetoric in which the courtship had to be conducted:

> Those confounded poets, with their celestially-terrene descriptions, did as much with me as the lady: they fired my imagination and set me upon a desire to become a goddess-maker. I must needs try my new-fledged pinions in sonnet, elegy, and madrigal. I must have a Cynthia, a Stella, a Sacharissa, as well as the best of them: darts and flames and the devil knows what must I give to my Cupid.   (L 31)

The same letter is also memorable for no less than twenty-nine lines of literary quotation, suggesting a certain element of pure intellectual exhibitionism.[23] In subsequent letters, Lovelace is nothing if not eclectic, although classical references outnumber native English ones.[24]

He nevertheless wears his learning lightly, and expresses contempt for the Latin scraps favoured by the 'motto-mongers among our weekly and daily scribblers' (L 530). His first letter to Belford moreover suggests a literary counterpart of his opening salvo to Clarissa, with its four lines of a Horace *Ode* (now in the original Latin), and five lines each from Dryden's *Don Sebastian* and *The Conquest of Granada*. The other *gentlemen* of *Clarissa* also draw their straws of classical learning to the stack, from James Harlowe's crude reference to Virgil's '*amor omnibus idem*' (L 50) to Lord M—'s dimly remembered Latin scraps (L 190) and Colonel Morden's untranslated passage from Juvenal (L 503).

Clarissa's first literary reference, on the other hand, is to Dryden's *Fables Ancient and Modern* (L 21); whilst her longest one reproduces the entire sixteen stanzas, or ninety-six lines, of Elizabeth Carter's *Ode to Wisdom*. Her other quotations include *A Midsummer Night's Dream* (L 98), Rowe's *Ulysses* (L 116), and *Paradise Lost* (comparing Belford with Satan, L 161). Her fourteen-line excerpt from Juvenal's *Satire* XV (L 218) is naturally quoted in translation.

On the evidence, then, it may seem wrong to suggest that the discourses of Lovelace and Clarissa are always mutually exclusive. And yet, one cannot deny the clear linguistic and stylistic contrasts between the aristocratic, secular, public, and classically educated *male* vision of Lovelace, and the bourgeois, religious, private, and demotically conditioned *female* vision of Clarissa. And in a writer so consummately skilful in representing either discourse, it is Clarissa's Christian world which prevails. Eventually, Lovelace even seems to scorn part of his classical heritage when he is overcome by Clarissa's sublimity ('Your Seneca's [sic], your Epictetuses, and the rest of your Stoical tribe, with all their apathy nonsense, could not come up to this', L 453).

Moral defeat also becomes a linguistic one, as affective reactions become ossified and emotions are reduced to mere stylistic *tics*. The once charismatic Lovelace, for whom verbal and physical seduction were long hardly separable, can ultimately only express himself in stale classicizing cliché: 'I am mad again, by Jupiter' (L 513); or 'would it please the Fates to spare [Clarissa]' (L 453). The heroine's physical and intellectual purity, conversely, are emphasized by a narrative which eventually records in full detail her apotheosis and subsequent canonization. At the end of her life, Clarissa finds exclusive solace in devotional literature: the inspiration for her final series of *Meditations* (L 364, L 399, L 413) is nothing less than the Old Testament itself, as exemplified by Job and the Book of Psalms.

Among the male correspondents, only Lovelace remains entirely unredeemed; and, central ethical questions aside, there is no mistaking Clarissa's frequently expressed contempt for his 'frothy insubstantiality', of which his writing is a lasting monument. What once seemed a brilliant, if cynical, intellectual detachment is transformed into the kind of obtuseness normally associated with the Harlowe males. The process is illustrated perfectly in Lovelace's misconstruction of the dying Clarissa's final flight of allegory ('I am setting out with all diligence for my father's house' L 421.1) as a reference to her earthly family. It is difficult to characterize the mind of a man who, after nearly two thousand pages of unrelenting persecution, believes so naively in a 'happy reconciliation'; *obsessive* is an obvious term, although it is tempting to add the word *thick*.

Belford, on the other hand, undergoes a religious and domestic conversion most clearly registered by the range and intensity of abuse it draws from an unrepentant Lovelace. This transformation, too, may be indexed in terms of literary quotations: altered by attending his dying friend Belton, he produces a letter surpassing even those of Lovelace in its number of literary references.[25] From this point onwards, one may trace Belford's rehabilitation process, in which his executorship of Clarissa's will and his recognized fitness to correspond with the formidable Anna are equally significant stages. In both contexts, Belford is effectively received into the ambit of the 'domestic'.

Among the male correspondents, only Lovelace matches the two women in either quantitative or qualitative terms; but he also shares more important affinities with Clarissa through the compulsive nature of his letter-writing, as well as in the self-confessed 'feminine' aspects of his own character. The shrewd Anna is the first to link the two points:

> That you and I, my dear, should love to write is no wonder. We have always from the time each could hold a pen delighted in epistolary correspondencies. Our employments are domestic and sedentary, and we can scribble upon twenty innocent subjects and take delight in them because they *are* innocent; though were they to be seen, they might not much profit or please others. But that such a gay, lively young fellow as this, who rides, hunts, travels, frequents the public entertainments, and has *means* to pursue his pleasures, should be able to set himself down to write for hours together, as you and I have heard him say he frequently does, that is the strange thing. (L 12)

From a perspective which sees letter-writing as (en)gendered by female social exclusion under a patriarchal order ('our employments are domestic and sedentary'), Anna later also offers what sounds like an essentialist argument in favour of women writers in general ('since the pen, next to the needle, of all employments is the most proper and best adapted to their geniuses', L 529). Here, however, she would appear to be absorbing a more general observation made by Clarissa, whom she also quotes approvingly:

> 'Who sees not, would she say, that those women who take delight in writing excel the men in all the graces of the familiar style? The gentleness of their minds, the delicacy of their sentiments (improved by the manner of their education) and the liveliness of their imaginations, qualify them to a high degree of preference for this employment: while men of learning, as they are called (of mere learning, however), aiming to get above that natural ease and freedom which distinguish this (and indeed every other kind of writing), when they think they have best succeeded are got above, or rather *beneath*, all natural beauty'.   (L 529)

Such validation and valorization of female discourse in *Clarissa* points once again towards the process of feminization in eighteenth-century fiction argued in Nancy Armstrong's *Desire and Domestic Fiction* and elsewhere. The latter, it will be recalled, claimed that specific female ideals were formulated and the virtues of the new woman were prescribed predominantly in courtesy books, educational treatises, and *domestic fiction*. It also featured an extensive analysis of *Pamela* (seen as the archetypal synthesis of fiction and conduct book). Had she found time (or perhaps space), Armstrong could surely have reinforced her argument by a reading of *Clarissa*.

There remains to be added a brief formal postscript on the issues of gendered sensibility and erudition in *Clarissa*. The present chapter (with others in the study) sometimes accepts uncritically a number of traditional narrative conventions, most obvious of which is the existence of an *author*, who also 'creates' autonomous individual *characters*; modern readings more frequently emphasize a constantly shifting interplay of voices and ideologies – internal and external – within discourse.[26] Here one may briefly ignore this critical divide, however, to remember that it *is* after all Richardson who is *doing all the voices*. With Fielding's more universal 'lawyer of 4,000 years' in *Joseph Andrews*, on the other hand, one senses that (in each occupational sphere, at least) there may only *be one voice to do*.[27] It is this mimetic illusion that Richardson's later compilations and extrapolations effectively undermine, and Fielding's modestly innovative *Amelia* attempts to reinforce. Once again, the sense of two complementary literary *parabolas* is strong.

Grandison *and the Epistolary Convention*

The final section of this chapter considers the third polarity of eighteenth-century fiction suggested in the introduction: that of first- and third-person narrators. The concentration of this discussion on *Grandison* is easily justified, for it surpasses even *Clarissa* in complexity, if not in depth and intensity. For systematic comprehensiveness, in fact, *Grandison*'s relation to the epistolary novel seems something like that of Bach's *Art of Fugue* to the polyphonic tradition. In neither case is there subsequently much to add.

It would have been fascinating to read the ten-year-old Richardson's epistolary reprimand to a litigious widow, or the love-letters written for three young women (unknown to each other) to their respective sweethearts. Another loss is the early correspondence, mentioned in the letter to Stinstra, with 'a Gentleman greatly my superior in degree, & of ample Fortunes, who, had he lived, intended high things for me'. There is even some hint of the gentleman's contribution to this exchange:

> Multitudes of Letters passed between this Gentleman & me. He wrote well, was a master of ye Epistolary Style: Our Subjects were various: But his letters were mostly narrative, giving me an Account of his Proceedings, and what befell him in ye different Nations thro' which he travelled.[28]

One may only speculate on what this correspondence might have contributed to Sir Charles Grandison's chronicle of Italy. On the other hand, these authentic letters were apparently as formative for the young Richardson as he later hoped his own fictional ones would be for the world. The epistolary habit seems engrained, and it would have been difficult to find anyone better suited to compile the *Familiar Letters*. With *Pamela*, however, Richardson faced more seriously the problem of reconciling didactic intent with generic requirements. Here it is also worth reconsidering the process that gradually transforms letter fiction into journal, since it anticipates a number of issues fundamental to Richardson's method. Apart from a few enclosures, the first part of

Pamela I actually contains just thirty-two letters, although Letter XXXII itself (open-ended) and Letter XXXI (a hybrid of various narrative elements) barely qualify for the term; according to definitions, then, letters account for between just a third and a quarter of the *first* volume of *Pamela I*. The rest is journal.

There is also a gradual increase in the length and scope of the letters; longest of the first thirty are Letter XXIII (vignettes of four gentlemen neighbours) and Letter XXIX (the story of the three bundles). The detailed external description of the former provides the first embryonic example of third-person narrative, whilst the obsessive quality of the latter ('I must write on') anticipates the 'compulsive scribbler' co-terminous with the Richardsonian heroine. The two examples are still far, of course, from the lengthy narrative sequences or exhaustive self-dramatization of *Clarissa* or *Grandison*. Letter XXXI – twice as long as any of its predecessors – is an important turning-point, however, with Pamela's 'Verses on going away', Mr B.'s letter to her father, an editorial insertion, and a four-page narrative link that abandons epistolary convention entirely. It is as if the author were confronting, for the first time, both the full dramatic potential and the great practical limitations of his chosen form.

No more genuine letters are completed, and, after eighteen pages, Letter XXXIII modulates into a journal of captivity. After this point, Pamela compiles a kind of 'personal record' (no longer for instant communication), and writing begins to acquire a greater figural significance. This is particularly true of the famous scene where the heroine has her letters literally stashed about her, and the impetuous Mr B. threatens to remove them by force (p. 271). For metaphor hunters, Pamela now *is* her correspondence; for connoisseurs of hidden puns, her secrets are, at last, likely to be be revealed.

Drugged before being raped, Clarissa, on the other hand, *is* presumably stripped, although her written words also acquire an enhanced significance – more monumental than ornamental – beyond the grave (and even beyond the pages of the novel). In the former respect, great energy is expended by Clarissa's admirers in collecting her complete correspondence and making it available to those whose needs (or deserts) are greatest. In the latter context, her 'Book of Meditations' (originally bequeathed to her friend and confidante, Mrs Norris) takes on an independent existence.[29] Not merely Clarissa's legacy to a friend, the meditations now become Richardson's own peroration to the great public. This increasing transparency of the editorial convention, I shall later argue, is closely related to the question of first- and third-person narrators, and even to broader issues of *author* and *authority*.

As a mere object lesson in epistolary technique, *Clarissa* may actually be the least interesting of the three great novels, lacking either *Pamela*'s formal ingenuousness or *Grandison*'s technical versatility. Most obviously, it has increased structural complexity through its four major correspondents and numerous minor ones; and since the main group is so articulate, there are opportunities in other letters for the humorous character pieces Richardson had occasionally allowed himself in the *Familiar Letters*. But even with his major correspondents, Richardson shows great capacity for generic flexibility: some passages, for example, are set out as stage dialogue; not to mention imaginative projection: Lovelace's verbal pyrotechnics on the subject of marriage licences (L 444) are worthy of the notorious Earl of Rochester himself. This particular letter is all the more extraordinary in view of Richardson's theory of writerly identification as explained to Lady Bradshaigh: 'I am all the while absorbed in the character. It is not fair to say – I, identically I, am anywhere, while I keep within the character.' For a writer originally troubled even by the ethics of writing fictional 'lies', the emotional ambivalence generated by impersonating libertines and sexual predators must have been considerable. It is reasonable to suspect that such moral, as well as technical, pressures finally persuaded Richardson to abandon all 'editorial' pretence and asssume the role of author proper.

Grandison contains far less high drama than *Pamela* or *Clarissa*, and yet, in purely formal terms, it is in some ways the most interesting of all Richardson's novels: it thus stretches the conventions of letter fiction to breaking-point. The typography of stage dialogue (beginning with the heroine Harriet Byron and the Grandison sisters in Volume I) is familiar from *Clarissa*; the lengthy absences of any letter recipient whatsoever (Harriet offers a detailed account of proceedings 'journal-wise' in Volume VII) recalls *Pamela*. But the various eavesdroppings and redactions ('The bishop gave me the following dialogue . . .' is a classic *incipit*) produce a new textual complexity. And when *Grandison*'s encounter with Pollexfen is reproduced in a signed twenty-page transcript from a shorthand writer installed in the closet (Vol. II, pp. 247–68),[30] editorial ingenuity may have reached new heights.

The most characteristic intricacies of *Grandison*, however, are the Chinese-box-like sequences of correspondents. In one memorable example (from Volume V), Mrs Beaumont (an English lady in Florence) writes about the invalid Clementina (Harriet's Italian rival) to

Grandison, who then reports to his mentor Dr Bartlett in England. Bartlett forwards the letter to Charlotte Grandison ('Lady G.'), who sends it in turn to her sister Caroline ('Lady L.'), at which point the external reader learns the contents (just before Harriet herself). Here perhaps, to revive the analogy with Bach, is Richardson's equivalent – in terms of complexity – of the triple mirror fugue.

Far from showing any of the ingenuousness attributable to the 'editor' of *Pamela*, however, *Grandison* is even self-consciously ironic about epistolary convention, as in Harriet's comments on what is required to write up half-an-hour's conversation ('I am amazed at the quantity, on looking back. But it *will* be so in narrative Letter-writing', Vol. III, Letter XVI). Charlotte occasionally carries this circumstantial tendency to the point of parody, as when recording an exchange with her sister:

Lady L.	'Sufficient to the day is the evil thereof.'
Ch.	Well observed. – Words of Scripture, I believe. – Well – *evil thereof.* –
Lady L.	Never, surely, was there such a creature as you, Charlotte –
Ch.	That's down, too. –
Lady L.	Is that down, *laughing* – That should not have been down – Yet 'tis true.
Ch.	*Yet 'tis true* – What's next?
Lady L.	Pish –
Ch.	*Pish.* –

(Volume VI, Letter IX)

The passage even seems to anticipate Fielding's parody of epistolary conventions in *Shamela*. More significant (if less amusing), on the other hand, are those parts of *Grandison* which make the reader forget letter fiction entirely: Harriet's history of the Grandisons, filling almost eighty pages of Volume II, is the obvious case.[31]

It is not unlikely that a writer of Richardson's genius, torn between the intimacy of the private correspondent (say Watt's famous 'realism of presentation') and the detachment of the social historian (the corresponding 'realism of assessment'), might arrive at the kind of formal synthesis offered by *free indirect discourse* (FID).[32] Examples of this technique, however, are surprisingly few; they are also largely confined to the last major novel. The very syntactic ambiguities of the form make it liable to sightings in the most unlikely places, but in several passages from *Grandison* it is unmistakable. In Volume I, for example, Harriet

relays an account (originating with Mrs Reeves) of Sir Hargrave
Pollexfen's request to marry her:

> He had had, he told my cousins, a most uneasy time of it, ever since
> he saw me. *The devil fetch him, if he had had one hour's rest. He never
> saw a woman before whom he could love as he loved me. By his soul, he
> had no view, but what was strictly honourable.*
>
> He sometimes sat down, sometimes walk'd about the room,
> strutting and now-and-then adjusting something in his dress that
> nobody else saw wanted it. *He gloried in the happy prospects before him:
> Not but he knew I had a little army of admirers: But as none of them
> had met with encouragement from me, he hoped there was room to flatter
> himself that he might be the happy man.*   (Letter XVII [my emphasis])

As the italics indicates, the passage alternates free indirect speech with
reported speech and conventional diegesis or 'telling', a process that
continues for another page. A decisive factor in the adoption of the
form may have been the fact that the scene is initially mediated by
another *speaker*: Mrs Reeves presumably gave her account, in either
direct or indirect speech, and Harriet herself made the relevant adjust-
ments. Free indirect discourse in *Grandison* does not, however, develop
into the consistent rhetorical device it becomes for Austen. Among the
few other unambiguous examples, one may cite Charlotte's report to
Harriet of an argument with Lord and Lady L. over her treatment of
Lord G.:

> *Where was poor Lord G. gone?*
> Poor Lord G. is gone to seek his fortune, I believe.
> *What did I mean?*
> I told them the airs he had given himself; and that he was gone
> without leave or notice of return.
> *He had served me right, ab-solutely right,* Lord L. said.
> *I believed so myself. Lord G. was a very good sort of man, and ought not
> to bear with me so much as he had done: But it would be kind in them,
> not to tell him what I had owned.*   (Volume IV, Letter XXXVII
> [my emphasis])

The apparently arbitrary alternation of FID with reported speech fairly
reflects the occasional, even inconsequential, role of the technique in
Grandison. The two passages quoted are the most interesting examples
in the novel, and it is notable that one concerns the unspeakable

Pollexfen, whilst the other features the 'bad' sister, Charlotte. FID was generally regarded as 'low style' in the eighteenth century, and its use in *Grandison* must have seemed unduly informal – even *racy* – to Richardson's readers; and for an author already sensitive to accusations of vulgarity, this may explain its rarity.

There is, however, an even more basic aspect to the rhetorical organization of *Grandison*. In the wake of *Clarissa*, Richardson was begged by admirers to attempt the portrait of a *good man*, and obligingly embarked on what could only be an ungrateful task. He seems nevertheless to have been pulled inexorably towards ingrained feminocentric perspectives, since the novel essentially develops round its English *heroine* (despite her more glamorous Italian counterpart), and might justly have been called *Harriet*, by analogy with *Pamela* and *Clarissa*. Such claims are based on a close analysis of the epistolary structure of the novel.

Although roughly equal in length to *Clarissa*, *Grandison* contains barely half as many letters: more precisely, 312 against 592. The average letter is thus far longer, continuing a tendency already apparent in *Clarissa* with respect to *Pamela*, and doubtless reflecting the broader perspectives of what Harriet called 'narrative Letter-writing'. More actually *happens* in *Grandison*, even if it is not always of a nature to interest the modern reader. Of the 312 letters, 187 are written by Harriet; and with the exclusion of the fifth volume – set almost entirely in Italy, and allowing her only five out of forty-five letters – the proportions become even more striking, at 182 of 267 (or almost 70 per cent).

There are, in addition, forty-four letters specifically addressed *to* Harriet, whilst all the other letters (without exception) eventually come into her hands. Richardson thus perfects a structure of narrative legitimization – an effective, if highly personal, integration of authority and novelty – that began its evolution in *Clarissa*: Harriet now becomes *fons et origo*, a kind of narrative clearing-house. Richardson also creates a 'Byronic' *heroine* in many ways as significant as her more dazzling true-life counterpart, perhaps even anticipating the classic Jamesian 'centre of consciousness' by some 150 years.

After *Grandison*, there is one more major work, the *Maxims* of 1755; or, to quote its full title: *A Collection of the Moral and Instructive Sentiments, Maxims, Cautions, and Reflexions, Contained in the Histories of Pamela, Clarissa, and Sir Charles Grandison*. Not content with merely extracting his moral plums, the *author* now rewrites, expands, and even supplements them, providing the whole with an index, under such headings as 'Friendship', 'Platonic Love', and 'Conjugal Piety'. A contemporary admirer of Richardson praised the 'modestly *anonymous* author' of the *Maxims*, and compared him (less modestly) to the Roman biographer Plutarch.[33] This now seems to discount entirely the original significance of 'writing to the moment', not to mention the vicarious pleasures – for author or reader – of identifying with fictional characters. Richardson is also now enshrined in the annals of conventional historiography. A modern scholar describes the *Maxims* more judiciously as 'the final flower of Richardson's literary activity', linking them with the older tradition of conduct books.[34] Both judgements would have probably pleased the author.

On the fictional front, Richardson continued to toy with a certain 'History of Mrs Beaumont' until 1757. A lady of this name plays a minor role in *Grandison* and may be identical with an old flame from the author's youth mentioned in a letter to his friend Lady Bradshaigh:

> I own the *Life* of a *certain person*, was what I had set my heart upon. I thought it might be form'd into a story, partly True, partly Fictitious, and yet there are objections. I am afraid you would be rein'd in too close by families now in being, fearing to give offence.[35]

It is not clear when Richardson wrote the surviving fragments of the story, but it is interesting to note that the author now seemed to be thinking in terms of dramatized biography rather than another epistolary novel.

There is one more fragment to consider: the novelist's correspondence with a certain Warwick attorney and financial huckster called Eusebius Silvester, over the years 1754–9. This survives in a sequence of forty-five unpublished letters, marked as a 'Warning Piece to Posterity' (Richardson was apparently duped by this gentleman).[36] A notable feature of the Silvester correspondence is the amount of manuscript comments and markings by an increasingly sceptical Richardson; these seem to suggest the novelist's awareness of the rhetorical ambiguities inherent in his original epistolary form. Far from being a window on the writer's heart, the intimate letter – he now realizes – is a treacherous document which the reader must confront with due caution. The marginalia also mark the return of explicit editorial comment: conspicuous in *Pamela*, marginalized in later editions of *Clarissa*, and successfully integrated in *Grandison*.

Jocelyn Harris remarked pointedly of the *Maxims* that 'Richardson retreats even more unhappily to the general principles with which he had already begun'[37] and the same might be claimed for the last fragments. In spite of the formal solutions which had seemed to allow the integration of male author (and the legacy of *authority*) with female novelist (and the promise of something *new*), some ultimately imponderable synthesis of ethics and personal psychology drags Richardson back to the didactic and homiletic traditions from which he had sprung. At this point, his parabola is complete.

5
Two Literary Parabolas (ii): Fielding from *Jonathan Wild* to *Amelia*

Fielding's prose production, like Richardson's, could also be said to form a parabola, even if its shape is neither quite as symmetrical or as simple to trace as that inscribed by his great rival. Formally and ideologically, however, the two curves may be broadly characterized as inversions of each other, as the following brief comparison suggests.

Each of Fielding's major fictional works has either a rough analogue or even a close literary counterpart in Richardson's output.[1] The mock-heroic *Jonathan Wild*, published in 1743 but substantially complete before the appearance of *Joseph Andrews*, is thus grounded in satirical techniques used by Fielding long before he ever thought he would be reduced to writing novels (or 'histories' as he initially called them); Richardson's *Familiar Letters*, in contrast, draws on a didactic tradition (exemplified by his own *Apprentice's Vade Mecum*) that was equally remote from classic realist fiction, if at the other end of the literary–documentary continuum. The relation of *Pamela* (1740) to both Fielding's parody *Shamela* (1741) and – although some critics minimize its spoof element – *Joseph Andrews* (1742) is even clearer. *Tom Jones* (1749) was published under the shadow of *Clarissa*, the last volume of which appeared in 1748, and the two novels are obviously the works by which their respective authors are ultimately judged.

Amelia (1751) is in some ways a response to *Clarissa*, where Fielding tried to do something radically new: if not literally 'feminocentric', it is at least his first fiction where the protagonist is more prominent than the ironic narrator; *Sir Charles Grandison* (1753–4), Richardson's portrait of a 'good man', meanwhile shifts the gender focus in the opposite direction, even if all the novel's letters are still mediated through its English heroine. By this point, exhaustion seems to have set in for both writers, although Fielding's posthumous travel memoir, the *Journal of a Voyage to Lisbon* (1755), moves one step further from the 'comic epic in prose', prizes the Greek *historian* Herodotus above the *poet* Homer, and finally produces an extended prose narrative (albeit non-fictional) in the first person. Richardson, on the other hand, at last abandons his pretence of editing other people's letters and collects his 'own' *Maxims* (1755) from the three novels, thus returning to the undisguised homiletics of his early writing.

The remainder of the present chapter discusses each of Fielding's four major prose fictions. It shows how *Jonathan Wild* is generated almost entirely by literary conventions habitual to the young Fielding, while *Joseph Andrews* develops and attempts to apply a specific theoretical model. It then presents *Tom Jones*, with its consolidation of techniques developed in *Joseph Andrews*, as the triumph of *authority* rather than *novelty*; and finally, *Amelia*, for all its attempted innovation, as not venturing to the point of exclusive *first*-person narrative, far less to the free indirect discourse embryonic in Richardson and his female followers.

Jonathan Wild

Jonathan Wild was published in 1743 in the collection known as *The Miscellanies*, but substantially completed some years before this date.[2] The life of Fielding's anti-hero, a notorious contemporary gangster and racketeer, was also chronicled by Defoe as well as providing the model for Peachum in John Gay's fabulously successful *The Beggar's Opera* (1728). Fielding's Wild starts his career in a sponging-house and becomes leader of a gang of thieves, taking the lion's share of the profits and shopping any subordinate who questions his authority. His main scheme, however, is to ruin his old schoolfellow, the jeweller Heartfree; this includes tricking Mrs Heartfree into leaving the country and then claiming that her husband has murdered her. Heartfree is rescued from the scaffold at the eleventh hour and the now unmasked Wild is hanged in his place.

Further detail is superfluous, since Fielding's account was above all a lightly veiled political allegory, related to the ironic presentation of his protagonist as a 'great man': Sir Robert Walpole, Britain's most powerful political figure for twenty years (1723–42), and long Fielding's personal *bête noire*, was widely known by this title. Occasional references to the 'prime minister' (normally unflattering comparisons to the criminal protagonist) underline this link, since the now conventional term for Britain's head of government was first applied ironically to Walpole.[3]

Fielding's earliest published work does not suggest the innovative force he was to exert on eighteenth-century fiction. Occasional verses for the coronation and birthday of George II, and a burlesque poem called *The Masquerade*, are roughly contemporary with his first staged comedy, *Love in Several Masques* (1728). There is also a reworking of Juvenal's misogynistic *Sixth Satire*, later published in the *Miscellanies* but – according to the author – 'originally stretched out' in his teens. Fielding's second play, *The Author's Farce* (1730), was published under the pseudonym of 'Scriblerus Secundus'; the original Martin Scriblerus was invented by the group of Tory writers and intellectuals gravitating almost a generation earlier round Swift and Pope. Fielding refers to a six-hundred line manuscript in imitation of Pope's satirical poem *The Dunciad* and, as late as 1752, he projected another *Dunciad*, where the protagonist was to be the hack writer and minor novelist 'Sir' John Hill.[4]

The attachment to formal satire, then, was never entirely eclipsed by an involvement with what Francis Coventry was to call the 'new species of writing'.[5] The 1730s were nevertheless years of remarkable theatrical triumphs, with particular emphasis on farce and burlesque, the ballad opera and the rehearsal play. The latter form, with its characteristic author-within-a-play, may actually be a model for the self-consciously obtrusive narrators in the novels. Fielding was not entirely happy with these successes, however, and would have preferred greater recognition for his five-act comedies. In the Prologue to *The Modern Husband*, for example, he attempts to dissociate himself from burlesque.[6]

There is perhaps an analogy between Fielding's progress on the stage and in the novel. If his ambition to become a serious dramatist was often overshadowed by a facility for writing farce, then his evolution as a serious novelist was also initially checked by a natural propensity for burlesque.

Apologies for the latter are hardly necessary in the case of the politically motivated *Jonathan Wild*, however, although the technique does eventually get a very long run in Fielding's fiction. Traditionally, burlesque involved depicting the actions of high characters in low language: Scarron's *Virgile travesti*, in its various English translations, was one of the best known examples. In the *burlesque nouveau* of Boileau's *Le Lutrin*, on the other hand, low characters are depicted in high language. The latter defines the technique used consistently in the presentation of

Wild, although, since the satirical target is the mighty Walpole, Fielding is implicitly tied to the traditional pattern ('low for high') as well.[7] The 'great statesman' is thus compared to the 'common thief', the one with his 'palaces and pictures', the other with his 'whores and fiddles' (p. 18). 'Cities, courts, gaols or such places' (p. 19) are satirically elided, as are 'conquerors, absolute princes, statesmen and prigs [thieves]' (p. 42). In his youth, on the other hand, Wild completes a Grand Tour of seven years (presumably transportation) in 'His Majesty's plantations in America', while his later residence of Newgate prison is a 'castle'; and gentlemen will find honour 'in the field' (i.e. as pickpockets) or 'on the road' (i.e. robbing coaches) (pp. 21–2).

Fielding explains the techniques of burlesque himself in the Preface to *Joseph Andrews*, assuring the reader that he uses it there for the diction alone, and not for the sentiments or characters. It is a dubious claim, for the newer form of burlesque at least, also known from Pope's day as 'mock-epic' or 'mock-heroic', still survives in *Amelia*. One might even suggest that, from Fielding and Smollett through most of the classically educated (or simply Fielding-inspired) male *authors* of the eighteenth century, mock-epic is virtually a 'default mode'. It informs the classicizing texture of much conservative novelistic discourse.

At the very beginning of his own ironic pseudo-biography, Fielding refers to the biographers of antiquity (Plutarch, Nepos, Suetonius etc.) and their subjects ('an Aristides or a Brutus, a Lysander or a Nero').[8] The names dropped here initiate a steady trickle of classical references and (untranslated) Latin tags. There is no need to cite all of the quotations here, although one of them might serve as a suggestive point of departure for a discussion of their significance in Fielding's writing. In Book I, ch. ix, Miss Laetitia Snap is portrayed as deceitful, lascivious and promiscuous – and literally dirty – in the best tradition of Juvenalian misogyny. Below her various petticoats she wears a grubby undergarment, whose colour is described by a tag from Ovid:

– Qui color albus erat nunc est contrarius albo.   (p. 27)

One can almost manage this tag without editorial help ('What was white in colour is now the opposite of white'), although the point hardly seems worth a Latin quotation, and it is tempting to ask who the latter was meant to amuse or impress. The answer is obvious, for the narrative clearly presupposes a classically educated male readership.

On some occasions, however, the textual irony and ambivalence seem to transcend Fielding's own intentions. When Wild fails in the attempt to end his own life at sea, for example, the narrator comments on the capriciousness of Nature:

> Be it known then that the great Alma Mater, Nature, is of all other females the most obstinate, and tenacious of her purpose. So true is that observation:
>
> *Naturam expellas furca licet, usque recurret.*
>
> Which I need not render in English, it being to be found [sic] in a book which most fine gentlemen are forced to read.   (p. 79)[9]

There is a wink at the 'fine gentlemen' who remember their lessons, a nudge for those who have forgotten, whilst the ladies (like Fielding's recurrent banes, the clerks and apprentices) are presumably beneath consideration. One suspects that Fielding either did not know, did not remember, or did not care that most male readers – and virtually all female ones – would not have understood his Latin tags.

Fielding's natural alignment with the *hieratic* over the *demotic*, the literary over the documentary, or – quite simply – authority over novelty, does not need labouring. It is nevertheless useful to consider these tendencies in more explicitly gendered terms. There is thus a moment in Chapter IX when Wild goes to court Miss Laetitia Snap, and the narrator expresses disgust at her pendulous breasts ('without stays or jumps', p. 26). This may simply reflect the inconveniences of eighteenth-century female dress, although it is difficult not to interpret these objections at a metaphorical level. In this passage, the narrator's objection to 'uncontrolled liberty' is presumably just anatomical, but three pages later the identical concept ('loose freedoms', p. 29) is used to describe Laetitia's sexual promiscuity: she is, to use a suitably classi-cizing cliché, the hero's 'Achilles heel', cuckolding him both before and after marriage. Behind the aesthetic objection, then, may lie a more insistent moral one – patriarchal judgement on the unconfined female; or even a psychological one – in terms of the threat to male identity posed by the woman who, as it were, lets it all hang out.

It is a good point at which to look more closely at Fielding's con-structions of women. In the passage just cited, he again apostrophizes his male reader:

> Here, reader, thou must pardon us if we stop a while to lament the capriciousness of nature in forming this charming part of the creation designed to complete the happiness of man.   (p. 29)

'[C]harming part of the creation' reflects a typically patronizing andro-centric view and, in fact, the narrator goes on to remark that half a yard of ribbon in the hat of a *beau* 'shall weigh heavier in the scale of female affection than twenty Sir Isaac Newtons!' (p. 29).[10]

The most significant female figure in *Jonathan Wild*, however, is Mrs Heartfree. If Thomas Heartfree represents a moral counterfoil to Wild, and therefore an ethically rather than a psychologically moti-vated character, then Mrs Heartfree is little more than an appendix to her husband. Heartfree is duly presented within the ironic conventions of the narrative: 'He was possessed of several great weaknessses of mind, being good-natured, friendly and generous to a great excess', etc. (p. 46).

Fielding can sustain this kind of ironic inversion with ease, although his method becomes more problematic in the case of Mrs Heartfree, commonly regarded as:

a mean-spirited, poor, domestic, low-bred animal, who confined herself mostly to the care of her family, placed her happiness in her husband and her children, followed no expensive fashions or diver-sions, and indeed rarely went abroad, unless to return the visits of a few plain neighbours, and twice a year afforded herself, in company with her husband, the diversion of a play, where she never sat in a higher place than the pit.   (pp. 46–7)

Here, textual ironies proliferate. In the tradition of indirect satire, the first two lines at least are clearly a critical reflection on vulgar public opinion. Since Mrs Heartfree represents positive values, the reader is expected to make certain mental substitutions: replacing 'mean-spirited', say, by *docile*; 'poor' by *without independent means*; 'low-bred' by *without social pretentions*, etc. The whole passage then comes to reveal what narrator and author apparently prized: a domestic drudge without fortune, opinions or ambitions of her own. It recalls Fielding's early poem 'To a Friend on the Choice of a Wife':

May then she prove, who shall thy Lot befall,
Beauteous to thee, agreeable to all.
Nor Wit, nor Learning proudly may she boast.[11]

The passage thus conceals a second layer of irony, behind or beyond the author–narrator's intentions, and perhaps – in terms of the modern reader's own ideological preconceptions – even a third, for Martin

Battestin also warns against reading Fielding ahistorically by modern sexually egalitarian standards.[12]

There is a short dramatic coda for the destinies of Heartfree's women, when one of his daughters is married off to the loyal family servant, Friendly, at the age of nineteen, while the other remains to 'dedicate her days to [her father's] service'. Both daughters, then, were on the way to becoming 'mean-spirited, poor, domestic, low-bred animal[s]' like their mother! More interesting, however, is Mrs Heartfree's own story in Book IV. The account of her adventures after she is separated from Wild on the abortive flight to Holland lasts twenty pages, or over a tenth of the narrative, and is significant – amongst other things – for being Fielding's longest *continuous* first-person narrative until Mrs Atkinson's story in *Amelia*, and the first one of any length (except Shamela's letters) to express a female point of view.[13]

Mrs Heartfree's saga of sexual harassment might seem an unambiguous indictment of male aggression, but for the grotesque and almost comic effect of its sheer repetitiveness. Having survived the importunities of Wild (ending in attempted rape), Mrs Heartfree is then subject to the advances of the more refined French captain (pp. 142–3). This is followed by a brutal episode with the master of an English man-of-war (p. 144), who treats his passenger 'with the insolence of a bashaw to a Circassian slave'. She forestalls another rape attempt by making the captain drunk, and accepts the support of a 'gentleman-protector', who stays with her through subsequent shipwreck, but who – once on dry land – assaults her himself. She is saved from this predicament by a wild hermit, who initially treats her with great deference, but then makes his own passionate declarations (although without use of force). She is now rescued by three sailors from the shipwreck, who display mild sexual interest before escorting her to the local town. Here, the local chief magistrate (known as the Schach Pimpach) makes his own proposal (p. 160) but, once refused, does not renew his suit; for in those parts, Fielding pointedly notes, 'as it is no shame for women . . . to consent to the first proposal, so they never receive a second'. She finally returns to England with yet another English man-of-war, whose captain, although a 'gallant man', does not importune her unduly.

It is an extraordinary sequence for a mere twenty pages, and the frequency of the attacks tends to compromise the seriousness of the account, bringing it dangerously close to farce. The story may ultimately be more memorable for purely formal elements, since – within such a narrow compass – Fielding seems to touch on the fictional repertoire of most of his great contemporaries. The passage thus jars slightly with the surrounding narrative by reflecting something of the formal realism associated with the first-person narratives of Defoe. The sufferings of beleaguered female chastity are the province of Richardson; the vignette of the brave lieutenant, waiting twenty-five years for a command but always losing out to the 'bastards of noblemen', belongs to Smollett. And finally, Mrs Heartfree's narrative is eventually transformed into a fantastic Swiftian satire of the traveller's tale.[14]

Mrs Heartfree's story, then, hardly explores the full subjective implications of feminocentric discourse. There are other short pieces of first-person narrative in *Jonathan Wild*, but these are grounded in theatrical convention rather than autobiographical or epistolary form.[15] Wild, the great manipulator, is also an essentially theatrical figure, although – like that other great fixer, Walpole – he is more stage manager than lead actor. The analogy is developed at some length in the course of the novel:

> for the stage of the world differs from that in Drury Lane principally in this – that whereas, on the latter, the chief figure is almost continually before your eyes, whilst the under-actors are not seen above once in an evening; now, on the former, the hero or great man is always behind the curtain, and seldom or never appears or doth anything in his own person. He doth indeed, in this GRAND DRAMA, rather perform the part of the prompter, and doth instruct the well-drest figures, who are strutting in public on the stage, what to say and do.   (pp. 113–14)

In spite of the first-person account of Mrs Heartfree and its various theatrical impulses, however, *Jonathan Wild* is the most homogeneous of Fielding's four major fictions. Its mock-heroic conventions have the consistency of Smollett's *Ferdinand Count Fathom*.

Shamela *and* Joseph Andrews

The immediate material conditions for converting Fielding from dramatist to novelist were provided by the theatrical censorship of the Licensing Act of 1737;[16] the particular impulse seems to have been the extraordinary success of Richardson's *Pamela*. Fielding could doubtless have accepted the presence of the book on every lady's dressing-table, or smiled at the naïve villagers of Slough sounding the church bells to celebrate Pamela's wedding; to hear the novel praised from the pulpit by an Anglican bishop, however, was clearly too much for him.[17]

His anonymous satire is directed at both moral and technical issues. The former were the target of a number of 'anti-Pamelas' in the 1740s, although no-one perhaps distils the moral ambivalence of Richardson's heroine as amusingly as Fielding does through Shamela's own words:

> I am resolved now to aim at it. I thought once of making a little Fortune by my Person. I now intend to make a great one by my Vartue.   (p. 342)[18]

The occasional awkwardness of epistolary conventions, on the other hand, is parodied in Fielding's version of a Richardson seduction scene, as Pamela lies in bed with the housekeeper:

> Mrs. *Jervis* and I are just in Bed, and the Door unlocked; if my Master should come – Odsbobs! I hear him coming in at the door. You see, I write in the present Tense, as Parson *Williams* says.
>
> (p. 12)

Moral and formal reservations are then wittily combined in the description of Shamela packing prior to departure – the corresponding account in *Pamela* is equally circumstantial, but not without pathos:

> Mrs. *Jewkes* went in with me, and helped me to pack up my little All, which was soon done; being no more than two Day-Caps, two Night-Caps, five Shifts, one Sham, a Hoop, a Quilted-Petticoat, two Flannel Petticoats, two pair of Stockings, one odd one, a pair of lac'd Shoes, a short flowered Apron, a lac'd Neck-Handkerchief, one Clog, and almost another, and some few Books: as ... *The Whole Duty of Man*, with only the Duty to one's Neighbour, torn out. The third volume of the *Atalantis. Venus in the Cloyster: Or, the Nun in her Smock. God's Dealings with Mr. Whitefield* ... Some Sermon-Books; and two or three plays, with their Titles, and Part of the first Act torn off.   (p. 344)

The formal satire of the opening lines underlines a rejection of the comprehensive detail required by 'formal realism', as well as a distrust of the intense subjective states it is used to convey.[19]

Historical interest aside, the move from *Jonathan Wild* to *Shamela* is essentially one from literary squib to literary parasite; *Joseph Andrews* promised more than this. In this neat inversion of the Pamela story, Lady Booby develops a passion for her handsome young servant, Joseph, and dismisses him when he does not respond. On his way home to the West Country, he meets the local parson coming to London in an attempt to get his sermons published; the pair are later joined by Joseph's sweetheart, Fanny, and the three undergo numerous adventures before completing the broad country–town–country movement of the narrative.

Joseph Andrews also has a famous Preface, widely seen as a landmark in fictional poetics, although – as implied below – it may also be regarded as one of the more over-rated statements in the history of the English novel: sharper, perhaps, than the bland generalizations preceding *Ferdinand Count Fathom* (containing Smollett's only explicit reference to the novel as genre), but ultimately less illuminating than the Preface to *Roderick Random*. Whatever the case, Fielding's apology is at least remarkable in its ability to reconcile the apparently contradictory claims of literary pioneer and sustainer of an established tradition.[20]

But the title-page of *Joseph Andrews* contains a more explicit literary acknowledgement ('Written in Imitation of the *Manner* of *Cervantes*, Author of *Don Quixote*'), inviting today's reader to find analogies between the two authors beyond those traditionally proposed (sunny humour, whacky chapter headings and a testy old Don transformed into a lovable old English parson). Less obviously, Cervantes – before turning to prose fiction – also proved a mediocre poet, besides producing numbers of short theatrical *Interludes* considerably more successful than his full-blown *Comedias*; Fielding was similarly the author of some unremarkable verse, before discovering a talent better suited to farce than to serious drama.

The true equivalent to *Joseph Andrews* may, in some respects moreover, be Cervantes's *Exemplary Novels*, with their juxtaposition of radical narrative experiment and more traditional models: the collection of twelve *novelas* was not published until 1613, although a number were certainly written before the first part of *Don Quixote* (1605). Fielding's bold claim to originality for *Joseph Andrews* ('this kind of Writing, which I do not remember to have seen hitherto attempted in our own Language') also recalls the Preface to the *Exemplary Novels*.[21] Only in terms of subsequent literary reputation, perhaps, is the obvious link between Cervantes and Fielding provided by their respective masterpieces, *Don Quixote* and *Tom Jones*.

With its discussion of references to literary models, classical learning, and other issues dear to Fielding, however, the Prologue to *Don Quixote* has a special interest in the present context. Cervantes envied Fielding nothing in terms of classical humanist education, and also anticipates the English writer in his defensive tone towards what was new and unorthodox, rather as if each man felt himself involved in some precarious kind of literary slumming. The Preface to *Don Quixote* is in the form of a dialogue between the author and an anonymous friend, whose iconoclasm obviously exercises a function as Cervantes's artistic *alter ego*. On the subject of learning, for example, the friend is far less respectful than Fielding:

> you have no reason to go begging sentences from philosophers, counsel from Holy Writ, fables from poets, speeches from orators, or miracles from saints. You have only to see that your sentences shall come out plain, in expressive, sober and well-ordered language, harmonious and gay, expressing your purpose to the best of your ability, and setting out your ideas without intricacies and obscurities.
>
> (p. 30)

Cervantes's anonymous counsellor seems to be advocating a style rather plainer than Fielding's self-conscious pastiche – an early *demotic* perhaps – whilst an earlier comment ('you have only to make use of imitation, and the more perfect the imitation the better your writing will be') also suggests a more conscious commitment to the concept of realistic imitation or *mimesis*. On the question of Latin quotations, so prominent in Fielding's fiction, the friend is even more scathing:

> all you have to do is to work in some pat phrases or bits of Latin that you know by heart, or at least that cost you small pains to look out.   (p. 28)

With these expedients, the friend cynically remarks, 'they may even take you for a scholar'.

The respective rhetorical strategies of the two authors are revealing. Whilst Cervantes constructs an anxious, almost deferential authorial *persona*, gleefully undermined by a highly sceptical counter-narrative, Fielding (behind the good-natured banter) is actually fairly peremptory about his views. One senses that, in terms of urbanity and ironic detachment, the English master is for once well and truly finessed.

For this reason, it may be better to examine the substance rather than the rhetoric of Fielding's Preface. He begins by aligning his *History* (never a novel or romance) with the hypothetical lost comic epic of Homer, a work which – according to Aristotle – 'bore the same relation to Comedy which his *Iliad* bears to Tragedy' (p. 3). The argument is then elaborated:

> Now a comic Romance is a comic Epic-Poem in Prose; differing from Comedy, as the serious Epic from Tragedy; its Action being more extended and comprehensive; containing a much larger Circle of Incidents, and introducing a greater Variety of Characters.   (p. 4)

In view of the likely respective lengths of stage comedies and comic epics, Fielding's three distinguishing features are hardly startling. The passage may in fact capture something of neo-classical theory at its most arid, and it is difficult to avoid irreverent comparisons with the pedantic list by Shakespeare's Polonius on mixed theatrical genres.[23] Fielding then goes on to distinguish his 'comic Epic-Poem' from 'serious Romance':

> It differs from the serious Romance in its Fable and Action, in this; that as in the one these are grave and solemn, so in the other they are light and ridiculous: it differs in its Characters, by introducing persons of inferiour rank, and consequently of inferiour Manners, whereas the grave Romance, sets the highest before us; lastly in its Sentiments and Diction, by preserving the Ludicrous instead of the Sublime.   (p. 4)

The new trio of distinctions is also unremarkable, but most notable perhaps for the implication that persons of lower social rank must necessarily be ridiculous.[24]

Fielding then compares comic and burlesque, drawing an analogy between 'comic history' and *caricatura* in painting, referring to his friend Hogarth. By this link, together with a later one to Garrick, Fielding projects a virtual realist *triumvirate* of the eighteenth-century arts. Here, too, apparent clarity of exposition barely survives a brief excursion into aesthetic relativism. From the perspective of psychological realism, Fielding's comic characters were indeed an advance on Jonsonian 'humors', although – to adopt E. M. Forster's classic distinction – they now seem decidedly more 'flat' than 'round'.[25] Similarly, Hogarth today is often regarded as master of a form of *caricature*; whereas it would have been interesting to compare Garrick's style with the naturalistic delivery of late twentieth-century theatrical praxis.

The latter half of the Preface requires less attention here. Its main concern is the subject of ridicule, with its famous judgement: 'The only

Source of the true Ridiculous (as it appears to me) is Affectation' (p. 6).
This is clearly included to justify the character of Parson Adams who, in
his 'perfect simplicity', is comic but never ridiculous in the author's
eyes. The point is well taken, since Adams's enlightened paternalism
(with allowances for comic exaggeration and a quixotic confusion of
books and 'real life') is close to Fielding's own.

As this brief account suggests, it is difficult to leave the Preface to
Joseph Andrews without some sense of anti-climax. Far from casting its
author exclusively as a bold innovator, it often suggests a self-conscious
and even over-defensive regard for established literary tradition. In his
close concern with genres and precedents, Fielding seems to be casting
around for a literary pedigree for this, his first (published) foray into the
novel, an initially sub-literary form in eighteenth-century England. If
Richardson's fiction can be regarded as transcending the narrow
homiletic modes from which it emerges, then Fielding's might be
viewed less kindly as retrogressing from prestigious classical forms into
a kind of literary limbo between ancient and modern.

Posterity fortunately tends to judge Fielding less on theoretical
pronouncements than on actual performance, and the canonic status of
Joseph Andrews reflects an ability to go beyond the prescriptivism of its
Preface. Modern responses to the novel are generally influenced by one
of two critical perspectives: a reading of the novel as Christian allegory,
and a renewed insistence on its parodic element in relation to *Pamela*.

The first of these approaches is associated with Martin Battestin,[26]
who begins with the simple onomastic associations of the names *Abraham
Adams* (the first man, or the old testament patriarch) and *Joseph*
Andrews (the later patriarch who resisted the charms of Potiphar's wife
in Egypt): Charity (Adams) and Chastity (Joseph) then embark on a
physical journey between town and country, simultaneously figuring
life's spiritual journey, according to a hallowed Christian trope. The
most obvious problem here, apart from the additional presence of the
hero's sweetheart Fanny, is Joseph's surname of Andrews. The reader
may turn at this point, then, to the kind of historically and generically
more sophisticated approach linked with Claude Rawson.[27]

According to this perspective, the element of anti-Pamela satire
remains strong. For most of the novel, Joseph is assumed to be the
brother of Richardson's heroine, whose parents – Gaffer and Gammer
Andrews – later make a brief appearance, although Pamela's true sibling
is Fanny. Joseph's own chastity, on the other hand, is probably to be
accepted at face value, although it is not ultimately a serious proposition
for a male protagonist, unless one is the author of *Grandison*. A hint of

Fielding's casual attitude towards male chastity may be gained from *Shamela* in the parodied seduction scene:

> he run up, caught me in his Arms, and flung me upon a Chair, and *began to offer to touch my Under-Petticoat.* Sir, says I, you had better not offer to be rude; well, says he, no more I won't then; and away he went out of the Room. I was so mad to be sure I could have cry'd.
>
> (p. 329; my emphasis)[28]

There is doubtless an element of pure linguistic parody here, although this does not preclude some characteristic Fieldingesque sexual banter. Not only is Richardson a bad moralist, then, but Squire Booby – at four removes from the object desired – is no great seducer either.

The irony which permeates Fielding is, by definition, exclusive, in the sense that it means one thing to the enlightened few and something else to the many; parody, in the Augustan tradition shared by Pope, Swift and Fielding himself, was a means of self-definition. In practice, as Rawson forcefully argues, it distinguished a true *author* from 'cits, dunces or canting vulgarians who wrote works about servant girls trapping their masters into marriage'.[29] History has its own irony here, of course, since Fielding was to marry his own heavily pregnant cook-maid only five years later.

Sharply contrasted as the two above perspectives are, neither the emphasis on Christian allegory nor a stress on textual parody contradicts the view of *Joseph Andrews* as a formally, rather than psychologically, motivated narrative predicated on *literary* sources. The opening chapter thus continues the learned references of the Preface by praising the classical *Biographers*, Plutarch and Cornelius Nepos, to the detriment of such modern *Historians* as Richardson or the actor and playwright Cibber. The neglect of the former category is explained with characteristic irony by their 'being written in obsolete, and, as they are generally thought, unintelligible Languages'; here is a virtual continuation of the battle of the Ancients and the Moderns.[30] In Fielding (and also, incidentally, in Smollett), it sometimes seems, a man weak in his Latin verb conjugations must be an impostor, and probably a scoundrel, too. Parson Adams triumphantly swaps verses with one such figure at the house of the country justice (Book II, ch. xi); whilst the sexually ambivalent Beau Didapper replies to Adams's quotation from Horace with the comment that he 'did not understand *Welch*' (Book IV, ch. ix). The highest compliment Adams can pay the modestly talented Joseph, on the other hand, is to acknowledge his potential for studying Latin.

Ignorance of Latin, in fact, is a significant cultural differential between Fielding's contemporary male audience and his twentieth-century public of either sex. *Joseph Andrews* regularly assumes a familiarity with the language (at least in its gentlemen readers) rarely met today even among its scholarly editors. There is a significant shift in *Tom Jones*, where the still frequent Latin quotations are now followed by English translations; *Amelia* tends to lapse into old habits. The most conspicuous examples of Fielding's classicizing tendencies are his apostrophes and invocations, his parodies of the extended epic simile – one thinks of the amorous Mrs Slipslop as 'hungry Tygress' or 'voracious Pike' (Book I, ch. vi); these are the passages to which Fielding was referring when he claimed to use burlesque in diction alone, although even this limited exposure is too much for some modern readers.

From Book II of *Joseph Andrews*, however, the presence of *Don Quixote* is increasingly prominent. Structural similarities noted between the two novels include the battle at the inn punctuating Leonora's story (Book II, ch. v) and the spilt hog's blood producing the same horrific sights as the punctured wineskins in *Don Quixote*. The night farce at Booby Hall echoes Cervantes, even as it anticipates Chaplin. The assault on Adams by a pack of hounds offers a mock-epic battle for the benefit of Fielding's 'Classical Reader', while the roll of the dogs' names recalls the catalogue of armies in virtually every serious epic as well as in Don Quixote's early encounter with a flock of sheep.[31] The discussion of biography which begins Book III shows an intimate knowledge of *Don Quixote*, particularly the digressions of Part I, as well as making detailed references to the contemporary French novelists Lesage and Marivaux.[32]

Literary in quite another sense is the sensational ending of the novel. When Fielding finally remarshals his characters at Booby Hall in Book IV, Fanny is revealed by a passing pedlar as the kidnapped daughter of Gammer and Gaffer Adams; the momentary *frisson* of potential incest is dispelled, however, when Joseph, too, proves a changeling and the son of the rural gentleman Mr Wilson, introduced in Book III. Attentive romance readers have been prepared for this by the insistence on Joseph's fair skin (Book I, ch. xiv) and his soft white hands (Book I, ch. xv). Ian Watt linked Fielding with Defoe and Richardson not only for his formal realism, but also for his rejection of traditional plots. With an itinerant Irish pedlar for *deus ex machina*, an incest scare for *crisis*, a strawberry birthmark for *anagnorisis* (or recognition) and a double-changeling device for *peripeteia* (or reversal), these seem wild claims to make for *Joseph Andrews*. And in fact, where *Tom Jones* and *Clarissa* merit thirty-five pages each in Watt's *Rise of the Novel* (and *Pamela* over forty), *Joseph Andrews* – rather like an embarrassing relative – is kept well in the background with only three.

Another of Watt's famous hypotheses was the legal analogy, according to which the new fictional discourse would have the verisimilitude of evidence in a court of law. And however incredible his plots, Fielding – by one of those literary ironies to which he is often subject – clearly knew more about that particular institution than any English novelist before or since. But this belongs more to the story of *Tom Jones*.

Tom Jones

Tom Jones represents a substantial shift from the intimate, even parasitical, relationships of its predecessors to other literary works. Shorn of its rich intertextual accretions, Fielding's novel is the simple story of an attractive but headstrong young man of unknown parentage raised in luxury on an idyllic country estate. He falls in love with the daughter of a neighbouring landowner, but incurs the hatred of the estate's presumptive heir, who manages to get him expelled. After a series of adventures on the open road, the hero, with his faithful companion and servant, arrives in London. Here, cruel circumstances and crueller human agency conspire against him, until he sinks to a point where he is about to be hanged – before a dramatic reversal restores his fortunes (and his fortune).

This hardly suggests a plot rated by Coleridge, together with those of Sophocles's *Oedipus Tyrannus* and Ben Jonson's *The Alchemist*, as 'one of the three most perfect . . . ever planned'. Such planning is most conspicuous, however, in the extraordinary symmetries of the novel.[33] In broadest terms, Fielding's second comic epic in prose is divided into eighteen books, with three equal parts of six books each. Part I is set in the country, at Paradise Hall under the benign rule of Squire Allworthy; Part II takes place on the open road, featuring the picaresque adventures of Tom and Partridge; Part III unfolds in the great metropolis of London. The mathematical centre of the narrative features the inn scenes at Upton, in Books IX–X. There are two major digressions in the novel, the stories of the Man of the Hill and of Mrs Fitzpatrick, symmetrically placed in Books VII and IX, respectively. Such architectonic proportion is then sustained by a host of smaller symmetries.

At the beginning of Book V, Fielding's narrator claims to be opening a 'new vein of knowledge' and goes on to explain that 'this vein is no other than that of contrast'. And the contrasts and conflicts of *Tom Jones* are indeed reinforced by a complex grid of cultural binarisms: town and country, Whig and Tory (or Jacobite); of thematic polarities: reason *versus* emotion, duty *versus* passion; and, above all, of simple character oppositions: Tom the hero and Blifil the anti-hero; the good Squire Allworthy and the brutish Squire Western; the Christian disciplinarian Thwackum and the free-thinking Square; together with an almost infinite regress of fathers and sons, fathers and daughters, masters (or mistresses) and servants, and more or less star-crossed lovers. Finally, there are the extraordinary twists, reversals and coincidences running through the novel, which were probably the real motivation for Coleridge's judgement.

It is unlikely that all the conflicts and contrasts of *Tom Jones* will become apparent on a first reading, and this very point suggests the significance of such intricate plotting: for perhaps in no other eighteenth-century narrative does the novel's *design* (or form) reflect so accurately the author's *designs* (in the sense of intentions). Fielding is particularly sensitive to the special relation of the parts to the whole; and, in a characteristic outburst, at the beginning of Book X, warns the unsympathetic critic that

> to presume to find Fault with any of its Parts, without knowing the Manner in which the Whole is connected, and before he comes to the final Catastrophe, is a most presumptuous Absurdity.[34]

Behind Fielding's witty polemic with his reptile of a critic, however, lies a profound metaphysical parallel. The fact that the design of the whole may seem unclear to the reader mirrors a conventional Augustan belief in a rational and divinely organized universe, whose purpose is similarly unclear to humanity. The latter idea finds its perfect expression in Pope's *Essay on Man*:

> All Nature is but Art, unknown to thee,
> All Chance, Direction, which thou canst not see;
> All Discord, Harmony, not understood;
> All partial Evil, universal Good.[35]

The 'omniscient' narrator, then, is nothing less than equivalent to the omniscient deity. In addition to such massive ideological underpinnings, however, *Tom Jones* also has an increasing groundwork of biographical and historical data. The central sections of the novel are set 'at the very time when the late rebellion was at its highest'. In 1745, the exiled Stuart pretender, Prince Charles Edward ('Bonnie Prince Charlie'), had returned from exile, raised an army in the Scottish Highlands and marched on London. He was halted at Derby, driven back over the border and crushingly defeated at Culloden in 1746. This effectively closed a phase of English history beginning with the restoration of the Stuart monarchy in 1660. Constitutional conflict had intensified under Charles II and peaked during the reign of his brother James, provoking the premature rebellion instigated by Charles's natural son, the Duke of Monmouth, and the final overthrow of James in 1688. A Whig parliament invited William of Orange (ironically married to James's daughter Mary) to replace him. When William and Mary's own daughter, Anne, died childless, the Act of Settlement (1701) ensured that the new pattern of Protestant constitutional monarchy would continue with the House of Hanover.

A number of the writers in this study were deeply implicated in these historical events. If Behn's unswerving Stuart loyalty ran to a spell as government agent in Antwerp, then Defoe – along with a number of his classmates from the Stoke Newington Academy – had been out in the abortive Monmouth uprising. Even Richardson's father, compromised by his sympathies for Monmouth, had beaten a strategic retreat to Derbyshire, where the novelist was born. Smollett – a Scot who nevertheless supported the Hanoverian cause – published his impassioned poem 'The Tears of Scotland' in 1746, in the wake of cruel English reprisals following the Battle of Culloden. The loyal Hanoverian Fielding was actively involved in government propaganda, writing a series of political pamphlets in the autumn of 1745 and launching a weekly paper, *The True Patriot*, later in the same year. In December 1747, moreover, he launched another pro-government paper, *The Jacobite's Journal*, using the comic persona of John Trott-Plaid, a diehard Stuart supporter.

Fielding was in the middle of *Tom Jones* when the rebellion broke out, and subsequently altered the time-scheme of the novel to accommodate it. When Tom is thrown out of Paradise Hall in the autumn of 1745, he thus goes north to enlist with the Redcoats and meet the invasion; there is a comic misunderstanding here, since Partridge – a Jacobite sympathizer – assumes that his master is going to join the Young Pretender. Squire Western, another closet Jacobite, hates the 'Hanover Rats' and their Whig supporters (personified by his sister) and toasts the exiled Stuart 'King over the Water'. The heroine Sophie is mistaken for Jenny Cameron, traditionally if rather fancifully cast as the lover of Bonnie Prince Charlie.

The historical material of *Tom Jones* blends with a number of traditional literary forms: Christian pastoral, in the pre-lapsarian Paradise Hall before expulsion from this west-country Eden; classical epic, modified by Homeric parody and burlesque; romance plotting and picaresque incident. That the elements blend so well must be partly ascribed to a new confidence and assurance on Fielding's part. The novel is conspicuous, in fact, for its emphasis on *authority*, a recurrent element in the introductory chapters to the eighteen books of the novel. From the initial metaphor of the 'Bill of Fare' (Book I) to the final analogy of the completed journey (Book XVIII), these prefaces effectively constitute an ambitious accumulative poetics. Within this context, Fielding's concerns are broadly literary rather than specifically novelistic through his constant citation of classical example and precedent: here are Homer and Virgil, the satirists Horace, Persius and Juvenal and a host of 'ancients' from Aristotle to Longinus; occasionally reinforced by such 'moderns' as the satirists Pope, Swift and Samuel Butler, or the dramatists Vanbrugh and Congreve.

Fielding thus continues a prescriptive labour begun in *Joseph Andrews*, where the opening to Book II ('Of Divisions in Authors') best reflects his characteristic complex of irony, reservation and qualification. Here as on many occasions, however, Fielding is as revealing for his hidden ideological assumptions as for anything self-consciously clever he has to say. He thus genders what he will later describe with (mock) grandiloquence as the 'Science of *Authoring*' (Book II, ch. i):

> There are certain Mysteries or secrets in all Trades from the highest to the lowest, from that of *Prime Ministring* [sic] to this of *Authoring*, which are seldom discovered, unless to Members of the same Calling. Among those used by us Gentlemen of the latter Occupation, I take this of dividing our Works into Books and Chapters to be none of the least considerable.   (p. 78)

Authorship is explicitly gendered and then troped with an occupation where women were, by definition, distinctly under-represented. Literary and social precepts thus elide, anticipating the special force which the concepts of *author* and *authority* were to assume for Fielding, both in the world of *Tom Jones* and in his career outside.

To begin with the novel itself: the opening chapter of Book II playfully, but insistently, underlines one kind of authority Fielding has in mind:

for as I am, in reality, the founder of a new province of writing, so I am at liberty to make what laws I please therein. And these laws, my readers, whom I consider as my subjects, are bound to believe in and to obey; with which that they may readily and chearfully comply, I do hearby assure them, that I shall principally regard their ease and advantage in all such institutions: for I do not, like a *jure divino* tyrant, imagine that they are my slaves, or my commodity. I am, indeed, set over them for their own good only, and was created for their use, and not they for mine.[36]

To which, two comments may be added. Twentieth-century critics proposed various concepts – narrative *personae*, implied authors – to distinguish the self-conscious narrator from the name on a novel's title page. The valedictory essay in Book XVIII, on the other hand, complains of slanderous attacks by critics; particularly galling was to have 'the abusive writings of those very men fathered upon me, who in other of their works have abused me themselves with the utmost virulence' (p. 814). Rather than referring to any kind of 'implied author' or narrative *persona*, however, this suggests an unmediated reference to contemporary literary battles. The ironic mask is pretty thin here, as is the division between Fielding and his self-conscious narrator. Elsewhere in the novel, too, the differences are less in actual identity than in degrees of ironic distance.

The second point concerns the phrase *jure divino*, the abbreviated Latin term for the 'divine right of kings' or the 'absolute monarchy' associated by Whig constitutionalists with the Stuarts. It has already been noted how Fielding draws on the now classic comparison between the 'omniscient' narrator of a novel and the omniscient God of the universe; here, his political convictions allow a second analogy, linking the same responsible, painstaking narrator with an enlightened, constitutional monarch.

With authority goes legitimacy, the subject of the prefatory essay to Book IX:

> Among other good uses for which I have thought proper to institute these several introductory chapters, I have considered them as a kind of mark or stamp, which may hereafter enable a very indifferent reader to distinguish, what is true and genuine in this historic kind of writing, from what is false and counterfeit.   (p. 435)

In a period before Bank of England notes existed, when coin was scarce and frequently debased by clipping, the financial metaphor is powerful.[37]

Fielding's view of his own fictional discourse as a kind of legal tender deserves close attention.

Most of the rest of the essay, on the other hand, is a list of the qualities necessary for a good writer: 'genius' (here defined as powers of invention and judgement), a 'good share of learning' ('on the authority of Horace', no less!), and universal 'conversation' (i.e. wide experience of human-kind); all crowned by a 'good heart' and the capacity to feel. The Preface to Book XII continues in this prescriptive vein in distinguishing between borrowing and plagiarism, with particular reference to the classics:

> The ancients may be considered as a rich common, where every person who has the smallest tenement in Parnassus hath a free right to fatten his muse. Or, to place it in a clearer light, we moderns are to the ancients what the poor are to the rich.   (p. 552)

The debate on 'ancients' and 'moderns' lives on. Book XIII provides a lengthy mock-epic invocation to the muse, much delayed like that of *Tristram Shandy*, and indirectly acknowledging some of the same sources of inspiration as Sterne:

> Come thou, who hast inspired thy Aristophanes, thy Lucian, thy Cervantes, thy Rabelais, thy Moliere, thy Shakespear, thy Swift, thy Marivaux ...   (p. 608)

The invocation goes on to personify such writerly attributes as Genius, Humanity, Learning (once again) and Experience.

The two latter features are also the main concern of the Preface to Book XIV, provoked by the recent successes of certain unnamed writers lacking in both. Fielding's targets are clear two paragraphs later, however, in the suggestion that 'one reason why many English writers have totally failed in describing the manners of upper life, may possibly be, that in reality they know nothing of it' (p. 656). This particular argument is recognizable as the one commonly applied in the eighteenth century to Richardson by virtually anyone lower in the creative scale but higher in the social one – clearly a considerable field. After the customary swipe at the 'citizens and their apprentices' (Defoe and Richardson were star examples in both categories), Fielding hints at his own familiarity with 'high life', although this knowledge is unnecessary to his immediate purposes:

> this knowledge of upper life, though very necessary for the preventing mistakes, is no very great resource to a writer whose province is comedy,

or that kind of novels, which, like this I am writing, is of the comic
class. (p. 657)

Explicit snobbery is less interesting here than implied aesthetics. For the
arch-conservative Fielding maintains a hierarchic view of both literature
and life: as in *Joseph Andrews*, the lower orders are comic whilst only the
upper ones – if rarely – are capable of the heroic or the sublime. This is
also, incidentally, Fielding's most important ideological link with
Smollett: neither of these novelists is about to retail the intimate
thoughts of a whore turned thief (*Moll Flanders*) or a fifteen-year-old
servant girl (*Pamela*).

Two recurrent themes of the prefatory chapters, then, are authority
and legitimization, reflected in the prescriptive claims of the novel's
literary legislator. But the term legislator and the concept of authority
naturally had quite other referents for Fielding during the period in
which he was writing *Tom Jones*. The author's labours for the Hanoverian cause were rewarded in 1746 when the Duke of Bedford appointed
him High Steward of the New Forest in Hampshire, a job which
entailed the prosecution of poachers and other kinds of trespassers. This
was Fielding's first official government appointment and effectively
marks his definitive entry into to the ranks of the Establishment. In
November 1748, he was named Justice of the Peace for the City of
Westminster, and in the following year his authority was extended to
the County of Middlesex. He worked tirelessly in his new role, institut-
ing London's first organized police force, the 'Bow Street Runners',
and producing three important tracts between 1749 and 1753; the
best-known of these is his *Enquiry into the Causes of the Late Increase of
Robbers* (January 1751). Fielding's new proximity to crime and poverty
was to bear some literary fruit in *Amelia*. More interesting here, however, are the suggestive parallels between legal and literary authority.

Within his new *literary* province, then, Fielding adopted the position
of ruler and arbitrator, often using a *legal* terminology to defend
appropriation and justify exclusion. John Bender's *Imagining the Penitentiary* cleverly compared the shift from the open prison to the modern
organized penitentiary in the eighteenth century with that from the
open promiscuous narrative to the modern organized novel during the
same period. Both discourses are concerned, for example, with *sentences*
and *sentencing*; or, to use an analogy not considered by Bender,
Fielding disciplined and controlled social behaviour in his career as
magistrate, just as he attempted to discipline and control literary behaviour, whether by subjugating critics or castigating 'modern novel and

Atalantis Writers' (Behn, Manley, and Haywood).[38] The term that will cover both activities is *censor*.

Tom Jones has one final interesting example of Fielding's peremptory stance in Book XVIII: defending the probability of Allworthy's change of heart, he insists on the 'authority of authors', adding the warning that 'we insist upon as much authority as any author'. It is perhaps the most explicit association of the two concepts to be found in eighteenth-century fiction.

Amelia

It would be simplistic to regard Fielding exclusively as a literary author, steeped in the classics, modelled on Cervantes and drawing occasionally on Marivaux or the continental picaresque. Readers of the day recognized many non-literary elements in his novels, ranging from contemporary polemic to pure autobiography. *Amelia* is a suitable context in which to return to this documentary – even topical – element. It is the only one of the four major novels, for example, where Fielding partly abrogates the authority of the self-consciously literary and intrusive narrator. He largely abandons the comic epic for the sentimental and the pathetic; he also uses his professionally acquired knowledge of crime and vice in London to address legal and constitutional issues; and finally, he draws more closely than ever before on details from his own personal life.

The plot of *Amelia* is unusual for eighteenth-century fiction in concentrating on married life rather than courtship. After making a love match with the novel's heroine, Booth is sent with his regiment to Gibraltar. On his return to England, financial improvidence and the inadequate income of a lieutenant on half-pay precipitate economic crisis and imprisonment for debt; the attractive but virtuous Amelia is meanwhile pursued by various unscrupulous admirers, before a recovered inheritance resolves the couple's material problems. They live happily ever after in the country – presumably on Amelia's legacy.

The principal literary model for *Amelia* is, on Fielding's own admission, Virgil's *Aeneid*, and a number of parallels can be adduced beyond the common twelve-book division. Booth thus tells his story to his fellow prisoner, Miss Matthews, in Books II and III, and the pair become lovers in prison at the beginning of Book IV. He ends the relationship on release and predictably earns Miss Matthews's enmity. Aeneas had similarly related his own adventures to Dido, Queen of

Carthage, in Books II and III of the *Aeneid*, and the couple had con-summated their love in the equally inhospitable atmosphere of a cave. Aeneas later abandoned Dido, provoking the same reaction as that of Miss Matthews to Booth. Such clear parallels are not particularly frequent or obvious, however, in spite of Fielding's explicit references to the Latin poet; the latter include his puzzled response years later in the *Covent-Garden Journal* to the mixed critical reception for his final novel and 'favourite child'.

> I followed the Rules of all those who are acknowledged to have writ best on the Subject; and if her Conduct be fairly examined, she will be found to deviate very little from the strictest Observation of all Rules; neither Homer nor Virgil pursued them with greater Care than myself, and the candid and learned Reader will see that the latter was the noble model, which I made use of on this Occasion.
>
> (Battestin, p. 538)[39]

Fielding thus indirectly confirms his continued sympathy with the 'learned Reader', even as he extends the sociological scope of serious fiction, in anticipation of nineteenth-century naturalism and the prob-lem novels of Dickens. Only in *Tom Jones*, however, does he display a robust literary independence; by *Amelia* he seems to have reverted to a characteristic neo-classical prescriptivism; whilst the construction of 'Homer' as some eighteenth-century English gentleman poring over critical treatises to get the rules right may raise a smile.

In spite of Fielding's classicizing impulses, however, the documentary element in *Amelia* is strong. Samuel Richardson complained to Sarah Fielding that her half-brother wrote as if he had 'been born in a stable, or been a runner in a sponging house'; he particularly disparaged *Amelia* for its author's general dependence on personal experience for plots and characters, thus proving the 'impotence of his imagination'. Parallels between the 'Life' and the 'Works' are a gradually expanding element in Fielding's fiction. They are also a staple of Battestin's definitive, exhaustive biography, from its opening claim that 'Like the history of Tom Jones, his foundling hero, Henry Fielding's own story begins in Glastonbury, Somerset.' A number of identifications are then made in fairly categorical terms: in *Joseph Andrews*, for example, William Young, curate of East Stour, is the *original* of Parson Adams; Peter Walter, the Dorset land-steward, is the *model* for Peter Pounce, *etc.*[40]

In *Tom Jones*, real-life parallels are quite explicit. Fielding declares in the dedication that the character of Squire Allworthy is modelled on his patrons, Ralph Allen and George Lyttelton. Sophie Western is a tribute to his first wife Charlotte: 'one whose Image never can depart from my Breast, and whom, if thou dost remember, thou hast then, my Friend, an adequate Idea of *Sophia*'. To these may be added a number of authentic contemporary figures – such as Fielding's favourite landlords – all mentioned by name. The biographical links in *Amelia*, on the other hand, were suggested by the novelist's cousin Lady Mary Wortley Montagu, according to whom, Fielding had:

> given a true picture of himselfe and his first Wife in the Characters of Mr. and Mrs. Booth (some Complement [sic] to his own figure excepted) and I am persuaded several of the incidents he mentions are real matters of Fact.[41]

The iconography of the novelist also agrees closely with a humorous portrait of the hero in Book XI, when Colonel James questions his wife's portrayal of Booth as handsome:

> 'What, with a nose like the proboscis of an elephant, with the shoulders of a porter, and the legs of a chairman? The fellow hath not in the least the look of a gentleman, and one would rather think he had followed the plough than the camp all his life.'
>
> (Book II, p. 223)[42]

In reality, however, Booth's career is more probably a synthesis of elements from the author's own life and that of his father, General Edmund Fielding. Like Booth, the latter had married in face of parental opposition, had been retired from the army on half-pay, had been cheated at cards by a fellow officer, had failed as a gentleman farmer and become thoroughly familiar with bailiffs and sponging-houses. The early dates of Edmund Fielding's life also match the documentary element proper of *Amelia*, whose powerful social, legal and constitutional critique centres on a period ending in 1733, almost twenty years before the publication of the novel.

It is ultimately difficult to decide whether *Amelia* or *Tom Jones* is closer to Fielding's own life, when the autobiographical elements of the two novels are mediated through such contrasting narrative conventions. The role of authority in the two novels is also different. Perhaps nowhere in eighteenth-century fiction is there a more powerful conjunction between the concepts of author and authority than in *Tom Jones*, with Fielding in the first flush of his legal career and the full confidence of his novelistic one. In the 1750s, real-life judicial activities perhaps came to predominate: certainly, the *literary* magistrate and censor – in the form of the familiar self-conscious narrator – is less conspicuous in Fielding's final novel.

Amelia is the work where Augustan author most closely resembles modern novelist, although the transition is incomplete and the tension between authority and novelty is never resolved. The chapter headings are instructive here: some of them – 'Containing wise observations of the author, and other matters' (Book IV, ch. 3); 'Containing much heroic matter' (Book V, ch. 5); 'Which inclines rather to satire than panegyric' (Book VIII, ch. 6) – would not have been out of place in *Joseph Andrews*; other examples – 'Containing various matters' (Book V, ch. 7); 'In which the history goes forward' (Book IX, ch. 2) – have a lameness which suggests that this particular device had outlived its usefulness. What might replace the ironically self-conscious omniscient narrator is unclear. Fielding is still uninterested in the kind of circumstantial detail which filled the novels of Defoe and Richardson. He also remains reticent about the erotic dimension which was to preoccupy classic realist fiction for the next two centuries: 'we decline painting the scene', he announces, as Booth and Miss Matthews finally fall into each other's arms.

Fielding's most conspicuous attempts at fictional innovation appear in the narrative structure of *Amelia*, with a virtual crisis of authority emerging in the divisions between third- and first-person narrators: almost 30 per cent of the novel actually consists of first-person narration, with the personal accounts of Booth himself, his fellow prisoner Miss Matthews and the learned Mrs Atkinson (formerly Bennet), in addition to more than a dozen letters.

Miss Matthews's story, told to Booth in Book I – at about fifteen pages – is slightly shorter than Mrs Heartfree's in *Jonathan Wild*, but has none of the latter's comic repetitiveness. Her sordid tale of seduction and sexual exploitation, culminating in the stabbing of her lover, also has a characterizing function; for Miss Matthews will later play the role of seasoned commentator on Booth's much longer narrative (approximately a hundred pages) occupying the whole of Books II and III. These sections of the novel also have the strongest intertextual links with *Clarissa*: Amelia elopes with Booth rather than be forced to marry the wealthy Squire Winckworth; unlike Lovelace, however, Booth has honourable intentions. The most interesting formal element here is the first-person narrative of the *male* protagonist, to which a subsidiary *female* character plays the role of censor and adjudicator. Such a perspective has not occurred in any Fielding narrative before.

The third interpolated story (about half the length of Booth's account) is that of Mrs Bennet, or Atkinson after her marriage to Booth's old sergeant; the commentator is now Amelia. Authority male and classical have a central role in its relation, since Fielding explicitly thematizes the subject of female education and learning. Daughter of an Essex clergyman, Mrs Bennet becomes a 'pretty good mistress of the Latin language' as well as making 'some progress in the Greek'. The first fruits of these achievements are the bitter jealousy of a less literate aunt and the admiration of the penniless young curate who marries her. The climax of her story involves seduction, or rape, under sedation, by an unnamed lord after a masquerade. As a result of this episode, Mrs Bennet passes a sexually transmitted disease on to her husband, who dies shortly afterwards of other causes. It is hard not to see some form of implied retribution here: Mrs Bennet should perhaps have limited her education to needlework and playing the harpsichord.

The newly constituted Mrs Atkinson now acts as a dynamic foil to the more passive Amelia, but also constitutes one side of the novel's running debate on female learning. In Book VI, she thus speaks out against 'that great absurdity...of excluding women from learning', although without convincing her listeners:

> Though both Booth and Amelia outwardly concurred with her sentiments, it may be a question whether they did not assent rather out of complaisance than from their real judgment.   (Book VI, ch. 7)

Such cautious reservation is certainly close to Fielding's own position.

The comically pedantic Dr Harrison is also outwardly complaisant towards Mrs Atkinson. He cites the French classical scholar and translator Anne Dacier[43] as proof of female capacity, but only questions 'the utility of learning in a young lady's education' and speculates on the problems of a 'learned lady' and an 'unlearned husband'. Less sweetly reasonable at the next encounter, however, he purposely foments discord between Mrs Atkinson and her husband over this very issue. At this point, the reader is probably expected to register and query Mrs Atkinson's female learning without judgement rather than Dr Harrison's male learning without civility. And in the classic final chapter, where characters are rewarded according to their deserts, the omniscient narrator – rampant once again – sarcastically notes:

Mr. Atkinson upon the whole hath led a very happy life with his wife, though he hath been sometimes obliged to pay proper homage to her superior understanding and knowledge. (Vol. 2, p. 311)

Such smugness recalls Fielding's grotesquely patronizing 1744 Preface to his half-sister Sarah's *David Simple*. After three references to this 'little book' (without even the excuse of literalness, since it is a good hundred pages longer than *Joseph Andrews*), he comments on the 'Grammatical and other Errors in Style'; although 'no Man of Learning would think worth his Censure in a Romance; nor any Gentleman in the Writings of a young Woman' (p. 5) – an unintentionally ironic comment, since it is precisely what this particular gentleman does several times in his Preface. The reason for Sarah's lapses are clear enough:

the Imperfections of this little Book, which arise, not from want of Genius, but of Learning, lie open to the Eyes of every Fool, who has had a little Latin inoculated into his Tail. (p. 6)[44]

The airily self-effacing tone does not convince, and it is easy to believe Hester Thrale Piozzi's anecdote about Fielding's reaction when Sarah began to inoculate her own tail:

though they lived on the tenderest Terms *before*, yet after She had by their common Friend's Assistance made herself a competent Scholar, so as to construe the sixth Book of Virgil with Ease – the Author of Tom Jones began to teize and *taunt* her with being a literary Lady &c.[45]

Matters apparently deteriorated further when Sarah turned her attention to Greek: 'her Brother never more could perswade [sic] himself to endure her Company with Civility' (p. 381). Whether authentic or not, the story has a certain emblematic appeal. Taken together with the case of Mrs Atkinson, it is hard not to sense a certain apprehension on Fielding's part about educated women or female novelists: learned or ignorant, they would seem equally damned.

The comments are not grounded, moreover, in some ahistorically imposed version of political correctness, but reflect recurrent examples of insensitivity in Fielding's gendered rhetoric. There is, for example, his reaction to false attributions in the same Preface:

There is not, I believe, (and it is bold to affirm) a single Free Briton in this Kingdom, who hates his Wife more heartily than I detest the

Muses. They have indeed behaved to me like the most infamous Harlots, and have laid many a spurious, as well as deformed Production at my Door.[46]

This was also the writer who could boast to Richardson on the subject of the coy *Mrs Fame*: 'I have ravished her long ago, and live in a settled cohabitation with her in defiance of that Publick Voice which is supposed to be her Guardian, and to have alone the Power of giving her away' (p. 444). In a letter otherwise devoted to a discussion of *Clarissa*, whose heroine is abducted, drugged and raped, the choice of metaphor is unhappy.

Although more marginal to the plot, Mrs Atkinson's story is in some ways the most revealing of all three first-person intercalations. Whereas Miss Matthews and Booth effectively produce confessions, albeit constantly monitored by attentive listeners, the intense but humourless Mrs Atkinson is made to condemn herself out of her own mouth. Much of her account is thus traditional indirect satire of a tiresome (female) pedant.

There was no more fiction after *Amelia*. The *Journal of a Voyage to Lisbon*, published posthumously in 1755, is speculative rather than confessional autobiography: even here, then, a characteristic reticence and aloofness preclude the intimacy or circumstantiality of a fictional narrative like *Clarissa*. Fielding's literary trajectory thus remains incomplete. Whereas Richardson inscribes a complete parabola from the didacticism of the *Familiar Letters* through the aesthetically autonomous achievements of *Clarissa* and *Grandison* back to the authoritative direction of the *Maxims*, Fielding may reach a kind of no-*man's*-land by *Amelia*, but is still remote from the novel as feminized genre. 'I describe not Men, but Manners; not an Individual but a Species,' he had announced in the introductory chapter to Book III of *Joseph Andrews*; and the generalizing impulse of Fielding's literary models remains strong. Attempts to confine him within the strait-jacket of the classic realist novel do him as great a disservice as they do to his other great rival, Smollett.

There is a final suggestive analogy to be drawn between Fielding and Cervantes. The epicentre of *Tom Jones*, as noted previously, is the inn at Upton in Book IX. The climax of *Don Quixote* (Part I) also features an inn. The three troopers who arrive there in chapter 45 join a company already consisting of the landlord, his wife and daughter, the serving-maid Maritornes, Don Quixote, Sancho, two barbers, the priest, the aristocratic Ferdinand and Dorothea – together with three of Fernando's friends – the madman Cardenio and Luscinda, the Captive escaped from the Moors with his lover Zoraida, a judge and his daughter, Don Luis with four servants and at least one muleteer, besides the various attendants of the judge, who presumably lodge elsewhere. In the midst of all the activity engendered by such a company, the innkeeper still manages to spot two guests trying to leave without paying.

Whereas the Upton section of *Tom Jones* announces many of the parts in the novel later to be reconciled to the whole, the most memorable feature of the corresponding section of *Don Quixote* may be the final genial detail: for here, perhaps, is an allegory for the very randomness of fiction. Fielding's 'novelist as God' thus appears to confront and re-order Cervantes's universe conceived as contingency; and it is in this sustained creative analogy between omniscient narrator and omniscient God that Fielding – like Eliot and Joyce after him – seems most central to the history of English fiction.

Part II

Fictional Perspectives from Behn to Austen

6
Aphra Behn's *Oroonoko* and Daniel Defoe's *Moll Flanders*

Through its concern with issues of gender, race and class, *Oroonoko* was guaranteed the attention of late twentieth-century critics and theorists. Feminists emphasized the strong matrilinear claims of Behn in genealogies of the novel: a form supposed to have 'risen' with those 'fathers of the novel', Fielding and Richardson, in the 1740s – or even Defoe in the 1720s – was already emerging with Behn in the 1680s. New historicists seized on the ideological contradictions inherent in Behn's writing: Tory, royalist and elitist, she produces a radical, pre-feminist text sometimes regarded as a pioneering anti-slavery narrative. For these reasons alone, *Oroonoko* is a challenging starting-point for a series of individual readings.[1]

There are other grounds, too: her fiction displays in microcosm the shifting relations between *genre* and *gender* so central to English fiction from the Restoration to the end of the eighteenth century. From humble English origins, Behn spent a brief period of her youth in Surinam (where a possibly adopted relative was apparently governor-designate) and was briefly married on her return to England in 1664 (the mysterious Mr Behn may have been a Dutch merchant), before working as a government agent in Holland. Widowed and penniless, she later began writing for the theatre, producing at least eighteen plays over two decades, sometimes concealing her sex in order to gain greater freedom of expression.[2]

Her fiction then, like Fielding's, virtually represents a second literary career, the importance of which can hardly be over-rated. The feminocentric *Love-Letters Between a Nobleman and His Sister*, for example, is the first full-length pre-Richardsonian epistolary narrative, although its three separately published instalments seem to anticipate the slow emancipation of the English novel from the constraints of letter fiction. The first part of the *Love-Letters* (1683) is thus entirely epistolary, the second (1685) mixes third-person narrative with letter fiction, whilst the final volume (1687) has considerably fewer letters but a large amount of concealed historical material. *Oroonoko*, on the other hand, juxtaposes private and public domains, as its essentially heroic and highly literary mode is consistently punctuated by an accumulation of personal and documentary detail. The discursive techniques of a *novella* like *The Fair Jilt*, finally, are located at some point between the private sensibility of the *Love-Letters* (especially in the first two volumes) and the public performance of *Oroonoko*.

An obvious starting-point, then, is to relate Behn's fiction more clearly to conventional concepts of 'novel' and 'romance', before assessing the significance of the fact that *Oroonoko* was written by a woman. The omission of Behn from discussions of the novel was often based on fairly crude generic criteria: she wrote *romances* lacking the verisimilitude of the classic realist novel, or *novellas* simply lacking their length. Such superficial judgements raise hackneyed issues of terminology, although, in a study which emphasizes *genre*, the process is perhaps inevitable. The classic distinction between novel and romance appears in the Preface to Congreve's *Incognita* (1692), a short fiction published a mere four years after *Oroonoko*:

> Romances are generally composed of the Constant Loves and invincible Courages of Hero's, Heroins, Kings and Queeens, Mortals of the first Rank, and so forth; where lofty Language, miraculous Contingencies and impossible Performances, elevate and surprize the reader into a giddy Delight, which leaves him flat upon the Ground wherever he gives of, and vexes him to think how he has suffer'd himself to be pleased and transported, concern'd and afflicted at the several Passages which he has Read, *viz.* these Knights Success to their Damosels Misfortunes, and such like, when he is forced to be very well convinced that 'tis all a lye.[3]

Novels, on the other hand, 'are of a more familiar nature; Come near us, and represent to us Intrigues in practice ... not such as are wholly unusual or unpresidented'. The passage is often quoted by literary historians as a balanced, objective view of the categories 'romance' and 'novel' in terms of the fantastic *versus* the natural, or the ideal *versus* the real, although the non-specialist reader would certainly guess (to put it crudely) which line Congreve thought he was *in*. His comments actually reflect what Derrida would have called a 'violent hierarchy': an apparently balanced distinction, where one term will always remain privileged; and in fact, English now uses the word 'novel' both as a generic term for all fiction ('romance' included) and as a specific term for the classic realist tradition.[4]

The hidden assumptions of Congreve's definition are clear from the patronizing reference to the 'miraculous Contingencies and impossible Performances' that leave the reader deluded by his own credulity; this would actually seem a fair enough description of the *Odyssey*, too, although the classically educated Congreve – as opposed to the auto-didact Richardson – would probably have found the suggestion blasphemous. Modern readers, on the other hand, will often have difficulty in accepting the high-flown *Incognita* itself – brevity apart – as an application of its author's (novelistic) principles.

Lord Chesterfield, in an equally famous but more facetious comment, effectively reduces the distinction between romance and novel to a simple matter of length:

> I am in doubt whether you know what a Novel is; it is a little gallant history, which must contain a great deal of love, and not exceed one or two small volumes. The subject must be a love affair; the lovers are to meet with many difficulties and obstacles to oppose the accomplishment of their wishes, but at last overcome them all; and the conclusion or catastrophe must leave them happy. A Novel is a kind of abbreviation of a Romance; for a Romance generally consists of twelve volumes, all filled with insipid love nonsense, and most incredible adventures.[5]

Chesterfield's remarks recall Fielding's ironic dig at Behn in *Tom Jones*, where the Irish adventurer Mr Mclachlan is portrayed reading a novel by 'Mrs Behn' to recommend himself with the ladies, improve his understanding and fill his mind with good literature (p. 471).

A more objective appraisal of the relation of novel and romance appears in Clara Reeve's pioneering *Progress of Romance* (1785):[6]

> The Romance is an heroic fable, which treats of fabulous persons and things. – The Novel is a picture of real life and manners, and of the times in which it is written. The Romance, in lofty and elevated language, describes what never happens nor is likely to happen. – The Novel gives a familiar relation of such things, as pass every day before our eyes, such as may happen to our friend, or to ourselves; and the perfection of it, is to represent every scene, in so easy and natural a manner, and to make them appear so probable, as to

deceive us into a persuasion (at least while we are reading) that all is real, until we are affected by the joys or distresses, of the persons in the story, as if they were our own.   (Vol. I, p. 111)

Reeve's more balanced judgement is especially praiseworthy, since – in the same reductive terms applied to Congreve – she was decidedly *in* the line of romance; her first published fiction, *The Champion of Virtue: A Gothic Story* (1777), was reissued in 1778 as *The Old English Baron*, with a Preface describing it as 'the literary offspring of *The Castle of Otranto*'. Reeve's definition is also close to the conventional ones of modern dictionaries and literary histories.

As emerges below, Behn's *Oroonoko* is significantly located at some ambiguous interface of novel (or *novella*) and romance. Her story of the noble African, separated and later reunited with the woman he loves, tricked by an English captain into slavery in Surinam, deserted by fellow slaves in the rebellion he instigates, and cruelly executed by local planters, has a certain generic ambivalence. Initially, *Oroonoko* seems to accord perfectly with Congreve's definition, although exact correspondences begin to falter somewhere after 'lofty language'. Even the narrative's 'miraculous contingencies' and 'impossible performances' might seem recognizable romance features, were it not for Behn's frequent reliance on the conventions of authentic autobiography to legitimize her 'true history'. Reeve's element of vicarious indulgence ('…a giddy Delight…pleased and transported…') is also soon excluded; for, in spite of all its heroics and high-royalist rhetoric, Behn's indirect indictment of a slave-based mercantilism is not an exercise in escapism: ultimately, Oroonoko's story is, sadly, not 'all a lye'.

Chesterfield's smug comments are actually more suggestive than one might expect. *Oroonoko* meets their requirements as to length and subject, whilst the gallant lovers themselves encounter 'difficulties and obstacles' rarely surpassed in fiction. The conclusion of the story is a genuine *catastrophe*, in the sense of 'dramatic reversal' as originally applied to classical tragedy. The 'happiness' of the lovers cannot be of this world, but the gruesome conclusion represents a kind of apotheosis of romance, although one perhaps beyond the conception of the complacent Chesterfield.

Reeve, finally, whose study elsewhere reveals considerable insight into both novels and romances, ironically provides the most problematic definition of all. Besides such vague attributes as 'heroic fable' or 'lofty and elevated language', it has little that is applicable to *Oroonoko*, at all. It would be reassuring to believe that the narrative describes 'what never happens nor is likely to happen', but contemporary eye-witness reports confirm the worst. There is, for example, the barely literate account of one William Yearworth – steward at the very St John's Hill where Behn claimed to have lived while in Surinam – on the arrival of a slave ship from the Guinea Coast:

> Shee hase 130 nigroes one Borde; y^c Commanders name [is] Joseph John Woode; shee has lost 54 negroes in y^c viage. The Ladeyes that are heare liue att St Johnes hill.[7]

The casual conjunction of the slave trade with everyday domestic life certainly adds a new and sinister significance to Reeve's 'familiar relation of such things, as pass every day before our eyes'. What Reeve saw as mere readerly empathy ('such as may happen to our friend, or to ourselves'), moreover, is heightened by modern analogies between slavery and domesticity in a patriarchal society: woman *slaving* in the kitchen remains a modern cliché. Reeve's temporal perspective, on the other hand, is ambivalent. If *Oroonoko* is indeed 'a picture of real life and manners, and of the times in which it is written', then it can obviously no longer provide scenes which literally 'pass every day before our eyes'. The point seems a banal one, and yet it exemplifies the more general observation that a narrative regarded by one generation as a novel may be viewed by a later one as romance. Behn may actually have telescoped this historical process, by distancing what was essentially a 'familiar relation' until it does in fact seem a 'heroic fable' in the sense intended by Reeve. For, whatever Behn's true opinion of slavery may be in *Oroonoko*, she clearly expresses it in the language of heroic romance.

But Behn often proves as resistant to theorists as she does to critics; and her fiction, where *novel* effectively meets *romance*, is also a meeting-point for ideological discourses which might seem mutually exclusive. Here, in the very same text (to borrow the terminology of Watt), formal realism confronts poetic idealism; or alternatively (in the model elaborated by McKeon), *romance idealism* and *naive empiricism* converge, *aristocratic* and *progressive* ideologies clash. Any reading of *Oroonoko* would therefore do well to remember Behn's characteristic literary and ideological ambivalence.

In terms of the generic distinctions discussed in Chapter 2, then, *Oroonoko* contrasts the *literary* conventions of heroic romance and the *documentary* forms of the travelogue, a polarity underlined by the text's emergent biographical and *auto*biographical discourses: the biography of the noble slave is framed by the *auto*biography of the female protagonist. There is, in addition, a barely tapped *satirical* potential available through the detached and marginalized status of the protagonist, an African slave, and/or the narrator, a European woman: such alienated outsiders were always the perfect satirical foil, allowing a clinically detached view of more central and influential positions. With respect to the broad division proposed between male *authors* and female *novelists*, on the other hand, *Oroonoko* represents a curious compound: it undermines the initial *authority* of an ungendered (and therefore, by default, presumably male) narrator by deferring ironically to the *novelty* of a 'female pen', a pen clearly personalized, moreover, on a number of subsequent occasions. And in her writing as a whole, Behn seems able at least to register, if not actually to reconcile, these same distinctions of *genre* and *gender*.

If *Oroonoko* often surpasses Richardson or Fielding in ideological complexity, it also scrutinizes an alien other with a thoroughness rarely found in English fiction (outside Defoe) before Stevenson or Conrad. The contrasts in *Oroonoko* between the process of lofty, heroic *idealization* and a more down-to-earth process of *naturalization* are apparent from the narrator's opening words:

> I do not pretend, in giving you the history of this royal slave, to entertain my reader with the adventures of a feigned hero, whose life and fortunes fancy may manage at the poet's pleasure; nor in relating the truth, design to adorn it with any accidents, but such as arrived in earnest to him. And it shall come simply into the world, recommended by its own proper merits, and natural intrigues; there being enough of reality to support it, and to render it diverting, without the addition of invention.[8]

Initially, the naturalistic mode is stronger, in the sense that the non-literary or documentary element prevails. The narrative is thus legitimized partly by its status as 'eye-witness' account, and partly by its redaction of material allegedly derived from 'the mouth of the chief actor in this history'.

The presentation of *Oroonoko* as a 'true history' is not simply a rhetorical device; rather than attempt mere verisimilitude, it insists on authenticity, and therefore on one kind of *authority*. One may even break formalist taboos here, and simply conflate author and narrator into a historical figure called Aphra Behn. At an early point in the story, this author–narrator thus mentions 'glorious wreaths' of feathers obtained from the Indians of Surinam: 'I had a set of these presented to me, and I gave them to the King's Theatre, and it was the dress of the *Indian Queen*, infinitely admired by persons of quality' (p. 76). And there is still more blatant self-promotion in the final pages, after Behn's chance encounter in the forest with the Cromwellian regicide Colonel Martin, 'a man of great gallantry, wit, and goodness, and, whom I have celebrated in a character of my new comedy' (p. 132).

Such details contribute to *Oroonoko*'s significant autobiographical element, often realized as a kind of travelogue, with an extensive range of geographical, zoological, socio-political, and even anthropological observation. The most prominent of these passages is an introduction to the Surinam Indians and their environment at the very beginning of the account. Here are marmosets, macaws and parakeets, as well as more astonishing sixty-yard snakes – whose existence is nevertheless solemnly verified by reference to a skin preserved at *His Majesty's Antiquaries* (p. 75). The Indians are said to make poor slaves, however, and this observation allows a shift of scene to 'Coramantien' (or Koromantyn), the fort on the West African coast which provided a base for the Dutch, and later English, slave trades. African customs are not described in such detail as those of the Indians, although they are more fully integrated with the protagonist's story.

Back in Surinam, there is later a remarkable account of an eight-day expedition by barge to an Indian town. The detailed description of this cross-cultural encounter also has the unmistakable ring of authenticity:

> A little distant from the houses, or huts, we saw some dancing, others busied in fetching and carrying of water from the river. They had no sooner spied us, but they set up a loud cry, that frighted us at first. We thought it had been for those that should kill us, but it seems it was of wonder and amazement. They were all naked, and we were dressed, so as is most commode for the hot countries, very glittering and rich, so that we appeared extremely fine. My own hair was cut short, and I had a taffeta cap, with black feathers, on my head. My brother was in a stuff suit, with silver loops and buttons, and abundance of green ribbon. (p. 121)

Behn and her brother later play their flutes to the astonished Indians. The 'authority' of this and similar passages is not, however, guaranteed by some literary precedent from Virgil or Horace, but rather by well-documented empirical observation. *Authority* derives here from authenticity, and is actually based on the documentary discourse of *novelty*. The convergence of the two elements suggests once again the ambivalence characteristic of Behn's 'female pen', even as the latter strives to emulate male authority.

The 'literary' element of *Oroonoko*, on the other hand, is most conspicuous in the heroic presentation of the protagonist. The safety of the author–novelist on her ethnological expedition (at a moment when settlers and Indians are in open conflict) is thus guaranteed by the mere physical presence of Oroonoko, an unambiguous example of the prot-agonist's essentially heroic character. This aspect is emphasized from the initial presentation of Oroonoko in his African environment:

> he became, at the age of seventeen, one of the most expert captains, and bravest soldiers that ever saw the field of Mars; so that he was adored as the wonder of all that world, and the darling of the sol-diers. Besides he was adorned with a native beauty so transcending all those of his gloomy race, that he struck an awe and reverence, even in those that knew not his quality; as he did in me, who beheld him with surprise and wonder, when afterwards he arrived in our world. (p. 79)

The idiom established here anticipates several recurrent features in the narrative, the most obvious being the hyperbolic, even occasionally overblown, quality of Behn's heroic mode. A clear expression of this is her frequent use of *literary* (and above all *classical*) allusion for her terms of comparison. Oroonoko's defiance of the king's men when surprised in Imoinda's arms (p. 95) inevitably recalls the reaction of Launcelot discovered in a similar position with Guinevere; his apathy on the eve of battle (p. 99) suggests Ajax sulking in his tent outside Troy. Oroonoko's slave name is Caesar, and his reunion with Imoinda – 'Caesar swore he disdained the empire of the world, while he could behold Imoinda' (p. 112) – reproduces the traditional trope of the 'world well lost for love', familiar since Dido and Aeneas, or an earlier Caesar with Cleopatra; later, in Surinam, Caesar–Oroonoko embarks on a series of exploits (hunting tigers, wrestling with snakes) echoing the mythological labours of Hercules. In the subsequent slave rebellion, Behn's literary scope extends yet further: Oroonoko now inspires his followers by describing how 'one Hannibal a great captain', had cut his way 'through mountains and solid rocks' (p. 127) – although the underlying *topos* is probably the later conventionalized one of Moses setting his people free. And the execution *tableau*, where the narrator's mother and sister 'were by him all the while, but not suffered to save him' (p. 140), may even evoke the presence of Mary and Martha at Christ's crucifixion.

Such patently *literary* intertext in Behn's historico-biography is a clear counterpart to the *documentary* components of her autobiographical discourse. In another rhetorical strategy related to this process of idealization, Behn repeatedly minimizes the African origins of Oroonoko, to allow him a kind of honorary European affiliation. He thus possesses a 'native beauty transcending all those of his gloomy race' (p. 78) – *native* here apparently meaning 'inherent' rather than anything as awkward as 'indigenous'. There is 'nothing of barbarity in his nature', and the fuller description of Oroonoko leaves an almost comically partisan impression:

> he had heard of, and admired the Romans; he had heard of the late Civil Wars in England, and the deplorable death of our great monarch, and would discourse of it with all the sense, and abhorrence of the injustice imaginable.   (p. 80)

Of 'good and graceful mien', Oroonoko behaves 'as if his education had been in some European court'. The identification with European culture even extends, somewhat embarrassingly, to physical detail:

> His nose was rising and Roman, instead of African and flat. His mouth, the finest shaped that could be seen; far from those great turned lips, which are so natural to the rest of the Negroes.   (p. 81)

We are also told that Oroonoko's hair came down to his shoulders ('with the aid of art'), so that it is not difficult to imagine him as a kind of Guinea-coast surrogate Cavalier.

Behn's Europeanization of the African prince both draws attention to her own political ideology, and suggests a strong emotional investment in Oroonoko's story. Her politics might be defined as royalist, elitist, and patriarchal; for in spite of Virginia Woolf's famous suggestion that 'all women together ought to let flowers fall upon [her] tomb', Behn makes an awkward proto-feminist. A feminist icon today, Behn nevertheless upheld the ideology of Stuart absolutism against political radicalism and religious dissent; this is sometimes referred to euphemistically as the 'problematic' aspect of her writing.

On an even more personal level, Behn identifies the story of *Oroonoko* with the trial and execution of Charles I, whom she had always seen refracted through the same kind of heroic prism as her African 'royal prince'. Oroonoko thus comes to embody, as the dead king must often have done for the young Aphra, 'the last of his great race'. He is received at Parham House 'more like a governor than a slave', and given the royal name of Caesar; and to remove any remaining ambiguity, Behn insists that 'if the king himself (God bless him) had come ashore, there could not have been greater expectations by all the whole plantation' (p. 108). There may even be an unintentional moment of farce in Oroonoko's rash empirical experiment on an electric eel, like some latter-day King Charles – now the son – at his Royal Academy (pp. 119–20).[9]

It should also be noted, however, that Behn's 'true history' appeared in the very year that James II – another legitimate monarch – was overthrown by Parliament, and might therefore be seen as allegorizing the analogous story of a royal prince destroyed by inferior men. On a more mundane level, too, *Oroonoko* actually reproduces the partisan politics of post-Restoration Surinam, transforming them into simple moral referents within the structure of the narrative. Byam, the Whig governor, submits Oroonoko to the most brutal scourging; Trefry, the gallant Tory planter, expresses his abhorrence and later defies the governor; the well-meaning female narrator, on the other hand, excluded from political power, can only participate feebly in 'making a thousand professions of service' and 'begging as many pardons'.

Byam's subsequent behaviour certainly justifies Oroonoko's strong rhetoric in his efforts to foment a slave rebellion: 'shall we render obedience to such a *degenerate race* [my emphasis], who have no one human virtue left, to distinguish them from the vilest creatures?' (p. 126). The epithet is significant, since Oroonoko's attitude towards slavery is otherwise as 'problematic' as the narrator's. One of his earliest recorded actions is to present Imoinda with 'a hundred and fifty slaves in fetters' (p. 82); the imagination baulks at what she might have done with them, short of selling them on to the first passing English trader. The young Oroonoko is then betrayed into captivity by the very captain with whom he normally deals; once in Surinam, however, he is soon recognized by the other slaves as 'that prince who had, at several times, sold most of them to these parts' (p. 109). His subsequent reception, however, is not what the modern reader might have expected:

> from a veneration they pay to great men, especially if they know them, and from the surprise and awe they had at the sight of him, they all cast themselves at his feet, crying out, in their language, 'Live, O King! Long Live, O King'. (p. 109)

Very soon, Oroonoko is negotiating for his own release, offering either gold, or (what else) 'a vast quantity of slaves, which should be paid before they let him go' (p. 113).

On the basis of such details as these, the whole discourse of race in *Oroonoko* surely pleads for an alternative reading in terms, not of *black* and *white*, but rather of *noble* and *plebeian*, or – by analogy with literary divisions proposed elsewhere – hieratic and demotic. It is a distinction on which both protagonist and narrator regularly draw: if Oroonoko is the avatar of Behn's beloved Charles Stuart, then the mass of African slaves who betray him are the moral equivalent of the 'vile English mobile', his torturers. The construction of Oroonoko within the parameters of romance may occasionally assume proportions as extravagant as his Cavalier hair-style. After Imoinda receives the royal veil, for example, he displays a positively quixotic intensity:

'O my friends! Were she in walled cities, or confined from me in fortifications of the greatest strength; did enchantments or monsters detain her from me, I would venture through any hazard to free her.' (p. 86)

In contrast, one may recall Oroonoko's denunciation of his fellow slaves:

They suffered not like men who might find a glory, and fortitude in oppression, but like dogs that loved the whip and bell, and fawned the more they were beaten. That they had lost the divine quality of men, and were become insensible asses, fit only to bear. (p. 126)

The tone of invective used here curiously reproduces that used in the narrator's own account of the colony council ('such notorious villains as Newgate never transported...who...had no sort of principles to make them worthy the name of men', pp. 133–4). Or, as perfectly conveyed by the props of heroic romance: the English mob who attempt to crush the revolt have 'none but rusty swords, that no strength could draw from a scabbard', whilst the 'people of particular quality' oil their weapons and keep them in good order (p. 125).

Behn's counterpointing of black slaves and white masters with the more ambivalent categories of 'noble' and 'plebeian' overlaps with the earlier proposed categories of *genre* and *gender*. For, in terms of the first distinction, Behn's heroic romance involves the demonization of *all* villains (black or white) as much as the idealization of its hero. And in terms of the second one, *Oroonoko*'s feminizing tendencies reflect both the conventional troping of woman and slave, and the more specific rapport between the novel's protagonist and the female members of the colony. There are some suggestive details in this context, as when Behn explains how Oroonoko 'liked the company of us women much above the men', adding approvingly that 'he could not drink, and he is but an ill companion in that country that cannot' (p. 113).

One thus notes the emergence of another kind of nobility – based on sentiment – including Oroonoko and Imoinda, the narrator, and perhaps even the planter, Trefry, 'who was naturally amorous, and loved to talk of love as well as anybody' (p. 110)! *Oroonoko*'s open celebration of patriarchy's power and simultaneous critique of its brutality makes a heady mixture; here, again, is the clash of aristocratic and progressive ideologies allowed by the dialectic model of Michael McKeon. One only suspects that Behn, in her overturning of social categories, sometimes wavers between intellectual autonomy and an ideological complicity with English mercantilism, including the institution of slavery which helped to sustain it.

Roughly half-way through the narrative, on the other hand, Behn makes her famous aside that it was Oroonoko's misfortune 'to fall in an obscure world, that afforded only a female pen to celebrate his fame' (p. 108). Whether regarded as ironic, polemic, or even genuinely self-effacing, the remark often receives more attention than a partly contradictory one a few pages later, when Behn comments on the inhumane treatment of Oroonoko after his recapture: 'I suppose I had authority and interest enough there, had I suspected any such thing, to have prevented it' (p. 132); such lack of suspicion on her part seems singly ingenuous. Whatever the case, the *novelty* of Behn's female status as Oroonoko's biographer effectively contrasts here with her residue of *authority* as the governor-designate's daughter. The quotation also rekindles speculation about Behn's role in her own history, even if another personal reminiscence just before this passage might have been thought to clarify this point:

> My stay was to be short in that country, because my father died at sea, and never arrived to possess the honour [that] was designed him (which was lieutenant-general of six and thirty islands, besides the continent of Surinam), nor the advantages he hoped to reap by them, so that though we were obliged to continue on our voyage, we did not intend to stay upon the place.   (p. 115)

In reality, however, Behn's biography is notoriously obscure. Most of the details of her life remain uncertain, and there were once doubts over whether she had even *been* in South America.[10] Historical confusion about the novelist's whereabouts seems to parallel critical confusion over her ideological status, and one might compress both issues into the same rhetorical question: What, literally and figuratively, in fact *was* Behn's *position?*

The key to the ambivalence of Behn's writing may lie in qualities inherent in romance itself. The genre was privileged by Northrop Frye and relativized by Gillian Beer. It was also rehabilitated by Hubert McDermott, who follows the tradition from classical epic through its Byzantine transformations to the long-winded French romances of the seventeenth century, arguing along the way that most examples of the form were produced by men; it is only with the 'passionate' romances of Manley and Haywood (as opposed to the 'heroic' romances that bewitched Don Quixote) that the tradition becomes identified in the mind of the early eighteenth-century public with female writers and readers.[11]

Precise gender divisions are difficult – the most famous seventeenth-century *romancier* was, after all, Madeleine de Scudéry – but McDermott's arguments are still suggestive.[12] He nevertheless ignores one fundamental distinction between the two forms he discusses. The male author can move easily enough from heroic to passionate romance; for the domestic female novelist, however, the opposite trajectory is more difficult. The romantic idealization of *female* public activity would present no intrinsic problems; there is only a notable lack of such activity (in most women's lives) to idealize. Behn is surely making a not-so-veiled reference to such feelings of powerlessness when she has a highly engaged Imoinda fight at Oroonoko's side and shoot her envenomed arrow at the governor.

In terms of McDermott's thesis, Behn could well stand as a major transitional figure. Her juxtaposition of 'heroic' and 'passionate' romance is nowhere more obvious than in her mythological troping of Imoinda and Oroonoko: 'she was female to the noble male; the beautiful black Venus, to our young Mars' (p. 81). Or, as a modern best-seller has it: men are from Mars, women are from Venus. The distinction is worth pursuing. Oroonoko's intertextual links with the epic-heroic have already been noted; Imoinda, on the other hand, is a cultural construct anticipating the eighteenth-century sentimental romance. In a conspicuous example of eurocentrism, Behn locates her squarely within a bourgeois discourse of inviolate virginity. The original concern of Oroonoko is thus whether Imoinda is 'robbed of that blessing, which was only due to his faith and love' (p. 86); happily, she faces no such threat from the king's 'withered arms'.

Behn also contrasts the fictional range of heroic and passionate romance, respectively, in her neatly gendered choice of reading for her two lovers: 'I entertained him with the lives of the Romans, and great men, which charmed him to my company, and her, with teaching her all the pretty works that I was mistress of, and telling her stories of nuns' (p. 113). The main alternatives envisaged seem to be the Roman historian Plutarch *versus* the popular *Lettres portugaises*, although the 'pretty works that I was mistress of' may even suggest something from Behn's own fictional repertoire.[13] The latter, by implication, is passionate or feminine romance, although – as *Oroonoko* itself shows in the horrific death of Imoinda, for example – such divisions cannot always be rigidly maintained.

Behn actually had more personal ties with the conventions of romance. Her real-life *nom de plume* was identical to her *nom de guerre*: 'Astrea'. The pseudonym for the creator of amorous intrigues in literary London was also the code-name for the undercover agent in Antwerp – another striking convergence of the sentimental, or erotic, and the active, or heroic, although now in autobiographical discourse. For classically educated male readers, moreover, the chief referent of the name was probably the Greek goddess of justice; to intellectually deprived female readers it was doubtless the heroine of a French romance.[14] The point neatly underlines Behn's debt to the two romance traditions.

The romance of Oroonoko, as previously noted, none the less dovetails neatly with a realistic autobiographical mode. Something of the nature of this join can be seen from a brief comparison with another Behn *novella*, *The Fair Jilt*. Subtitled 'the History of Prince Tarquin and Miranda', the latter work is a distinctly *un*heroic tale of female opportunism and male imposture, set in an Antwerp familiar to Behn from her activities there as a government agent. Far more consistently than *Oroonoko*, *The Fair Jilt* is a third-person narrative, the few exceptions to the pattern representing simple authenticating devices rather than more personal intrusions: a jump forward here, a flashback there, and a characteristic *renvoi* at the end of the tale: 'Since I began this relation, I heard that Prince Tarquin died about three quarters of a year ago' (p. 72).

The most notable structural difference between the two *novellas*, however, lies in their respective temporal frames: *The Fair Jilt* regularly switches from past to present tense in the middle of a passage, as, for example, during the story of Prince Henrick, the young friar later compromised by Miranda:

'This young prince no sooner *saw*, but *loved* the fair mistress of his brother, and with the authority of a sovereign, rather than the advice of a friend, *warned* his brother Henrick (this now young friar) to approach no more this lady, whom he had seen; and seeing, loved.

'In vain the poor surprised prince *pleads* his right of love, his exchange of vows, and assurance of a heart that could never be but for himself. In vain he *urges* his nearness of blood, his friendship, his passion, or his life . . . ' (p. 35; my emphasis)[15]

Such tense shifts, by contrast, are entirely absent from *Oroonoko*. The possible models for Behn's usage of such a technique are several: Roman authors regularly employed what grammarians describe as the 'historic present', and the practice is also common in the oral tradition of the popular ballads. The aim in both contexts may be broadly defined as *dramatic* effect, and here surely is the ultimate explanation for Behn's use of the device: it obviously conveys the immediacy of the theatre, even literally employing the tense of *stage directions*.

Behn was a major dramatist of the Restoration period and seventeen of her plays are still extant, although only one of these is a tragedy; the latter, *Abdelazer*, she nevertheless dismissed as 'cold' and 'feeble'. It might be inferred, then, that the history of the 'royal slave' uses the *novella form* for the *material* of a heroic tragedy, a mode which Behn did not normally attempt on the stage.[16] *The Fair Jilt*, on the other hand, reveals clear analogies – both thematic and syntactic – with Behn's comedies of intrigue. This may be the true dividing line between the distinctive modes of the two fictional *novellas* as discussed here.

Oroonoko, then, remains a unique compound of the autobiographical and the historico-biographical; it cannot be read as exclusively 'documentary' or 'literary', like *Pamela* or *Joseph Andrews*, respectively, fifty years later. Behn also undermines divisions between male (or hieratic) *author* and female (or demotic) *novelist*, just as her anti-egalitarian categories of 'noble' and 'plebeian' overturned distinctions of man and woman, or master and slave. Some fifty years after *Pamela* and *Joseph Andrews*, a far greater female novelist was to complete an even more powerful synthesis than Behn's. Admittedly, Jane Austen probably wrote the epistolary *Lady Susan* in 1793 and the literary parody *Northanger Abbey* in 1797–8 – thus isolating the classic 'documentary' and 'literary' modes, respectively – but the formal compromise of *First Impressions* (later to become *Pride and Prejudice*) was finished by 1797.

Histories of the English novel traditionally revolve around Richardson and Fielding. It is a truism to suggest that both of these writers are more substantial than Behn, in almost any sense of the term. But they are also more *monolithic*; Behn's writing, on the other hand, often displays greater flexibility than either of her hitherto more illustrious successors; her *novellas* sometimes seem a veritable fictional laboratory, moving between the 'literariness' of the hieratic *author* and the 'documentation' of the demotic *novelist*.

Defoe: Moll Flanders

Born the son of a butcher and raised in a Dissenting family, Defoe is one of the most versatile and prolific of all English writers. His first significant work, the *Essay on Projects* (1697), is notable, among other things, for its advocacy of women's education; his first poetic success, *The True-Born Englishman* (1701), satirically defended William of Orange, England's foreign-born monarch. Better remembered today is Defoe's 1702 pamphlet *The Shortest Way with the Dissenters* (using the same kind of irony as Swift's 'modest proposal') and the three-volume *Tour Thro the Whole Island of Great Britain* (1724–7), a still highly readable account of the state of a nation. In a fictional context, Defoe produced a remarkable series of works over a short span of five years: *Robinson Crusoe* (1719), *Memoirs of a Cavalier* (1720), *Captain Singleton* (1720), *Moll Flanders* (1722), *A Journal of the Plague Year* (1722), *Colonel Jack* (1722) and *Roxana* (1724). Many scholars regard these seven narratives as the beginnings of the English novel; rather fewer note what an anomalous group they form.[17]

In technical, thematic, and ideological terms, Defoe provides an instructive contrast to Behn. His own romance of empire, *Robinson Crusoe*, deals obliquely with the institution of slavery, on which eighteenth-century mercantilism was largely grounded; it also provides some of the solid economic, and even linguistic, data absent from Behn's account. The closest point of contact with *Oroonoko* may ironically be Defoe's cultural construction of Friday, his own 'good native', in Europeanized terms which sound uncannily like Behn's description of her African prince:

He had a very good countenance, not a fierce and surly aspect; but seem'd to have something very manly in his face, and yet he had all the sweetness and softness of an European in his countenance too, especially when he smil'd.[18]

And when Friday's hair is described as 'long and black, not curled like wool', his skin as 'not quite black, but very very tawny', and his nose as 'small, not flat like the negroes', it might seem that Defoe had Behn's own portrait of Oroonoko in mind. In each case, the racial other is familiarized, and the process of Europeanization is complete.

Other Defoe texts besides *Robinson Crusoe* also evoke *Oroonoko*: *Captain Singleton*, with its journey across Africa to the Guinea Coast in the company of another noble African slave; or *Roxana*, for its consistent troping of female existence as slavery. *A Journal of the Plague Year*, on the other hand, with its pure 'documentary' form (only in the nineteenth century did it come to be regarded as a fictional text), contrasts sharply with *Oroonoko*'s more stylized 'literary' heroics. *Moll Flanders* may be the best basis for comparison, however, with both occasional links and more significant contrasts with Behn's novel. After the scourging of Oroonoko towards the end of the narrative, for example, Behn describes the council of Surinam planters as 'such notorious villains as Newgate never transported'. Moll herself, her highwayman husband, and even her own mother, were all transported from London's famous prison; and in 1703, just fourteen years after the publication of *Oroonoko*, Defoe himself spent five months there for writing *The Shortest Way with the Dissenters*. None of these four figures, fictional or historical, belonged to the cultural or ethnic groups treated sympathetically in *Oroonoko*; here, then, is one obvious example of polarization between Behn and Defoe. There are certainly more.

Of all eighteenth-century narratives, *Moll Flanders* thus suggests a minimum of explicitly 'literary models', classical or otherwise, and proclaims its direct descent from the early eighteenth-century journalistic substrata explored so thoroughly by J. Paul Hunter.[19] When Moll is finally sent to Newgate, there are thus none of the conventional overtones of the *epic* descent into the underworld familiar from Fielding or Smollett, and so many other writers of the period. In another literary context, the various reappearances of Moll's Lancashire husband at highly sensitive moments recall the coincidences of traditional picaresque narrative, but Defoe's use of this device is fairly sparing. In the general absence of widespread literary tendencies, then, it is predictably the demotic element which shapes Moll's narrative.

These are hardly original conclusions. After *The Rise of the Novel*, Defoe long seemed little more than the supreme example of 'formal realism' in eighteenth-century fiction; in this respect, Moll's theft of the apothecary's bundle (p. 164)[20] or the child's necklace (p. 166) are probably the most quoted passages in the entire novel. In either case, Defoe's writing wins little recognition here beyond what is due to faithful journalistic representation. For the necklace scene, he may not even receive this, in view of Moll's notorious attempt at self-justification:

> The last affair left no great concern upon me, for as I did the poor child no harm, I only thought I had given the parents a just reproof for their negligence, in leaving the poor lamb to come home by itself, and it would teach them to take more care another time.   (p. 167)

The passage is a kind of critical touchstone, encouraging two broad types of critical response. Some have seen it as reflecting an indiscriminate identification by the author with his protagonist, which is artistically 'bad'; and in this context, a writer producing the *Journal of the Plague Year*, *Colonel Jack*, and several hundred pages of miscellaneous writing in the same year as *Moll Flanders* (1722) can expect little sympathy from less prodigiously fertile academics. Or alternatively, Moll's words showed the masterly irony and artistic detachment of an author always in firm control; this, on the other hand, was aesthetically 'good', encouraging a kind of critical reading more in tune with the inflationary tendencies of modern academic overkill.

The position of Defoe in the history of the novel sometimes owes more to the vagaries of canon formation or to readers' generic expectations than to any more rigorous classification. Traditionally, *Robinson Crusoe*, *Roxana*, and *Moll Flanders*, at least, are rescued from the ambivalent status of fictional biography to be absorbed into the more prestigious category of the modern novel. Much of what remains of Defoe's output is regarded as (*super-* or *sub-*) journalism, and relegated to the attention of specialist scholars (currently coming to terms with widespread reattributions in the traditional Defoe canon). In the master plot of one authoritative guide: 'The novelist we know grew out of the journalist and political hack we have forgotten.' Almost half of the items traditionally included in the Defoe canon are now generally assumed to be written by other hands.[21] Even what remains, however, confirms that – in simple *quantitative terms* – Defoe is not principally a novelist, by any definition of the word; and, despite much received literary history, he is hardly one in evolutionary terms either: the fictional achievements of the years 1719–22 were followed by such substantial documentary or didactic non-fictional works as the *Atlas Maritimus & Commercialis* and *The Compleat English Tradesman*.

These tendencies invite consideration of Defoe's links with various forms of modern literary journalism. There are thus striking equivalents in his production for most of the sub-divisions of popular fiction proposed in John Sutherland's entertaining study of the contemporary best-seller:[22] the modern disaster scenario has a predecessor in the *Journal of the Plague Year*; the lightly disguised scandal chronicle recalls *Roxana*; the inside story of organized crime has its forerunners in Charles Johnson's *History of the Pirates* (1724: traditionally, at least, attributed to Defoe). And elsewhere, Defoe moves effortlessly between categories broadly compatible with such modern journalistic concepts as the 'docu-drama', the 'investigative feature', or the 'human interest story'. Defoe's Newgate memoirs for Applebee's *Weekly Journal* have even been regarded as a kind of early 'cheque-book journalism'.

Finally, whether we choose to argue for vicarious participation or mere literary deception on Defoe's part in his fictional narratives, the effect of an autobiographical impersonation like *Moll Flanders* anticipates a characteristically modern literary and journalistic hybrid: twentieth-century 'ghost-writing'.[23] For the latter is surely the most appropriate term to describe two recurrent features of Defoe's writing: the coherent form of the first-person 'proto-novel' (organized essentially, if not exclusively, around the chronology of a single life); and the strong sense of personal identification (but simultaneous self-effacement) which governs the author/editor's relations with his dynamic protagonist. It is a relationship endlessly reproduced between modern freelance journalists and vigorous but inarticulate sportsmen or movie stars.

Behn's heroic romance and Defoe's criminal autobiography also illustrate clearly the polarization of hieratic and demotic modes already previously argued for the early English novel, even as they invert conventional generic expectations of the male *author* and female *novelist*. For in some crude sense, surely, the educated male Defoe should be writing like Behn, or, at least, the 'unlettered' female Behn should be writing like Defoe. Of Behn's intellectual formation, little is known, although it was certainly modest by the standards of most of her male contemporaries. She knew French well (inviting conjectures that she may have been educated in a Belgian convent), but no Latin.[24]

Defoe is a different proposition. A considerable amount is known about the kind of education he would have received at the exemplary Stoke Newington Academy for the sons of Dissenters.[25] Lay students normally spent three years at this institution, whilst theological students spent five; Defoe, who was initially destined for the ministry, seems to have studied for four. In spite of curricular innovation in the fields of natural science and modern languages, teaching also followed the university tradition of the Medieval Trivium (rhetoric, logic, and Latin grammar) and Quadrivium (arithmetic, geometry, astronomy, and music).[26] The most important novelty, however, was the use of English, rather than Latin, as a medium of instruction. All told, Defoe was probably as competent a Latinist as Fielding, who must have had a certain amount of the language drubbed into him at Eton, before his year at the University of Leyden; Defoe is also quite a different case from Richardson (who often regretted his own lack of formal education), and can hardly be measured on the same scale as a genuinely unlearned Puritan Dissenter such as Bunyan.

In practice, Defoe does not pepper his *narrative* with Latin quotations like Fielding, but this surely reflects an attempt at convincing characterization of the *narrator–protagonist* rather than any ignorance on the part of the author. Moll, for example, is the product of a social environment where (female) illiteracy was widespread, and her account is only enabled through her adoption by the mayor's family:

> Here I continued till I was between seventeen and eighteen years old, and here I had all the advantages for my education that could be imagined; the lady had masters home to teach her daughters to dance, and to speak French, and to write, and others to teach them music; and as I was always with them, I learned as fast as they.   (p. 16)

Moll thus anticipates the upwardly mobile servant of another male-authored 'feminocentric' fiction a generation later. The first letter of Richardson's Pamela also legitimizes the heroine's subsequent narrative in much the same terms ('my lady's goodness had put me to write and cast accompts and made me a little expert at my needle, and otherwise qualified above my degree'). In terms of class and gender, then, Moll and Pamela were both special cases, whose voices would not normally have been heard.

Moll's narrative, on the other hand, is not simply a spontaneous account through a series of discrete episodes in interchangeable order. Although it alienates many modern readers by its lack of chapter divisions, the novel actually splits quite coherently into a number of sections roughly equal in length. One may thus note Moll's childhood, adolescence and first clandestine affair (pp. 7–25); her courtship by the younger brother, Robin (pp. 25–50); the story of her extravagant second husband (pp. 50–65); the introduction of the Virginia planter who turns out to be a half-brother (pp. 65–90); relations with the friend and repentant lover (pp. 90–108); with the financial adviser turned suitor (pp. 108–20); and with the fourth husband, Lancashire James (pp. 120–36); before the account of being pregnant and alone in London (pp. 136–62). Moll's later experiences as a thief are contained in two sections of roughly thirty pages each (pp. 162–92 and 204–36), punctuated by a last adventure with the passionate baronet (pp. 192–204). Also equal in length are the two final sections covering the spell in Newgate (pp. 236–64), followed by transportation and eventual prosperity in Virginia (pp. 264–95).

Moll's demotic antecedents hardly need labouring any more than her creator's bourgeois, mercantile background. With their common vitality and entrepreneurial dynamism, moreover, it seems inevitable that three centuries of readers should elide the two *personae*. But Defoe could also be comically subversive, and his satirical skills are often forgotten.[27] Both of these elements emerge in the representation of Moll, who – while ostensibly conforming to the expectations of formal realism – occasionally oversteps these limits to assume almost mythical proportions. She thus marries five husbands and sees three buried, producing twelve children (one of whom she seems to forget entirely). She exudes a primal energy, whilst two husbands die of lethargy.

Even more notable than the 'larger-than-life' or mythical dimension, however, are Moll's subversive tendencies. The satirical account of her trip to Oxford with her extravagant draper husband is a case in point:

> We saw all the rarities at Oxford; talked with two or three fellows of colleges about putting a nephew, that was left to his lordship's care, to the university, and of their being his tutors. We diverted ourselves with bantering several other poor scholars, with the hopes of being at least his lordship's chaplain and putting on a scarf.   (p. 53)

Such episodes make the Oxford visit a classic example of 'carnivalization', the tradition of hierarchic reversals traced by Mikhail Bakhtin from the Middle Ages and through the writing of Rabelais. By the same kind of comic inversion, Moll describes her own higher education as extended by 'crime school' for pickpockets (p. 175) and the 'college of Newgate' (p. 277). The ultimate social transgressions are undoubtedly her successful public excursions in the disguise of a man (pp. 185ff). This satirical dimension of *Moll Flanders* also implicitly deconstructs the 'straight' gallantry depicted in *Oroonoko*. With the Virginia planter Humphry who transpires to be her half-brother, for example, Moll engages in a poetic duel cut on glass. Extracted from its context, the poem underlines Moll's pragmatic views about human relationships; the odd-numbered lines are Humphry's, the even ones are Moll's rejoinders:

> You I love, and you alone.
> *And so in love says everyone.*
> Virtue alone is an estate.
> *But money's virtue, gold is fate.*
> I scorn your gold, and yet I love.
> *I'm poor; let's see how kind you'll prove.*
> Be mine, with all your poverty.
> *Yet secretly you hope I lie.*
> Let love alone be our debate.
> *She loves enough that does not hate.*
> (pp. 67–8; my emphasis)

In terms of the juxtaposition made in the present chapter, Moll's anti-heroics can again be read as an implicit rejection of the romantic ideology of Behn.

If the literary constructions of Oroonoko and Imoinda raise these two characters to the status of master race and ruling class, then Moll and her long-time husband, Lancashire James, inscribe a trajectory in precisely the opposite direction. Moll makes the trip to Virginia twice, fully understanding the economics of the place with its two main kinds of colonists: 'either, first, such as were brought over by masters of ships to be sold as servants; or, second, such as are transported after having been found guilty of crimes punishable with death' (p. 73). In practice, the two types are hardly differentiated: 'the planters buy them, and they work together in the field, till their time is out'. Distinctions between servants/convicts and genuine slaves, as Moll's narrative underlines at various points, are largely a matter of degree.

When Moll is transported with her husband, she thus anguishes over what to take with her:

> it was by no means proper for me to go without money or goods, and for a poor convict that was to be sold as soon as I came on shore, to carry a cargo of goods would be to have notice taken of it. (p. 266)

Two pages later, however, Moll dots every last 'i' by referring to her husband and herself as 'transported convicts, destined to be sold for *slaves*' (p. 268). The only major difference between the two groups, in fact, seems to be that the release of convicts was rather more likely, and certainly more rapid, than the manumittance of slaves. The latter were a property or tangible asset, however, which sometimes actually guaranteed them better treatment than indentured servants.

The economic underpinnings of both Virginia and, by extension therefore, Behn's Surinam, are made clearer when Moll and James spend a whole week comparing colonial prospects in Virginia and Ireland. James paints a rosy picture of the latter:

> He told me that a man that could confine himself to a country life, and that could but find stock to enter upon any land, should have farms there for £50 a year, as good as were [here] let for £200 a year; that the produce was such, and so rich the land, that if much was not laid up, we were sure to live as handsomely upon it as a gentleman of £3000 a year could do in England.   (p. 135)

The missing factor in James's utopian account of Ireland is clearly labour, and on this point, Moll's conditions for success in Virginia are rather more pragmatic ('carrying over but two or three hundred pounds' value in English goods, with some servants and tools', p. 134). But here, unlike the narrator of *Oroonoko*, she is less than explicit, and the real conditions of success appear uncannily in the text, without Moll ever consciously putting them there:

> I laid it down in *black and white*, as we say, that it was morally impossible, with a supposition of any reasonable good conduct, but that we must thrive there and do very well.   (p. 135; my emphasis)

Moll and James are irrefutably *white*, whereas the origins of the *black* contribution are not hard to imagine. With black slaves and white masters, prosperity will be assured.

Moll's calculating acquisitiveness is often considered to reflect accurately the sympathies of her creator. Against such conventional judgements, however, one may counter that Defoe is actually quite successful at *explicitly* excluding himself from the narrative. But this may only be achieved – in accordance with a classic tendency in modern ghost-writing – through a powerful *implicit* identification with the subject. The process is not unexpected, for here is a pro-mercantile, anti-aristocratic ideology consonant with the author's own; here, too, is a proto-feminism consonant with pronouncements elsewhere in other writings, such as the *Essay on Projects*.

After the death of her first husband, Moll describes her happy discovery of a well-bred but prosperous successor: 'at last I found this amphibious creature, this land–water thing, called a gentleman-tradesman' (p. 52). Forced to choose, Moll would doubtless have gone for the tradesman. She shows a sympathetic attitude towards James ('bred a gentleman, though he was reduced to a low fortune', p. 127), but her later remarks suggest what is, consciously or not, a patronizing attitude. When she has returned to Virginia with James, she makes her final comment on James's life-style, with irony but without rancour:

> The case was plain; he was bred a gentleman, and was not only unacquainted, but indolent, and when we did settle, would much rather go into the woods with his gun, which they call there hunting, and which is the ordinary work of the Indians; I say, he would much rather do that than attend to the natural business of the plantation. (p. 282)

As prosperity grows, however, Moll is able to humour her husband in every way, as suggested by one of those famous inventories of which Defoe and his more acquisitive protagonists were so fond:

> I took especial care to buy for him all those things that I knew he delighted to have; as two good long wigs, two silver-hilted swords, three of four fine fowling-pieces, a fine saddle with holsters and pistols very handsome, with a scarlet cloak; and in a word, everything I could think of to oblige him, and to make him appear as he really was, a very fine gentleman. (p. 293)

The irony here is good-natured, but doubtless heavy. Moll and her creator thus reduce the trappings of gentility to the hankerings of a spoilt child.

Behn and Defoe

Defoe has links with virtually every kind of early eighteenth-century professional writing, fictional or otherwise, although he is the only author from this vast field – and then only on the basis of one short productive burst – to have achieved canonic status. Among female novelists, the situation is different: together with Delarivier Manley and Eliza Haywood, Behn formed what one contemporary admirer called the 'Fair Triumvirate of Wits', notorious in the early eighteenth century and receiving ever-increasing attention today. Their erotic fiction also perhaps provided a negative model, in the sense of something to be avoided, for another less controversial trio of early eighteenth-century women writers: Penelope Aubin, Jane Barker and Mary Davys. And at one further remove, lies the pious didacticism of Elizabeth Rowe.

In his seminal account of popular fiction before Richardson, John Richetti traces five recurrent narrative patterns: the heroic or anti-heroic narratives of rogues and whores; the accounts of travellers, pirates and pilgrims; the scandal chronicles; the erotic and/or pathetic *novella*; and the novel of pious polemic.[28] Defoe personified, even as he transcended, the first three categories, in *Moll Flanders*, *Robinson Crusoe* and *Roxana*, respectively. The other two groups are better represented by Behn, Manley and Haywood.

Defoe's antecedents are inseparable from a wide range of demotic (and domestic) documentary traditions. His most famous narrative has no high 'literary' precedents, although it owed something to the 'true account' of one Alexander Selkirk, who spent four and a half years on an uninhabited Pacific island. Modern readings of *Robinson Crusoe* tend to find an allegory of economic man, a view that attracted Ian Watt (and even Karl Marx before him), or emphasize Defoe's connections with the tradition of spiritual autobiography. In the first instance, the novel recalls a host of Defoe's journalistic projects, such as *The Compleat English Tradesman* (1726), suggesting perhaps a kind of complementary 'complete English colonist'; in the second case, the obvious analogues are Bunyan's *Pilgrim's Progress*, or his more explicitly confessional *Grace Abounding*.[29]

The other five narratives from Defoe's most creative phase are similarly 'documentary' in inspiration. *Colonel Jack* (where the protagonist's picaresque adventures make him Defoe's closest male counterpart to Moll) and *Roxana* (with its tortured and shocking complicity between mistress and servant) correspond most closely, in their apparent originality and fictional autonomy, to conventional novelistic expectations. More generically ambivalent in this respect are *Captain Singleton*, which often seems a mere compilation of adventures from the author's wide reading, and the *Memoirs of a Cavalier*, where Defoe's account of a cavalry officer may be based on a first-hand document – and therefore constitute quite genuine ghost-writing. The

Journal of the Plague Year, finally, was regarded for nearly two centuries as an authentic eye-witness account, before it was discovered that Defoe had been an exiled five-year-old (or younger) at the time of the plague. The narrative was even convincingly advanced as a forerunner of the American 'new journalism' in the 1960s and of the non-fiction novel exemplified by Norman Mailer and Truman Capote.[30]

Where Defoe's fiction has its roots in such non-literary forms as miscellaneous journalism and Protestant homiletics, however, the three early female novelists are more influenced by French literary models: Ros Ballaster cites the full-scale Romance, the *histoire galante* or *nouvelle*, the *chronique scandaleuse* and the Love-Letter.[31] The first of these categories is decidedly marginal, and chiefly relevant in this study to the satire on the genre produced by Charlotte Lennox and discussed in Chapter 8. The other three forms are most effectively exploited in the fiction of Behn.

Her feminocentric *Love-Letters Between a Nobleman and His Sister*, for example, is a classic *histoire galante*, although its faintly disguised account of a notorious contemporary scandal also exemplifies the *chronique scandaleuse*. The shorter fiction, of which the best known example is *The Fair Jilt* (1688) discussed above, consists quite literally of *novellas*, or 'nouvelles', with predominantly erotic themes. Manley's flouting of conventional female roles, in her life as much as her writings, was as conspicuous as Behn's. Her specialty, however, was the *chronique scandaleuse*, including the *Secret History of Queen Zarah* (1705; 1711), a *roman à clef* sometimes published quite literally with a key, and the similarly libellous *The New Atalantis* (1709). Both of these works remain well outside the parameters of classic realist fiction, but also beyond the conventions of romance.[32] Eliza Haywood is more prolific, if less rewarding, than either Behn or Manley, although her characteristically torrid short romance *Love in Excess* (1719) was – together with *Robinson Crusoe* and *Gulliver's Travels* – one of the three most popular fictions before Richardson's *Pamela*. Savaged in Pope's great satire on literary dullness, *The Dunciad*, Haywood reformed in later years and produced several longer and sentimentally moral fictions, of which the best known today is *The History of Miss Betsy Thoughtless* (1751).[33]

Of the second and less celebrated trio, Penelope Aubin's sub-literary career of Grub Street hack, no less than her frantic episodic narratives, have suggestive parallels with Defoe. The stories of persecuted lovers – as in *The Noble Slaves* (1722) or *The Life of Charlotta du Pont* (1723) – can nevertheless be traced directly to French romances (Aubin was also a copious translator), and perhaps ultimately to the romance of antiquity.[34] True respectability for the woman novelist perhaps came with Jane Barker, whose debt to the romance tradition, French and Byzantine, is also clear in *Love's Intrigues* (1713) and *Exilius, or, The Banish'd Roman* (1715).[35] Exactly contemporary with Barker, and also interesting for her ambiguous status as a woman writer as much as for her versatile output, is Mary Davys, whose early dramatic experience – together with the comic talents displayed in *The Reform'd Coque't* (1724) and *The Accomplish'd Rake* (1727) – have routinely drawn comparisons with Fielding. The small fictional output of Elizabeth Rowe, finally, is difficult to relate to any of the foregoing, but should not be ignored for that. Her *Friendship in Death* (1723), commonly known by its sub-title of 'Twenty Letters from the Dead to the Living', is clearly modelled on the Greek writer Lucian's *Dialogues of the Dead*; Rowe's strong links with spiritual autobiography and Christian ideology, on the other hand, place her strategically between Defoe and Richardson.

John Richetti speculates on the cultural contexts that produced early eighteenth-century women's fiction, together with the kind of audience that received it. Such concerns are also developed by more recent feminist critics. Where Haywood is now largely a subject for literary sociology, Manley is particularly interesting in the context of gender politics. Her narratives read convincingly as political allegory, where sexual seduction in the private sphere is a metaphor for political exploitation in the public one: Ballaster actually discusses the motif of 'broken vows', as no less relevant in erotic relations than in post-Restoration political settlements. As with more celebrated male satirists such as Swift and Smollett, however, her topicality is sometimes a barrier to wider appreciation. It is in Behn, then, that English eighteenth-century fiction finds a precursor in many ways as significant as the more traditional triumvirate of Defoe, Richardson and Fielding.

7

Laurence Sterne's *Tristram Shandy* and Tobias Smollett's *Humphry Clinker*

Whether regarded as straight novel, anti-novel or meta-novel, *Tristram Shandy* reflects the progress of the form to date, even as it suggests future potential. Through judgement and commentary, or satire and parody, it thus reviews the technical and aesthetic possibilities of the genre, even if this process is not as methodical – and certainly never as self-consciously authoritative – as it is in the hands of Fielding. At the same time, however, Sterne's fiction is a strange mixture of parts, exploiting the mid-eighteenth-century vogue of sensibility, even as it draws on an older tradition of learned wit now most familiar from Swift.[1]

Born in Ireland to an Irish mother and a subaltern in the English army, Sterne attended Jesus College, Cambridge, an institution with strong clerical connections. Ordained into the Anglican Church immediately after graduation, he fretted in obscurity as the vicar of remote Yorkshire villages. His life was then transformed with the appearance of the first two volumes of *The Life and Opinions of Tristram Shandy* on 1 January 1760. At the age of forty-six, Sterne had published nothing except a short political satire (later withdrawn), and he produced relatively little afterwards, except seven more volumes of *Tristram Shandy* between 1761 and 1767.[2] Even the exceptions to this pattern have a curiously parasitical relation to his major work: a volume of sermons, using the identity of *Tristram Shandy*'s Parson Yorick (1760) and the eccentric travelogue of *A Sentimental Journey through France and Italy*, evolving from Volume VII of *Tristram Shandy* (1768). Even the posthumously published private journal, *Letters from Yorick to Eliza* (1775), returned to the literary persona created in *Tristram Shandy*. The centrality of one work to Sterne's life and literary career, then, is patent.

With Sterne, the concepts of 'literary' and 'documentary' modes acquire an entirely new dimension. The author's direct borrowings from earlier writers are extensive and occasionally border on plagiarism.[3] Scholars note such major stimuli on Sterne as the freakish *Voyage Round the World* (1692) by journalist and miscellaneous writer John Dunton, and Robert Burton's great medical-*cum*-philosophical treatise, *The Anatomy of Melancholy* (1621).[4] More routine support is suggested by the quotations (and misquotations) from Ephraim Chambers's *Cyclopaedia*.[5]

The Anatomy of Melancholy provides two of the mottoes for Volume V and another for Volume VII of *Tristram Shandy*, although a more pervasive influence can be shown by almost random quotations from the *Anatomy* itself. Burton's discussion of hydrophobia, for example, confirms that author's deep reverence for written authority:

> They that will read of them, may consult with Dioscorides, Heurnius, Hildesheim, Capivaccius, Forestus, Sckenkius, and before all others Codronchus, an Italian, who hath lately written two exquisite books on this subject.   (p. 124)[6]

A comment on the truism that 'love is blind', on the other hand, illustrates the same writer's sheer verbal exuberance:

> Every lover admires his Mistress, though she be very deformed of her self, ill-favoured, wrinkled, pale, red, yellow, tanned, tallow-faced, have a swollen Juggler's platter-face, or a thin, lean, chitty-face, have clouds in her face, be crooked, dry, bald, goggle-eyed, . . . black or yellow about the eyes, or squint-eyed.   (p. 737)

Burton's characteristic synthesis of learning and verbosity are then captured perfectly by Sterne in passages like his 'metaphysical' conceit comparing a man's body and mind to a jerkin and its lining:

> *Zeno, Cleanthes, Diogenes, Babylonius, Dyonisius Heracleotes, Antipater, Panœtius* and *Possidonius* amongst the *Greeks*; – *Cato* and *Varro* and *Seneca* amongst the *Romans*; – *Pantenus* and *Clemens Alexandrinus* and *Montaigne* amongst the Christians; and a score and a half of good honest, unthinking, *Shandean* people as ever lived, whose names I can't recollect, – all pretended that their jerkins were made after this fashion, – you might have rumpled and crumpled, and doubled and creased, and fretted and fridged the outsides of them all to pieces . . .   (III, 4)[7]

Such parody is also a fine example of how little is required to push Burton's scholarship over the epistemological divide into comic pedantry. The frequency of such writing in *Tristram Shandy* even suggests that it may constitute the novel's dominant narrative mode. The fact that Burton is also the one major inspiration that Sterne never directly acknowledges might even suggest an 'anxiety of influence', or a classic example of literary repression.

More widely recognized literary models for *Tristram Shandy* appear in Sterne's own invocation in Volume III ('By the tomb of *Lucian . . .* by the ashes of my dear *Rabelais*, and dearer *Cervantes*', III, 19). Among these three, the debt to Lucian's satirical dialogues and fantastic tales, combining wit and inventiveness, would certainly have been more apparent to classically educated eighteenth-century readers (the Greek writer's influence on Swift was even clearer) than to their less learned twenty-first-century counterparts.

In retrospect, too, Lucian's contribution is sometimes difficult to separate from that of Rabelais, a far more obvious presence in *Tristram Shandy*. Another disaffected cleric (like Burton, too, as it happens), Rabelais even anticipates Sterne in his publication pattern: five instalments, of which the last is a shorter single volume. The grand sequence of what is usually referred to as *Gargantua and Pantagruel*, like *Tristram Shandy* a potentially open-ended work, spans twenty years. The roughly equal-sized *Gargantua*, *Pantagruel*, *Tiers Livre* and *Quart Livre* are followed by a slightly shorter and more problematic *Cinquiesme et Dernier Livre*, whose authenticity is widely questioned. *Tristram Shandy*'s textual references to its French predecessor are quite detailed, although largely confined to the *Quart Livre*; they include 'Tickletoby's mare' (Rabelais's *Tappecue* or penis, *Quart Livre*, ch. xiii), the visit to the Oracle of the Holy Bottle Bacbuc (*Quart Livre*, ch. i) and Homenas, the Bishop of Papimany (*Quart Livre*, ch. xlviii). The broader example of Rabelais is apparent in the visual aspect of Sterne's lists, such as the roll-call of painterly qualities (III, 12), the ABC of love (VIII, 13) and gazeteer of Paris streets (VII, 18), as well as the pseudo-inventories of infant prodigies (VI, 2) or misogynists (VI, 30).

In the case of Cervantes, Sterne's response is more subtle: an even greater number of detailed textual references suggests a knowledge and understanding of *Don Quixote* remarkable even for an eighteenth-century English novelist. Some of these allusions, such as the linking of Parson Yorick's horse to Don Quixote's Rosinante and the latter's adventure with the Yanguesan carriers' mares (I, 10), the name of

Dulcinea and the plague of the Enchanters (I, 19), or the theft of Sancho's ass (VII, 36) are highly specific.[8] Others are broader, suggesting a whole ethics of reception: the melancholy Yorick associated with Don Quixote as 'knight of the woeful countenance'; Uncle Toby as a kind of English reincarnation of Cervantes's hero – in a line of 'benevolent humourists' descended from Parson Adams, with Toby's relation to Corporal in the mould of *Don Quixote*'s own master–servant relationship: his harmless hobby-horse of military campaigns recalling his avatar's passion for novels of chivalry.[9] While the serio-comic 'cervantick tone' of Yorick on his deathbed (I, 10) recalls Fielding's attempts at 'grave Cervantick humour' in *Joseph Andrews*: for many eighteenth-century readers this rather diffuse concept seems to have been exemplified by the comically slow but meticulous description of grotesque actions such as Dr Slop's fall from his horse into the mud (III, 29). It is a reminder, in any case, of how important a stimulus *Don Quixote* provided to the eighteenth-century English novel, particularly in the context of Fielding, Smollett and Sterne.[10]

Further borrowings, or at least significant references, in various contexts of *Tristram Shandy* include Erasmus (madness and the carnivalesque), Montaigne (speculation on abstruse subjects), La Rochefoucauld (ridicule of exaggerated seriousness) and even Sterne's exact contemporary, Voltaire (a shorter invocation in the first volume refers to 'CANDID and Miss CUNEGUND'S affairs'); while the allusions to classical authors would require a study apart.

The documentary dimension of *Tristram Shandy* is effectively a *pseudo*-documentary one, but no less interesting for that. Northrop Frye made a classic division of fictional narrative into the four constituent elements of novel, romance, confession and anatomy (eventually replacing the latter with the concept of 'Menippean satire').[11] The twentieth-century work widely experienced as the most completely satisfying, Joyce's *Ulysses*, so the argument runs, managed to include all four elements in abundance: the realism of the novel, the fantasy of romance (in its prototypical epic form), the intimacy of confession and the miscellany of anatomy.

The presence of all four dimensions could also be argued for *Tristram Shandy*: few realist novels match it for circumstantial detail, while the 'amours' of Toby and the Widow Wadman provide a classic (parody) romance. It is nevertheless the other two elements which predominate: the close links with Burton's archetypal English 'anatomy' have already been argued, whereas the confession in *Tristram Shandy* is relentlessly celebrated, exploited – and parodied. The eighteenth century

brought a proliferation of confessions, from traditional puritan expiations
to such scandalous memoirs as those of Smollett's Lady Vane (included
in *Peregrine Pickle*).[12] It is difficult to link Sterne directly with any of
these traditions, however, although there is conversely an astonishing
originality in the comprehensiveness of his own confessional mode. At
one point, Tristram refers admiringly to John Locke's *Essay Concerning
Human Understanding* (1690) as a 'history-book of what passes in a
man's mind' (II, 2), but the phrase would also be a fitting epitaph for
his own performance.

One of Sterne's modern editors has helpfully suggested that
Tristram Shandy contains three major narrative strands: events
surrounding Tristram's conception and birth; the lives of the two
Shandy brothers; and commentary on the process of writing itself.[13]
Volume I thus begins with Tristram's comic conception, followed by
the characterization of Uncle Toby through his hobby of fortification,
and that of Walter Shandy (initially) through his dogmatic attitudes
towards midwives and childrens' names. Volumes II and III, largely
structured round the group of men waiting anxiously for news of
Tristram's delivery upstairs, generally maintain this blend. Subsequent
instalments of the novel have more substantial digressions such as
Slawkenbergius's tale of a gigantic nose (Volume III) and the pathos of
Le Fever the soldier's story (Volume V). There is nothing to overturn
basic patterns, however, although the other four volumes each place
special emphasis on *one* of the three major male characters: Volume VI
deals at length with Walter's educational guide for his son, the Trista-
paedia; Volume VII (a kind of prototype for the *Sentimental Journey*)
covers the beginnings of a Grand Tour made by the adult Tristram;
Volumes VIII and IX, finally, concentrate on the story of Uncle Toby's
'amours' with the Widow Wadman.

In addition to this, Sterne interrogates and subverts the actual writing process throughout the novel. The dashes and asterisks are the most
conspicuous features of his idiosyncratic style; far more radical, however, are various typographical tricks – a marbled page to suggest
human motley, a black one for Yorick's coffin, a blank space for each
reader's personal portrait of the Widow Wadman; a series of squiggles
as an ironic comment on the progress of the narrative. The latter, need
it be added, is predictably slow, when the circumstantiality of the
correspondence in *Clarissa* is combined with the self-consciously
speculative narration of *Tom Jones*. A metafictional comment in the
middle of Volume IV, when Tristram is still on the first day of his life,
graphically illustrates this point:

I am this month one whole year older than I was this time twelve-month; and having got, as you perceive, almost into the middle of my fourth volume – and no farther than to my first day's life – 'tis demonstrative that I have three hundred and sixty-four days more to write just now, than when I first set out; so that instead of advancing, as a common writer, in my work with what I have been doing at it – on the contrary, I am just thrown so many volumes back – was every day of my life to be as busy as this –   (IV, 13)

And the fact that Tristram, on his own admission, needs two chapters for 'what passed in going down one pair of stairs' (IV, 10), merely underlines such comic speculation. There is, of course, a 'signpost' in this apparent muddle. Walter's traumatic experience of Tristram's conception (I, 4) is caused by Mrs Shandy's 'unhappy association of ideas' connecting the sexual act and the winding up the family clock: such combinations, Tristram points out, are the concern of the 'sagacious *Locke*' who claims they have 'produced more wry actions than all other sources of prejudice whatsoever' (I, 4).

Sterne warmly praises Locke's 'Essay upon the Human Under-standing' [sic], adding that many 'quote the book who have not read it, – and many have read it who understand it not' (II, 2). He refers twice in some detail to Locke's idea of duration and its simple modes, dramatizing his distinction between time divided objectively into conventional units and time experienced subjectively as a more elastic concept (II, 8). The most extensive reference to Locke nevertheless occurs with Walter's garbled attempts to explain this very distinction while the men wait anxiously for Mrs Shandy to give birth (III, 18). There then follows a ten-line paraphrase of Locke's *Essay*, suitably acknowledged by italics, although Toby remains none the wiser for such detail. Regarded variously as philosopher (from the *Essay*) or political thinker (from his *Two Treatises on Government*), Locke's relevance to *Tristram Shandy* may be that of a proto-psychologist. As hinted above, Sterne's definition of the *Essay* as a 'history-book of what passes in a man's mind' (II, 2) indirectly defines the scope and structure of his own narrative. For the method of *Tristram Shandy* has long been recognized as 'digressive' rather than 'progressive': it proceeds on the principle of the association of ideas, Toby's or Walter's certainly, but also Tristram's and, ultimately, those of Sterne himself.

The Locke–Sterne epistemological axis – the term does not seem too grandiose – is highly resonant. For, behind the clowning, *Tristram*

Shandy is also a book about how people *know*. The genial transposition of abstract philosophical (or psychological) theory into dramatic narrative terms is a significant dimension of the novel. Sterne's most illustrious fictional predecessor in this kind of writing may once again be his beloved Cervantes, whose *Don Quixote* can be partly seen as an extended commentary on Renaissance neo-Platonic theories of appearance and reality. A comparable example of this kind of fictional concretization in Cervantes would, then, be the incident of Mambrino's helmet (Part I, ch. 21). On the open road one day, Don Quixote sees an approaching knight wearing the mythical golden headpiece, while Sancho sees an itinerant barber wearing a brass basin to keep the rain off; the narrator Cide Hamete Berengeli reserves judgement, while Cervantes himself – serenely aloof – does at least enough to suggest his ironic awareness of such fundamental epistemological issues. The links between Cervantes and Sterne are increased by the presence of a structurally analogous male quartet for each novel: the same two brothers (or brothers-in-arms), a similar self-conscious narrator, functioning ultimately as dramatic extension or *alter ego* of a great comic genius within the European novelistic tradition.

In a twentieth-century context, the effects of the association of ideas in *Tristram Shandy* are close to those produced by the 'free association' techniques of classic psychoanalysis; which is merely to affirm once more the premise that the formal unity of the book is not chronological, but is provided by the mind of the narrator. It is the kind of unity explored and developed in Joyce's *Ulysses* (first through Bloom and finally in Molly's monologue) or in Woolf's *Mrs Dalloway*. From the association of ideas, moreover, it is only a step to human subjectivity in general, with Uncle Toby often passing as the epitome of a man who lives through feelings (and particularly exquisite ones at that). Sterne is a key figure in the cult of sensibility so widespread from the mid-eighteenth century, and the story of Le Fever and his orphaned son (VI, 6ff) is a *locus classicus* in this respect.[14] Equally celebrated in its day was the scene describing Toby's encounter with a fly:

> – Go, – says he, one day at dinner, to an over-grown one which had buzz'd about his nose, and tormented him cruelly all dinner-time, – and which, after infinite attempts, he had caught at last, as it flew by him; – I'll not hurt thee, says my uncle *Toby*, rising from his chair, and going a-cross the room, with the fly in his hand, – I'll not hurt a hair of thy head: – Go, says he, lifting up the sash, and opening his hand as he spoke, to let it escape; go poor Devil, get thee gone, why

should I hurt thee? – This world is surely wide enough to hold both thee and me. (II, 12)

Sterne's attitude towards sensibility here is complex and ambivalent. In both *Tristram Shandy* and *A Sentimental Journey* he mocks – or at least gently guys – the cult of feeling as much as he celebrates it. The fly incident even suggests that Sterne could achieve all three effects in a single episode.

The association of ideas is also Sterne's starting-point for characterization: for if Tristram himself remains a rather shadowy figure, of whom we know ostensibly everything but ultimately almost nothing, then his father and uncle are inversely prominent. It is sometimes suggested that the so-called *Life and Opinions of Tristram Shandy, Gentleman* are effectively the life of Uncle Toby and the opinions of Walter. Certainly, Sterne explicitly portrays Uncle Toby through his 'hobby-horse' of military fortifications (reconstructed lovingly on the bowling-green with his long-time servant, Corporal Trim). Associations of ideas here, and the private obsessions they reveal, are a regular source of comic misunderstandings, as in the confusion over a bridge in fortifications and the bridge of Tristram's nose (III, 23ff). Toby is contrasted with the dogmatic, pedantic Walter, a man who even has a system for the supposedly spontaneous activity of swearing. He must then, of course, watch each of his schemes go awry, whether it concerns the conception, delivery, christening or general education of his younger son. Certain elements in his *Trista-paedia*, such as his advocacy of auxiliary verbs as the 'north-west passage' to knowledge (V, 42), are as richly absurd as anything in the novel.

The issue of gender in *Tristram Shandy*, at least in terms of male *authors* and female *novelists*, may have been anticipated, if not prejudged, above. There are few eighteenth-century novelists (beyond such marginal figures as Thomas Amory) who can rival Sterne for 'learned wit', and such a propensity in his day was, almost by definition, the obvious product of a *gentleman*'s education. There are equally few novels, however, which devote as much attention as *Tristram Shandy* to the reader, whether actual or implied, and it is here that discussions of gender relations in Sterne should begin. The three hundred and fifty or so references include 'My Lord', 'Jenny', 'Madam', 'your worship', 'my dear anti-Shandeans, and thrice able critics, and fellow labourers... subtle statesmen and discreet doctors', 'Julia', 'your reverences', and 'gentry'. It sometimes seems, as one critic remarked, that the reader has invaded the book.[15] Sterne is obviously keenly aware of his audience, even anticipating such modern formalist concepts as the narrator and the narratée with his comic reference to 'jester' and 'jestée' (I, 12). If Tristram, the narrator/jester, is explicitly male, then there is a conscious gendering of narratée/jestée, with what seems a rough equilibrium between the sexes, although this apparent even-handedness only exists in quantitative terms.

For the constructions of gender implied by Sterne's narrative divisions are quite significant here. A number of his sexual jokes, like those of Kunastrokius and his 'whim-wham', Trim's offer to demonstrate 'strong-holds' to the chambermaid and cook, or Walter's dismissal of Susannah as a leaky vessel, are presumably aimed at male readers, even if the point is never openly made; discussion of affairs of the heart, such as Uncle Toby's 'amours' (VI, 29), are explicitly directed at women. A more covert – and perhaps therefore more noteworthy – division concerns critics, conventionally assumed to be men, whether the 'gentleman reviewers in *Great-Britain*' (I, 13) or the 'criticks and gentry of refined taste' (II, 2). Authority, whether narrator or narratée, is predictably male; the female counterpart is neither as intelligent or even as attentive. The demonstration that Tristram's mother is not a 'papist' (I, 20) is thus presumed to have escaped the careless *female* reader (' – How, could you, Madam, be so inattentive in reading the last chapter?', I, 20), who is ignorant into the bargain:

> – this is ænigmatical, and intended to be so, at least, *ad populum*. –
> And therefore I beg, Madam, when you come here, that you read on as
> fast as you can, and never stop to make any inquiry about it.   (I, 23)

An educated and intelligent elite is thus gendered as male, the ignorant mass as female, a division corresponding to gender stereotypes found elsewhere in the narrative. Walter is thus associated – or associates himself – with (male) 'reason' and his wife with a lack of it; and in the novel's other great example of sexual dualism, Uncle Toby is gallant and sensitive, while the Widow Wadman is a comic residue of the lubricious Eve figure.

A closer glance at the female characters in *Tristram Shandy* is revealing. For it is a notable feature of the novel that centre-stage is occupied by three eccentric male characters, each haunted by the spectre of sexual inadequacy; the sex in relation to which such inadequacy is defined remains marginal. The closest relationship in the novel is arguably that of Uncle Toby and his servant, Trim, although this tie is conditioned by social hierarchy and economic dependence. There is also genuine affection between Toby and Walter. As Tristram assures us, 'My father, I believe, had the truest love and tenderness for my uncle *Toby*, that ever one brother bore towards another' (I, 21); his only regret is the lack of a worthy foil for his dialectic. With Mrs Shandy, on the other hand, Walter's reactions fluctuate between irritation, exasperation, and even contempt. Tristram's mother, like some of the other marginalized female characters, actually conforms to traditional constructions of women bordering on stereotypes. Walter is exasperated, among other things, by his wife's inability to engage in any kind of meaningful debate, particularly in their regular 'beds of justice'. He dismisses her at one point as 'the truest of all the *Poco-curante's* [care-nothings] of her sex!' (VI, 20). During the delivery sit-in, he alludes to traditional ideas of male reason and female lack of it; or in view of the context for these deliberations, it is as if men conceived hypotheses, where women merely conceived children. The implication that the former activity might be the more valuable or fundamental of the two is not the least ridiculous of Walter's assumptions.

If Mrs Shandy is the empty-headed female, then, the Widow Wadman is merely devious. She schemes to entrap Toby, by infiltrating herself into his sentry-box and arranging to have her hand guided over his map. Her main preoccupation is the possible effect of Toby's wound on his sexual capacity. When a blissfully innocent Toby is enlightened by Walter on this point, he immediately ends the courtship. There is no imaginative identification with the Widow Wadman, who is simply presented as the sexually obsessed widow of male stereotype. Since she is referred to as a 'daughter of Eve' and her story is punningly described as 'matter copulative', the true sexual obsession might be thought to reside in author–narrator rather than in one of his less fortunate female creations.

At one point in the novel, however, during the events surrounding Tristram's birth in Volume II, the (en)gendering of narrative could be assigned a kind of metacritical dimension. Tristram's parents thus argue about who will assist at the delivery and where the event will take place. A compromise is reached on condition that Mrs Shandy is attended by her local village midwife rather than the more pretentious *accoucheur*, Dr Slop, preferred by Walter. Social historians have shown that the midwife's profession was undergoing a significant change in status in the course of the eighteenth century.[16] Traditional methods advocated by generations of local female midwives were being challenged by newer, if cruder, scientific 'improvements' from male obstetricians. The profession was evidently becoming re-gendered, as men now encroached on what was previously an exclusively female preserve. Outside the socio-economic context, however, it is tempting to read the whole process as an allegory of the 'birth' of the novel. Virginia Woolf, in speculating on woman's relationship to the new fictional form evolving in the eighteenth century, suggested that 'all old forms of literature were hardened and set by the time she became a writer'; the novel, however, still offered freedom, flexibility and new horizons to the female pen. But what was a potentially female form, in the hands of Behn, Manley and Haywood, was largely usurped by Fielding, Richardson and other practitioners of the 'new species of writing'. The canonic novelists before Jane Austen are men. Metaphors of both engendering and parturition, on the other hand, are commonplace in talk of literary origins (from 'fathering' a novel to the 'birth' of the genre); midwifery, moreover, seems potentially as fertile a trope as carnival or the penitentiary in the context of eighteenth-century fiction. The new gender distribution in novel-writing (whether in contemporary hack-work or modern canon-formation) would then be yet another example of male colonization of potentially female territory.

Humphry Clinker

Of the five canonic male eighteenth-century English novelists, Tobias Smollett is now the least read; he may actually be the first major English author to have passed from broad acclaim to antiquarian status without any intervening stage of genuine critical esteem.[17] Certain other biographical and literary-historical details are also important: the former because Smollett is not really an 'English' novelist at all, and the latter since his writing career lasted so much longer than those of his major contemporaries.

Born on the banks of Loch Lomond into the Scottish gentry, Smollett attended the local grammar school and was apprenticed surgeon after uncompleted studies at Glasgow University.[18] At the age of eighteen, he wrote a tragedy, *The Regicide*, on a Scottish historical theme; his first published pieces were the verse satires 'Advice' (1746) and 'Reproof' (1747), and another poem, 'The Tears of Scotland', lamenting harsh English reprisals after the Jacobite rebellion of 1745. By the age of nineteen, Smollett was in London seeking his fortune, first as a medical doctor, and later as a professional author. Subsequently, he spent most of his life in England, and even lived longer in France and Italy than he ever did in his native Scotland. Exile and the journey, together with the mythical return, are predictably powerful motifs in his fiction.[19]

Smollett's first novel, *Roderick Random* (1748), and his last, *Humphry Clinker* (1771), are divided by twenty-three years. Only Richardson, in the traditional eighteenth-century canon, comes close to such a long creative period: *Pamela* and *Grandison* are separated by fourteen years. Fielding's fiction from *Joseph Andrews* (1742) to *Amelia* (1751) spans nine years; Defoe's from *Robinson Crusoe* to *Roxana* only five; whilst the nine volumes of *Tristram Shandy* cover seven. Views of Smollett will vary greatly according to which novel is discussed (it is only unfortunate that none usually are), particularly when the widely separated first and last, rather than the three in between, are universally regarded as his most significant works.

After medical service in the English navy, and with little more than an unperformable tragedy and two Juvenalian satires to his name, Smollett produced *The Adventures of Roderick Random* in 1748: to unexpected critical acclaim. The novel's Preface, arguably more interesting and original than Fielding's for *Joseph Andrews*, locates its writer in a precise generic space between 'satire' and 'romance'; and the ensuing narrative has little of the (classic realist) novel, a word not even mentioned by Smollett before the preamble to *Ferdinand Count Fathom* (1753). *Roderick Random* follows the experiences of its young Scottish hero in search of a fortune – as aspiring author in London, surgeon in the Royal Navy, and miscellaneous adventurer (with or without the aid of his servant-companion, Strap). No amount of special pleading, by the author himself or by later generations of critics, can cancel obvious autobiographical links here. The next novel, the voluminous *Peregrine Pickle* (1751), can seem a tedious rehash of its predecessor, although certain structural innovations are worth noting: the switch from first- to third-person narrator, for instance, and the shift to an English protagonist, albeit without any of the attractive features or egalitarian tendencies of Roderick.

Smollett's next narrative is *Ferdinand Count Fathom* (1753). As the autobiographical impulse of the early novels fades and the psychological potential of letter fiction remains untapped, *Fathom* relies heavily on the structures of satire. More precisely, it is a monolithic (and occasionally sterile) exercise in 'mock-epic', largely after the manner of Fielding's *Jonathan Wild*. *Sir Launcelot Greaves* (1762), in turn, has an even more obvious satirical model in Cervantes's *Don Quixote*. These two novels are certainly Smollett's least successful, and give no hint of the great originality to come with *Humphry Clinker* (1771). The present section concentrates on Smollett's last novel, although – for reasons now evident – references to the earlier fiction will be necessary.

An initial comparison of 'literary' and 'documentary' modes clearly illustrates Smollett's extensive literary range. The Preface to *Roderick Random*, for instance, openly acknowledges the author's faith in a fictional hybrid of satire and romance:

> Of all kinds of satire, there is none so entertaining, and universally improving, as that which is introduced, as it were, occasionally, in the course of an interesting story.   (p. xxiii)[20]

The 'interesting story' is clearly the simple linear narrative of romance, for which Smollett then supplies an entertaining, if tendentious, pedigree. Its origins are thus said to lie in performances evolved for readers long 'debauched by the imposition of priest-craft', before the welcome advent of Cervantes, who converted romance to satiric purposes. Smollett then mentions 'other Spanish and French authors' who practised the same method. *Peregrine Pickle* deviates relatively little from these models.

Further evidence for the importance of literary models for Smollett comes from a glance at the novelist's simultaneous activity as translator and hack writer. His translation from the French of René Lesage's picaresque novel *Gil Blas* appeared shortly before *Roderick Random*; his version of Cervantes's *Don Quixote* was published in 1755. Between *Sir Launcelot Greaves* and *Humphry Clinker* almost a decade elapsed, and this period is marked by a shift from obvious literary models to more subtle documentary ones (Smollett's own as it happens): the fictional work immediately preceding *Humphry Clinker* is the highly topical, and thus occasionally inpenetrable, political satire *The History and Adventures of an Atom* (1769), although Smollett's last novel obviously owes more to his own epistolary travelogue, the *Travels through France and Italy*, published five years earlier.

There is a well documented craze for travel books in the England of the 1770s and 1780s, coinciding with an equally remarkable vogue for letter fiction. Where the latter is concerned, the entire 1740s – that formative decade in the history of English fiction – produced barely a dozen epistolary novels of note, whereas the year 1771 provided more than twice that number, in addition to *Humphry Clinker*. Of guides to continental travel, on the other hand, there was a regular supply throughout the century, beginning with Addison's *Remarks on Several Parts of Italy* (1705).[21] Smollett's own characteristically splenetic contribution to the genre attracted much attention, and that not always positive: one contemporary actually suggested that the *Travels* might more reasonably have been called 'QUARRELS through France and Italy for the cure of a pulmonic disorder'.[22]

The *Travels* are clearly a major documentary model for *Humphry Clinker*, and a brief comparison of the two texts is revealing. The forty-one letters of the former divide roughly according to setting, whether the open road or the major stopping-points on the various journeys. With exactly double the number of letters, *Humphry Clinker* achieves the same balance. Certain minor figures in the *Travels*, such as Father Graeme, a Scottish priest from *Peregrine Pickle*, or Père Charles, a thieving Capuchin friar from *Roderick Random*, are already familiar to Smollett's readers. The techniques of caricature – a drunken lawyer in the *Travels* (letter 2) or Narcissa's grubby aunt (*Roderick Random*, ch. 45) – are common to both Smollett's fiction and his travel writing, not to mention the genial synthesis of the two which is *Humphry Clinker*.

The themes of exile and return also underpin both the fictional and the documentary mode. The last letter of the *Travels*, headed 'Boulogne', thus happily anticipates the traveller's return to England:

> I am at last in a situation to indulge my view with a sight of Britain, after an absence of two years; and indeed you cannot imagine what pleasure I feel while I survey the white cliffs of Dover, at this distance.[23]

The reaction here is quite literally novelistic, since it matches that of Count Fathom on a similar occasion:

> When he beheld the white cliffs of Albion, his heart throbbed with all the joy of a beloved son, who after a tedious and fatiguing voyage, reviews the chimneys of his father's house.[24]

The Scottish hero of *Roderick Random* returns to claim his birthright; and the rhetoric of homecoming is even more striking (if only implicit) in *Humphry Clinker*, when the author's *alter ego*, the Welshman Bramble, visits Smollett's native Scotland.

Literary status aside, however, the major differences between the *Travels* and *Humphry Clinker* are structural. The forty-one letters of the former are dispatched by a single correspondent to apparently four addressees, thirty-three to the same anonymous recipient, whose identity remains unclear. The eighty-two letters of *Humphry Clinker*, on the other hand, are produced by five individuals, each for a specific fictional addressee. Twenty-seven (or just under a third) are written by Bramble, the irascible and neurasthenic *pater familias*, to a country neighbour and fellow Welshman; twenty-eight are sent by his lively, self-opinionated nephew Jery, to an Oxford college friend; whilst the remaining twenty-seven are divided between three female correspondents: eleven from Bramble's niece, the romantically sensitive Lydia; ten from the latter's cantankerous aunt, Tabitha Bramble; and ten more from Tabitha's maid, the lively Win Jenkins. The five make their leisurely progress via Gloucester, Bristol, and Bath to London (where Clinker's own expedition begins), and thence through Yorkshire to Edinburgh and the Scottish Highlands before the return, by Glasgow, Carlisle, and Manchester, back home to Wales.

A glance at the individual interests of the five correspondents casts interesting light on the respective strengths of the novel's literary and documentary modes. A classic eighteenth-century 'original', with equal doses of misogyny and hypochondria, Bramble nevertheless produces a fairly conventional travelogue: conventional, that is, in subject matter – if not always in tone – for, until his arrival in rural Scotland, he finds little positive to say. Letters 4 to 7 (in his own sequence) thus describe the dirt and confusion of Bath; letters 9 and 11 deplore the urbanization of London; letters 15 and 16 record disillusion with the Gothic architecture of York Minster and the general appearance of Durham; while letter 17 criticizes Edinburgh (beginning predictably with its smells). About half-way through the correspondence, however, Bramble's identity as a Welshman allows the requisite distance for an external view of the English (letter 14), echoing a strategy frequently used in the *Travels*, with its anonymous British correspondent's caustic views of the French. Only arrival in the Scottish Highlands produces a mellower tone. There is even a poignant note (together with a certain existential ambivalence) when the fictional Bramble and his party visit Cameron House, the real-life Smollett family seat.[25]

In marked contrast, Bramble's nephew is responsible for almost all the elements of story and intrigue in *Humphry Clinker*, even as he mixes social observation with comedy and critical detachment. Taken as a whole, his narrative actually has a curious similarity to the kind of generic hybrid developed by Smollett in *Roderick Random* more than twenty years earlier. The train of events described by Jery thus alternates breathtakingly between comedy, satire and romance, with the cruder or more farcical elements occasionally relieved by scenes appealing to the new sensibility of the later eighteenth century. It is Jery, for instance, who jubilantly describes each attempt of Tabitha to find a husband (a tribute to the tenacity of Smollett's 'old maid' motif), and who comments with amused detachment on the more unlikely turns of the romance subplots. 'Every day is now big with incident and discovery' (p. 331), he remarks on the unmasking of one transparent disguise. Or, on the sensational triple marriage at the end of the novel, he concludes like some master of the revels: 'The fatal knots are now tied. The comedy is near a close; and the curtain is ready to drop' (p. 346).

Male *authors* might be expected to eclipse female *novelists* in the abrasive and archaic world of Smollett. As Mrs Barbauld remarked scathingly of *Roderick Random*: 'Much of the work is filled up with low jokes, and laughable stories, such as, one may suppose, had been circulated in a club over a bottle.'[26] It is nevertheless possible, as demonstrated below, to extract significant female subtexts from most of Smollett's fiction, even from a novel with the apparently crude sexism of *Humphry Clinker*.

In the latter, the individual narratives of Bramble and Jery suggest a well articulated and clearly identifiable division of labour, while the letters of the three female correspondents are more problematic. It has already been noted that their combined total is exactly equivalent to the number written by Bramble alone (and one less than those of Jery). These data should nevertheless be supplemented by some reference to actual quantities of text. In a modern paperback edition of the novel (running to 350 pages without the preliminary correspondence between editor and bookseller), the relative shares of the three writers (calculated to the nearest page) are as follows:

Bramble	135pp
Jery	166pp
Lydia	25pp
Tabitha	6pp
Win	17pp

Smollett's Tabitha Bramble has been described as a cartoon figure to whom 'language itself was almost totally alien';[27] and whatever the truth of this claim, it does seem that (together with Lydia and Win) her opportunities for practice are limited.

The question of gender in Smollett's novels may be related to his images of women, or – in a later theoretical idiom – his constructions of femininity. It is no exaggeration to speak here of a strong misogynistic streak, and for a writer so sensitive to classical precedents, there is a rich tradition on which to draw. In the context of Smollett's fiction, Juvenal's sixth *Satire* once again supplies a virtual blueprint. In both writers, unmarried females are promiscuous, whilst married ones torment their hen-pecked husbands. Juvenal is also particularly bitter about women who invade traditional male preserves:

> most intolerable of all is the woman who as soon as she has sat down to dinner commends Virgil, pardons the dying Dido, and pits the poets against each other, putting Virgil in the one scale and Homer in the other. The grammarians make way before her; the rhetoricians give in; the whole crowd is silenced; no lawyer, no auctioneer will get a word in, no, nor any other woman.[28]

The passage could well be a portrait of the heroine Narcissa's aunt (*Roderick Random*), that grotesque caricature of the female intellectual.

Misogyny apart, Smollett's generally male-oriented perspective was well captured in an amusing proto-feminist critique almost a century ago:

> The hero falls in love with a beautiful lady, not over seventeen, and there is a conflict between lust and chastity. The hero, balked of his prey, travels up and down the world where he meets with a series of adventures, all very much alike, and all bearing little on the main plot. At last fate leads the dashing hero to the church door, where he confers a ring on the fair heroine, a paltry piece of gold, the only reward for her fidelity, with the hero thrown in, much the worse for wear, and the curtain falls with the sound of wedding bells in the distance.[29]

This rather reductive account draws largely on *Roderick Random* and *Peregrine Pickle*. Such patterns are then progressively abandoned, although – in the form of Wilson's story, for example – vestiges of them remain even in *Humphry Clinker*.

Hardly surprisingly, perhaps, Smollett's fiction generates a significant number of counter-narratives (from potential *female* novelists among his own characters, one might suggest) which subvert the crude phallocentrism of their *male* author. The process begins with the enterprising Nancy Williams in *Roderick Random*, although the 'Memoirs of a Lady of Quality' in *Peregrine Pickle* are the most obvious example of such disruptive elements.[30] Such intrusions are implicitly ideological and ultimately suggest female resistance to male discourse. They are particularly prominent in *Humphry Clinker*, although the initial profiles of the three female correspondents are not promising. For, in the crudest terms, the women represent experience without literacy (Tabitha), literacy without experience (Lydia), and a notable lack of either (Win).

The latter's correspondence (ten letters, seventeen pages) is sometimes praised for its representation of nonstandard English, although it is surely more significant for its use of misspellings as veiled satirical commentary: overdressed Bath servants are described as 'devils in garnet', while their mistresses are ruined by diabolical luxury, or the 'power of sattin' (letter 19). The 'banes of marridge' called between Tabitha and Lismahago are a cynical pun on the nuptial state, while the joining of couples in 'the holy bands of mattermoney' wittily recalls the economics of the eighteenth-century marriage market.

Tabitha's correspondence (six letters and not quite six pages) is often indistinguishable, stylistically or psychologically, from that of her maid, and both women are the vehicle of Smollett's scatological wit. The latter incidentally stands comparison with that of Sterne himself, particularly regarding the latently erotic imagery of Methodism. Win thus urges her fellow maid to prepare for the arrival of the newly saved Clinker ('pray without seizing for grease to prepare you for the operations of this wonderful instrument, which, I hope, will be exorcised this winter upon you and others at Brambleton-hall', p. 156); Tabitha, in turn, recommends Clinker to Mrs Gwyllim the housekeeper ('that he may have power to penetrate and instill his goodness, even into your most inward parts', p. 275).

Tabitha and Win here are hardly more than extensions of Smollett's own scatological humour. Less obviously comic but more thematically significant is the character of Bramble's niece Lydia (eleven letters and twenty-seven pages). An ingenuous and sentimental seventeen, the classic age of the Smollett romantic heroine, Lydia does not initially seem a very original creation. Four of her letters are merely point-by-point revisions of topographical accounts by Bramble. Her relationship with 'Wilson', her disguised admirer, provides a good half of the romance subplot, although this material is narrated by, and even generally focalized through, Jery.

The two male correspondents regularly pass judgement on Lydia, and on women in general, fluctuating between condescension (Jery) and outright scorn (Bramble). But Lydia's actions ultimately contradict her weak self-image. Her strongly maintained convictions about 'Wilson' ('I am still persuaded that he is not what he appears to be: but time will discover,' p. 37) recall the similar defiance of male authority by Fanny Price in *Mansfield Park*, with regard to Henry Crawford. Her intelligence also emerges clearly from a comparison of her first letter – written as a helpless orphan, to her ex-governess – with the second more calculating one to her confidante, Letty. From other evidence, too, the reader must form opinions of Lydia at odds with those of Bramble and Jery: thus, her comment on a ladies' coffee-house at Bath where 'conversation turns upon politics, scandal, philosophy, and other subjects above our capacity' (pp. 69–70) can only be read as wittily ironic comment.[31] And Lydia also possesses physical courage, reacting to a case of sexual harassment with a 'box on the ears' that sends her assailant reeling across the room (p. 295).

The most telling detail in Lydia's characterization, however, may be a structural irony in the text itself. Bramble and Jery continually undermine romance convention, but they are ultimately revealed as simply poor readers of the genre. For whereas in *Don Quixote*, giants were 'only' windmills, and opposing armies 'only' sheep, *Humphry Clinker* actually finds reality enhancing appearances: the Jewish pedlars and itinerant actors really *are* the long-awaited prince in disguise. What is transparent to Lydia remains opaque to Bramble and Jery, and it is the heroine's reading of events which is finally vindicated. Here, finally, is a feminine romance in the middle of Smollett's bottle stories.

Sterne and Smollett

In literary history, the name of Sterne is often synonymous with the eighteenth-century literary vogue of sensibility, although this simple correspondence has already been questioned, and the validity of the link may ultimately depend on the relative significance attached to *A Sentimental Journey* and *Tristram Shandy*. While the former is undoubtedly a key work in the context of a fashionable cult, the latter satirizes its excesses even as it recognizes its virtues. In her *Progress of Romance* (1785), proto-critic Clara Reeve actually placed *Tristram Shandy* with Swift's *Gulliver's Travels* (1726), Robert Paltock's *The Life and Adventures of Peter Wilkins* (1751) and Thomas Amory's *The Life of John Buncle* (1756) in a category she called 'Novels and Stories Original and Uncommon'. Paltock's novel was described in its day as 'the illegitimate offspring of no very natural conjunction betwixt *Gulliver's Travels* and *Robinson Crusoe*'; Amory's is a synthesis of erotic Utopia and antiquarian compendium.[32] Perhaps *Tristram Shandy* is the only common link here, with its fantastic grotesque in the style of Paltock and eccentric miscellany after Amory. Northrop Frye's *Anatomy of Criticism*, on the other hand, followed Reeve in linking Sterne with Swift as examples of 'Menippean satire' or 'anatomy'.[33]

In the context of sensibility, Sterne is a literary heir to Shaftesbury's notions of human benevolence and Rousseau's cult of spontaneous emotions, but in novelistic terms he anticipates Brooke, Mackenzie and Pratt.[34] Henry Brooke's *The Fool of Quality* (5 vols, 1765–70) provides a model of emotionally correct responses as its colourless hero moves through selected scenes of eighteenth-century life. Brooke's literary career otherwise illustrates the consequences of longevity: a man who was the friend of Swift and suffered, like Fielding, from the stage censorship of the Licensing Act, lived to endorse a one-volume abridgement of *The Fool of Quality* (1781) by the Methodist John Wesley.

More celebrated than Brooke was Henry Mackenzie, author of *The Man of Feeling* (1771). The worldly education of its quixotically ingenuous protagonist, Harley, is the classic exposition of what Johnson described as 'the fashionable whine of sensibility'. But after *The Man of the World* (1773), portraying Harley's antithesis, the amoral Sir Thomas Sindall, and the epistolary novel *Julia de Roubigné* (1777), Mackenzie stopped writing fiction entirely at the age of thirty-two. Sir Walter Scott, the first major novelist-critic, nevertheless regarded Mackenzie as a Sterne without the 'wild wit' or 'buffoonery and indecency', and this literary coupling remains prominent in conventional literary histories. The radical William Godwin incidentally underlined the reactionary side to Mackenzie's sensibility by sub-titling his own novel *Fleetwood* (1805) 'The New Man of Feeling', although the kind of conservatism targeted here would not have troubled Scott.

The highly derivative Samuel Pratt, who also published under his stage name of Courtney Melmoth, owes a similar debt to Mackenzie, but ultimately a larger one to Sterne. If his first novel, *The Pupil of Leasure* (1776), is structurally an evocation of Mackenzie's *The Man of the World*, then its successor, *Travels of the Heart* (1777), is – as its title suggests – a fairly slavish imitation of *A Sentimental Journey*. *The Vicar of Wakefield*, the one novel proper of Oliver Goldsmith, appeared in 1766, the year before the ninth and last volume of *Tristram Shandy*. Structurally and stylistically, however, the most conspicuous model for *The Vicar of Wakefield* is Fielding's *Joseph Andrews*. But if Goldsmith's attitude to sensibility is ambivalent – mingling tender sympathy with gentle irony – then the literary trail once again leads to Sterne.

As will emerge in Chapter 10, no such ambivalence is apparent in the attitudes of Jane Austen. The title alone of her first published novel, *Sense and Sensibility*, underlines the centrality of the issue for her; the experiences of Marianne Dashwood, the over-sensible sister, suggest its dangers.[35] Austen, of course, could appreciate the delicate feelings of the Richardsonian hero, and her *Juvenilia* include a short dramatic adaptation of *Grandison*; but other apprentice works, including the presumably early *Northanger Abbey* and the *Sanditon* fragment, also find in sensibility a particularly fruitful target of satire. A literary circle is thus complete.

The decline of sensibility perhaps threw other aspects of *Tristram Shandy* into greater relief. Sterne was predictably spurned by a more prudish nineteenth century, clearly unconvinced by Tristram's assurances that a nose meant no more or less than a nose. A spectacular rehabilitation then occurred among both critics and novelists in the course of the twentieth century. From being a literary oddity, the work was raised to the status of proto-novel by the Russian formalist critic Viktor Shklovsky.[36] This theorist much admired the novel for its self-referential element, as well as its exposition and interrogation of fictional techniques. Such 'baring of the device', as Shklovsky called it, also defined the interest of Sterne for Robert Alter. The latter saw Sterne as the forerunner of such postmodern writers as Calvino and Borges, through a common interest in self-conscious narrative and metafictional issues.[37]

In the broader context of twentieth-century anglophone fiction, moreover, Sterne's meticulous coverage of everything that passes within a man's (though not of course a woman's) mind obviously anticipates Joyce and his 'stream of consciousness technique'.[38] An even more obvious successor of Sterne, however, is Salman Rushdie. The comic opening of *Midnight's Children* (1981), with its insistence on the exact hour of the protagonist's birth, recalls the precision surrounding the account of Tristram's conception. Rushdie's narrator and *alter ego*, Saleem Sinai, moreover preserves each year's events in a single chapter like one more jar of *Special Formula* pickle. Tristram, who also dreamed of endless annual instalments, would certainly have understood Saleem's temporal obsessions in his 'chutnification of history; the grand hope of the pickling of *time*' [my emphasis].[39]

The modern interest in *Tristram Shandy* hardly applies to the fiction of Smollett, whose profile in the history of the novel is quite overshadowed by Sterne's. The only reservation to such claims concerns the broad fictional sub-genre of the *picaresque*, although Smollett's relation to this generates as much critical heat as Sterne's to the cult of sensibility.[40] All of Smollett's novels have thus been proposed at some time as authentic picaresque, with pride of place usually going to *Roderick Random* or *Ferdinand Count Fathom*. Certainly, the former has some of the elements identified in a classic essay on picaresque by Claudio Guillén: it is a first-person pseudo-autobiography, an odyssey which moves horizontally through space and, to some extent, vertically through society; its structure is loosely episodic, its protagonist virtually an orphan.[41]

But the mere setting of the open road, with accompanying scenes of low life, are not sufficient grounds in *Roderick Random* – any more than in *Tom Jones* – for speaking of picaresque. *Roderick Random* has a strong admixture of romance: far from being a classic *pícaro*, or 'rogue', its protagonist is a handsome, well-educated young man, spared the worst physical indignities and provided with a servant-companion; he marries a stereotypically beautiful but passive romance heroine after a dramatic *anagnorisis* or recognition, through which he discovers his lost father. With regard to *Humphry Clinker*, the concept of the picaresque is even less relevant, although vestiges of the genre remain in the story of Clinker himself. The latter's mysterious origins and physical appearance (a skin 'fair as alabaster') are nevertheless conventional attributes of one more romance hero. Like *Joseph Andrews*, he carries the marks of gentility on him.

Percy Adams made a suggestive distinction between static and dynamic narrative, the domestic and the peripatetic or itinerant. Ronald Paulson identified the former with the interior settings of 'drawing rooms, hallways and bedrooms'; Coleridge wrote similarly of a 'close, hot, day-dream world'. Northrop Frye's archetypal scheme similarly contrasted the 'idyllic world of happiness and security' with the 'demonic or night world', or simply, narratives of the garden and narratives of the river.[42] Defoe (with *Roxana* after *Moll Flanders*) or Fielding (whose *Amelia* follows *Tom Jones*) were partly able to cross this divide. Sterne's apparent familiarity with both worlds may, on the other hand, be deceptive: whereas *Tristram Shandy* is quite literally a narrative of 'drawing rooms, hallways, and bedrooms', *A Sentimental Journey* is largely a journey in the mind.

Of all eighteenth-century writers, however, Smollett is surely the one most closely associated with the dynamic adventure story, or the 'narrative of the river'. He and Richardson thus seem to remain entrenched on their respective sides of this divide. In a spirit of compromise regarding the picaresque debate, then, Smollett's omnipresent journey motif and 'low scenes' might therefore be categorized as a kind of 'soft' or pseudo-picaresque, if not quite simply peripatetic narrative. But Smollett's narrator-persona is ultimately more traveller rather than *pícaro*: observer hero (Roderick), participating anti-hero (Peregrine or Fathom), quixotic seeker (Greaves) – and finally, fierce Juvenalian or milder Horatian satirist (functions largely split between Bramble and Jery).[43]

Such concepts are useful in constructing the somewhat meagre eighteenth-century genealogies of Smollett. One common fictional traveller of the period was the 'spy', the foreign or external observer of 'manners', as exemplified by Montesquieu's *Lettres persanes* (1721) or Goldsmith's *Citizen of the World* (1762). Roderick and Count Fathom, the Smollett protagonists normally identified most closely with the picaresque, are also outsiders providing an anatomy of English life. Through the *History and Adventures of an Atom*, on the other hand, Smollett also contributes to a group of tales with non-human narrators: the obvious immediate predecessor is Lesage's *Le Diable boiteux* ('The Devil upon Crutches'); the earliest one is Apuleius's *Golden Ass*, the only Latin novel of antiquity to survive in its entirety. Satirical observation and nonhuman narrator are notably combined in two novels by Smollett's contemporaries: Francis Coventry's *Pompey the Little* (1751), where the narrator–protagonist is a lap-dog, and Charles Johnstone's *Chrysal; or, The Adventures of a Guinea* (1760 and 1765).

In the nineteenth century, Smollett's reputation declined drastically and never really recovered. An important stimulus to John Surtees (who, in turn, stimulates few twentieth-century readers) and the early novels of Dickens, the spirit of Smollett hardly seems to survive beyond the satirical fictions of an Evelyn Waugh, or the literary pastiche of John Barth's *The Sot Weed Factor*.

In spite of their respective forms of originality, however, neither *Tristram Shandy* nor *Humphry Clinker* will reward participants in one more specific critical quest: the search for examples of free indirect discourse. Although a number of eighteenth-century novelists apparently avoided the device as vulgar, or confined it to isolated comic passages involving 'low' characters, neither the free-spirited Sterne nor the outspoken Smollett would presumably have had any such inhibitions. There is, in fact, a presumed example of FID in the first volume of *Tristram Shandy* (using the older punctuation convention of inverted commas), to record public reaction to Parson Yorick's new horse:

> The story ran like wild-fire. – 'The parson had a returning fit of pride which had just seized him; and he was going to be well mounted

once again in his life; and if it was so, 'twas plain as the sun at noon-day, he would pocket the expence of the licence, ten times told the very first year: – so that every body was left to judge what were his views in this act of charity.'   (I, 10)

In line with the hypothesis that most eighteenth-century writers con-sidered free indirect discourse (if not by that name) as only suitable for low scenes, the above passage thus becomes a comic evocation of the *vox populi*.

A further explanation for the rarity of FID in Sterne, however, is that the device is normally precluded by the use of the first-person autobio-graphical mode. The latter, at least, reached new stylistic heights, so that Virginia Woolf could write with awe of the sheer intimacy of Sterne's writing:

> the very punctuation is that of speech, not writing, and brings the sound, the associations of the speaking voice in with it. The order of the ideas, their suddenness and irrelevancy, is more true to life than to literature. . . . Under the influence of this extraordinary style the book becomes semi-transparent. The usual ceremonies and conven-tions which keep reader and writer at arm's length disappear. We are as close to life as we can be.[44]

Examples of such effects in *Tristram Shandy* are legion, although one might recall the disarming intrusion following the remarks on climate and character, where Tristram and Sterne himself could hardly be closer:

> – that observation is my own; – and was struck out by me this very rainy day, *March* 26, 1759, and betwixt the hours of nine and ten in the morning.   (I, 21)

But such sudden personal entries into what Frye classified as the fictional anatomy then have an uncanny resemblance to that earlier and quite different *Anatomy*, as when Burton announced his intention of discuss-ing other kinds of obsession:

> these more properly belong to *Melancholy*, of all which I will speak apart, intending to write a whole book of them.   (pp. 124–5)

The same stylistic and aesthetic considerations suggested for Sterne also apply to Smollett. His most personal narratives are the travelogues, whether documentary like the *Travels* or fictional as in *Humphry Clinker*; in neither case, however, would the formalities of current epistolary convention allow the raciness of free indirect discourse.

Smollett is not a rich source for authentic FID either, although he is master of another fairly similar technique. There is thus a scene in *Roderick Random* which conveys brilliantly the erotic tensions between the hero and his employer's wife and daughter:

> this good office I ow'd not to any esteem or consideration she had for me, but solely to the desire of mortifying her daughter, who on this occasion observ'd, that *let people be never so much in the right, there were some folks who would never do them justice; but to be sure they had their reason for it, which some people were not ignorant of, although they despised their little arts.*   (pp. 99–100; my emphasis)

With its blend of straight narration and oblique impersonation, the passage suggests the classic Bakhtinian polyphony (complete with 'hidden polemic') denoted by the Russian term, *skaz*.[45] *Skaz* refers to *somebody else's speech*, although it is not so much the oral mode of delivery that is important as the author's recruitment of an alternative voice. Such passages are probably the nearest Smollett, in turn, comes to the technique of free indirect discourse, discussed more fully in the final chapter.

Smollett, the irascible narrator of the *Travels through France and Italy*, is satirized in *A Sentimental Journey* as 'the learned Smelfungus'. *Tristram Shandy*, in turn, is rather trivialized in a series of comments in the *Critical Review* (some of these certainly by Smollett), as mere imitation of Rabelais. Connections between the two authors are otherwise meagre. Sterne and Smollett are therefore linked here more for their contrasts than their affinities. The novels discussed are nevertheless sometimes considered the last two landmarks of eighteenth-century fiction before the emergence of Jane Austen. The following two chapters should help to dispel such assumptions.

8

Charlotte Lennox's *The Female Quixote* and Frances Burney's *Evelina*

There are good grounds for discussing Lennox's *The Female Quixote* with Burney's *Evelina*, whether in terms of the similarities or the differences between the two novels. In the first respect, both novels feature naïve heroines from sheltered rural environments, forced to live through a painful socialization process, with all its attendant public embarrassment. Some form of sentimental education is central here, thus anticipating the concerns of the female *Bildungsroman* or 'novel of formation' proper, perfected by Jane Austen – who, incidentally, praised both of these writers.

On the other hand, the two novels also illustrate the binary distinction argued in this study between 'documentary' and 'literary' modes, demotic and hieratic impulses – or, quite simply, first- *versus* third-person narratives. Seen in these terms, Burney's epistolary (and therefore first-person) narrative, linked to the greatest private diary of the eighteenth century seems remote from Lennox's cautionary tale (with its 'omniscient' third-person narration), grounded in the conventions of parody and satire. For, in the latter respect, *The Female Quixote* is committed to a traditionally classical, and even specifically *Roman*, genre. As a result, its didactic intent is not always camouflaged by the kind of mimetic wizardry which the modern reader associates with Defoe or Richardson, not to mention Austen. In literary terms, moreover, the narrative also has a clearly parasitical relationship to the vast corpus of French heroic romances, which Lennox obviously knew intimately. Behind these, finally, lies the equally explicit literary model of Cervantes.[1]

Lennox (1729/1730?–1804) was born Charlotte Ramsay, the daughter of an English army officer.[2] She spent her adolescence in New York province, and her American reminiscences form the basis of her action-packed first novel, *The Life of Harriot Stuart*, published in 1751. For a short period before the publication of *The Female Quixote* (1752), she worked as an actress; for many years afterwards, she produced translations from the French; both activities were partly impelled by marriage to an impecunious Scot. After two undistinguished sentimental novels, she produced no more fiction for over thirty years, until the almost forgotten *Euphemia* in 1790. As her first epistolary novel, with a return to now topical American subjects (both Colonial and Native) and the introduction of some equally fashionable Gothic elements, *Euphemia* was nothing if not speculative. One contemporary reviewer also dismissed it as the kind of absurd romantic fantasy which the younger Lennox would have given short shrift.

The 'Adventures of Arabella', providing the sub-title of *The Female Quixote*, are generally unremarkable. Arabella's father, a Marquis banished from court, wishes to marry off his daughter to a favourite nephew, Mr Glanville; the heroine is less concerned about this parental imposition than about her suitor's disregard for the niceties of romance convention. On the premature death of the Marquis, Arabella (now alone with her servant, Lucy) becomes ward of Glanville's father and companion to his sister, both of whom arrive for an extended visit. Glanville's friend Sir George, a local baronet, becomes an admirer of Arabella. The highly episodic narrative is now generated through the resulting series of dramatic character pairings: Arabella and Lucy (a classic master/mistress and servant relationship); the two female cousins (*ingénue* and *coquette*); and the two gentlemen (Glanville, who suffers with Arabella, and Sir George, who mischievously humours her). A gradual cure for the heroine beckons when the action moves to Bath and the heroine is befriended by a wise and sympathetic Countess; the same Countess plays no part, however, in the abrupt but morally expedient *catastrophe*, or dramatic resolution, which occurs in London shortly afterwards.

Lennox's first and most obvious literary model is Cervantes. There are straightforward echoes of Don Quixote's delusions in the kind of scene where Arabella mistakes local haymakers for a band of kidnappers (Book IV, ch. 4), or confuses distant trees with knights on horseback (Book II, ch. 10). More interestingly, Arabella's sharpness on a number of topics *outside* heroic romances (see below) also reflects contemporary English readings of Don Quixote's character: typically considered ridiculous in the seventeenth century and sublime in the nineteenth, he was widely regarded in the age of sensibility as a fountain of wisdom and fine feelings in virtually any context except novels of chivalry.[3]

The Female Quixote also resembles *Don Quixote* in its initially episodic, even fragmentary, pattern grounded in parody and satire. There is a brief etiology of Arabella's disturbance (the early loss of her mother, extensive solitude in the country) every bit as sketchy as her Spanish predecessor's; after which both novels – *Don Quixote* initially, *The Female Quixote* consistently – use a limited number of formal devices rather than any psychological motivation for advancing the narrative: for Lennox, these include the conceptual misunderstandings already noted (Edward the gardener's boy mistaken for a knight in diguise is another example), and the frequent misreading of visual cues (in Arabella's confrontations with her various male suitors). Just as frequently, however, the confusion is semantic, with two common variants. According to the first of these, verbal misinterpretations arise from Arabella's habit of interrupting her interlocutor in mid-sentence before the exact sense of the argument is clear; and, more ingeniously, there are occasions when a misunderstanding centres on the ambiguities of particular words, such as 'histories' and 'favours', as in one spirited exchange between Arabella and Miss Glanville (Book II, ch. 9).[4]

The wide reliance on such generative devices fails to provide *The Female Quixote* with much dramatic momentum, or any other kind of sustaining power. In chapter 10 of Book I, for example, Arabella's father, the Marquis, rides out to take the evening air and falls from his horse (p. 35); his subsequent confinement allows the unsupervised Arabella to banish her cousin from the house (p. 36); the Marquis recovers overnight (p. 37), and learns with dismay of his nephew's departure (p. 38). The whole sequence thus lasts three pages. The scale of events recalls the early chapters of *Don Quixote* and the knight's first excursion before the introduction of Sancho, when Cervantes does not seem to have envisaged much more than a short literary parody. A later chapter heading of *The Female Quixote*, 'Containing some curious Anecdotes' (Book II, ch. 9), might actually provide an emblematic heading for the whole novel's piecemeal progress. Only in an episode such as the extraordinary appearance of the weeping Cynecia in Richmond Park does the narrative prove capable of mystery or suspense: Cynecia is, in fact, an actress hired by Sir George to discredit his rival, Glanville. There is a fitting musical analogue for the fragmentation of *The Female Quixote* in comparison with a later more intricately plotted high realist fiction: it suggests the 'Theme and Variations' before the advent of classical sonata form.

There are many other incidental details linking *The Female Quixote* with its Spanish avatar, such as the prominence of the priest in both narratives, the planned burning of the offending novels (an event only partly realized in *Don Quixote*) and, most conspicuously of all, the increasing involvement of Sir George Bellmour (like Sampson Carrasco) in the discourse of romance. He thus provides a mock personal 'History', occupying most of Book VI; a parody pastoral romance, with its burlesque of generic convention; and the concluding *History of the Princess of Gaul* (Book IX, ch. 4). All of these recall the long digressions in the first part of *Don Quixote*, related structurally or thematically in varying degrees to the main narrative. And finally, Lennox's obviously prodigious knowledge of French romances, like Cervantes's intimacy with the novels of chivalry, suggests a complexly ambivalent relation to the satirical target.[5]

Beside the protagonist of Lennox's novel, however, there is one other character with an obvious Cervantine analogue: Arabella's servant Lucy, the dramatic equivalent of Sancho Panza. Without the rich ambiguity of Don Quixote's squire and only occasionally falling under the influence of her mistress, she is generally introduced as a rational, sceptical, even *demotic* voice. Just occasionally, too, she manages to combine elements of convert and apostate, ingenuously confronting a heroic and *secular* code with a pragmatic but *Christian* one, as when Arabella seems resigned to letting Sir George die of unrequited love:

> To be sure, Madam, returned *Lucy*, your Ladyship knows what you ought to do better than I can advise your Ladyship, being that you are more learned than me: But, for all that, I think it's better to save Life than to kill, as the Bible-Book says; and, since I am sure your Ladyship is a good Christian, if the Gentleman dies for the Want of a few kind Words, or so, I am sure you will be troubled in Mind about it.   (p. 176)

The innocently ironic tone of the first sentence invites discussion of Lennox's pervasive use of satire. The latter, in *The Female Quixote*, is occasionally formal or *direct*, but predominantly *indirect*. The distinction here is the conventional one between a satiric voice addressed either straight to the reader, or to a formal *adversarius* within the text; and satire where characters or groups unwittingly render themselves ridiculous by what they say or do. There is a fairly benign example of the first type (in what is actually called a 'Chapter of the Satyrical Kind') when Arabella, the satirical *persona*, comments to Miss Glanville, her *adversarius*, on the ladies of Bath:

> What room, I pray you, does a Lady give for high and noble Adventures, who consumes her Days in Dressing, Dancing, listening to Songs, and ranging the Walks with People as thoughtless as herself? How mean and contemptible a Figure must a Life spent in such idle Amusements make in History? Or rather, Are not such Persons always buried in Oblivion, and can any Pen be found who would condescend to record such inconsiderable Actions?   (p. 279)

The effect of the passage is clearly enhanced by such sound views coming from a character otherwise regarded as deranged; or, from what might be called the method-in-madness dimension. The feature is also a staple of Cervantes.

The novel's more widespread *indirect* satire, on the other hand, is often inseparable from the stylistic parody of French heroic romances. Conspicuous examples of literary pastiche thus occur in Arabella's letters ('Whatever Offence your presumptuous Declaration may have given me, yet my Resentment will be appeased with a less Punishment than Death', p. 192). Book V, ch. 3. Miss Glanville herself, Arabella's future sister-in-law, provides some of the best examples of indirect satire, as in her comment on the Countess, whose intelligent concern first sets Arabella on the road to recovery:

> The Countess of —— is very well, to be sure, said Miss *Glanville*, yet I don't know how it is, she does not suit my Taste – She is very particular in a great many Things, and knows too much for a Lady, as I heard my Lord *Trifle* say one Day: Then she is quite unfashionable: She hates Cards, keeps no Assembly, is seen but seldom at Publick Places; and in my Opinion, as well as in a great many others, is the dullest Company in the World.   (p. 333)

There is also more topical *direct* satire, bordering on a kind of literary in-fighting and continuing a tradition running from Pope's *Dunciad* through Swift and Fielding. Here, too, are the first hints of an English literary pedigree for Lennox's novel. She mocks Grub Street and the London *literati* only a year after Smollett's grotesque 'Society of Authors' in *Peregrine Pickle*, and lets Glanville rag Sir George Bellmour for his misfired heroic parody, to which Sir George replies that he already has sufficient stock to set up for an author, and provides a satiric version of a hack's inventory.[6] And at this point, Lennox appears to assume Glanville's voice in order to settle some literary scores of her own:

> Nay, then, interrupted Mr *Glanville*, you are qualified for a Critic at the *Bedford* Coffee-house; where, with the rest of your Brothers, Demy-wits, you may sit in Judgment upon the Productions of a *Young*, a *Richardson*, or a *Johnson*. Rail with premeditated Malice at the *Rambler*; and, for the want of Faults, turn even its inimitable Beauties into Ridicule.   (pp. 252–3)

The hero of this particular exchange is clearly the editor of the *Rambler* himself, and Lennox's close friendship with the great Dr Johnson is well attested.[7] Johnson wrote the dedications for a number of her works, and Lennox's interest in the type of the novel-reading heroine also has Johnsonian echoes. The motif is already present in *The Life of Harriot Stuart*, where the heroine's mother complains that 'these horrid romances have turned the girl's brain' (p. 420); but the subsequent sketch of a deluded romance-reader called Imperia in Johnson's *Rambler*, no. 115 (23 April 1751) suggests a process of mutual stimulation between the two writers.

In 1751, on the other hand, the year before her novel appeared, Lennox met and was advised by Richardson. In this case, there is even a surviving correspondence on *The Female Quixote*, where Lennox refers intriguingly to an earlier planned conclusion requiring a third volume. Richardson advised against this move:

> The method you propose, tho' it might flatter my Vanity, yet will be thought a Contrivance between the Author of Arabella, and the Writer of Clarissa, to do credit to the latter; and especially if the Contraste will take up much Room in the proposed 3d Volume.[8]

The exact nature of the 'method' proposed remains a mystery, although it has been suggested that Lennox might have intended to imitate *Don Quixote* and *Clarissa* simultaneously by giving Arabella 'a fatal illness, a consequent realization of the follies of romances, and an exemplary, virtuous death' (p. 426). The fact that the original Preface to the fourth volume of *Clarissa* condemns romances, whilst the novel itself is such an outstanding example of moralistic fiction, may reinforce this hypothesis. Such theories are mere speculation, however, and Lennox's novel ends brusquely with its mixture of disquisition and sermon. As it stands, it is hard to avoid the impression that *The Female Quixote* has failed to emulate *Clarissa* by fully integrating the 'natural' and the moralistic; its elliptical conclusion, which suggests a literal rejection of Richardson for Johnson, certainly reflects the ultimate preference of a didactic, ethically motivated fiction based on literary models (and not only *Don Quixote*) over a 'natural', psychologically motivated narrative derived from 'non-literary' sources.

The conclusion, then, is certainly abrupt and unmistakably (perhaps quite literally) *Johnsonian*: the good doctor may have actually written it himself.[9] It is highly likely that Lennox's rubric (*Being in the Author's Opinion, the best Chapter in this History*) is a literary compliment, implying that Johnson's contribution was at least substantial.

Whatever the truth about this particular section, it clearly echoes what – for the present argument – are perhaps even more significantly Johnsonian opinions, those in Arabella's speech at Bath Assembly Rooms:

> The Ugliness of Vice, reply'd *Arabella*, ought only to be represented to the Vicious; to whom Satire, like a magnifying Glass, may aggravate every Defect, in order to make its Deformity appear more hideous; but since its End is only to reprove and amend, it should never be address'd to any but those who come within its Correction, and may be the better for it: A virtuous Mind need not be shewn the Deformity of Vice, to make it be hated and avoided; the more pure and uncorrupted our Ideas are, the less shall we be influenc'd by Example. A natural Propensity to Virtue or Vice often determines the Choice; 'Tis sufficient therefore to shew a good Mind what it ought to pursue, though a bad one must be told what to avoid. In a Word, one ought to be always incited, the other always restrain'd.
>
> (p. 277)

Arabella's sentiments are identical to those in a celebrated piece by Johnson urging that, in all writing, 'chastity of sentiment ought doubtless to be observed, and purity of manner to be represented'.[10] Johnson generally opposed the representation of vice, in what today might be called 'naturalistic' fiction, and was particularly concerned by 'mixed characters' where vice and virtue were portrayed in the same person; he was unlikely to be upset by *The Female Quixote*, although it is difficult to imagine the extraordinary achievement of *Clarissa* within the parameters of a Johnsonian aesthetic.

There is a slightly comic postscript to this particular debate, provided by the Italian ex-patriate writer Joseph Baretti. This scholar, translator and man of letters once exchanged language lessons with Lennox, and was also a long-time friend of Johnson's. He even wrote an 'Ode to Charlotte Lennox', which complains of a baleful Johnsonian influence on her fiction.[11] Poor Baretti was perhaps looking for a romantic *novelist*, but only found a didactic *author*.

The comparison between the Johnson of *Rasselas* and the Richardson of *Clarissa* is fruitful. The Preface to Volume I of *Clarissa* thus attempted to disarm those critics who would 'apprehend hurt to the morals of youth from the more freely-written letters', and insisted that the novel's two libertines, Lovelace and Belford, often make reflections on each other consistent with 'reasonable beings who disbelieve not a future state of rewards and punishments'; although one need only read Lovelace's uproarious parody of the marriage licence, or his irreverent related project of short-term marriages renewable each Valentine's Day, to suspect that Richardson has far exceeded his ethical brief, and is – perhaps unconsciously – celebrating his own inventive powers.

Terry Eagleton has speculated cleverly on the moral ambivalence the prudish Richardson must have felt in his highly convincing presentation of Lovelace;[12] and yet, by twentieth-century standards, *Clarissa* scores modestly on prurience, and even the most sensitive general readers have normally abandoned the novel for its preachiness as much as for its length. Morally edifying as its intention certainly was, however, Richardson's 'History of a Young Lady' is not quite didactic in the manner of *Rasselas*, Johnson's 'philosophical tale": the distinction between *ethically* and *psychologically* motivated fiction is again helpful. The author of *Clarissa* would doubtless have considered himself as ethically motivated as Johnson, although it is often his psychological insights which startle the modern reader. *The Female Quixote*, on the other hand, can be located more solidly in the ethical camp.

The relevance of this short literary digression is clearest from a glance at the latter part of Lennox's novel. When the narrative follows a classic eighteenth-century pattern by shifting the action to Bath, the satirical scope is enlarged, as is the potential for social embarrassment. Arabella's social rank ensures some tolerance for her eccentricities, but only the anonymous Countess (Book VIII, ch. 5) shows any genuine compassion for the heroine. Having been addicted to romances in her own youth, the Countess is well suited to undertake the heroine's rehabilitation. Initially even willing to converse in heroic style, herself, she nevertheless expresses relief that current 'Customs, Manners, Habits, and Inclinations' exclude the kind of adventure Arabella has read about. She then raises the issue of historical authenticity, but with a subtle ambivalence which implicates modern scepticism as much as romantic excess: 'such is the strange Alteration of Things, that some People I dare say at present, cannot be persuaded to believe there ever were Princesses wandering thro' the World' (p. 326). She finally returns to the semantic dimension with a warning about the 'free and licentious' modern associations of the word 'adventure' (p. 327); one wonders how the two women would have reacted to the comparable semantic shift in the phrase 'making love', between Lennox's day and our own.

The first encounter between Arabella and the Countess occupies two whole chapters, and there is every reason to expect a slow but effective cure. In the next chapter (Book VIII, ch. 8), however, the Countess is called away, never to return, and the scene shifts rapidly to London, concluding what is by far the shortest book in the novel. After some brief satire of London life, the story moves on rapidly to a climax, when Arabella plunges into the Thames to escape yet another party of presumed ravishers. Her cure is now effected by the 'Pious and Learned Doctor', with methods far less convincing than those of the brilliant Countess. This might be regarded as the victory of Johnsonian morality over Richardsonian psychology. The sentimental resolution of the narrative is as abrupt and perfunctory as the pathological one, as Arabella makes a declaration to Glanville strangely similar in style to the language she has used throughout the novel:

> To give you myself, said she with all my remaining Imperfections, is making you but a poor Present in return for the Obligations your generous Affection has laid me under to you; yet since I am so happy as to be desired for a Partner for Life by a Man of your Sense and Honour, I will endeavour to make myself as worthy as I am able of such a favourable Distinction. (p. 382)

If Dr Johnson had been a woman, he might have proposed like this. Glanville is understandably reduced to silence.

In historical perspective, then, *The Female Quixote* occupies an important position in that minor tradition in English fiction of satirical Quixotic imitations. The present study, particularly in the context of Smollett, has already noted the often conflictual narrative demands of satire and realism in eighteenth-century fiction; the question will return in no less a novelist than Austen, whose *Northanger Abbey* fails to achieve either the structural complexity of *Mansfield Park* or the impression of psychological depth found in *Emma*.

It is nevertheless pointless to condemn Lennox for a failure to achieve certain naturalistic effects which may have been quite foreign to her intentions. The purpose of the present discussion is not to judge Lennox by arbitrarily imposed aesthetic norms, but merely to reiterate that her novel is more *ethically* than *psychologically* motivated, an partial consequence of her dependence on a *classical* and *literary* model: that of satire. The same episodic pattern is typical, after all, in other explicitly satirical fiction of the proto-canon such as *Roderick Random* or *Peregrine Pickle*. By the same criteria, *The Female Quixote* would remain a pleasant enough minor classic, comparable perhaps to that other Quixotic imitation, *Sir Launcelot Greaves*, except that Smollett's novel is undoubtedly the weakest of his five, and Lennox's the strongest of hers.

To move beyond such bland judgements, however, it is necessary to speculate more freely, to look for subtexts and counter-narratives in *The Female Quixote*, to read – as it were – between the lines or against the grain. The two most obvious subversive readings of this kind are predictably gender-related. Passing comparisons between *Don Quixote* and *The Female Quixote* have hitherto largely ignored one essential distinction between the two novels: the sex of the respective protagonists and their creators. Lennox is clearly concerned to mediate a number of social conflicts facing young women of her day in the contexts of courtship and marriage – and most women, after all, had few other 'contexts'.

What is probably the crucial subtext of the novel, and thus complementary to the rehabilitation of the heroine from French romances, emerges with the arrival of Arabella's cousin, Charles Glanville, intended by the Marquis as his daughter's future husband. Arabella's initial reaction is predictably formulated in heroic terms: 'What Lady in Romance ever married the Man that was chose for her? In those cases the Remonstrances of a Parent are called Persecutions' (p. 27), but also accurately evokes increasing contemporary demands for companionate marriage after courtship by consent, to replace the arranged marriage under parental duress.[13] Arabella assures her father that she will obey him in 'all just and reasonable Things', on the assumption that he would 'never attempt to lay any Force upon her Inclinations'. Since Arabella has not met her cousin since she was eight, however, and the Marquis is described rather ominously as 'being perfectly assured of her Consent whenever he demanded it', it is as easy to admit the reasonableness of the supposedly deranged heroine as it is to share her misgivings.

When Glanville finally arrives, he is respectful enough by eighteenth-century standards of courtesy, although these will clearly not satisfy Arabella; together with her apparently extravagant behaviour, however, she makes a highly prophetic remark: '[I] shall be very well contented if I escape the Persecutions which Persons of my Sex, who are not frightfully ugly, are always exposed to' (p. 48). Her comment here seems to prefigure whole modern histories of sexual intimidation and harassment. Austen's Fanny Price, a far more self-effacing heroine, was to complain similarly sixty years later about male arrogance and presumption:

> Let him have all the perfections in the world, I think it not to be set down as certain, that a man must be acceptable to every woman he may happen to like himself.[14]

In the course of the novel, Arabella's concern about male attention might seem to reach paranoid proportions: anticipating a classic Freudian analytic gambit, she interprets explicit sexual interest at face value, but simultaneously assumes that the alternative of apparent indifference only indicates male concealment or repression; at one point, for example, she suspects a romantic (read erotic) interest on the part of her guardian uncle. There are nevertheless good reasons, then or now, for attributing consistent confusion of this kind to male behavioural patterns as much as to female paranoia. For Lennox captures exquisitely the central incongruity of courtship when the injured Arabella is taken up into the chaise of a young gentleman (Book II, ch. 11), who, 'being extremely glad at having so beautiful *a Creature in his Power*, told her she might *command him in all she pleased*' (emphasis added). Here, surely, is the paradox of erotic relations, the whole dynamic of *Clarissa* even, distilled into a mere three lines.

Arabella, and Lennox herself, seem to have an acute sense of an attractive young woman's ambiguous position in a male-dominated world. Arabella's chief tormentor, Sir George, out hunting is thus depicted at one point as 'a keen Sportsman, eagerly pursu[ing] the Game' (p. 154): in a writer extremely sensitive to polysemy, such a remark probably need no further comment. In an echo of the same metaphor, Hardy's Tess is seduced a century and a half later in the oldest *chase* [i.e. 'wood' or 'pursuit'] in England. Arabella's own sensitivity, which makes her see potential sexual abductors at every point, could even be read as a conditioned response to eighteenth-century male fetishism over female virginity.

One of the key fictional tropes for the latter, enshrined by *Pamela*, is the 'jewel' and Lennox has already been quite explicit in connecting the economic and the erotic; for, in a brilliant inversion of Fielding's acquisitive Shamela, she has Sir George 'meditating on the Means he should use to acquire the Esteem of Lady *Bella*, of whose Person he was a little enamoured, but of her Fortune a great deal more' (p. 129). Thus, the female novelist's exposure of male motivation is a neat inversion of the male author's interpretation of female impulses.

But Lennox's pointed subtext of eighteenth-century courtship patterns co-exists with a subversive counter-narrative on education. A seventeen-year-old girl brought up in rural isolation with a vast library of French romances cannot be expected to have a great awareness of classical culture. What little she possesses is limited to the heavily revisionist versions of ancient history supplied by her preferred reading. Even this is enough, however, to puncture the scholarly pretensions of the pedantic Mr Selvin at Bath.[15] Such satirical passages can seem tedious to the modern reader, but it is worth remembering again how jealously possessive gentlemen could be about their classical education. The fact clearly rankled with many intelligent women: in *Evelina*, Burney's Mrs Selwyn – surely the name is no coincidence – similarly exposes a group of university-educated wits over their inability to quote an ode of Horace.

With the introduction of the Countess, however, Lennox goes beyond simple male sham to question the uncritical adulation of heroic or chivalrous ideals, whether in ancient civilization or feudalism, an issue also dear to Richardson:

> The same Actions which made a Man a Hero in those Times, would constitute him a Murderer in These – And the same Steps which led him to a Throne Then, would infallibly conduct him to a Scaffold Now. (p. 328)

And to Arabella's astonished query as to whether the 'Heroes of Antiquity' are really bad, she responds: 'Judging them by the Rules of Christianity, and our present Notions of Honour, Justice, and Humanity, they certainly are.' Both Arabella and the Countess thus echo sentiments related to that ideological shift in later eighteenth-century fiction identified as the feminization of the novel.

The obvious counter-narrative to entrenched patriarchy, in Lennox's day no less than our own, is the utopia of equal opportunity for all, regardless of class or gender. And in the latter context, Glanville senior pays a fulsome tribute to Arabella's wit: 'if she had been a Man, she would have made a great Figure in Parliament, and ... her Speeches might have come perhaps to be printed in time' (p. 311). Much of the irony inherent in such a comment was not available to Arabella's future father-in-law: it would be almost two centuries before the wit of any woman could be heard in a parliament, whereas preferment would presumably have been a simple formality for the far duller Sir Charles; by way of a metafictional joke, on the other hand, all of Arabella's speeches, including her less lucid ones, are indeed printed, and generally stand comparison with anything the narrative offers by way of male authority.

The Female Quixote actually contains two other subsidiary female narratives, although one of these remains purely potential: the story of the pregnant Miss Groves, innocently extracted by Arabella from her maid (Book II, ch. 5), and Arabella's version of her own story – to be ghosted by Lucy (Book III, ch. 5) – a project left unrealized. The first of these accounts, as already suggested, is partly motivated by the author's wish to exploit the semantic ambiguities of words such as 'adventure' or 'favour'. Its surface comedy lies in the ingenuous Arabella's inability to understand what has actually *happened* to Miss Groves: in crudest terms, if she is incapable of understanding what it might mean for Miss Groves to have a 'story' *behind* her, she is certainly unable to appreciate how her two 'trips in the Country' for a lying-in might have been caused by stories *in front of* her as well. In terms of a gendered critique, however, the original question might be reformed to ask what actually *has* happened to Miss Groves: inviting not a self-righteous clucking at an indiscretion where the chief fault seems that of being discovered; but speculation on the seduction and deceit which may have led to this particular chain of circumstances. The modern reader is naturally at liberty to extract such subtexts from *The Female Quixote*: such processes may even be a pre-requisite for a twentieth-century recuperation of the novel.

The non-realization of the second female narrative derives from Lucy's inability ever to achieve the recital of Arabella's experiences ('it is not such simple Girls as I can tell Histories', p. 121). Lucy's failure could be read as an indirect comment on the narrative strategies available in *The Female Quixote*. Lennox rejected a first-person narrative from the mouth of either Arabella or Lucy, in favour of a detached, all-purpose extradiegetic third-person narrator. Her ultimate failure to write a naturalistic novel rather than an exemplary tract may be connected with this insistence on maintaining full narratorial authority.

It is one of the lasting achievements of Burney's *Evelina*, on the other hand, that it exemplifies precisely this naturalism in the form of a letter fiction.

In conclusion, then, *The Female Quixote* is a prime example of an eighteenth-century fiction with an even parasitical dependence on literary sources. It is also an exclusively third-person narration – although by a woman writer – suggesting that here, in some ways, there may have been a *novelist* aspiring to be an *author*. And the latter proposal is not entirely facetious: Lennox never produced another novel to match *The Female Quixote*; but in the very next year she began publishing her notorious *Shakespear Illustrated; or, The Novels and Histories, on Which the Plays of Shakespear Are Founded, Collected and Translated* (3 vols, 1753–4), with its harsh strictures on the dramatist's misuse of his own sources.[16] This is prescriptivism run riot, and even Lennox's sympathetic first biographer baulks at such 'pseudo-classical standards of Probability, Decorum, and Poetical Justice'.

Evelina

The structural and ideological poles proposed for eighteenth-century fiction are also evident in Burney's *Evelina*. In terms of the *patrician/ plebeian* or *hieratic/demotic* oppositions, for example, Burney's first novel is even remoter than *The Female Quixote* from the authoritative assumptions of a Fielding. It is, after all, an epistolary novel – and thus a first-person narrative; most of the letters are supplied, moreover, by the timid, self-effacing heroine, ambiguously linked with the twenty-six-year-old subject of a voluminous private journal.[17]

The specifically *demotic* character of *Evelina* is also virtually ensured by the mere fact of the writer's sex, if further reinforced by her education and socio-economic background. The daughter of Britain's first musicologist, Burney was born in King's Lynn in 1752, the publication year of Lennox's *The Female Quixote*. Her unpromising intellectual beginnings (at the age of eight, she was still unable to read) were combined with a painful reticence: she burned all her early works, including a manuscript novel, in 1767. By the age of twelve, however, she was exploiting her father's excellent library; and – more significantly still – only four years later, shortly after destroying her juvenilia, she began her diary. Elements of the lost novel, entitled *The History of Caroline Evelyn*, apparently survive in the first four letters of *Evelina*, published in January 1778. By this point, Burney had been keeping her diary for ten years; she was to continue it for another fifty, to provide one of the most remarkable social documents of the eighteenth century.[18]

Like Lennox's, Burney's novel-writing career spanned five decades; unlike Lennox's, it evolved remarkably over this period. After *Evelina*, Burney abandoned the epistolary method to produce *Cecilia* (1782), perhaps the finest novel of manners before Austen, but also – with its complex plot of a young woman's inheritance conditional on retaining her maiden name – a fable of feminine identity. *Camilla* (1796), nominally another courtship novel, further extends the writer's social and psychological range. Almost twenty years later, Burney published her massive and many-sided *The Wanderer; or, Female Difficulties* (1814): set against the background of the French Revolution, her final novel is also her most explicitly feminist work in its study of the meagre range of economic choices available to the unmarried middle-class woman in England.

At its simplest, *Evelina* is – as its subtitle emphasizes – the story of a young woman's entry into the world.[19] Brought up in the rural seclusion of Howard Grove by her over-protective guardian, Villars, the orphan Evelina is apparently the unacknowledged daughter of the wealthy Sir John Belmont. Her move to London with the daughter and granddaughter of Villars's friend Lady Howard is therefore not merely a young woman's conventional coming out, but another more literal quest for female identity. Her experiences in London amply justify views of the novel as an epic of social embarrassment and, less frequently but just as prominently, of sexual harassment. The first element is generated by the heroine's relations to Lord Orville, Burney's male paragon, suggestively equidistant in time between the protagonist of *Sir Charles Grandison* (1753–4) and Darcy in *Pride and Prejudice* (1813); it is compounded by experiences with her vulgar maternal grandmother, Mme Duval, and the latter's circle, in scenes sometimes recalling the Price family of *Mansfield Park*. In the context of sexual harassment, however, Evelina's scourge, Sir Clement Willoughby, shares little more than a name with the villain of *Sense and Sensibility*. For *Evelina* is a remarkably explicit novel: the two London sections of Volume I, the new London episodes of Volume II – after a brief interlude at Howard Grove – and the dramatic climax of the novel at Bristol Hotwells and Clifton, are worlds away from Austen's self-proclaimed two square inches of ivory.

It seems remarkable that such a respectable critic as Walter Allen could once refer disparagingly to Burney's limited scope in terms of 'tea-parties'.[20] The idea is amusing, although the same crude kind of caricature would logically reduce Fielding's novels to rather drunken young men entering the wrong bedrooms in country inns; neither definition is quite the whole story. Within the conventions of sentimental narrative, among which the heroine's chastity remains paramount, *Evelina* at least is a remarkable chronicle of ill humour, aggression and physical violence, more reminiscent of *Roderick Random* than *Pride and Prejudice*. No Jane Austen heroine, for example, is ever physically accosted by a man or thrown on the protection of prostitutes in a public place; and even then, largely focused through the journal of a timid *ingénue*, *Evelina* is necessarily limited by Burney's own autobiographical parameters. There is even less time for tea-parties in *The Wanderer; or, Female Difficulties*; whilst Burney's real-life female difficulties included a mastectomy performed in her own kitchen without anaesthetic, an operation described in detail in her own journal.

Despite the novel's epistolary form and its author's own remarkable journal, however, literary modes are still initially as prominent as their documentary counterparts; for *Evelina* has one of the most substantial prefaces in eighteenth-century fiction, with Burney anxiously defending the *novel* as genre, even as she genders the *novelist* as male:

> In the republic of letters, there is no member of such inferior rank, or who is so much disdained by *his brethren* of the quill, as the humble Novelist: nor is *his* fate less hard in the world at large, since, among the whole class of writers, perhaps not one can be named, of whom the votaries are more numerous, but less respectable.
>
> Yet, while in the annals of those few of our predecessors, to whom this species of writing is indebted for being saved from contempt, and rescued from depravity, we can trace such names as Rousseau, Johnson, Marivaux, Fielding, Richardson, and Smollett, no *man* need blush at starting from the same post, though many, nay, most *men*, may sigh at finding themselves distanced.   (p. 7; my emphasis)

As eighteenth-century prefaces go, Burney's follows those of *Joseph Andrews* or *Roderick Random* in their concern for literary pedigree, without entirely rejecting those of *Robinson Crusoe* or *Pamela* in their anxious moral justifications. Remarkable here is the emphatic triple dismissal of writer (*the humble novelist*), the text (*depravity*) *and* the reader (*less respectable*) in one fell swoop; only the writer is later effectively redeemed. There is presumably some ironic exaggeration here, although Burney's gendering of these experiences is probably quite unconscious. The passage provides an interesting contrast to the spirited defence of novels made in chapter 5 of *Northanger Abbey*, with its beautiful compliment to Burney's *Cecilia* and *Camilla*:

> only some work in which the greatest powers of the mind are displayed, in which the most thorough knowledge of human nature, the happiest delineation of its varieties, the liveliest effusions of wit and humour are conveyed to the world in the best chosen language.

The narrative voice here is as forthright as anything in the Austen *Juvenilia*, although the novelist does shelter behind a fictional character. Burney herself remained more ambivalent on the issue of imaginative fiction, however, later even insisting that *Camilla* was not a novel at all, but a 'work' in which characters and morals were put into action. And in the Preface to *The Wanderer* (1814), exactly contemporary with Scott's *Waverley*, she was still apologizing for the novel as genre.

The Preface to *Evelina* nevertheless acknowledges a group of six illustrious predecessors. In this, it recalls the opening chapter of *Ferdinand Count Fathom*, where a similarly defensive Smollett offers no less than seven 'ancients' and seven 'moderns' in an attempt to forestall possible accusations of indelicacy. *Evelina*, although not as bland as is often assumed, hardly needs this kind of special pleading. There is good reason, however, to regard the six authors listed as reflecting, in roughly ascending order, their respective degrees of relevance to Burney's first novel. In the case of Rousseau, she is presumably thinking of his *Julie, ou la Nouvelle Héloïse* (1761), a highly successful epistolary romance.[21] Johnson, in contrast, was the literary figure Burney knew best, on a purely personal level, although the reference here might be read more as respectful homage than practical acknowledgement. Marivaux, most recognized in England at the time for the sentimental but realistic *Vie de Marianne* (1731–41), also seems to have more diffuse literary links with Burney; he is omitted entirely from the author's subsequent recapitulation of her literary mentors: 'enlightened by the knowledge of Johnson, charmed with the elequence of Rousseau, softened by the pathetic powers of Richardson, and exhilarated by the wit of Fielding, and humour of Smollett' (p. 9).

The influence of Fielding on Burney, however, is pervasive, although it is not always easy to define. When *Evelina* was published, Fielding was still a literary yardstick for many, and the tradition of linking the two novelists dates from early comparisons in no way detrimental to Burney: the early reception of her first novel was enthusiastic. In broadest thematic terms, there are analogies between Fielding and Burney in such classic topics as the *art* versus *nature*, or *town* versus *country* debates. More concretely, one may point to various theatrical elements or visual effects in *Evelina* which probably reflect an absorption of Fieldingesque techniques (as well as Burney's own dramatic gifts). A prominent example is the *vignette* or *tableau*, in which the exact expression or physical reaction of each participant is listed, such as one scene where Sir Clement Willoughby's attempts at conversation are met with stony silence: 'Mr Smith seemed afraid, young Branghton ashamed, M. Du Bois amazed, Madame Duval enraged, and myself determined not to interfere' (p. 209).

The major intertextual relations of *Evelina*, however, point unambiguously to Richardson, and – more surprisingly – to Smollett. Burney doubtless had her eye on the latter in her more grotesque and farcical scenes, such as the first confrontation between Captain Mirvan and Mme Duval (Volume I, ch. 14), or the fall of Mme Duval and M. Dubois into the mud (Volume I, ch. 16). The long and complicated hoax, by which Captain Mirvan sends Mme Duval off after M. Dubois, to have her assaulted and left bound in a ditch, recalls the practical jokes of *Peregrine Pickle*; the violent emotions and physical aggression, as when Mme Duval slaps Evelina and spits in the captain's face, seem to echo *Roderick Random*.

In certain structural features, in fact, Smollett provides even more significant parallels: after she has exploited the crude but limited farcical potential of Captain Mirvan, Burney introduces a more rewarding narrative foil in Mrs Selwyn, who is thus able to carry the novel's harshest satire, without compromising the affability of the heroine. This literary division is exactly analogous to the one existing between the young protagonist and the misanthrope, Cadwallader, in the second half of *Peregrine Pickle*: in a kind of generic split, Smollett can rechannel some of Peregrine's satirical venom, even if his hero's priggishness seems to remain beyond cure. Evelina is neither venomous nor priggish, and, for these very reasons, a genuine satirical foil is indispensable for a writer as shrewdly critical and comically talented as Burney.

To conclude the analogy between *Evelina* and Smollett: it is rather as if Burney were letting *Humphry Clinker*'s much patronized Lydia Melford tell her own story in full detail; whilst the reactions of Jery Melford, Smollett's main satirical foil, followed Mrs Selwyn in *Evelina* by being thoroughly subsumed within the heroine's own correspondence. And a final parallel with Smollett is Burney's constant recourse to the most blatant romance conventions of true love, courtship and marriage; and not for simple motives of parody, or even indirect satire, as in *The Female Quixote*, but as a fundamental structural device, with all its potential for excitement and suspense. The obvious parallel here is again *Roderick Random*.

As already suggested, however, Burney's most important predecessor is Richardson, both in terms of epistolary form (whether letter or journal) and in overall thematics (courtship, marriage, and the broader socialization process of the young heroine). There is a lurking paradox here, since *Evelina*'s epistolary mode – in its literary debt to Richardson – is also indirectly reliant on 'non-literary' or 'documentary' forms. There is no reason, however, to repress such an apparent contradiction. By Burney's day, the elements of my original fictional matrix are becoming blurred: it is still possible to identify later eighteenth-century novels with predominantly literary or non-literary models, respectively, but it is also necessary to recognize a kind of fictional self-reflexivity: as the eighteenth-century proto-canon emerged, Burney could also follow in the path of a *literary* giant like Richardson, himself almost exclusively conditioned – through both education and temperament – by the mimetic power of *non-literary* forms. By the time of Austen, who could draw on the tradition of Richardson *and* Burney, as much as that of Fielding *and* Lennox, the distinction is further subverted, so as to become virtually meaningless.

The question of classical literary models emerges most conspicuously in the second volume of the novel. It centres round the issue of satire, with the introduction of Mrs Selwyn, the 'lady of large fortune' who takes Evelina to Bristol Hotwells for her health. The heroine's account of her new companion is revealing in several ways:

> Mrs. Selwyn is very kind and attentive to me. She is extremely clever; her understanding, indeed, may be called *masculine*; but, unfortunately, her manners deserve the same epithet; for, in studying to acquire the knowledge of the other sex, she has lost all the softness of her own. In regard to myself, however, as I have neither courage nor inclination to argue with her, I have never been personally hurt at her want of gentleness; a virtue which, nevertheless, seems so essential a part of the female character, that I find myself more awkward, and less at ease, with a woman that wants it, than I do with a man. She is not a favourite with Mr. Villars, who has often been disgusted at her unmerciful propensity to satire. (pp. 268–9)

The entire passage, like many in Burney, has a density of allusion and depth of implication to rival Austen. Mrs Selwyn's cleverness is indirectly characterized as uncommon to her sex, although, in the light of influential contemporary advice to women, the novelty may lie less in the possession than in the display of such intelligence.[22] A financially independent widow, Mrs Selwyn has long been absolved from strict adherence to roles imposed by men, whether father, husband, or suitor; she regularly speaks her own mind, whatever the cost to fragile male egos.

Evelina's own exemption from attack, which she herself attributes to lack of combativeness, may actually owe more to a nature generally free from social vices: Lord Orville also largely escapes Mrs Selwyn's satire for the same reason. It is unsurprising, on the other hand, that Mrs Selwyn is unpopular with the pompously patriarchal Villars. Evelina's own reservations about her companion are based entirely on gender expectations: Mrs Selwyn displays none of the 'softness' or 'gentleness' associated with the female sex, suggesting that Burney's proto-feminism – however sharp – is not revolutionary. Rather than censuring women for behaviour she regarded as masculine, for example, she might have exposed in men some of the very qualities she reductively perceives in women. Such an approach would certainly have corresponded more closely to the kind of feminization process which social historians have traced in eighteenth-century life, and critics and theorists have found in eighteenth-century fiction.[23]

In the present context, however, the most interesting detail in Evelina's description may be the explicit *gendering* of Mrs Selwyn's intellect: the association of the 'propensity to satire' with a *masculine* understanding is no coincidence. Quintessentially classical (and the one unambivalently Roman literary genre) as already suggested, satire is also, by historical association, a predominantly masculine technique, even if Manley was an able enough satirist to collaborate with Swift.[24] In its more ephemeral form of 'raillery', satire is condemned in both *The Female Quixote* and *Evelina*, as well as by Johnson and Richardson, the respective chief ideological mentors of the two novels.

By a neat structural irony, however, it is precisely male ignorance of a classical satirist which motivates one of Mrs Selwyn's earliest attacks in the third volume of the novel. When each of Mrs Beaumont's dinner guests is asked to propose the topic of a wager, Mrs Selwyn suggests the prize go to '*him* who can repeat by heart the longest ode of Horace' (p. 290). Neither the aristocrat, Lord Merton, nor the parliamentarian, Lovell, is able to quote a line. The joke highlights a common source of resentment among eighteenth-century women of letters (it was also noted in the context of *The*

Female Quixote) about proprietorial male attitudes towards the classics. It is a point close enough to the writer's heart to recur in subsequent novels.[25] Burney herself received Latin lessons from no less a teacher than Dr Johnson, although she had mixed feelings about spending 'so much time to acquire something I shall always dread to have known'. The novelist's father found Latin 'too masculine for Misses'.[26]

And if Burney was sensitive about her knowledge of Latin, she was made to feel equally self-conscious about her satirical gifts. The immediate successor to *Evelina* was not, in fact, *Cecilia* but an unperformed comedy entitled 'The Witlings'.[27] Even at the age of twenty-six, Burney still seems quite reconciled to paternal censorship, and her own response is conciliatory: 'I would a thousand times rather forfeit my character as a writer, than risk ridicule or censure as a female'.[28] Such sentiments invite reconsideration of the ambivalent relationship between the heroine of *Evelina* and the autobiographical subject of the *Early Diary, 1768–78*. Burney's novel has already been characterized as an epic of social embarrassment; and even the most cursory review of the writer's private reactions immediately around publication reveals uncanny similarities of voice and phrase between Burney and her fictional heroine: 'I am frightened out of my wits from the terror of being attacked *as an author*, and therefore *shirk*, instead of *seeking*, all occasions of being drawn into notice'; 'Let them criticise, cut, slash without mercy my book, and let them neglect me; but may God avert my becoming a public theme for ridicule.'[29]

It seems inevitable to regard *Evelina* as in some way autobiographical, although parallels between the novel and the life in Burney probably refer almost exclusively to moods and sentiments rather than to concrete events: at precisely the age when the timid and self-effacing Evelina made her entry into the world, for example, the similarly timid and self-effacing Burney began her own early journal addressed to a 'Nobody'. There is simply no eighteenth-century narrative, not even Richardson's imaginative projections, which conveys as convincingly as Burney's first novel *or* early journal what a young woman felt or experienced. And here, perhaps, Walter Allen redeems himself with a more perceptive comment, even if it suggests an acquaintance with Burney limited to *Evelina*:

To read Miss Burney is rather like having a mouse's view of the world of cats: the cats are very terrifying, but the mouse's sense of the ridiculous could not be keener.[30]

Further light may be thrown both on Burney's generic relations – whether autobiographical impulses transformed, or satirical ones repressed – and on her family relations – a case, perhaps, of paternal authority flouted – by a return to the text itself.

Evelina is, above all, an epistolary novel: perhaps, together with *Clarissa* and *Humphry Clinker*, one of the three most formally satisfying examples of a quintessentially eighteenth-century form. Modern criticism tends to use the term interchangeably with the newer coinage, 'letter fiction', although it is worth considering whether there is anything to be gained in attempting to distinguish between the two labels. The 'epistle', both from classical times (Pliny the Elder) and in the Christian tradition (St Paul), had a certain formality; it was suitable, even consciously intended, for some kind of 'publication', or at least wider dissemination. 'Letter' is the generic term, but can also be reserved for a more private and intimate form of writing. In the latter sections of *Clarissa*, on the other hand, the heroine's correspondence assumes canonic status (the Epistles of St Clarissa, as it were) as it is passed around among the other characters, and even Pamela's later writings acquire great authority and prestige. If one uses the distinction suggested above, then, *Pamela* and *Clarissa* are '*letter* fictions' fast transformed into true '*epistolary* novels'.

On the other hand, letters often presume a respondent as much as a recipient. *Clarissa*, with its complex structure concentrated on two corresponding couples, is the classic example of the former; but even *Humphry Clinker*'s five letter-writers each have a cleverly individuated *implied* receiver. Richardson's first novel is less interesting here; unlike *Pamela*, however, *Evelina* does not gradually modulate (or, arguably, even degenerate) into a journal, but follows a presumably preconceived pattern, as a brief structural analysis will illustrate.

Of the thirty-one letters in the first volume, the expository first nine are examples of genuine reciprocal correspondence, with Villars (the heroine's elderly guardian) and Lady Howard (her equally aged patroness) supplying four each. Evelina's only contribution at this stage is a request to accompany Lady Howard's daughter and granddaughter to London. Letters 10–23 actually constitute a London *journal* sent in instalments to Villars, with the sole exception of letter 15, where Villars passes judgement on events to date. Letter 24 expresses the guardian's relief at his ward's safe return to Howard Grove, after which there is another exchange of letters between Villars and Lady Howard (letters 27–31) on the possibility of Evelina gaining her father's recognition; Evelina (letter 30) expresses characteristic alarm at the idea.

Of the thirty letters in the second volume, no less than twenty-four are by Evelina; the remainder – with the exception of number 4, where Sir John Belmont denies paternity – are from Villars. The journal structure is now more prominent than ever: letters 1–3 and 5 thus provide an account of Howard Grove, before three letters of advice from Villars; the major part of the narrative (letters 9–24) then covers the month Evelina spends with her London relatives. Villars punctuates the new London series with a homily in letter 18, and terminates it by welcoming Evelina home in letter 25. With the heroine now installed at Berry Hill, her last five letters are necessarily addressed to Lady Howard's granddaughter, Maria Mirvan.

The twenty-three letters of the third volume, finally, are weighted even more heavily in the heroine's favour, with nineteen to Villars's three, the remaining item being a letter written by Evelina's long-dead mother. Here, too, the narrative divisions are simple, with letters 1–3 coming from Bristol Hotwells (where Evelina is sent with Mrs Selwyn to improve her health), and the remainder addressed from Mrs Beaumont's house in neighbouring Clifton. The whole is briefly punctuated by a little more of Villars's commentary (letters 6 and 12) and concluded by his consent to Evelina's marriage (letter 22).

Evelina, then, could be regarded as a letter fiction fast transforming itself into a journal, albeit one organized in instalments for the greater convenience of its two internal readers, Villars and Lady Howard. The point throws interesting light on the recurrent issue of first- and third-person narrators. The epistolary novel presupposes a first-person narrator (or narrators) by definition. When the novel's two early and elderly correpondents, Villars and Lady Howard, focus entirely on Evelina, however, the effect of such perspectives, particularly with the censoriously didactic Villars, is not unlike that of an authoritative third-person narrator. The growing marginalization of Villars at the expense of Evelina in the course of the novel could then be seen as representing a gradual subversion of third-person 'omniscience' by these new perspectives. Such claims are also substantiated by simple numerical evidence. The share of Evelina's guardian, Villars, and the family friend, Lady Howard, over three volumes is fourteen, five, and three letters respectively; or, in simple quantitative terms, over 20 per cent of the first volume, and barely 5 per cent in each of the remaining two.

The small number of letters by Lady Howard and Villars makes additional analysis easier, and, since the former never writes directly to Evelina, attention may be confined to the latter. The immediate impression here is that Villars was hardly Evelina's ideal correspondent:

his patience must have been sorely tried by the Pamela-like trivia of his ward's early letters.[31] To her credit, Evelina seems aware of her own limitations: 'pray excuse this wretched stuff I write, perhaps I may improve by being in this town, and then my letters will be less unworthy your reading' (p. 28). Her self-awareness grows rapidly, in fact, and soon it is Villars's responses which are not always adequate to Evelina's letters. He stiffly acknowledges his ward's reports, but offers little else beyond a lugubrious comment on London: 'the dissipation in which I find you are involved fill[s] me with uneasiness' (p. 55).

Villars later writes to welcome Evelina back to Howard Grove (Volume I, letter 24), offering some banal reflections on town *versus* country:

> Alas, my child, the artlessness of your nature, and the simplicity of your education, alike unfit you for the thorny paths of the great and busy world. The supposed obscurity of your birth and situation, makes you liable to a thousand disagreeable adventures. Not only my views, but my hopes for your future life, have ever centered in the country.   (p. 116)

Unremarkable for its recycling of a hoary neo-Augustan *topos*, the passage is more interesting for its total repression of any form of gender awareness on the part of the writer; or, as a more astringent modern gloss might put it, 'you've been kept naive and ignorant, so you have no prospects; the fact you're a nobody will expose you to constant sexual harassment and exploitation; and I'd always intended you should stay at home and look after me, anyway!' It is unsurprising that some readers have even seen Burney as satirizing the over-fussy paternal figure; the circumstances of her own life certainly provided material.

Villars has two more letters in Volume I, that to Lady Howard being by far the longest he ever writes. It is notable for an unwavering advocacy of patriarchal authority, as exemplified by the promise to Evelina's mother, '*That her child, if it lived, should know no father, but myself, or her acknowledged husband*' (p. 125), and his horrified opposition towards suing Sir John Belmont over Evelina's paternity ('A child to appear against a father! – no, Madam', p. 128). Again, it is not hard to see the figure of Dr Burney behind such sentiments. Villars's own aims are quite restricted:

> My plan, therefore, was not merely to educate and to cherish her as my own, but to adopt her as the heiress of my small fortune, and to

bestow her upon some worthy man, with whom she might spend her days in tranquillity, chearfulness, and good-humour, untainted by vice, folly, or ambition. (pp. 126–7)

Since Evelina's new friend, Mrs Selwyn, procures in a couple of weeks the recognition that neither Villars nor Lady Howard could obtain in seventeen years, both filial duty and social deference might seem over-rated.

Villars's three letters to Evelina at Howard Grove (Vol. II, letters 6–8) before her departure to London include a little officious advice: 'Remember, my dear Evelina, nothing is so delicate as the reputation of a woman: it is, at once, the most beautiful and most brittle of all human things' (p. 164). His subsequent censure of Macartney, 'the Scotch poet' ('he should endeavour by activity and industry to retrieve his affairs; and not pass his time in idle reading', p. 216), suggests further limitations in empathic ability.

The final volume contains just three more letters from Villars: the first includes the uncompromising edict against further contact with Lord Orville ('You must quit him! – his sight is baneful to your repose, his society is death to your future tranquillity!' p. 309), which causes Evelina such social embarrassment and emotional turmoil; the second advises capitulation in face of the false Miss Belmont ('the birth of my Evelina will receive a stigma, against which honour, truth, and innocence may appeal in vain!' p. 337). From this point onwards, Evelina effectually exercises independent judgement: in the case of Lord Orville, paternal authority is undermined; and where Sir John Belmont is concerned, the final reconciliation is on Evelina's initiative. Villars's final task is to sanction the marriage to Orville, although he keeps heroine and reader in suspense until the last letter proper of the novel. By now, however, the marriage arrangements are made, and so well have Evelina and Mrs Selwyn managed things, that Villars's consent is a pure formality.

With their exclusive focus on Evelina, the letters of Villars acquire a kind of narrative authority analogous to the moral authority he exercises as guardian. And just as this moral authority is questioned by a series of unfortunate judgements in the course of the novel, so his narrative authority is similarly undermined as it becomes increasingly marginalized. The polarity proposed for eighteenth-century fiction between male *authority* and female *novelty* is thus replicated, where *Evelina* is concerned, by an analogous division between third- and first-person narrators.

Lennox and Burney

Despite their obvious structural and generic differences, there is an abiding impression of unexpected similarities between the two novels. Two specific parallels each illustrate a kind of structural *chiasmus* or 'cross-over' in this respect.

In the first instance, both novels provide a seemingly endless sequence of confusion and misunderstanding. *Evelina* is not the only epic of social embarrassment; the pattern is central to *The Female Quixote*, too, although here it normally involves the heroine's suitor, Glanville. A turning-point is then reached in each novel when the respective co-protagonists, Burney's Lord Orville and Lennox's Arabella, become subject to the same kind of confusion, themselves: in each case, the process marks a kind of sympathetic participation across barriers of class and/or gender and lays the basis for the sentimental resolution of the novel. The second type of cross-over concerns the narrative conventions of the two novels. *The Female Quixote* begins with a conventionally omniscient third-person narrator, and *Evelina* uses the intimacy of the private journal. Lennox then introduces a number of subordinate first-person narratives, together with an indirect metafictional critique of the third-person form; Burney, on the other hand, gradually marginalizes Villars's voice and simultaneously erodes his authority, which is tantamount to privileging *first-* over *third-* person narrative.

A final parallel between the two writers regards their respective careers: as noted above, both produced novels over a period of five decades. With its partly outmoded satirical frame, Lennox's formally most successful work constitutes a literary dead-end; for Burney, on the other hand, the points of intersection with other eighteenth-century novelists are so many as almost to defy classification. Some literary relations of both writers are considered below.

The Female Quixote belongs to a group of eighteenth-century 'Quixote novels', which would include Smollett's *Sir Launcelot Greaves* and Richard Graves's *The Spiritual Quixote* (1773), as well as such anonymous productions as *The Country Quixote* (1785), *The Amicable Quixote* (1788) and *The Political Quixote* (1797). From the turn of the century came Charles Lucas's *The Infernal Quixote* (1801), attacking Godwin's *Political Justice*, as well as Eaton Stannard Barrett's *The Heroine*, warmly praised by Jane Austen and providing another precursor of *Northanger Abbey*.[32] The most obvious English antecedent of *The Female Quixote* is Fielding's *Joseph Andrews* (1742), described on the title page as 'Written in Imitation of the Manner of Cervantes': like that of Parson Adams, Arabella's knowledge of the world is derived entirely from books. But since the good parson is unlikely to be seduced, while his favourite guide is the Greek dramatist Aeschylus, detailed comparisons are unhelpful.

A more pertinent predecessor of Arabella is the romance-reading Nancy Williams in Smollett's *Roderick Random* (1748). Roderick's sometime ally and companion had been seduced as a young girl, apparently victim of a sensibility enflamed by novel-reading. Her development corresponds closely to contemporary constructions of femininity, inscribed within the vicious circle of female education: if a woman had none, she would remain ignorant and foolish; if she had any at all, particularly of a sentimental kind, her 'natural' susceptibility as a woman would expose her to sexual exploitation.[33] The novel-consuming female is an eighteenth-century fictional stereotype, with the disturbing hidden assumption that many young women's problems are merely due to unsuitable reading. It is notable that, after her own early novel-reading heroine Catherine Morland, Jane Austen was never so simplistic again.

A broader and shrewder inventory of female difficulties, even before she explicitly used the phrase for the sub-title of her last novel, appears in the fiction of Burney. A major point of reference between Richardson and Austen, she can be inserted into most genealogies of the late eighteenth-century novel: the pre-feminist novel, the novel of manners, the novel of sentiment, or the didactic novel linked to the contemporary tradition of courtesy books. All of these elements can in turn be related to a tendency identified by prominent social historian Lawrence Stone, and elaborated by leading literary theorist Nancy Armstrong: the *feminization* of eighteenth-century life. The latter concept is linked with new forms of autonomy and, above all, new kinds of relations between the sexes, reflecting what Stone calls 'affective individualism' and the 'companionate marriage'.[34]

Such issues are reflected in the great amount of contemporary fiction dealing with courtship; critic Katherine Sobba Green has listed forty-nine important examples of this feminized genre.[35] Besides *Pamela* and *Clarissa*, the six major novels of Austen, and three each of Lennox and Burney (including, of course, *The Female Quixote* and *Evelina*), the list would include fiction by Collyer, Haywood, Frances Brooke, Mackenzie, Smith and Edgeworth. To the modern reader, a narrative of conventional courtship may not seem a promising vehicle for a fundamental questioning of gender roles; the form was not, however, beneath the consideration of the Jacobin novelist Holcroft, in *Anna St Ives* (1792), the radical Inchbald, *A Simple Story* (1791), or the revolutionary Wollstonecraft (*Mary*, 1788; and the unfinished *Maria; or, The Wrongs of Woman*, 1798).

In practice, the time between a young woman's 'coming out' into society and her subsequent marriage represented her only period of social ascendency. Green borrows a distinction from *The Dialogic Imagination* by the Russian theorist Mikhail Bakhtin, between two 'language categories' contributing to personal formation: one of these is a fixed prior discourse ('religious, political, moral; the word of a father, of adults and of teachers'); the other is a language of internal persuasion which pushes an individual towards autonomy ('denied all privilege, backed up by no authority at all, and . . . frequently not even acknowledged in society').[36] The young nubile woman is most obviously caught between these conflicting voices. And to move from the protagonist to the writer: the two voices also correspond to the distinction frequently made in this study between the discourses of *authority* and *novelty*.

At a formal level, Green also argues that this new feminocentric fiction rejects the 'masculine' plot of pursuit and seduction for the 'feminine' plot of courtship and marriage (p. 13). Such a definition is well-suited to such early examples of the genre as Mary Collyer's two volumes of *Felicia to Charlotte* (1744/1749), with their treatment of courtship (and even subsequent marriage) in epistolary form.[37]

The insistence on the feminine courtship plot also characterizes the two late and best-known novels of the newly reformed Eliza Haywood: *The Fortunate Foundlings* (1744) and *The History of Jemmy and Jenny Jessamy* (1753). After Lennox's *Henrietta* and *Sophia*, the next major courtship novel is probably Frances Brooke's *The History of Emily Montague* (1769), although the issue is never quite so central here as in *Evelina*.[38] Among the six novels of Sarah Scott, courtship is most prominent in *The Test of Filial Duty* (1772), but quite absent from the better-known didactic and utopian *Millennium Hall* (1762). In a novelist with Scott's life-long interest, fictional and real, in the economically independent all-female community, moreover, too much critical emphasis can be attached to the courtship *topos*. The same is not true, however, of Mackenzie's third and final novel, the epistolary *Julia de Roubigné* (1777), whose two volumes are evenly divided between the heroine's courtship and unhappy marriage.

Green also discusses a number of lesser-known novelists such as Jane West and Amelia Opie, but two more substantial writers in the category of the courtship novel are Charlotte Smith and Maria Edgeworth. The former, sometimes regarded as a proto-Gothic or even a political radical, draws on the courtship plot in *Emmeline* (1788) and *Ethelinde* (1789), as does the Irish regionalist Edgeworth in at least four novels: *Belinda* and *Angelina* (1801), *Manoeuvring* (1809) and *Patronage* (1814). Both of these novelists are discussed further in the context of the Gothic at the end of the following chapter.

9

Ann Radcliffe's *The Mysteries of Udolpho* and William Godwin's *Caleb Williams*

In traditional histories of the novel, the last three decades of the eighteenth century normally receive far less attention than any of the seven before. After its 'birth', 'rise' or 'origins' (tastes in metaphor vary), the novel seems to lose its appeal until the arrival of Jane Austen and the beginnings of a recognizably classic realist tradition. The main victims of this critical neglect have been the Gothic novel and the politically radical novel of the late eighteenth century; the most celebrated examples of each tendency are juxtaposed in the present chapter. It was earlier noted that, of the male proto-canon, Smollett had the longest fiction-writing career. Between *Roderick Random* (1748: a year before *Tom Jones*) and *Humphry Clinker* (1771: three years after *A Sentimental Journey*) there was an interval of twenty-three years; the literary and conceptual gap seems even greater. If one now moves forward another twenty-three years exactly, there is a striking literary coincidence. The year 1794 saw the publication of two epoch-making novels, superficially quite diverse, but with interesting literary parallels: Ann Radcliffe's *The Mysteries of Udolpho* and William Godwin's *Caleb Williams*.

The differences between the two books are clear enough. The former, if not the prototype then certainly a high point of the Gothic novel, has a particular interest for modern feminist scholars, but was largely ignored by earlier (male) arbitrators of literary taste. *Caleb Williams*, on the other hand, is the classic *roman à thèse* by a major late eighteenth-century philosopher and political radical. Some might make a crudely reductive distinction between literary escapism for female readers and social propaganda for male ones. But there are more genuine points of contact. *Udolpho* is the prime example of a literary genre: it deals in mystery, terror and suspense, although these elements transcend conventional Gothic trappings of secret passages in gloomy castles. It also always provides a naturalistic explanation for even the deepest of mysteries. *Caleb Williams*, on the other hand, has its own forms of mystery and suspense, so that it has sometimes been advanced as the original detective novel. Relevant here is Godwin's claim to have written the three volumes of the novel in reverse order: the first two parts thus answer the challenge of motivating the catastrophe of the third volume. The classic detective story begins with a murder in the first chapter (in *Caleb Williams* it arrives in chapter 11), and then reconstructs events leading up to it. Suspense and deferral, then, are among the more obvious common features of the two novels discussed in this chapter.

Ann Radcliffe's *The Mysteries of Udolpho* is the high point of a brief novelistic career stretching from the apprentice work of *The Castles of Athlin and Dunbayne* (1789) through *A Sicilian Romance* (1790) and *The Romance of the Forest* (1791) to the artistic triumphs of *The Mysteries of Udolpho* (1794) and *The Italian* (1797); there is also a posthumously published sixth novel, *Gaston de Blondeville* (1826).[1] Besides its central position in Radcliffe's own output, *Udolpho* is also paradigmatic for Gothic fiction in general, although – in chronological terms – it appeared a generation after Horace Walpole's *The Castle of Otranto* (1764), and was anticipated by a number of other narratives elaborating the conventions of the genre.[2] By an irony of literary history, on the other hand, interest in the novel has often been limited to the fact that it is the object of critical comment and literary parody in Jane Austen's *Northanger Abbey*. Since Austen's remarks are often appreciative and her parody never malicious, however, literary and historical relations between the two novels are ambivalent; they thus recall those between *Don Quixote* and that similarly neglected but seminal novel (of chivalry), the anonymous *Amadis of Gaul*.

It is nevertheless difficult to regard a narrative as long and complex as *Udolpho* simply in terms of the Gothic. Even the title is misleading: in a four-volume work of fifty-seven chapters, barely a quarter of the action takes place in the grim Apennine castle prefiguring General Tilney's abbey in Austen's Cotswolds. Slightly more chapters (admittedly with occasional relief from outdoor scenes) are actually set not in Udolpho, but in the Château-le-Blanc, attractive Languedoc seat of the Count de Villefort, surrogate father to the heroine, Emily St Aubert. The title of the novel invites further reservations. Château-le-Blanc has as many mysteries as Udolpho, while Udolpho in turn has other elements quite as shockingly dramatic as its canonic Gothic mysteries.

Volume I of the novel is largely the record of Emily's journey from her native Gascony through the Pyrenean foothills to Rousillon and Languedoc, a restorative trip she makes with her father after the loss of his wife, Emily's mother. By the end of the volume, Emily has lost her father, too, and made a brief acquaintance with the French castle that will play such a significant part in the last two volumes. Emily's new guardian, her aunt Mme Cheron, marries the villain of the novel, Montoni, who carries both women off to Italy – first to Venice, and ultimately (although not until midway through the second volume) to his gloomy Apennine home. The aunt fails to survive the period of incarceration at Udolpho, although Emily eventually escapes, together with another prisoner, the French soldier Du Pont, and two servants. On their return to France, the four are shipwrecked off the coast of Languedoc, and find shelter precisely in Château-le-Blanc. The links between the two castles are ingenious if far-fetched, and although Udolpho does not feature directly in the last volume and a half, it is closely involved with a new crop of mysteries.

If *Udolpho* is not exclusively a Gothic novel, then, at least in the reductive sense satirized in *Northanger Abbey*, the question remains of what else it might be. The division between literary and documentary modes, argued consistently throughout this study, throws some light on this question. To begin with the second dimension: the most obvious 'documentary' tendency in Radcliffe is the use of contemporary travel literature to provide an extensive and detailed topography. Emily's family home is thus on the banks of the Garonne in Gascony, and the tour she undertakes with her father (a kind of 'sentimental journey' regendered and transposed from the eighteenth to the sixteenth century) contains precise geographical references.[3] The terrors of Udolpho in Volume III form the Gothic core of the novel, and, even after the heroine's escape from the castle, the narrative never entirely recovers its strong element of travelogue, although Emily's flight from Montoni takes her through Italy and back to France.[4]

Generations of readers have fastened on anomalies and anachronisms in Radcliffe's account of her heroine's education and travels – Emily learning English in the 1580s to read the great poetic tradition of that language, Montoni taking a private box at a Venetian opera house: there was little poetic tradition in England and no public opera anywhere at the time. Radcliffe is more convincing in her physical descriptions, however, and pays particular attention to local flora; all quite admirable in one who only left her native country once, and then went no further than Holland and Germany.[5] A different kind of 'documentary' element, on the other hand, is French and Italian landscape painting: Radcliffe often cites Poussin and Lorrain, while *Udolpho* expressly acknowledges the seventeenth-century Italian painter Salvatore Rosa (p. 30).[6]

Like most women novelists of the eighteenth century, Radcliffe had a modest education, in the sense that it was circumscribed by a society even more patriarchal than our own. But her French heroine, with her own study and full access to her father's library, is an anomalous compound of sixteenth- and eighteenth-century ways. Besides English, she knows both Italian and Latin (unusual attainments for a woman in Radcliffe's own day) and takes volumes of Petrarch and Horace with her on tour. During her stay at Udolpho, she also comforts herself with her 'favourite Ariosto' (p. 284). Among such striking literary indicators, a crucial point can easily be missed. Sensitive and intelligent young women had little opportunity for foreign travel in Radcliffe's day; one of the novelist's major documentary sources, Hester Thrale Piozzi, was fortunate in this respect to marry an Italian.[7] Like a broader education at home, the subsequent Grand Tour was normally the prerogative of gentlemen. It is enough to remember the succession of scenes in eighteenth-century fiction where self-important young men favour a predominantly female audience with reminiscences of their European travels, from Richardson's Mr B. and Pamela to Godwin's Squire Forester and Emily Melville. Radcliffe's landscapes are within the reach of any of her readers today, but the travel experiences undergone by her strange amalgam of sixteenth- and eighteenth-century heroine are an imaginative projection of something denied to generations of women. Their dramatic effect should not be underestimated.

In literary terms, by contrast, Radcliffe is not conspicuously indebted to any major writer, and has few links with the heavier classical genres of satire and (mock)-epic appropriated by male authors and discussed above in the second chapter. Her chief claim to 'literariness' probably lies in the careful choice of epigraphs for each of the novel's fifty-seven chapters.[8] From the chapter headings, it is only a brief transition to the odd score of poems by the novelist herself, ranging from short sonnets to longer pieces of up to a hundred lines. But these elements are not the sum total of Radcliffe's literary impulses, although it is misleading to speak here of 'literary sources' or even 'influences'. More fruitful, however, is the concept of 'intertextuality', emphasizing the fact that any work is inevitably created from a complex network of cultural associations and allusions, shared by writer, reader and text.[9] And in this context, Radcliffe's late eighteenth-century literary sensibility (itself often lost to the twentieth-century reader) is then projected incongruously onto a late sixteenth-century environment. For these reasons alone, *Udolpho* would be a rewarding object of intertextual study.

Many structural features of Radcliffe's novel would thus have been identified by contemporary readers, at least at some half-conscious level, with a fictional tradition which, by the end of the eighteenth century, was now rich and varied. At the centre of this network, for example, are the stories of Emily and her long-suffering suitor, Valancourt. Emily's fate, as an economic pawn subject to constant psychological pressure and (just occasionally) more explicit sexual threat, cannot have failed to recall the archetypal persecuted female of eighteenth-century fiction, Clarissa Harlowe. The tyranny and greed of Montoni echoed the attitude of the Harlowe men, while the false suitor and would-be rescuer, Count Morano, has obvious analogies with Lovelace. Like Clarissa, Emily arouses envy and resentment by her economic autonomy through inherited property; and for this, she suffers the same kind of harassment and vilification. Unlike her predecessor, however, Emily's defences are never explicitly religious, even if she does retire at one point to a convent.[10]

The story of Valancourt, on the other hand, does not ultimately suggest the struggle of a penniless younger son of the sixteenth-century French nobility, but rather that of an eighteenth-century Englishman apparently gone astray among the fleshpots of the city: a possible model here is Fielding's Tom Jones. Valancourt, however, is only really guilty of gambling excesses, rather than being 'totally depraved'; he thus resists the charms of various Parisian ladies, never being reduced to accepting money – far less, sexual favours – as Jones had from Lady Bellaston.

Similarly, the comically loquacious servants with their endlessly protracted stories are perhaps a literary throwback to Horace Walpole, who in turn claimed to have found the type in Shakespeare. When the servant is combined with a mistress, moreover, as in the case of Emily and Annette, it is difficult not to think of a long tradition of master/mistress–servant pairings back through Tom Jones and Partridge or Sophie Western and Honor, and perhaps ultimately to Don Quixote and Sancho Panza.

Even Radcliffe's Italians – passionate, perfidious and vengeful – draw on a long tradition of national stereotypes, freely transposed from Machiavelli into Elizabethan drama. Once again, Richardson provides an interesting intertextual link. Like Radcliffe, he travelled little (never apparently leaving England), although this does not prevent him from setting several books of *Sir Charles Grandison* in Italy, from depicting a dramatic Alpine crossing like Radcliffe's, or from creating his own stereotypically hot-headed Count. And in his *Dramatis Personae* for the same novel, as earlier noted, he divides his characters rather primly into the three categories of 'Men', 'Women' and 'Italians'. For Radcliffe, too, Montoni's fellow conspirators and a number of lively Venetian ladies seem a race apart from her more sedate and dignified French characters (perhaps the novelist's surrogate English).

A reader, at the turn of the twentieth century, of a novel written in the eighteenth and set in the sixteenth, will naturally endow *Udolpho* with even greater intertextual complexity than did Radcliffe's contemporaries. Such points are again a useful reminder that the concept of the Gothic is not an all-embracing or exhaustive key to the novel. From an objective review of the plot, for example, one might easily assume that the novel's Gothic conventions existed merely to support a far more insistent thematic dimension: that provided by the many kinds of (normally patriarchal) tyranny and coercion to which Emily and other (normally female) young people are subjected. After the death of her father, in fact, Emily's existence is one of almost endless constraint and duress. In a series of intrigues, almost farcical in their frequency were they not so grotesque, Valancourt's suit is first dismissed by Emily's suspicious and mercenary aunt, then forcibly accelerated as Valancourt's social connections are discovered, before being finally postponed and terminated when the aunt's new husband, Montoni, has other plans for his stepdaughter. These include marriage to Count Morano, a minor Venetian nobleman, before even his suit is rejected on economic grounds.

In the Udolpho section, too, the greatest suspense is possibly produced not by the novel's Gothic machinery, but by the cruel campaign to which Montoni subjects first his wife, and later Emily, to make them sign away their French estates (will they or won't they sign?). Mme Montoni is literally harassed to death by her sadistic husband, whose treatment of Emily is hardly kinder. Even after her flight from Udolpho, Emily is subjected to the now honourable, if no less insistent, suit of the Chevalier Du Pont. The latter, moreover, is supported by Emily's father figure, the Count de Villefort, who prematurely condemns Valancourt on the basis of false reports. Such passages, then, transcend mere Gothic sensation to address the more mundane concerns of the eighteenth-century novel of manners. Succeeding generations of Radcliffe's readers cannot have been unaware of Austen-like subtexts behind the more obvious targets of satire. The orphan Emily's room on the backstairs of her aunt's house seems to anticipate the situation of Fanny Price in *Mansfield Park*; Emily's mistaken first impression of Count Morano moves into the territory of *Pride and Prejudice*; Count de Villefort's premature dismissal of Valancourt recalls similarly ill-judged advice on Captain Wentworth in *Persuasion*.

But the most interesting intertextual crux may be the romance tradition itself. Arguments have been made for a more extensive concept of the term 'parody' – based on the term's etymological origin of 'counter-song' – to include a kind of authorial complicity, rather than mere formal ridicule, with regard to the target text.[11] Thus, Cervantes had a genuine admiration (perhaps even a weakness) for the romances of chivalry he ostensibly ridiculed; in the *auto de fe* organized by the priest in *Don Quixote* (Part I, ch. 6), a number of such novels are spared from the flames, while Cervantes's own final work, *Persiles y Sigismunda*, was as fantastic as anything he ever parodied.[12] Similarly, Austen has a great admiration for Radcliffe, whom she certainly regards as exemplary in her field.

Radcliffe, too, on the other side of the romance divide from, say, Lennox – or even Burney – occasionally displays ambivalent feelings. One expression of this is her praise of Ariosto, a writer who displayed a similar ambivalence three and a half centuries earlier; it is not just Emily who admires the Italian poet's inimitable synthesis of rich fantasy and ironic detachment. The Radcliffe narrator also allows the servant, Annette, to ridicule chivalry ('it is no business of mine to look gruff, and fight battles', p. 392), much as Catherine Morland deplores conventional male history. And exchanges between the grotesque Ugo and Bertrand, Emily's escort from Udolpho to Tuscany (Volume III, ch. 6), place male codes of honour in a particularly ridiculous light.[13]

There is a richly suggestive episode in the final volume, concerning Château-le-Blanc's 'haunted room'. The enterprising servant Ludovico offers to spend the night there, armed with a sword against human intruders and confidently sceptical about supernatural ones. By the morning he has inexplicably disappeared. To deepen the mystery (or resolve the servant crisis), the Count de Villefort and his son Henry then spend a night in the room themselves. They emerge unscathed but shaken the next morning, categorically refusing to describe their experiences. There are natural, if long deferred, explanations for all these events. But the same double episode also introduces an amusing – and surely conscious – structural parallel: when brave Ludovico (incidentally sharing his given name with Ariosto) begins his vigil, he takes a volume of Provençal stories with him for amusement. One of these is inserted verbatim into the narrative, which should at least have made the servant susceptible to further supernatural hints.[14] The Count, on the other hand, when he watches, takes a volume of Tacitus, that most ironically detached and sceptical of Roman historians. Here is an emblematic contrast between the worlds of romantic imagination and classical reason.

Such distinctions are not, however, always so clearly maintained in the surrounding narrative. The Countess de Villefort's favourite 'saloon' in Château-le-Blanc thus contains a faded tapestry with Provençal verses; and with the double wedding in the final chapter, the Carolingian romances are effectively rehabilitated by the rapid fabrication of a new tapestry. Valancourt and Emily, moreover, are clearly the archetypal romantic lovers; even the unfortunate Du Pont, who escorts his lady through every danger from Udolpho to Provence – only to have his suit rejected – is another throwback to the age of chivalry. *Udolpho*, then, is not exclusively or ingenuously 'Gothic'. Its parallel situations of two young women (first Emily, and then the Lady Blanche) each persecuted by a jealous stepmother (Mme de Cheron and the Countess de Villefort) even suggest intertextual links with traditional folk-tale motifs. More significantly, however, the novel provides a veiled critique of women's socio-economic and legal status at the end of the eighteenth century and thus, indirectly, a reflection on the same status in any other age.[15]

Not even the novel of manners, however, can account for all the residual effects of Radcliffe's novel, although one structural device may go further towards explaining its force. A number of theorists have thus argued for the significance in narrative of a kind of 'literary unconscious', something situated not in the reader or even the author, but belonging to the text itself.[16] In *Udolpho*, too, the concept seems quite promising; the focal point of such a discussion might be the novel's almost obsessive recourse to the device of 'narrative deferral'.

Perhaps more than any other novelist, Radcliffe relies on the elements of mystery and suspense. Initial examples of the technique, even before the appearance of Udolpho and Château-le-Blanc, might include the lute music in Emily's garden at La Vallée (Vol. I, ch. 1), the picture preserved by St Aubert (Vol. I, ch. 2), the papers he asks his daughter to burn without reading (Vol. I, ch. 7), and the music at St Aubert's funeral (Vol. I, ch. 8). The two castles themselves then generate other more substantial episodes: the story of Signora Laurentini, former owner of Udolpho (Vol. II, ch. 5), the picture behind the veil (Vol. II, ch. 6), the disappearance of Laurentini from Château-le-Blanc (Vol. IV, ch. 7); and this is without further specifying numerous minor examples of secret doors and passages, distant music, ghostly presences, disembodied voices or horrid groans. For each of these mysteries, great or small, there is a natural explanation long deferred.

It is notable, however, that suspense is not limited to the 'haunted' rooms, or 'supernatural' appearances gently ridiculed by Jane Austen in *Northanger Abbey*; it also applies to virtually any and every other aspect of the narrative. In these less sensational contexts, in fact, one might perhaps speak simply of 'delayed resolutions'. One could even argue, moreover, that this characteristic narrative deferral is the most conspicuous structural feature of *Udolpho*. It applies not only to the novelist–narrator's own habit of postponing natural explanations for apparently supernatural events; it also concerns the sub-narratives directly related by characters in the novel.

An obvious example here is the story of Dorothée, the housekeeper at Château-le-Blanc. When Emily returns (Vol. II, ch. 12) to the castle she had once seen while travelling with her father, she raises the question of the mysterious music she had heard on that occasion. Dorothée is reluctant to discuss it, merely remarking cryptically that Emily reminds her of the late Marchioness (p. 491), thus launching the next mystery in the tale. Her explanation to Emily is actually deferred to the next volume (Vol. IV, ch. 3), where it begins with much attention to atmosphere ('I wonder what it is makes my old limbs shake so, tonight', p. 523). Even now, however, there are elements of the story which Dorothée refuses to divulge, although she takes Emily to the late Marchioness's room. Here, incidentally, there seems to be a new supernatural incident when a pall moves, and all Emily's reserves of rationality are required: '"Time", she added, "may explain this mysterious affair"' (p. 537) – a phrase which might even serve as a motto for Radcliffe's whole method.

The pattern is typical for *Udolpho*. It recurs with the abbess's story of the mad nun, Agnes (Vol. IV, ch. 4), the finale of which is also predictably deferred: 'I cannot tell you now, but, if you think it worth your while, come to my cell, tonight' (p. 575), another paradigmatic Radcliffe formula. Such narrative deferral, then, is an ubiquitous feature of the novel: in literary terms, to the extent of virtual self-parody; in psychological ones, to the point of compulsion. It is worth asking, therefore, whether the pattern has any consistent motivation, and the answer to this question may lie in the character of Emily herself.

Emily is an extremely sensible and rational young woman. Her adored father and almost every other mature figure she encounters warn her against the dangers of excessive sensibility and the foolishness of vulgar superstition. Emily has effectively learned the lesson. She has the advantage of an excellent private education, together with a sound moral and affective base. Thus armed against life's deceits, she might reasonably be assumed to merit – and even to be able to create for herself – a comfortable and dignified existence. She has no identifiable vices, no extravagances of taste, and wins the love of a young man of similar emotional and intellectual constitution. That such a promising future does not immediately materialize obviously provides Radcliffe with the stuff of a novel, through the kind of interaction which has been wittily defined as 'narrative and its discontents': the latter referring to elements that are existentially unwelcome, but fictionally highly desirable for their contribution to the plot.[17] But it may also reflect some objective correlative in the 'real world', or the eighteenth-century England so inadequately disguised as sixteenth-century France.

The ultimate source of Emily's suffering in this sense, then, is not a series of Gothic props initially without rational explanation – and to a modern generation familiar with *The Silence of the Lambs*, heavy breathing beyond a locked door (as in Vol. III, ch. 9) is an even less likely source of terror; it is, rather, the vile treatment to which she is subjected by a number of older adults, particularly Montoni and her aunt (Mme Montoni's position changes from persecutor to persecuted, of course, when she refuses to sign over her property to her husband). After this, however, there is no sense of retribution, but only the more general penalty suffered by Montoni, who ultimately carries his defiance of the Venetian republic too far. His death is never specifically regarded as punishment for the way he has treated his wife (and Mme Montoni's own death is not mentioned again). Radcliffe may give us plenty of romance, but does not try to fob us off with poetic justice.

The chastening conclusion, then, is that Emily's excellent moral preparation and far from negligible education cannot in fact protect her against constraint and tyranny. This is a question that the benignly accommodating Radcliffe, unlike her more radical female contemporaries, never fully confronts; this, in fact, might be her own repressed subtext, and explain why the motif of narrative deferral seems almost a compulsive element in her own writing. For the indirect political lesson of *The Mysteries of Udolpho* is that individual action is not enough to overcome an arbitrary and despotic world. For this, some kind of collective solidarity, together with an explicit new political ideology, is required; and these, of course, are the very issues confronted by Godwin in both the *Enquiry Concerning Political Justice* and his novel *Caleb Williams*, written to illustrate it.

William Godwin, Caleb Williams

Godwin's reputation rests on two interconnected works, a novel and a political treatise; neither could have been anticipated from the writer's early formation.

Son of a Dissenting minister and product of a strictly Calvinist upbringing, Godwin claimed to have read Bunyan's *Pilgrim's Progress* by the age of five, the whole of the Bible a couple of years later, and to have studied so voraciously that he would sometimes not leave the house for weeks. After a brief and largely frustrating career in the ministry himself, Godwin was converted to atheism and political radicalism by reading the French free-thinkers d'Holbach, Rousseau and Helvetius.[18] In the same year (1783), he began a new career as a pamphleteer. By the end of the decade, he had matured into a significant political journalist writing on the side of such revolutionaries as Thomas Paine, and intersecting at many points with the so-called Jacobin novelists discussed at the end of this chapter. He also became a pivotal figure in radical circles, with a wide literary acquaintance, including Coleridge, Wordsworth and Shelley.[19]

Godwin's own account of the composition of *Caleb Williams* (1794), included in the 1832 edition of his novel *Fleetwood* (1805), is as helpful as any critical summary.[20] The author had finished his major non-fictional work, the revolutionary *Enquiry Concerning Political Justice*, in January 1793, and then decided to attempt a 'book of fictitious adventure' with a 'very powerful interest'. The precise nature of this interest is identical to that behind the *Enquiry*: 'a general review of the modes of domestic and unrecorded despotism by which man becomes the destroyer of man' (p. 3). Godwin also describes how he wrote the three volumes of the novel in reverse order: beginning with the adventures of a fugitive desperately involved in a story of flight and persecution; then developing the dramatic motivation for this pursuit (knowledge of a murder); and finally, explaining how the murderer, a seeming paragon of virtue, could have ever committed such a crime.

Such a calculated, even programmatic, approach, according to which the initial fable is expanded to a kind of social anatomy, seems to mark

Godwin, too, as an ethically rather than psychologically motivated writer, more 'literary' than 'popular': or, to shift the parameters slightly, an *author* rather than a *novelist*. On the other hand, certain analogies with earlier demotic traditions in eighteenth-century fiction are striking. Godwin's initial motivation for adopting the novel form – to propagate 'a truth highly worth to be communicated to persons whom books of philosophy and science are never likely to reach', p. 3) – echoes Richardson's justification for *Pamela*; his Nonconformist background, with its rigorous educational discipline, has parallels with Defoe's almost a century earlier. The humble station of Caleb recalls both Pamela and Moll Flanders.

With regard to more explicit 'literary' or 'non-literary' sources, Godwin provided further useful hints in the same 1832 Preface: 'it was ever my method to get about me any productions of former authors that seemed to bear on my subject' (p. 351). The books he mentions here are nevertheless largely outside the standard literary canon, and seem to lean more towards the documentary.[21] The protagonist's experiences in prison in the second volume, moreover, draw on criminal cases recorded in the annals of the *Newgate Calender*.[22] And in Volume I, Hawkins, father and son, are persecuted by Squire Tyrrel through the notorious Black Act (1723), legislation originally introduced to curb poaching, but later widely used as a catch-all device to suppress any undesired political activity. Behind all this, however, looms Godwin's self-created non-literary impulse: *Caleb Williams* was originally a sub-title for *Things as They Are*, reaffirming the novel's relation to the political blueprint, in the *Enquiry Concerning Human Justice*, for how things could be.

On the other hand, Godwin's *Fleetwood* Preface also acknowledges more conventionally 'literary' interests: 'no works of fiction came amiss to me, provided they were written with energy' (p. 352), and *Caleb Williams* is in fact demonstrably saturated in an eighteenth-century narrative tradition. The novel is thus defined as a series of 'adventures', recalling Smollett's *Roderick Random*, although the major intertextual links are undoubtedly Richardson and Fielding.

In the first context, the analogies between Godwin's aristocratic despot, Falkland, and Richardson's Sir Charles Grandison are particularly striking: they include Falkland's long stay in Italy (Grandison spends several years there), his role as Lady Lucretia's English teacher (Grandison had tutored the Lady Clementina) and the jealous reaction of her suitor Count Malvesi (Grandison provokes similar reactions in the Count of Belvedere). In addition, Falkland becomes an object of infatuation for the defenceless orphan, Emily (Grandison arouses similar feelings in his ward). And when the latter is held captive by Squire Tyrrel (like Pamela by Mr B—), abducted by Grimes (like Clarissa by Lovelace), and rescued by Falkland himself (like Harriet by Grandison), Emily seems to run through much of Richardson's fictional repertoire in one particularly eventful chapter.[23] But the most significant link between the two novels is a contrastive one, as Godwin radically revises Richardson's portrait of the 'good man'. The portrait is also refracted through a number of eighteenth-century fictional paragons, from Burney's Lord Orville to Elizabeth Inchbald's Dorriforth (*A Simple Story*, 1791); Frances Sheridan's Orlando Faulkland (*Memoirs of Miss Sidney Biddulph*, 1761) even seems to have given Godwin a name.[24]

Ultimately, however, the echoes of Fielding may be even stronger: Caleb himself cites *Tom Jones* and *Jonathan Wild*; and elsewhere, Godwin's picture of a venal and reactionary squirearchy, particularly in the contexts of political elections and magisterial duties, draws on techniques of irony and indirect satire familiar from *Joseph Andrews*.[25] Another parallel with Fielding, and also incidentally Smollett (*Jonathan Wild* and *Ferdinand Count Fathom* immediately spring to mind) is the plethora of classical references and (mock)-heroic tropes. Squire Tyrrel is a 'rural Antaeus' or a Hercules (p. 21); his scheming partner at the local assembly is his 'fair inamorata' (p. 23), a favourite Smollett trope; the newspaper editor who rejects Caleb's first literary efforts is an 'Aristarchus'; the housekeeper of the robber band is an 'infernal Thalestris' (p. 222).[26]

Mock-heroic elements also link *Caleb Williams* with that archetypal literary parody, Cervantes's *Don Quixote*, although the English 'Quixote novels', from *Joseph Andrews* to *Northanger Abbey*, are obviously closer relations. The concept of 'chivalry' is particularly insidious in *Caleb Williams*, however, since it directly motivates much of the anti-social or deluded behaviour of the novel. Caleb himself admits his early 'attachment to books of narrative and romance' (p. 6), and the insatiable curiosity this breeds is largely responsible for his downfall. For Emily, on the other hand, with her head turned by Falkland, '[a]ll was fairy-land and enchantment' (p. 48). The ultimate perversity of the cult, in Godwin's eyes, nevertheless appears in the behaviour of Falkland himself, 'pervaded with the groundless romances of chivalry' (p. 101) and ironically portrayed as author of an 'Ode to the Genius of Chivalry' (p. 27), obsequiously received in the local assembly rooms.

Unlike *Don Quixote* or even *Northanger Abbey*, however, with their ambivalent parody and even partial nostalgia, *Caleb Williams* is quite uncompromising in its indictment of the 'poison' of chivalry. It is, after all, Falkland's obsession with remaining the 'true knight' (p. 101), with his honour and reputation intact, that prompts the murder of Tyrrel, the destruction of the Hawkinses, and the relentless persecution of Caleb. The central idea of the novel ('message' is hardly too crude a term) is the need to extirpate an aristocratic code of *honour*, and replace it by an egalitarian one based on universal justice.

But perhaps the most striking 'literary' motifs in *Caleb Williams* appear in certain formal elements of the narrative. Godwin thus introduces a series of self-consciously ironic incidents during the protagonist's long flight in the third volume: in rapid succession, Caleb first comes across a handbill offering a £100 reward for his apprehension (p. 230), then overhears a conversation about himself (p. 244), and is subsequently asked for information, unwittingly, by his own pursuers. His attempt to make a fresh start in a Welsh country idyll is then foiled when the relentless Gines distributes a defamatory *History of Caleb Williams*. And in an even more ingenious narrative turn, Caleb is finally ruined by the fruits of his own labours: obsessed with stories of young men escaping from the gallows (another staple of Fielding and Smollett plots), he attempts to earn a living by selling redactions of French and Spanish picaresque tales remembered from Cartouche and *Guzmán de Alfarache*.[27] But it is precisely these stories of persecution which enable the same Gines to recognize and trace the author, when he finds the manuscripts on the premises of his brother, the London printer. There is even greater structural irony when Caleb buys a paper from a hawker (p. 278) – the latter's sales-pitch is quoted verbatim for twelve lines – where his alleged criminal exploits are listed.

At this point, Godwin's narrative play introduces various examples of a kind of 'mirror-text', best illustrated by a final example from the end of the novel.[28] Here, Caleb is convinced that Falkland's trunk contains nothing less than a narrative of his crime with its 'concomitant transactions', all of which could eventually 'redeem the wreck of his reputation' (p. 326). By this juxtaposition of (fictionally) 'real' and 'imagined' narratives, Godwin introduces an ironic playfulness that has become a postmodern commonplace; in the eighteenth century, it is associated more exclusively with the structural ironies of Fielding or Sterne. Such games also distinguish the self-consciously literary Godwin from the more unequivocally documentary Radcliffe.

The main parallels between the two novels nevertheless lie elsewhere. In formal terms, they revolve most obviously around a heavy reliance on suspense, and this not merely within the frame of Gothic convention, but in a more general atmosphere of constant narrative expectation. *Caleb Williams* may even surpass *The Mysteries of Udolpho* with its unbroken tissue of such hints ('I little suspected'... 'it will soon be perceived'), together with more emphatically expressed intentions.[29] In the case of *Udolpho*, it was argued that 'suspense' was not simply Gothic machinery but a kind of pathologically induced narrative deferral: an attempt to avoid the unpleasant conclusions that would have tended to emerge through any more realistic thematic resolution. It is interesting to speculate whether some similar form of unconscious motivation occurs in *Caleb Williams*, too. One possible interpretation is to see Godwin's own narrative deferrals as a kind of 'diegetic compensation': if, as he claimed, the three volumes of the novel really were composed in reverse order, then the constant reference to something to be revealed might be an attempt to repress the fact that, for Godwin, all was already quite literally revealed – in draft in his desk drawer as it were.

The massive reliance on suspense is the most obvious formal analogy between the two novels. There is another thematic link, however, centring quite simply on the issues of oppression and coercion. In Godwin, these concerns are obvious enough in his comprehensive, almost programmatic, anatomy of tyranny: he had, after all, promised a 'general review' of the various forms of despotism. And there are indeed *three* (named) squires – in addition to nameless magistrates, *three* principal victims and even *three* additional (unnamed) Justices of the Peace.

The first volume of *Caleb Williams* is dominated by the story of Squire Tyrrel's cruelty towards his cousin and dependant, Emily. Incapable of guile, she is crushed by 'the oppression of despotism', in defiance of a naive belief in natural justice ('nobody is punished for doing what is right', p. 52) and in spite of her brave rhetoric of freedom ('imprison my body, but not my mind', p. 60). Radcliffe's Emily is most obviously persecuted for her refusal to sign over property to her self-appointed guardian, Montoni, although an important secondary cause is her refusal to submit to an enforced marriage, the very motive for the sufferings of Godwin's Emily. The archetypal eighteenth-century narrative of an avaricious family pressurizing a daughter in this way is once again *Clarissa*.

Godwin's main subsidiary example of socio-economic tyranny concerns the yeoman farmer, Hawkins, a case without any direct parallel in Radcliffe. When Hawkins is ejected by his landlord for voting against him in a county election, his cause is espoused by Tyrrel, although less from any sense of justice than as a personal vendetta with Hawkins's old landlord. Hawkins later falls foul of Tyrrel, too, and is persecuted by 'wealth and despotism', to the point that he compares himself to the 'poorest neger' (p. 74) in his lack of personal freedom.

The second and third volumes of Godwin's novel then emphasize Caleb's own story. The earlier facile distinction between the 'bad squire' and the 'good squire' now disappears, as Falkland proves more evil than anything encountered so far. The tropes used to depict his behaviour proliferate wildly. As he begins his relentless pursuit of his ex-protégé, now in possession of a dangerous secret, Falkland becomes an 'omnipresent God' with his 'lynx-eyed jealousy and despotism': the echo of the Old Testament ('I the Lord thy God am a jealous God') is unmistakable. The Biblical patriarchy in which the young Godwin was saturated is thus conflated with the social and political oppression which the mature Godwin attacked.

Even with obvious differences of gender and (in theory) historical period, then, there are strong thematic links with *Udolpho*. *Caleb Williams* incidentally provides one more explicit parallel to Radcliffe's Emily St Aubert with the story of Laura Denison in Volume III. Grand-child of an exiled Neapolitan nobleman, Laura has grown up in the remote Welsh village where Caleb tries to begin a new life. She resembles Radcliffe's heroine in her orphan status and in the strong imprint received from her father. She has cultural achievements remarkable for her sex and station, having 'taught herself to draw, to sing, and to understand the more polite European languages' (p. 301).[30] Laura's propensity for goodness is innate: 'she had no idea of honour or superiority to be derived from her acquisitions; but pursued them from a secret taste' (p. 301); Emily St Aubert has a similar fund of natural virtue. Both Godwin's central portrait of victimization and his subsidiary examples seem strategically chosen to reflect a range of cases, portraying what the anarchist Godwin regarded as the clash between natural man and the 'man of artificial society'. Radcliffe herself clearly lacked such an uncompromising ideological agenda; her gender politics are not as vociferous, but possibly no less effective.

At this point, however, one may consider more covert parallels between the two novels by returning to the trope of narrative deferral. A similar kind of tension to that found in *Udolpho* also operates in *Caleb Williams*, although the phenomenon now has quite different ideological causes. On Godwin's own evidence (p. 351), he began writing his narrative in the third person, but eventually switched to the first person (a method retained in most of his subsequent fiction). Godwin discussed this change of method nearly forty years later in a revealing comment:

It was infinitely the best adapted, at least, to my vein of delineation, where the thing in which my imagination revelled most freely, was the analysis of the private and internal operations of the mind, employing my metaphysical dissecting knife in tracing and laying bare the involutions of motive, and recording the gradually accumulating impulses, which led the personages I had to describe to adopt the particular way of proceeding in which they afterwards embarked.

(p. 351)[31]

Striking here is the conflation of author and narrator, with its resulting paradox. If Godwin was intent on producing a kind of surgical anatomy of human motivation, here surely was a good reason for using a detached, extradiegetic (i.e. external) viewpoint – a third-person narrator – rather than an intradiegetic first-person voice. Such criticisms do not, incidentally, deny the subtlety or complexity of Godwin's narrative. Like earlier demotic writers, for example, he is careful to naturalize his humble narrator's highly articulate performance. Pamela's literacy would have been unusual in Richardson's day, as would that of Moll Flanders a generation earlier. Caleb's social origins are as lowly as those of Pamela or Moll, and his induction into a literate world is comparable to that of Moll (brought up in the mayor of Colchester's family), or Pamela (instructed by the mother of Mr B.): he is installed as the amanuensis of the local squire, Fernando Falkland.

Caleb Williams also belongs to a group of novels characterized by what may be called 'double articulation'. Beginning with a portrait of Falkland, it later comes to concentrate on the *effect* of Falkland's character on the protagonist. The sensational events of the third book tend to eclipse Falkland, although the latter returns quite literally with a vengeance in the concluding trial scene. Such double articulation is common enough in twentieth-century fiction, be it Marlow and Kurtz in *Heart of Darkness* or Nick Carraway and Gatsby in *The Great Gatsby*, where it literally involves a 'frame narrator' between the real-life author and the central events. The original of the pattern is not found in any of the proto-canonical novels, however, but rather in Behn's once again seminal *Oroonoko*: here, too, the narrative is poised between object (an African slave presented within the time-worn conventions of heroic romance) and subject (a female observer drawing on a newer and more typically female autobiographical mode). The relative importance of the two components may even be reflected in the respective titles used by Behn and Godwin: *Oroonoko* named for the agent, and *Caleb Williams* for the narrator.

But Godwin's technical solutions are not always problem-free. In practice, they produce the sort of literary hybrid where the first-person narrator becomes a kind of editorial figure. The paradox is worth pursuing briefly. From the very outset, *Caleb Williams* is syntactically an unambiguous first-person narrative, although the entire first volume is effectively a redaction (by Caleb) of material provided by Falkland's steward, Collins. Caleb recognizes this anomaly at the end of the first chapter,[32] and again at the end of Volume I when he suddenly announces, 'I shall endeavour to state the remainder of this narrative in the words of Mr Collins', as if admitting slightly ruefully that he had previously failed to do so.

Rather belatedly, too, after such unmotivated interpolations as the story of Emily, the second volume begins with yet more 'editorial' assurances:

I have stated the narrative of Mr Collins, interspersed with such other information as I was able to collect, with all the exactness that my memory, assisted by certain memorandums I made at the time, will afford. I do not pretend to warrant the authenticity of any part of these memoirs, except so much as fell under my own knowledge, and that part shall be given with the same simplicity and accuracy that I would observe towards a court which was to decide in the last count upon everything dear to me.   (p. 111)

Godwin's comparison with a court of law has several ironic echoes. In the first instance, it is notable that the narrative is much dominated by trial scenes, where the hero's protestations of truth are consistently rejected and the false testimony of others is readily accepted. In this light, Caleb's faith in legal procedure, no less than his belief in narrative transparency, may seem naive and unfounded. Or, to stay with the courtroom analogy: for all the special pleading there is no satisfactory *representation*, and *justice* is hardly done.

Secondly, and from a strictly formal perspective, Caleb's new approach – after the narrative inconsistencies of the first volume – seems rather a case of closing the narratological door after the horse has bolted. Such an impression is reinforced by a subsequent comment of Caleb's in the second volume:

It will also most probably happen, while I am thus employed in collecting the scattered incidents of my history, that I shall upon some occasions annex to appearances an explanation which I was far from possessing at the time, and was only suggested to me through the medium of subsequent events.   (p. 124)

This seems little more than a pre-emptive damage limitation exercise. Godwin's occasionally crude (authorial) interventions are thus a far cry from Radcliffe's epistemologically naïve (but novelistic) narrative solutions.

The implications of this short digression on narrators and narrative authority are in fact far-reaching. It could be argued, quite simply, that Godwin – archetypal liberal and champion of the oppressed – paradoxically exerts some form of tyranny over his own tale. The self-justifying stratagems of his chief narrator hardly differ, in fact, from those of the tyrannical Squire Forrester at the beginning of Volume II:

> It will also most probably happen, while I am thus employed in collecting the scattered incidents of my history, that I shall upon some occasions annex to appearances an explanation which I was far from possessing at the time, and was only suggested to me through the medium of subsequent events.   (p. 124)

Such comments suggest that narrative omniscience (like its real-life counterpart of socio-political omnipotence) is hard to relinquish.[33] And in the third volume, the very speed with which a large number of purely external events unfold probably marginalizes, or simply camouflages, editorial problems, although there are now also signs that Godwin may be tiring of any narrative impositions at all. 'I hasten to the conclusion of my melancholy story' (p. 313), he announces in the penultimate chapter, and this aim is much advanced by the return of Collins, providing further useful opportunities for cutting a few narrative corners.

The fact that Godwin occasionally seems to be both 'omniscient' narrator and (in the person of Caleb) 'partial' memoirist reaffirms a deep complicity between author and narrator–protagonist. There is an ideological conclusion asking to be drawn: an author who fulminated for most of his life against every form of tyranny was perhaps reluctant to assume total and undisguised authority over his own narrative. Fielding, it was earlier noted, had no such inhibitions. There is thus one final comparison to be made between *Caleb Williams* and *The Mysteries of Udolpho*. Philosopher, polymath and political radical, Godwin might initially seem a more exciting subject than the less intellectually dazzling Radcliffe. And yet it might also be argued that, while the creator of *Udolpho* achieves a creditable naturalization of the events of her *story* (in contrast to certain other Gothic novelists who resort uninhibitedly to the supernatural), then Godwin is less successful in naturalizing the structure of his *discourse*.[34]

Radcliffe and Godwin

Each of the two writers also produced a critical essay of interest in the present context. Radcliffe's posthumously published 'On the Supernatural in Poetry'[35] attempted to distinguish between the concepts of 'terror' and 'horror' in the Gothic novel:

> Terror and horror are so far opposite, that the first expands the soul, and awakens the faculties to a high degree of life; the other contracts, freezes and nearly annihilates them. I apprehend, that neither Shakespeare nor Milton by their fictions, nor Mr Burke by his reasoning, anywhere looked to positive horror as a source of the sublime, though they all agree that terror is a very high one.[36]

Or, more simply, Radcliffe was the great exponent of good healthy terror, while her contemporary Matthew 'Monk' Lewis specialized in genuine horror. Burke's essay, cited here, is the major statement of the new aesthetic underlying Radcliffe's own conception of the Gothic. Ironically, the person Radcliffe admired as a philosopher of the sublime was also the very man excoriated by Godwin as a political reactionary, and probably supplied the model for Falkland in *Caleb Williams*.

The Godwin essay, a short piece from a vast *oeuvre* and not published until the 1980s, is entitled 'Of History and Romance'.[37] Arguing the superiority of moral over literary truth, Godwin suggests provocatively that the best kind of history may be one where 'a scanty substratum of facts and dates' was combined with 'a number of happy, ingenious and instructive inventions' (p. 368). And since history is 'little better than romance under a graver name', then it is worth inquiring more closely into that branch of literature which is quite explicitly invented, i.e. the romance or novel (Godwin seems to regard the terms as interchangeable). Or as he paradoxically concludes:

> The writer of romance then is to be considered as the writer of real history; while he who was formally called the historian, must be contented to step down into the place of his rival ... (p. 372)

Such subversion, or even literal inversion, of traditional literary hierarchies brings Godwin startlingly close to contemporary narrative theorists and metahistorians. Beside Radcliffe's more prosaic efforts, then, 'Of History and Romance' is something of a *jeu d'esprit*. But the two essays and their authors are central reference points to at least a dozen of the writers in this survey.

One authoritative account of Gothic fiction initially defines the category merely as a group of novels written between the 1760s and the 1820s.[38] Other definitions of the field tend to emphasize one of three elements: a kind of work related to a recognizable movement in cultural history known as the Gothic revival; a fictional sub-genre defined more restrictively in terms of certain plot features; or a simple aesthetic reaction to conventional fictional realism. The three characteristics are not mutually exclusive, and their relative prominence tends to vary according to the work discussed. There is thus a proto-gothic sequence in Smollett's *Ferdinand Count Fathom* (1751), although Horace Walpole's *The Castle of Otranto* (1764) is recognized as the first Gothic novel proper.[39] This story of a dynastic struggle set in medieval Italy is notable for its regular recourse to the supernatural: a talking portrait, a bleeding statue, a gigantic helmet that crushes the heir of the usurper Prince of Otranto, to mention only a sample from a novel stronger in sensational events than in psychological interest. The novel was also part of the author's all-embracing Gothic project, which included the rebuilding of his Twickenham home of Strawberry Hill, thus placing Walpole in the first and third categories as defined above.

In terms of plot structure, however, 'Gothic' unites a series of novels written between the 1760s and the 1820s. Beside Walpole and Radcliffe, the key authors here are Clara Reeve, Matthew Lewis, C. R. Maturin and Mary Shelley; of more marginal significance as Gothic novelists are the sisters Harriet and Sophia Lee, Charlotte Smith and Godwin himself. There are further interesting parallels between the lives of Walpole and William Beckford, another wealthy connoisseur and man of letters, who constructed his own elaborated Gothic fantasy (Fountain Hill, largely completed by 1809). Beckford's oriental tale of *Vathek*, originally written in French, is another uncompromising rejection of realistic fiction, although the latter point may be the limit of its Gothic connections.

A more genuine successor to Walpole, then, is Clara Reeve, also a pioneering literary critic with her *Progress of Romance* (1785). Awkwardly framed as a series of nightly debates between three speakers, this work nevertheless provides a survey of eighteenth-century fiction in terms of the 'novel' and 'romance' with a clear partiality for the latter. Her first novel, *The Champion of Virtue, a Gothic Story* (1777), republished in 1778 as *The Old English Baron*, attempts to correct what she saw as the supernatural indulgences of Walpole. Reeve also wrote a historical novel, *The Exiles; or, Memoirs of the Count de Cronstadt* (1788), where Gothic elements are insignificant, and three heavily didactic letter fictions where they are non-existent. She produced one more semi-historical novel, *Memoirs of Sir Roger de Clarendon* (1793), before returning to pedagogical concerns with *Destination* (1799). *The Old English Baron* aside, then, she has little to do with Gothic.

The combination of historical characters, fictional events and Gothic machinery is in fact more the province of Sophia and Harriet Lee. Sophia's *The Recess* (1783), sub-titled 'A Tale of Other Times', features the lives of two historically unrecorded daughters of Mary, Queen of Scots: one marrying the Earl of Leicester, the other falling in love with the Earl of Essex; both predictably persecuted by Queen Elizabeth. The long title of her second novel, *A Hermit's Tale, Recorded by His Own Hand, and Found in His Cell, by the Author of the Recess* (1787) includes a number of classic Gothic props. Harriet wrote two novels of her own, as well as contributing ten of the twelve stories of *The Canterbury Tales* (5 vols, 1797–1805), the collaborative effort which brought the sisters fame. In this collection, Harriet's 'The Old Woman's Tale, Lothaire' is the most obviously Gothic.

The high point of Gothic fiction, as already suggested, occurs in the 1790s with the advent of Mrs Radcliffe. Both financially and artistically, she was the most successful practitioner of the genre: she received astronomical advances for her later works, but was also described by Sir Walter Scott as 'the first poetess of Romantic fiction'.[40] Godwin, on the other hand, is more marginal to the Gothic novel, and Radcliffe's most significant rival was Matthew 'Monk' Lewis. Lewis's sensational novel *The Monk* is sometimes seen as heralding a kind of Gothic revolution, although its heavy use of the supernatural might be considered a return to Walpole. But where *The Castle of Otranto* narrowly misses (if it does not actually achieve) comic absurdity, *The Monk* has a genuine line in horror, which earned its young author his nickname and ensured that the book was generally expurgated until well into the twentieth century. Radcliffe's next novel, *The Italian* (1797), is a riposte to *The Monk*, in terms both of its renewed insistence on rational explanation for all its mysteries, and of its emphasis on 'terror' rather than 'horror'.

Neither Gothic terror nor Gothic horror had a central place in literary canons for nearly two centuries, however, and the exciting re-evaluations of Radcliffe and her contemporaries are largely the work of modern feminist critics. Anne Williams, for example, argues that 'Gothic' and 'Romantic' are indivisible, and that Gothic – 'like the human race' – has a male and a female genre:

> in the feminine Gothic the heroine exposes the villain's usurpation and thus reclaims an exposed space that should have been a refuge from evil but has become the very opposite, a prison. The masculine Gothic gives the perspective of an exile from the refuge of home, now the special province of women.[41]

The second part of the definition seems made for Charles Maturin's *Melmoth the Wanderer* (1820), a gloomy tale of a pact with the devil. According to Williams, the female plot of Gothic fiction typically expresses the 'rage and terror that women experience within patriarchal social arrangements, especially marriage' (p. 136). This in turn is a fair description of Emily St Aubert's experiences in *Udolpho* and explains why Charlotte Smith can also be viewed as a precursor of Radcliffe. Of Smith's ten novels, five of the first six are sentimental adventure stories, including *Emmeline* (1788) and *Ethelinde* (1789). Only *Montalbert* (1795), with its partly Italian setting and its abduction plot featuring a remote castle, has substantially Gothic elements: its publication the year after *Udolpho* may reflect a keen awareness of market trends. *Desmond* (1792) and *The Banished Man* (1794) are political novels dealing with the French Revolution and its aftermath. *Marchmont* (1796) and *The Young Philosopher* (1798), harsh attacks on social injustice, are clearly overshadowed by Smith's personal bitterness over a substantial family legacy denied her for thirty years. The radical element brings Smith closer to Godwin, and her links with Gothic remain incidental.

After the decline of Gothic in the 1820s, even Radcliffe's *The Mysteries of Udolpho* was hardly known beyond the parody of the novel in *Northanger Abbey* (1818). But Austen had a healthy respect, even admiration, for Radcliffe; and by an irony of literary history, her posthumously published novel appeared in the same year (1818) as what is arguably the most famous of all Gothic fictions, Mary Shelley's *Frankenstein*.

Godwin also has a wide range of literary relations: these include a group of 'philosophical radicals' or so-called Jacobin novelists, including Thomas Holcroft, Robert Bage and Elizabeth Inchbald. There are further intimate links with other women novelists of the period, several of whom he proposed to and one of whom, Mary Wollstonecraft, he eventually married.

There is an enormous breadth to Godwin's writing. Of the fiction, only *Caleb Williams* is well known, but there were actually eight other novels in a vast literary output. These included three historical romances, *Imogen* (1784), *St Leon* (1799) and *Mandeville* (1817), set in Ancient Britain, the sixteenth and seventeenth centuries, respectively, and not without miraculous elements. Slightly better known is *Fleetwood; or, The New Man of Feeling* (1805), a story of what Godwin called 'common and ordinary adventures', revisiting the cult of sensibility represented by the Scottish novelist Henry Mackenzie. *Fleetwood* also marks Godwin's gradual shift of interest from the uncompromisingly political to the more generally moral and psychological, neatly symbolized by his promotion of 'Caleb Williams' from sub-title to main title – in place of 'Things as They Were' – in a later edition of that novel.

The closest novelist to Godwin, both ideologically and personally, is Thomas Holcroft, son of a shoemaker, sometime stableboy, itinerant actor, and the most clearly proletarian writer in the corpus since Bunyan. Three of his four full-length novels, *Alwyn* (1780), *The Adventures of Hugh Trevor* (1794–7) and *The Memoirs of Brian Perdue* (1805) are highly mobile, peripatetic narratives, with picaresque elements reminiscent of Smollett and Fielding; the first two of these are also, rather paradoxically, letter fictions in the manner of Richardson. Holcroft's finest novel, *Anna St Ives* (1792), is the chief point of contact with Godwin; and although the novel is generally overshadowed by *Caleb Williams* in literary histories, it actually preceded it by two years, just as Holcroft was an intellectual inspiration to Godwin, rather than the reverse. With its active and uninhibited heroine, however, *Anna St Ives* could also be classified with the radical women's fiction of the late eighteenth century, Jacobin or not.

Robert Bage also combines the social comedy of Fielding and Smollett with the epistolary form of Richardson; and uses the resulting synthesis in his first four novels for a less strident political radicalism than Godwin or Holcroft. His most important novels, *Man as He Is* (1792) and *Hermsprong* (1796), portray both the American and French revolutions sympathetically: *Hermsprong* confronts Edmund Burke's reactionary *Reflections on the Revolutions in France* (1790), and thus brings Bage even closer to Godwin.

Elizabeth Inchbald's relation to Godwin and the Jacobin novel also derives from both personal acquaintance and ideological content. Her two novels, *A Simple Story* (1791) and *Nature and Art* (1796), thus reverse a tendency noticeable in Godwin by moving from acute psychological observation to more explicit ideological commitment. Less significant as novelist than as social critic, on the other hand, is Mary Wollstonecraft: her first political essay, *A Vindication of the Rights of Man* (1790) – like some of Godwin's writing – is expressly directed at the reactionary politics of Burke; her next work, *A Vindication of the Rights of Women* (1792), had even greater originality and significance. Wollstonecraft's only complete novel is the early and heavily autobiographical *Mary* (1788); even more politically explicit was the posthumous and unfinished *Maria; or, The Wrongs of Women* (1799).

10

Jane Austen's *Northanger Abbey* and *Mansfield Park*

Even if the known details of Jane Austen's biography were not so familiar, there would be little to tell. The seventh child of a High Tory Anglican clergyman, the writer grew up and later resettled in rural Hampshire, where she seems to have been happy; in the interim, she lived five years with her family in Bath, and briefly – on her father's death – in Southampton: places where she was clearly less happy.[1] The relative uneventfulness of Austen's life always seems implicit in subsequent literary judgements, where there is of course a great deal to tell. Several much-quoted tags (the 'two square inches of ivory', or the 'two or three families in a country village') record Austen's own self-deprecating assessment of her range. The novelist's first – and for long her only – substantial critic, Sir Walter Scott, noted in his journal another comment that has become famous:

> The Big Bow-wow strain I can do myself like any now going, but the exquisite touch which renders ordinary commonplace things and characters interesting from the truth of description and the sentiment is denied to me.[2]

Mark Twain was less appreciative: 'Every time I read 'Pride and Prejudice' I want to dig her up and hit her over the skull with her own shin-bone'; although, by his own admission, he seems to have been a compulsive reader. Other comments, like those of James ('little touches of human truth') or Conrad ('What is there in her? What is it all about?'), are more intentionally patronizing than Scott's.

George Steiner provides a more measured indictment of Austen's presumed limitations:

Entire spheres of human existence – political, social, erotic, subconscious – are absent. At the height of political and industrial revolution in a decade of formidable philosophic activity, Miss Austen composes novels almost extraterritorial to history.[3]

There is perhaps a little scholarly myopia in this implied reproach of a Hampshire clergyman's daughter for not writing a philosophical counterblast to Kant's *Critique of Pure Reason* or a direct *riposte* to the revolutionary Tom Paine. There is also a critical tradition which can be seen as a counterpart to Steiner's thinly disguised frustration. According to this, public drama is admittedly excluded, and private emotion repressed, from Austen's fiction, but this is from conscious choice rather than any culturally conditioned restriction. Through her brothers in the navy, her refugee sister-in-law from France's revolutionary reign of terror, or even the fairy-tale destiny of her adopted brother Edward – not to mention the raw realities of birth and death endemic to eighteenth-century life – the novelist had much more material at her disposal, but chose to ignore it. The latter arguments nevertheless leave many unconvinced.

Thanks to adaptations for cinema and television, Austen's six major novels currently enjoy a familiarity undreamed of for any earlier, and most subsequent, English fiction. Significant details of their composition and publication are not, however, always understood. Chronologically, *Northanger Abbey* appeared after Austen's death, but actually belongs with the two earlier novels *Sense and Sensibility* and *Pride and Prejudice*; only the second of the posthumously published novels, *Persuasion*, was written after *Emma* and *Mansfield Park*. *Sense and Sensibility* (1811) started life as *Elinor and Marianne* in 1795; *Pride and Prejudice* (1813) was begun as *First Impressions* in 1796, completed in 1797 and unsuccessfully submitted for publication under this name in the same year. *Northanger Abbey* (1817), *Susan* in an earlier draft, was sold to Crosby & Co. in 1803, but, for reasons unknown, was not published; in 1809, the novelist's brother Henry bought the manuscript back for the original price of £10. Some scholars suggest that the novel itself was written in 1798/9, although a comment in Austen's own prefatory 'Advertisement' ('thirteen years have passed since it was finished, many more since it was begun') suggests it may contain some of the earliest writing from any of the six major novels.

The corresponding dates for the three later books are simpler: *Mansfield Park*, begun in 1811 and published in 1814, was followed by *Emma* (1814/1815) and *Persuasion* (1816/1817). To these, however, must be added two unfinished works; *The Watsons* (abandoned in 1804) and *Sanditon* (1817); of particular interest in the present context, finally, is the short epistolary novel *Lady Susan*, perhaps written in 1795, together with a considerable body of *Juvenilia* produced in the novelist's teens. All of Austen's writing is relevant to the present chapter, although the chief emphasis is placed on *Northanger Abbey* and *Mansfield Park*, as representative examples of Austen's two great creative phases.

In addition to the chronological gap, however, there is a gulf between the two novels in generic terms. *Northanger Abbey*, like much of the *Juvenilia*, is thus grounded on literary models, and reflects the essentially parasitic modes of satire and parody. Even *Sense and Sensibility*, Austen's first major narrative, seems to shift between burlesque and 'serious novel'; the respected Austen scholar Walton Litz describes it as 'a youthful work patched up at a later date, in which the crude antitheses of the original structure were never successfully overcome'. Litz also notes earlier eighteenth-century novels, such as Maria Edgeworth's *Letters of Julia and Caroline* (1795) or Elizabeth Inchbald's *Nature and Art* (1796), with a similar kind of moral polarity: Austen's own memorably spelt *Love and Freindship* is another example.[4]

And yet much of this same parody and burlesque is both expressed *in*, and even sometimes directed *at*, epistolary form, the narrative convention most readily associated with private, documentary modes. A first glance at the *Juvenilia* suggests that Richardson is the central impulse, whether as literary model or satirical target. *Volume the First* thus includes *Amelia Webster* and *The Three Sisters*, short parodies of Richardsonian letter fiction. *Volume the Second*, with *Love and Freindship* (15 letters and 63 pages) and *Lesley Castle* (9 letters and 57 pages), has more substantial examples of the same tendency; in addition, the five set pieces of *A Collection of Letters* – including 'From a Young lady crossed in Love to her Freind' and 'From a young Lady in distress'd Circumstances to her freind' – presumably have one eye on Richardson's own *Familiar Letters*. There was even a very short dramatization of *Grandison*, a work which Austen obviously knew intimately. Only the longer piece of *Volume the Third*, 'Catharine, or The Bower', forsakes the Richardsonian mode entirely and points to the shrewdly authoritative Fieldingesque external narrator familiar from the later fiction.[5]

Sense and Sensibility, in its earlier form of 'Elinor and Marianne', was an epistolary novel; the final version still quotes eight letters and refers to another dozen. 'First Impressions', the early draft of *Pride and*

Prejudice, may have had similar origins: the published novel includes twenty-one letters, and mentions or implies as many more. There may, in fact, be a significant moment in *Lady Susan* (variously dated 1795 or 1805) where Austen reacts against the restrictions of epistolary form, much as Richardson did in the first volume of *Pamela*, the difference being that Austen later abandoned the form. Here, after participating in a series of nineteen perfunctory exchanges, the more conventional Catherine Vernon produces a letter twice as long as anything before it, with extensive *verbatim* quotations from Austen's most outrageous heroine; letter 24 (out of 41) is even longer, with extensive dialogue set out in a form that has little suggestion of letter fiction.

Apart from illustrating an evolution in narrative technique, however, such examples also reaffirm the existence, by Austen's day, of a long and substantial fictional tradition on which the novelist could draw. There are now, in fact, other impressive *literary* models – not least, Richardson and Burney – which show the budding novelist how to exploit *documentary* ones.

But letter-writing in the eighteenth century, fictional or otherwise, was also a gendered activity. Henry Tilney in *Northanger Abbey* refers to the 'easy style of writing for which ladies are so generally celebrated' (p. 13).[6] Extreme letter-writing facility in a man, as also appears from Clarissa's earlier comments on Lovelace, was conversely a suspect talent. Gender may again be linked with genre, then, and not only in etymological terms. Comparisons have already been made between male *authors*, with their implication of 'authority', and female *novelists* with their promise of something 'new', although – in view of the sex of Fielding and Richardson – the terms 'hieratic' and 'demotic' were proposed as a more useful terminological distinction between the two tendencies. In practice, however, there is a high correlation between demotic mode and female gender in canonic eighteenth-century fiction, although Austen once again confounds all easy generalizations.

The complexity of her fiction is nowhere more apparent than in modern critical trends, according to which she is often seen as a kind of proto-feminist radical. An antidote to such ahistorical approaches may be found with reference to the political realities of late eighteenth-century England. In the country's tense social climate following the French Revolution, most English writers were polarized into the 'Jacobin' (or radical) and 'anti-Jacobin' (or conservative) camps. Austen would belong unambiguously to the second group, with the reactionary *Mansfield Park* being the great anti-Jacobin novel.[7] Austen herself is, then, a 'latecomer to an established, highly stylized feminine genre',

with Burney and Edgeworth as her most significant immediate predecessors; she may also be placed in an even longer tradition of Tory
women's writing going back to Aphra Behn and Mary Astell.[8]

Ideologically, Austen is also close to Fielding; and in literary terms,
paradoxical as it may seem, she is even closer to the admittedly arch-Tory
but also sexually uninhibited Behn. For in spite of her innate conservatism, Behn is still the great fictional innovator of the (long) eighteenth
century. Austen stands in much the same relation to the nineteenth,
with two literary characteristics particularly prominent in her own case:
the first is an aesthetic commitment to the novel as form, which is
almost Jamesian – without pseudo-pedigrees like Fielding or moral
reservations like Burney; the second is a consolidation of perhaps the
major technical innovation of classic realist fiction, the use of Free
Indirect Discourse. It is, of course, this latter stylistic hybrid which first
transcends, and then virtually supercedes, the third binarism underlying
this study: the contrast between first- and third-person narrators. This
aspect of Austen's fiction is discussed in detail below.

Northanger Abbey, as any literary history will remind us, begins as a
send-up of Gothic romances, with Radcliffe's *The Mysteries of Udolpho*
as the chief target. Such a parasitical relationship suggests, moreover,
that this particular Austen novel should be classified emphatically with
those eighteenth-century texts generated primarily by literary rather
than non-literary or documentary sources or impulses: say *Joseph
Andrews* or *The Female Quixote*. That Austen certainly appreciated this
kind of literary exercise is clear from her comments in letters both on
Lennox's novel and on that lesser known satire of sensational romances
and their susceptible readers: Eaton Stannard Barrett's *The Heroine*.
The Female Quixote, she writes in 1807, 'now makes our evening enter-
tainment; to me a very high one, as I find the work equal to what
I remembered it', suggesting she read the work more than once; *The
Heroine* she describes as 'a delightful burlesque, particularly on the
Radcliffe style'.[9]

Austen's references to novels and novelists are fairly frequent, quite
explicit and generally well-known. For the scholar hoping to extract
a coherent poetics, on the other hand, the *Letters* are disappointing.
There are numerous remarks on contemporary novelists, confirming
that Austen was an avid novel reader, and – at least among intimates –
unashamed of her enthusiasm for the form. As the references themselves go, the comments on Fielding and Richardson (let alone Defoe,
Sterne, or Swift) are perfunctory. Opinions on various contemporary

writers are sometimes more revealing, although they normally reflect highly personal reactions rather than reasoned critical comment. The letters reveal predictably moderate tastes, shunning the extremes of both heavy didacticism and wild sensation. Of Hannah More's *Coelebs in Search of a Wife*, for example, Austen thus writes rather dismissively:

> You have by no means raised my curiosity after Caleb [*sic*]; My disinclination for it before was affected, but now it is real; I do not like the Evangelicals. – Of course I shall be delighted when I read it, like other people, but till I do I dislike it.   (p. 256)

In the revised version of the early 'Catharine, or The Bower' (in *Volume the Third* of the *Juvenilia*) the heroine's prudish aunt offers More's novel to her independently-minded ward. A novel by the Irish novelist Sydney Owenson (Lady Morgan), on the other hand, finds Austen in her most facetious vein:

> We have got *Ida of Athens* by Miss Owenson; which must be very clever, because it was written as the Authoress says, in three months. – We have only read the Preface yet; but her Irish Girl does not make me expect much. – If the warmth of her Language could affect the Body it might be worth reading in this weather. –   (p. 251)

Some of the most detailed, if ambivalent, comments are reserved for Mary Brunton's *Self-Control* ('an excellently-meant, elegantly written Work, without anything of Nature or Probability in it'), together with jokes about writing 'a close Imitation' as soon as she can:

> my Heroine shall not merely be wafted down an American river in a boat by herself, she shall cross the Atlantic in the same way; & never stop till she reaches Gravesend.   (p. 423)

Irony is mixed with admiration, but an earlier comment in another letter ('I am looking over Self Control again', p. 344) suggests that – like Mark Twain – she, too, had read and *re*read her author. The most important contemporary novelists for Austen are clearly Burney and Edgeworth, although there is not much detailed comment on either of these writers. Far from signalling authorial indifference, however, the nature of Austen's remarks probably suggests that, for one who does not set herself up as a professional critic, further judgement may be superfluous. In the same way, Austen does not presume to criticize *Tom*

Jones, although she knows it well enough to remember the colour of the hero's clothes when he is wounded.

In terms of literary influences, critics find no shortage of candidates for Austen's novels. There is even a widespread tendency to regard eighteenth-century English fiction as no more than an evolutionary process required to produce a Jane Austen: it is a dangerous over-simplification, although Ian Watt did suggest more judiciously that Austen combined Richardson's realism of presentation with Fielding's realism of assessment.[10] This important triangular relationship is worth a further glance. And nothing demonstrates more vividly the contrasting approaches of Fielding and Richardson than their handling of one particular variation of the courtship *topos* – unwanted male attentions to the heroine – in *Tom Jones* and *Clarissa*, respectively. Fielding's version of this scene is the *description* of an interview between Sophie Western and Blifil, as offered by Fielding's extradiegetic, or external, narrator in *Tom Jones*:

> Mr Blifil soon arrived; and Mr Western soon after withdrawing, left the young couple together. Here a long silence of near a quarter of an hour ensued: for the gentleman, who was to begin the conversation, had all that unbecoming modesty which consists in bashfulness. He often attempted to speak, and as often suppressed his words just at the very point of utterance. At last out they broke in a torrent of far-fetched and high-strained compliments, which were answered, on her side by downcast looks, half bows and civil monosyllables. Blifil from his inexperience in the ways of women, and from his conceit of himself, took this behaviour for a modest assent to his courtship; and when to shorten a scene which she could no longer support, Sophia rose up and left the room, he imputed that, too, merely to bashfulness, and comforted himself, that he should soon have enough of her company.   (Book VI, ch. 7)

Despite the highly literary narrator, there are obvious theatrical echoes, with Blifil as comic stage villain and Sophie as the persecuted, but ultimately inviolable, heroine. One might also emphasize the carefully balanced antitheses of the narrator's rhetoric, all suggesting a passage that is aesthetically constructed rather than psychologically motivated, external social observation rather than internal intimate analysis.

In stark contrast is the *dramatization* of an identical context in Clarissa's meeting with Solmes, as recalled in a letter to the heroine's friend and *confidante*, Anna Howe:

I went down this morning when breakfast was ready with a very uneasy heart . . . wishing for an opportunity to appeal to my mother in hopes to engage her interest in my behalf, and purposing to try to find one when she returned to her own apartment after breakfast – But, unluckily, there was the odious Solmes sitting asquat between my mother and sister, with *so much* assurance in his looks! – But you know, my dear, that those we love not cannot do anything to please us.

Had the wretch kept his seat, it might have been well enough: but the bent and broad-shouldered creature must needs rise and stalk towards a chair; which was just by that which was set for me.

I removed it at a distance, as if to make way to my own; and down I sat, abruptly I believe; what I had heard all in my head.

But this was not enough to daunt him. The man is a very confident, he is a very bold, staring man! Indeed, my dear, the man is very confident.

He took the removed chair and drew it so near mine, squatting in it with his ugly weight, that he pressed upon my hoop – I was so offended (all I had heard, as I say, in my head) that I removed to another chair. I own I had too little command of myself. It gave my brother and sister too much advantage. I dare say they took it – But I did it involuntarily, I think. I could not help it – I knew not what I did.   (Letter XVI)

With its insistent physicality, and a tormented sensibility further empha-sized by fragmented syntax, the scene from *Clarissa* is paradoxically more dramatic than the corresponding episode in *Tom Jones*, or may at least be regarded as more psychologically than aesthetically motivated.

Ian Watt must also be credited for first juxtaposing these two scenes, although the unwanted courtship *topos* is a commonplace in eight-eenth-century fiction.[11] For another classic example, one need look no further than *Caleb Williams* (Vol. 1, ch. 7), when Squire Tyrrel selects the uncouth Grimes as a husband for his cousin Emily. Godwin exploits the full dramatic potential of the episode: from Emily's cool rejection of Tyrrel's original scheme ('I am very happy as I am: why should I be married?'), to Grimes's grotesque presumption ('As coy and bashful as you seem, I dare say you are rogue enough at bottom. When I have touzled and rumpled you a little, we shall see'), to the comic juxtaposi-tion of Emily's formal register – '[she] began . . . to thank Mr Grimes for his good opinion, but to confess that she could never be brought to favour his addresses' (p. 54). Godwin's final dismissal of Grimes ('he was always accustomed to consider women as made for the recreation of men') is more ideologically explicit than anything Fielding offers on Blifil. By and large, however, the scene has more of the social comedy of *Tom Jones* than the emotional trauma of *Clarissa*.

Predictably, for a novelist of manners, the unwanted proposal is also a staple of Austen, reflecting in microcosm something of the novelist's range and subtlety. The best known example is Elizabeth Bennet's efficient dismissal of Mr Collins in *Pride and Prejudice* (ch. 19): the form of unmediated dialogue used here is closer to Richardson's epistolary monologue, but the element of social comedy – Collins's pomposity, his airy assumptions of female reticence, his final disabuse by Elizabeth – is closer to Fielding. With Fanny Price's refusal of Henry Crawford in *Mansfield Park*, on the other hand, the ingredients are reversed: the original scene (ch. 31) is pure Fieldingesque *diegesis* or 'telling'; Fanny's 'double distress' only appears directly when she must explain to the austere Sir Thomas Bertram (ch. 32) how she could refuse such a catch as Henry; here, even the fragmented syntax recalls Clarissa's voice. Between them, the two passages provide a genial synthesis of Fielding and Richardson.

There are other effective variations on the courtship theme, such as the clever thematic inversion in *Sense and Sensibility*, with Willoughby's letter extricating himself from involvement with Marianne: at the exact central point, and in the most excruciating scene, of the novel, Marianne 'almost scream[s] with agony' (ch. 29). The proposal of Mr Elton in *Emma*, on the other hand, surpasses even *Pride and Prejudice* in its farcicality, not least for the suitor being emboldened by 'Mr Weston's good wine' (ch. 15). But the most remarkable reworking of the *topos* is surely the double experience of Captain Wentworth and Anne Elliott in *Persuasion*. The first occasion is striking even by Austen's standards for the total perfunctoriness of the account:

> Half the sum of attraction, on either side, might have been enough, for he had nothing to do, and she had hardly any body to love; but the encounter of such lavish recommendations could not fail. They were gradually acquainted, and when acquainted, rapidly and deeply in love. It would be difficult to say which had seen highest perfection in the other, or which had been the happiest; she, in receiving his declarations and proposals, or he in having them accepted.[12]

Wentworth's renewed suit in writing eight and a half years later, on the other hand, is simply the most dramatic episode in all of Austen's fiction:

> You pierce my soul. I am half agony, half hope. Tell me not that I am
> too late, that such precious feelings are gone for ever. I offer myself
> to you again with a heart even more your own, than when you
> almost broke it eight years and a half ago.   (p. 223)

Here, in complete seriousness, is a declaration as passionate as anything
by the Brontës; it is also, ironically enough in a writer always suspicious
of emotional excess, in intimate letter form.

The marriage proposal at the climax of *Northanger Abbey* is tame by
comparison, generated as it is by a blend of parody and burlesque. The
'anxious, agitated, happy, feverish Catherine' (four adjectives are not
the norm in Austen) sets out on the momentous walk with Henry,
during the course of which:

> She was assured of his affection; and that heart in return was
> solicited, which, perhaps, they pretty equally knew was already
> entirely his own; for, though Henry was now sincerely attached to
> her, though he felt and delighted in all the excellencies of her charac-
> ter and truly loved her society, I must confess that his affection
> originated in nothing better than gratitude, or, in other words, that
> a persuasion of her partiality for him had been the only cause of
> giving her a serious thought.   (p. 198)

The narrator then proceeds to comment rather skittishly:

> It is a new circumstance in romance, I acknowledge, and dreadfully
> derogatory of an heroine's dignity; but if it be as new in common life,
> the credit of a wild imagination will at least be all my own.   (p. 198)

Sadly, the sudden intrusion of the first person, absent to this point in
the text, may owe more to youthful lack of nerve in an erotic context
than to any more deliberate concept of anti-romance.

In spite of these technical (or perhaps temperamental) limitations,
however, Austen is a dedicated novelist. There is thus a spirited call for
writerly solidarity in chapter 5 of *Northanger Abbey*: 'Let us not desert
one another; we are an injured body' (p. 21) comes significantly from
the authorial *persona her*self. The sense of corporate identity ('From
pride, ignorance, or fashion, our foes are almost as many as our
readers', p. 21) suggests, moreover, that the formal distinction between
anonymous narrator and Austen herself need not be urged too
strongly. Against the fashionable cant that dismisses a book as 'only

a novel', the novelist–narrator makes an ironic rejoinder to the effect that it is:

> only some work in which ... the most thorough knowledge of human nature, the happiest delineation of its varieties, the liveliest effusions of wit and humour are conveyed to the world in the best chosen language.   (p. 22)

Austen's spirited defence of novelists singles out Burney's *Cecilia* and *Camilla*, together with Edgeworth's *Belinda*, for individual praise. It is also worth noting that the kinds of writing to which the novel is favourably compared include not only the 'nine-hundredth abridger of the History of England' (perhaps a reference to Goldsmith) or an overlauded editor of Milton, Pope, or Prior, but the very essays of the *Spectator*. All are significantly male productions and receive far shorter shrift than Radcliffe herself, the ostensible target of Austen's parody in the novel.

There is, of course, some risk in equating the narrator's opinions in *Northanger Abbey* too literally with those of the writer, since the authorial *persona* of the novel might reflect the kind of self-consciousness reminiscent of Fielding's facetious narrator in *Tom Jones*. Here, once again, the distinction between literary and non-literary impulses is helpful. The layers of Austen's irony are often complex, and any acceptance of the above comments at face value follows quite naturally from an exclusive emphasis on the *literary* inspiration of Austen's narratives: in this context, reflecting the parasitical mode of the parodist. For the passing comments of the latter do not normally presume a painstakingly conceived, psychologically motivated, narrative *persona*, or even an 'implied author'; they tend rather to represent unmediated author and authority.

An alternative approach to such passages, stressing the narrator's formal independence from the 'real' author, is not simply the result of modern critical overkill, but is also encouraged by the mature Austen's characterization technique. For even the most perfunctory reading of *Northanger Abbey* suggests that Henry Tilney soon becomes more than just the author's mouthpiece, a simple benchmark for desirable ideological norms; whilst, by the time of *Mansfield Park*, Austen's texts have become so complex that it is a simple academic exercise to deconstruct any holistic reading at all, or to refute any monolithic interpretation. Together with the other two late novels, then, *Mansfield Park* suggests emphatically the consummate novelist and the new.

Northanger Abbey's 'Advertisement, by the Authoress' confirms that the work was written over a long period. It is hazardous to speculate on which parts of the novel come from which period, although it seems equally cowardly not to try. Thus, Henry's long list of Gothic clichés as he and Catherine approach Northanger Abbey ('We shall *not* have to explore our way into a hall dimly lighted by the expiring embers of a wood fire – *nor* be obliged to spread our beds on the floor of a room without windows, doors, or furniture' [my emphasis], p. 124) can only be introduced by negatives: what is *not* about to happen. The catalogue suggests an only partially successful attempt on Austen's part to naturalize key elements of her parodic enterprise. Or, in other words: if Catherine *had* accumulated any 'normal' experiences to relate, these would have little relevance in a narrative supposedly ridiculing Gothic excesses; whereas, if there *were* any genuinely sensational events, recounting them would then have involved some form of complicity with Gothic conventions rather than any kind of reaction against them. It is a form of generic tension which lies at the heart of many eighteenth-century narratives trying to negotiate the ambiguous terrain between satire and realism.

The ultimate incompatibility of parody or satire and psychological realism can be illustrated by returning to *Don Quixote*, the first great European novelist to confront this dilemma. Cervantes is saved by his greater generic flexibility: for, much critical opinion to the contrary, he was frequently writing simple anti-romance rather than any kind of realistic fiction. It is enough to try to transpose what is arguably the most famous episode of the novel, Don Quixote tilting at the windmills, into naturalistic visual terms. Like such similarly graphic scenes as Gulliver being tied down by the Lilliputians, it is made for Hollywood special effects rather than *ciné-vérité*. Even a writer as late as Smollett – before *Humphry Clinker* at least – remains well on the traditional side of the romance–realism divide: he thus described *Roderick Random* as a '*Romance* in two small volumes'. In Austen, on the other hand, every scene can be literally – even visually – naturalized. Contemporary cinema and television have, in fact, gone far towards doing so.

In the light of the novel's lengthy gestation period, certain elements of *Northanger Abbey* may literally represent a pre-novelistic discourse. Catherine's loss of the use of her candle is thus a fairly crude satire of Gothic sensationalism:

> The dimness of the light her candle emitted made her turn to it
> with alarm; but there was no danger of its sudden extinction, it had

yet some hours to burn; and that she might not have any greater difficulty in distinguishing the writing than what its ancient date might occasion, she hastily snuffed it. Alas! it was snuffed and extinguished in one.   (p. 135)

The trope of sudden reversal even seems to echo one of the eighteenth-century novel's grosser parodic scenes ('Mrs. *Jervis* and I are just in Bed, and the Door unlocked; if my Master should come – Odsbobs! I hear him coming in at the Door'), occurring in Fielding's *Shamela*.[13]

Such elements contrast markedly, for example, with a subtle exchange between Henry and Catherine on Isabella Thorpe's flirtation with the other Tilney brother. Henry is the first speaker:

'I understand: she is in love with James, and flirts with Frederick.'

'Oh! no, not flirts. A woman in love with one man cannot flirt with another.'

'It is probable that she will neither love so well, nor flirt so well, as she might do either singly. The gentlemen must each give up a little.'

After a short pause, Catherine resumed with 'Then you do not believe Isabella so very much attached to my brother?'

'I can have no opinion on that subject.'

'But what can your brother mean? If he knows her engagement, what can he mean by his behaviour?'

'You are a very close questioner.'

'Am I? – I only ask what I want to be told.'

'But do you only ask what I can be expected to tell?'

(pp. 118–19)

The passage either anticipates, or – depending on dates of composition – actually *is* late vintage Austen. Its implied competing discourses include (at least) Catherine's naive idealism, Henry's measured scepticism and, of course, some kind of intrinsic ethical standards embraced by the writer. The force of the passage is nevertheless rooted in characterization – that is, in psychological rather than ethical motivation. Here is the fully fledged novel of manners, with a carefully crafted exchange of almost Jamesian refinement. As dialogue, it stands comparison with Sheridan or Wilde.

In other scenes, such as the great discussion of Gothic novels in chapter 14, the mechanics of parody and the subtleties of characterization are not so easily separated. In response to Catherine's jibe that 'gentlemen read better books', Henry mounts a spirited defence of *Udolpho*, claiming to have read it in two days with his hair standing on end all the time. Ironically patronizing as this seems, Henry may be a more naive reader than he would like to think. A self-proclaimed expert on most subjects from landscape painting to the contemporary political scene, he can blithely attribute a more extensive knowledge of Gothic romance to the educational advantages of his sex: 'Consider how many years I have had the start of you. I had entered on my studies at Oxford, while you were a good little girl working your sampler at home!' (p. 83). Here, apparently, is an unambiguous admission of gender divisions on Henry's part.

But Henry's self-irony has its limits: there is a recognition of educational opportunities and privileges enjoyed, but without questioning the male monopoly of their use (or misuse). Henry does not apparently imagine that things could ever be otherwise; and, although personal interpretations will certainly differ here, Austen herself does not seem to be criticizing this ideological blind spot, either. Once again it is difficult to unravel the complexities of textual irony, although later authorial comments on gender roles in informal disussion ('A woman especially, if she have the misfortune of knowing any thing, should conceal it as well as she can', p. 86) may also suggest some proto-feminist awareness of gender roles on Austen's part.

One abiding impression of *Northanger Abbey*, on the other hand, is the author's patent respect for Radcliffe: she finds fault less with *The Mysteries of Udolpho* than with some of its sillier contemporary admirers. Anticipating revisionist readings of Gothic at the end of the twentieth century, moreover, Austen even achieves a revisionist *writing* of this mode at the beginning of the nineteenth. When Henry suddenly understands the nature of Catherine's suspicions about his father, for example, he reacts in horror: 'Remember the country and the age in which we live. Remember that we are English, that we are Christians' (p. 159). Catherine learns fast, and her later paean to the 'central part of England' is arguably as enthusiastic as anything offered by the complacent Henry. From here on, the narrator assures us, '[t]he anxieties of common life began soon to succeed to the alarms of romance' (p. 161). It is precisely at such moments, however, that the dangers of reading Austen without due attention become clear. For Catherine's remarks then shade off into some classically understated comments on the Tilney family:

> she would not be surprised if even in Henry and Eleanor Tilney, some slight imperfection might hereafter appear; and upon this

conviction she need not fear to acknowledge some actual specks in the character of their father, who, though cleared from the grossly injurious suspicions which she must ever blush to have entertained, she did believe, upon serious consideration, to be not perfectly amiable. (p. 161)

The General is, in fact, a mercenary monster, whose patriarchal tyranny rivals that of the worst Gothic villain; such unspeakable behaviour is as possible in Austen's world as it is in Radcliffe's. And if the hero's romantic declarations (never explicit) were probably tame by the standards of Captain Wentworth in *Persuasion*, then the real climax of *Northanger Abbey* lies in Henry's blatant defiance of his own father to be able to make them: perhaps the only occasion in all of the major novels when the authority of the defective father figure is so clearly portrayed *and* so openly flouted. Austen is now firmly located in the world of parental oppression so familiar from the social context of authentic non-parody feminine Gothic.

Mansfield Park

With *Mansfield Park*, the distinction between literary and documentary sources finally breaks down, as does the related distinction between 'hieratic' and 'demotic' modes; or even male *author* and female *novelist*. Ideologically, there is not much new in the novel; technically, however, Austen's development is spectacular. Besides her use of free indirect discourse – noted above and discussed below – these innovative elements also include the wide use of figural devices within the narrative. There are no obvious literary sources in *Mansfield Park*, and far less a target text as in *Northanger Abbey*, whereas the insights and achievements of such major fictional forebears as Richardson, Fielding and Burney have been so seamlessly absorbed, that it is difficult to speak in simple terms of influence.

There are other more obvious structural and thematic analogies between *Northanger Abbey* and *Mansfield Park*, which can also be extended to Austen's other major fiction. All six novels are thus English prototypes of the female *Bildungsroman* – or 'novel of education' – in which the heroine is taken through a painful socialization process towards marriage and social integration.[14] One great contrast between the two novels, however, is that existing between the surprisingly candid Catherine Morland and the timidly self-effacing Fanny Price.

Readers upset by the passivity of Fanny Price seem to assume an ideal norm among Austen's female protagonists that is difficult to locate in practice. Elizabeth Bennet is the obvious popular favourite, although the sharp outspokenness and animal vitality that charm most modern readers would doubtless have troubled many contemporaries; even a more mature Austen found the novel 'rather too light, and bright and sparkling', and it is clearly Elizabeth who provides this sparkle. The plausibility of Elinor and Marianne Dashwood, on the other hand, is often compromised by their schematic role as emblems of 'sense' and 'sensibility'. Catherine Morland has a few memorable individualizing traits with her youthful preference for 'cricket, base ball, riding on horseback, and running about the country' (p. 3), but – as archetypal *anti-heroine* – still has a blatantly ideological function like the Dashwood sisters. This naturally allows her some freedom as an outspoken satirical foil, as in her famous dismissal of conventional historiography as '[t]he quarrels of popes and kings, with wars or pestilences, in every page; the men all so good for nothing, and hardly any women at all – it is very tiresome' (p. 84). Emma Wodehouse, on the other hand, one of Austen's most psychologically convincing protagonists, is introduced defensively as the heroine that no-one but her creator will much like.

Only Anne Elliot of *Persuasion* would seem to strike a traditional balance between mere docility and total self-effacement, and the catastrophic results of her attitude – initial loss of the man she loves – are plain to see. It is sometimes suggested that *Persuasion*, for all the new and uncharacteristic sensitivity to the sublime, has a few jarring passages and might have been further polished had time permitted. *Emma*, the most claustrophobic of the major novels, is conversely appreciated for certain technical refinements; a seminal essay by Wayne Booth in this context examined the novelist's 'control of distance', that is, her conscious attempt to mould the reader's sympathies for the heroine.[15]

Mansfield Park is closer to *Emma* by way of its technical achievements than it is to *Persuasion* for any form of aesthetic innovation. Among the immediate family resemblances between *Northanger Abbey* and *Mansfield Park*, on the other hand, the common choice of a house for the title seems the most striking: of all the other fiction, only the adolescent 'unfinished Novel in Letters', *Lesley Castle*, shares this distinction. In practice, however, this superficial similarity conceals a more significant opposition; for the Tilneys' home in the Cotswolds, as noted above, only really exists as an inventory for everything which it is *not*; *Mansfield Park*, on the other hand, is an equally obvious index of something which unambiguously *is*. Tony Tanner ingeniously links all of the novel's standard group of defective parents and nubile children with the great house, classifying them as guardians, inheritors and interlopers. And beyond mere bricks and mortar, the house is also an 'edifice of values'.[16]

Setting is an important ingredient in the 'formal realism' which characterizes the English classic realist novel. The seat of Mansfield Park has its closest antecedent in *Tom Jones*'s Allworthy Hall, in the sense of the house standing as metonym for a certain social order, a concrete symbol for an entire way of life: rural and traditional, conservative and hierarchic. But *Mansfield Park* the novel has an even more complex topography than *Tom Jones*. The home of the Bertrams, or the 'great house' is clearly related to a whole matrix of authentic, solidly specified houses which move fleetingly or rest more permanently within its orbit. These spacial relations are clearly defined within the high-realistic conventions of the narrative: 'scarce half a mile' from Mansfield, for example, is the parsonage, home of the Grants, and the means of introducing the disruptive Crawfords into Mansfield life; at a slightly greater distance is the white house provided by Sir Thomas for Mrs Norris. 'Only eight miles' beyond Mansfield Park, but more tenuously linked, is Thornton Lacey, where it is assumed Edmund will live after ordination.

'Ten miles of indifferent road' then brings us to Mr Rushworth's seat of Sotherton Court, momentarily entering Mansfield's orbit, whilst possessing its own constellation of houses: the Brighton house taken for a few weeks after Mr Rushworth's marriage; Maria's town house in Wimpole Street to compensate for the London house her mother had given up; the smaller house to which Mrs Rushworth might be expected to retire on her son's marriage. More topographically marginal, on the other hand, are the Price home at Portsmouth, the 'establishment' in another country for the disgraced Maria and Mrs Norris, the various refuges of Mr Yates and Julia during their elopement, perhaps even the floating home of Fanny's brother William, on the *Antwerp*; more ontologically remote, finally (in the sense that they never actually materialize), are Stanwix Lodge, which Henry Crawford has fantasies of renting, or the cottage that Fanny would share with William in her own family romance.

The full thematic significance of all these houses in *Mansfield Park* emerges most clearly in two of the novel's central metaphors for social change. The first of these is the activity of 'improvement'; centred primarily on the disastrous modifications made to Sotherton Hall by the foolish Mr Rushworth, this thoughtless uprooting and destruction of tradition had profoundly negative associations for Austen. The second of these motifs, reflecting the novel's concern with territorial appropriation and its tendency to regard social identity in terms of a house, is 'establishment'. This frequently used and highly pregnant word in the context of the novel contains several interrelated meanings, including the process of acquiring a seat such as Mansfield; the state of social stability associated with such an acquisition; *and* the material consolidation resulting from this dual process.

Houses are then also associated with the rage for amateur theatricals. The 'itch for acting' is brought to Mansfield by Mr Yates from another country house, Ecclesford; when problems of casting arise, Tom claims that vacant roles can easily be filled by 'six young men within six miles of us' (p. 170). Parsonages and 'houses' of worship form another thematically loaded topographical set: Mansfield parsonage, the significantly disused Sotherton chapel, Edmund Bertram's future home of Thornton, Mrs Price's refuge of the family church at Portsmouth. Readers may ultimately constitute their own sets almost at random – fashionable town houses, comfortable country seats, places of public assembly; or they may expand the original matrix, to include such marginal elements as the Sneyds at Albion Place, the Andersons of Baker Street, or the Miss Owens of Peterborough, bringing ever fresh contingents of marriageable daughters presumably caught up in ever new manifestations of sibling rivalry in ever new courtship rituals.

The extraordinary topographical complexity and precision of *Mansfield Park* can be read in various ways: the final embodiment of Watt's *formal realism* in the fiction of the eighteenth century, the 'solidity of specification' integral to F. R. Leavis's concept of moral seriousness, or simply as the crowning example of Austen's (*pseudo-*)documentary or quasi-sociological modes; for it is easy to imagine that the environment of *Mansfield Park* must exist somewhere on a genuine map.

With the young people's performance of *Lovers' Vows*, on the other hand, Austen enters a new area of novelistic convention: that of 'mirror text' or *mise en abîme*.[17] The latter term is derived from heraldry and denotes that portion of a coat of arms which repeats in miniature the design of the whole shield, although it should be noted that the element reproduced is almost never identical to the original. The figurative device of *mise en abîme* would appear to be a universal literary pattern, with perhaps the most famous example in English literature appearing in *Hamlet*'s 'play within the play'. With the amateur theatricals in *Mansfield Park*, Austen's internal duplication is generically further from her surrounding text than Shakespeare's: for here are two different literary forms, a drama within a novel. The precise nature of the aesthetic and psychological effects of *mise en abîme* are highly complex and speculative matters, although it could be argued that the convention of the omniscient author itself may ultimately be the most profound and fundamental example of the device: for the author–narrators of *Tom Jones* or *Pride and Prejudice* effectively enjoy the same relation to their text as the conventional Christian God does to *His* universe; here, in either case, is the ultimate authority.

There are other lesser patterns of interior duplication within *Mansfield Park*. In merely formal terms, however, there can be little doubt of the reality-enhancing effect of fictional characters engaged in interaction with real literary texts, including ones familiar to the reader. It is, after all, one of the elements in *Northanger Abbey* which helps even this novel cross a basic realistic threshold. There is a classic exchange in this context between Catherine and Isabella Thorpe, with their broad survey of Gothic novels and brief comment on Richardson's *Grandison* (p. 25). In practice, however, *mise en abîme*, may be too inflated a term for some of the barely 'naturalized' references to writers in the earlier novels, with their roots in eighteenth-century burlesque. Elinor's comments to her highly-strung sister in *Sense and Sensibility* are a case in point:

> 'Well, Marianne, . . . for *one* morning I think you have done pretty well. You have already ascertained Mr Willoughby's opinion in almost every matter of importance. You know what he thinks of Cowper and Scott; you are certain of his estimating their beauties as he ought, and you have received every assurance of his admiring Pope no more than is proper. (p. 79)

Here, surely, is mere youthful satire of fashionable literary tastes. In *Mansfield Park*, on the other hand, literary reference is a totally integrated index of character, as in the case of Henry Crawford, who reads Shakespeare so beautifully. For there is then an ironic counterpoint between dramatic excerpts used purely to train elocution in well-educated children and the wide-scale erotic sublimation evident in the home performance of the sentimental melodrama *Lovers' Vows*. Henry's dramatic talents then become highly suspect: 'whether it were dignity or pride, or tenderness or remorse, or whatever were to be expressed, he could do it with equal beauty' (p. 335). He will ultimately use his talents for a totally amoral kind of improvised theatre in his declared intention of making the heroine, Fanny, fall in love with him.

But the actual staging of *Lovers' Vows* may use *mise en abîme* in another sense; for this episode offers an additional reflection – a kind of metacritical comment – on narrative genres. The young people represent the speech and thought processes of Kotzebue's characters in unmediated first-person form; *Mansfield Park*, in turn, generally portrays its own characters – whether by quotation or summary – through mediated third-person narrative. The second part of this broad contrast is not quite accurate, of course, since the novel has increasing recourse to the kind of syntactic hybrid of free indirect discourse. Briefly mentioned in previous chapters in discussing texts where its role was more marginal, the technique must now be considered more fully in the context of Austen, with whom it acquires major significance.

The so-called 'style indirect libre' was first identified and analysed in detail by the Swiss linguist and pupil of Ferdinand de Saussure, Charles Bally, in 1912.[18] For a brief recapitulation of what the French term describes, one may compare the following three simple sentences:

1. He made a firm promise: 'I'll be home for dinner.'
2. He made a firm promise that he'd be home for dinner.
3. He made a firm promise; *he'd be home for dinner.*

The first sentence is identified as 'direct speech', and the second as 'indirect speech'; the difference has long been understood, ever since the Roman grammarians, who distinguished between *oratio recta* and *oratio obliqua*, respectively. The third formulation, a kind of synthesis of the other two, is the structure to which Bally was referring, and is normally described in English as 'free indirect speech' or 'free indirect discourse' (FID): it thus keeps the flavour, even the identical words of the original discourse, but uses the syntax of reported speech. Some theorists have regarded it as a stylistic effect allowed by a kind of universal grammar, and have found examples of it in many languages and as early as the Middle Ages. Others have been more cautious about the antiquity of a form which, by its very nature, is often syntactically ambiguous: in the above comparison, for example, (3) only differs from (2) by a paltry conjunction. The acid test, however, is to reconvert such passages to the hypothetical direct speech they invoke; and there would actually have been nothing distinctive enough in the specific example here to guarantee that it ever constituted anybody's exact words.[19]

The first context in which FID occurs with some consistency is the *Fables* of La Fontaine in the seventeenth century, although the technique is more widely linked with the 'rise of the novel' in the following century.

It thus appears with regularity in Rousseau's *Émile* (1762), and is subsequently prominent in German fiction (particularly Goethe's *Elective Affinities* of 1809); the most frequent user of the technique in the French novel is Flaubert. An earlier, if less frequent, practitioner in English fiction is precisely Jane Austen. Before Austen, the device is relatively rare, however, leading to something of a critical treasure hunt in the field, as scholars attempt to identify a form regarded – in retrospect at least – as evidence of technical subtlety and innovation. Two obvious questions here are why the technique *does* occur fairly infrequently before Austen; and why, finally, she herself uses it so effectively. The latter questions may be answered simultaneously with reference to some of the novels analysed in earlier chapters.

There are embryonic examples of FID in Behn's *Oroonoko*, when the narrator records examples of the hero's oratory:

> He told them it was not for days, months, or years, but for eternity; there was no end to be of their misfortunes. *They suffered not like men who might find a glory, and fortitude in oppression, but like dogs that loved the whip and bell . . .* (p. 126)

> He told them that he had heard of one Hannibal, a great captain, had cut his way through mountains and solid rocks, and should a few scrubs oppose them, which they could fire before them? *No, 'twas a trifling excuse to men resolved to die, or overcome.* (p. 127; my emphasis)

The same syntax is never used more ambitiously, however, to represent the kind of internal monologue also described suggestively by Dorrit Cohn as 'psycho-narration'.

There are then isolated cases in Fielding and Smollett, several in Richardson, and a rather larger number in the fiction of Burney.[20] The sole putative example from *Joseph Andrews* concerns the dinner in Book III, chapter 2, where Parson Adams gives a long discourse on Homer, before asking his host for the story of his life:

> Adams told him it was now in his power to return that Favour; for his extraordinary Goodness, as well as that Fund of literature he was Master of, which he did not expect to find under such a roof, had raised in him more Curiosity . . . (pp. 178–9)[21]

More striking is a passage by Smollett, discussed in Chapter 7 in the context of *skaz*.[22] To the example from *Roderick Random* cited there, one may add Wilhelmina's indignant outburst in *Ferdinand Count Fathom* when confronted by an irate father:

> [she] began to hold forth upon her own innocence and his unjust suspicion, mingling in her harangue, sundry oblique hints against her mother in law, importing that *some people were so vitiously inclined by their own natures, that she did not wonder at their doubting the virtue of other people; but that these people despised the insinuations of such people, who ought to be more circumspect in their own conduct, lest they themselves should suffer reprisals from those people whom they had so maliciously slandered.*   (p. 94; my emphasis)

Any attempt to re-create the speaker's words is nevertheless problematic: for the passage is as much *burlesque* (heightening Wilhelmina's presumably far more incoherent original outburst) or *skaz* as FID.

There are also a few clear examples of FID in Godwin's *Caleb Williams*, as when Emily asks Grimes for help in her escape from Tyrrel Place:

> It showed very little gratitude, to desire him to disclose to other people his concern in this dangerous affair. For his part, he was determined in consideration of his own safety never to appear in it to any living soul. If Miss did not believe him when he made this proposal out of pure good-nature, and would not trust him a single inch, she might even see to the consequences herself. He was resolved to condescend no further to the whims of a person who in her treatment of him had shown herself as proud as Lucifer himself.   (p. 63)

Although clearly all FID in syntactic terms, the above passage is equally problematic: converted into direct speech, most of it would surely be beyond the capacity of the inarticulate Grimes, from whom it supposedly originates.

Examples of the technique from *Grandison* were quoted in Chapter 5 to illustrate that novel's remarkable formal range, from extreme 'writing to the moment' to what is effectively third-person extradiegetic narrative. Somewhere between these two extremes lies FID, as in Harriet's account – at second hand – of a courting visit from Sir Hargrave Pollexfen:

> He had had, he told my cousins, a most uneasy time of it, ever since he saw me. The devil fetch him, if he had had one hour's rest. He never saw a woman before whom he could love as he loved me. By

his soul, he had no view, but what was strictly honourable.

(Vol. I, Letter XVII)

The common denominator of the quotations from Fielding, Smollett and Godwin is their comic mode. And even if Pollexfen is not a comic figure, he is clearly an undignified one – particularly after the loss of three front teeth at the hands of Grandison. This may hint at the answers to questions posed at the beginning of this brief survey. The clear implication emerges that FID is a rather 'low' stylistic device, at least in the eyes of canonic eighteenth-century male (or hieratic) authors who are largely uninterested in the minute representation of individual thought-processes in fictional characters anyway. This is exactly what *did* interest Richardson, of course, although his use of intimate letters largely precludes the necessity of this kind of psycho-narration. Examples do occur in his fiction, however, the further epistolary convention is stretched: virtually non-existent in *Pamela*, they are rare in *Clarissa*, and most prominent in *Grandison*.

More obviously, FID appealed to the typical female (or demotic) eighteenth-century novelist of manners, interested in subtle emotional or psychological distinctions, and using a third-person narrator – or, in the case of letter fiction, lengthy enough third-person narrative embedding – to allow extended passages in this form. Besides Richardson, the pioneers of the technique are, in fact, Frances Brooke, Sheridan, and Burney: but the Burney of *Cecilia* and *Camilla* rather than the early epistolary *Evelina*. The technique reaches its apogee in Austen. One might even propose FID as a gendered stylistic marker, characteristic of the female novelist, whereas the colloquial, oral, potential of *skaz* largely remains the province of the male author.

Roy Pascall gives an admirable summary of the preconditions in Austen's fiction which might have encouraged the development of FID. It focuses on a small group of people of similar social class and cultural background; plots consist almost exclusively of characters' changing attitudes towards each other, so that their thoughts and feelings are integral elements of the story; the narrator – non-personal and non-defined, but both story-teller and moralist – is then given access to these thoughts and feelings. Pascall demonstrates convincingly, moreover, that *Mansfield Park* represents the most varied and effective use of FID among the six novels.[23] It also contains a wide range of formal variants, of which three may be illustrated here.

On many occasions, Austen uses quotation marks for what is clearly free *indirect* speech; a good example is the early scene between

Edmund and a homesick Fanny, with its transition from third-person narrative to FID:

> It was William whom she talked of most and wanted most to see ... *'William did not like she should come away – he had told her he should miss her very much indeed.'* 'But William will write to you, I dare say.' *'Yes, he had promised he would, but he had told* her *to write first.'* 'And when shall you do it?' She hung her head and answered, hesitatingly, *'she did not know; she had not any paper.'*
>
> > (p. 52; my emphasis)

Although the passage ends in dialogue, there is a clear difference, indicated by tenses and pronominalization, between the direct speech of Edmund and the indirect speech of Fanny.

A more conventional representation of the form, although still with snatches of third-person narrative, occurs in the report of Sir Thomas Bertram's reservations about adopting Fanny:

> *Sir Thomas could not give so instantaneous and unqualified a consent.* He debated and hesitated; *– it was a serious charge; – a girl so brought up must be adequately provided for, otherwise there would be cruelty instead of kindness in taking her from her family. He thought of his own four children – of his two sons – of cousins in love, &c.;* – but no sooner had he deliberately begun to state his objections, than Mrs. Norris interrupted him.   (p. 43)

The most original examples of all, however, are the record of thought processes, as when Fanny learns – with mixed feelings – that Henry Crawford (after the trauma of his marriage proposal) has gone on to procure William his commission in the navy:

> She was feeling, thinking, trembling about every thing; – agitated, happy, miserable, infinitely obliged, absolutely angry. *It was all beyond belief! He was inexcusable, incomprehensible!– But such were his habits, that he could do nothing without a mixture of evil. He had previously made her the happiest of human beings, and now he had insulted – she knew not what to say – how to class or how to regard it.*   (p. 305; my emphasis)

Here is genuine free indirect *discourse* rather than speech: a subtle instance of 'psycho-narration' or narrative monologue.

There is no need to prolong the list of examples. It may be emphasized instead that Austen's use of FID is more than a mere technical resource; as previously hinted, it may have ideological significance, too. FID is rare in Fielding and Smollett, and never found in a serious context; Richardson has it more frequently, but – with his characteristic cultural cringe – was probably wary about over-using what was obviously considered a colloquial, even vulgar, device. Godwin, who is politically more radical than any of his eighteenth-century predecessors, still has a more conservative view of language and similarly avoids FID; his case may be partly analogous to that of the so-called pre-romantic poets, full of new yearnings, but in search of a new idiom within which to express them. FID is the major formal innovation in eighteenth-century fiction and, for this reason, the achievements of Austen in the novel could even be compared to those of Wordsworth in poetry. If she has not championed the 'language of common *man*' – like Wordsworth, famously, in the Prelude to the *Lyrical Ballads* – then she has, more authentically than any of her predecessors, recorded the language and thought-processes of the sensitive and intelligent (gentle)*woman*.

Austen's fiction is widely regarded as a watershed between eighteenth-century narrative and the modern realist novel. There are persuasive arguments to support this view, some of which may be related to the three broad interconnected binarisms developed in this study.

The first of these divisions was grounded on the relative prominence of 'literary' and 'non-literary' (or documentary) impulses in an individual writer or even a particular work. It thus contrasted the classical and public, or formal, literary genres of epic and satire with the modern and private, or informal, non-literary genres of letter and journal. The first category could be enlarged by the addition of newer European literary models such as Rabelais, Cervantes, the European picaresque and Swift; and the second could be extended with reference to a vast range of didactic writing and journalistic ephemera. With respect to the proto-canonic names of eighteenth-century fiction, for example, this would pit Fielding (drawing on Homer, Virgil, Swift, Lucian, Cervantes) or Smollett (Horace, Juvenal, Rabelais, Lesage and more Cervantes) against the ghost-writing of Defoe or the epistolary conventions of Richardson.

Such formal divisions are naturally contentious, not only because of the notorious diffuseness of most generic groupings, but also because of the inevitably subjective – even arbitrary – nature of distinctions between 'literary' and 'non-literary'. A number of miscellaneous forms that might seem to fit the second, or 'documentary', category would thus paradoxically fall within the boundaries of the highly learned 'anatomy' or 'Menippean satire', as defined by Northrop Frye. It is also hard to find a writer of either sex who belongs exclusively to one side or the other of this divide. For a practical example, one need look no further than Sterne. Who would argue with confidence that *Tristram Shandy* is grounded predominantly in formal literary or informal non-literary impulses, however these terms are defined? The most intimate and personal of narratives, the archetypal 'novel of consciousness' or – to borrow Tristram's description of Locke's *Essay Concerning Human Understanding*: a 'history book of what passes in a man's mind' – is also the ultimate expression of a tradition of learned wit from Rabelais to Swift, with a particular debt to Robert Burton's *Anatomy of Melancholy*. The only response to such qualifications was to open a new critical front.

The second binarism of this study was grounded in the links between the terms *genre* and *gender*: in Latin and some of its linguistic descendants – but not in English – the two words are identical (Latin *genus*, Italian *genere* and Spanish *género*). This prompted a discussion in Chapter 2 of whether certain literary forms are extrinsically gendered. It was suggested there that, for purely cultural rather than any ultimately essentialist reasons, epic and satire were essentially male genres, while the letter and the private journal were female ones. Other literary forms, such as the drama or the romance, were not so easy to classify. The most intrusive eighteenth-century borrowings for today's reader are undoubtedly those from classical literature; the latter was also a quarry which, because of contemporary cultural and educational practices, was almost exclusively limited to men. On the other hand, most of what was genuinely innovative in the period from Behn to Austen seemed to come not from classically schooled and intellectually assertive men, but rather from more modestly educated and more discreetly insistent women.

This prompted two more etymological couplings, linking the concepts of 'author' and 'authority', and then those of 'novelist' and 'novelty'. Once again, the link is particularly noticeable in the self-consciously facetious but firmly authoritative narrators of Fielding. Women writers such as Behn, Manley or Haywood, generally denied the opportunity of academic education or (in the last two cases) foreign travel, tended to produce fiction modelled on non-literary, documentary or even 'informal' discursive practices such as the letter, private journal or confession. An additional tentative distinction was then made between male *authors* and their traditional authority and female *novelists* with their implied promise of something new. Such a conception seemed undermined, however, by the fact that four of the most celebrated feminocentric fictions of the first half of the eighteenth century – *Moll Flanders* and *Roxana* (pseudo-autobiographical confessions), *Pamela* (letter-fiction-*cum*-journal) and *Clarissa* (epistolary monument) – were actually produced by men. This anomaly was nevertheless removed by refining the original crude distinction between male *authors* and female *novelists* to a broader but often co-terminous one between *hieratic* and *demotic* modes. Among writers of the former group, Fielding regularly linked women, on intellectual grounds, with his twin banes of 'clerks and prentices' (Smollett and Sterne were hardly less patronizing). It may be noted that, if Defoe was generally more, but – as a bankrupt businessman – sometimes rather less than a clerk, then Richardson the master-printer began his career quite literally as an apprentice. Here is the foundation for a firm distinction between 'hieratic' and 'demotic' writers.

The broad division between the literary, hieratic *author* and the non-literary, demotic *novelist* was extremely suggestive when applied to the entire oeuvre of Fielding or Richardson in Chapters 4 and 5, respectively. But these two chapters also demonstrated the viability of the third and final binarism underlying this study: the division between third- and first-person narratives. Fielding partly relinquished the explicit authority of his third-person narrators to produce something more radically novelistic in *Amelia*; Richardson, by the time of *Grandison* and the collected *Maxims* that followed it, seemed increasingly intent on imposing some kind of direct authority on the growing autonomy of his first-person correspondents. Neither, however, really bridged the formal gap imposed by the choice of first- or third-person narrator, respectively.

Such monolithic tendencies were not so much in evidence, however, in the paired readings which constitute the second part of this study; and with the arrival of Austen, all three binarisms are undermined and finally superseded. Outside the context of parody and burlesque, her six novels do not obviously demonstrate classical literary prototypes, or even the later European influences – Cervantes, Lesage, Rabelais, Swift – so prominent in eighteenth-century English fiction. The most obvious points of literary reference, instead, belong to a domestic tradition exemplified by Fielding, Richardson and Burney. But these writers themselves, by Austen's day, are on the way to becoming institutionalized, if not canonized; so Austen can paradoxically draw on English literary models (in the case of Burney or Richardson) of 'non-literary' fiction. In this way, she also virtually obliterates the distinction between male, or hieratic, authors and female, or demotic, novelists.

But the most radically original aspect of Austen's writing was the specific formal advance by which she elided the distinction between first- and third-person narrators: her use of free indirect discourse, as discussed above.

The three binary constructs I have consistently imposed on English fiction of the long eighteenth century are open to criticism – and, naturally, even to outright rejection. In one sense, however, they are only the 'bath-water' of this study. The 'baby' is a hopefully even-handed account of a number of major novels and certain cultural processes which raised them to canonic (or *sub*-canonic) status. This should not be thrown away. For the body of this survey offers another perspective on what is often called the feminization of the novel. In terms of both personal achievement and subsequent influence, Richardson and Fielding remain the key figures at the heart of the period. Of at least equal significance, however, are Behn, the great innovator, and Austen, the great consolidator – in what Bakhtin described as 'the sole genre that continues to develop, that is as yet uncompleted'.

Appendix A

Mrs Barbauld's The British Novelists *(1810 and 1821)*

		vols
Samuel Richardson	*Clarissa* (1747–8)	1–8
	Sir Charles Grandison (1753–4)	9–15
Daniel Defoe	*Robinson Crusoe* (1719)	16–17
Henry Fielding	*Joseph Andrews* (1742)	18
	Tom Jones (1749)	19–21
Clara Reeve	*The Old English Baron* (1778)	22
Horace Walpole	*The Castle of Otranto* (1764)	
Francis Coventry	*Pompey the Little* (1751)	23
Oliver Goldsmith	*The Vicar of Wakefield* (1766)	
Charlotte Lennox	*The Female Quixote* (1752)	24–5
Samuel Johnson	*Rasselas* (1759)	26
John Hawkesworth	*Almoran and Hamet* (1761)	
Frances Brooke	*Lady Julia Mandeville* (1763)	27
Elizabeth Inchbald	*Nature and Art* (1796)	
	A Simple Story (1791)	28
Henry Mackenzie	*A Man of Feeling* (1771)	29
	Julia de Roubigné (1777)	
Tobias Smollett	*Humphry Clinker* (1771)	30–1
Richard Graves	*The Spiritual Quixote* (1773)	32–3
John Moore	*Zeluco* (1786)	34–5
Charlotte Smith	*The Old Manor House* (1793)	36–7
Frances Burney	*Evelina* (1778)	38–9
	Cecilia (1782)	40–2
Ann Radcliffe	*The Romance of the Forest* (1791)	43–4
	The Mysteries of Udolpho (1794)	45–7
Robert Bage	*Hermsprong* (1796)	48
Maria Edgeworth	*Belinda* (1801)	49
	Belinda (cont.)	50
	The Modern Griselda (1805)	

Note that the first edition of Clara Reeve's *The Old English Baron* was published as *The Champion of Virtue, A Gothic Story* (1777).

Appendix B

The Dictionary of Literary Biography, *Volume 39 (two parts):* British Novelists, 1660–1800, *ed. Martin C. Battestin (Detroit: Gale Research, 1985)*

Thomas Amory (1691?–1788)
Penelope Aubin (1685–c.1731)
Robert Bage (1728–1801)
Jane Barker (1652–1727?)
William Beckford (1760–1844)
Aphra Behn (1640?–89)
Arthur Blackamore (1679–?)
Frances Brooke (1724–89)
Henry Brooke (1724–89)
John Bunyan (1628–88)
Frances Burney (1752–1840)
John Cleland (1710–89)
Mary Collyer (1716?–83)
William Congreve (1670–1729)
Francis Coventry (1725–54)
Mary Davys (1674–1732)
Thomas Day (1748–89)
Daniel Defoe (1660–1731)
Henry Fielding (1707–54)
Sarah Fielding (1710–68)
William Godwin (1756–1836)
Oliver Goldsmith (1731/2–74)
Richard Graves (1715–1804)
Elizabeth Griffith (1727?–93)
Eliza Haywood (1693?–1756)
'Sir' John Hill (1714?–75)
Thomas Holcroft (1745–1809)
Elizabeth Inchbald (1753–1821)
Samuel Johnson (1709–84)
Charles Johnstone (1719?–1800?)
Harriet (1757–1851) and Sophia Lee (1750–1824)
Charlotte Lennox (1729/1730–1804)
Matthew Gregory Lewis (1775–1818)
Henry Mackenzie (1745–1831)
Delarivière Manley (1672?–1724)
Robert Paltock (1697–1767)
Ann Radcliffe (1764–37)

Clara Reeve (1729–1807)
Samuel Richardson (1689–1761)
Elizabeth Rowe (1674–1737)
Sarah Scott (1723–95)
Frances Sheridan (1724–66)
Charlotte Smith (1749–1806)
Tobias Smollett (1721–71)
Laurence Sterne (1713–68)
Jonathan Swift (1667–1745)
Horace Walpole (1717–97)
Mary Wollstonecraft (1759–97)

Appendix C

The Chadwyck–Healey database of English fiction (1700–1780)

Thomas Amory	*John Buncle*
Penelope Aubin	*Charlotta du Pont*
	Count Albertus
	Count de Vinevil
	Lady Lucy
	Lucinda
	Madam de Beaumont
	The Noble Slaves
Jane Barker	*Bosvil and Galesia*
	Exilius
	The Lining of the Patch-Work Screen
	A Patch-Work Screen
Frances Brooke	*Emily Montague*
	Lady Julia Mandeville
Henry Brooke	*The Fool of Quality*
Frances Burney	*Evelina*
John Cleland	*Memoirs of a Woman of Pleasure*
Francis Coventry	*Pompey the Little*
Mary Davys	*The Accomplish'd Rake*
	The Cousins
	Familiar Letters Betwixt a Gentleman and a Lady
	The Lady's Tale
	The Reform'd Coquet
Daniel Defoe	*Captain Singleton*
	Colonel Jack
	The Farther Adventures of Robinson Crusoe
	A Journal of the Plague Year
	Memoirs of a Cavalier
	Moll Flanders
	Robinson Crusoe
	Roxana
Henry Fielding	*Amelia*
	Jonathan Wild
	Joseph Andrews
	A Journey from This World to the Next
	Shamela
	Tom Jones

Sarah Fielding	*The Countess of Dellwyn*
	David Simple
	David Simple, Volume the Last
	The Cry
Oliver Goldsmith	*The Vicar of Wakefield*
Richard Graves	*The Spiritual Quixote*
John Hawkesworth	*Almoran and Hamet*
Eliza Haywood	*Anti-Pamela*
	Betsy Thoughtless
	The British Recluse
	Fantomina
	The Fatal Secret
	The Force of Nature
	The Fortunate Foundlings
	Idalia
	The Injur'd Husband
	The History of Jemmy and Jenny Jessamy
	Lasselia
	Love in Excess
	The Masqueraders
	The Rash Resolve
	The Surprise
Samuel Johnson	*Rasselas*
Charles Johnstone	*Chrysal*
Charlotte Lennox	*The Female Quixote*
	Harriot Stuart
Henry Mackenzie	*Julia de Roubigné*
	The Man of Feeling
	The Man of the World
Mary de la Rivière Manley	*The Adventures of Rivella*
	Memoirs of Europe
	The New Atalantis
	The Power of Love
	Queen Zarah
Robert Paltock	*Peter Wilkins*
Clara Reeve	*The Old English Baron*
Samuel Richardson	*Clarissa* (1st edn)
	Clarissa (3rd edn)
	Familiar Letters
	Pamela (1st edn)
	Pamela (6th edn)
	Sir Charles Grandison
Sarah Scott	*Millennium Hall*
	Sir George Ellison
Frances Sheridan	*Conclusion of the Memoirs of Miss Sidney Biddulph*
	The History of Nourjahad
	Sidney Biddulph
Tobias Smollett	*Adventures of an Atom*

	Ferdinand Count Fathom
	Humphry Clinker
	Peregrine Pickle
	Roderick Random
	Sir Launcelot Greaves
Laurence Sterne	*A Political Romance*
	A Sentimental Journey
	Tristram Shandy
Jonathan Swift	*Gulliver's Travels* (Faulkner (ed.) 1735)
	Gulliver's Travels (Motte (ed.) 1726)
Horace Walpole	*The Castle of Otranto*

Note that the successor to this collection is a CD-ROM rather misleadingly entitled *Nineteenth-Century Fiction*, although it actually covers the period 1781–1900. Most of Burney, all of Austen, as well as Gothic, Jacobin and other fiction of the Romantic period is therefore rather awkwardly separated from the eighteenth-century database.

Notes

Chapter 1   Critics and Theorists

1 There is a critical reading list at the end of this study; the number of scholars listed there is pointedly restricted to the number of eighteenth-century novelists cited in Chapter 2. The present chapter attempts a more detailed review of a number of critics and theorists who have formed or reformed the ways in which we think of eighteenth-century fiction.

2 Dorothy Van Ghent, *The English Novel: Form and Function* (New York: Harper and Row, 1953). The 'Essays in Analysis' also cover *Tristram Shandy* among eighteenth-century novels. Terry Eagleton in *The Rape of Clarissa* (Oxford: Basil Blackwell, 1982) refers to the hard-boiled scepticism of Van Ghent's discussion of *Clarissa* (pp. 64–5).

3 The opening words of her 'Introduction' ('*The subject matter* of novels is human relationships in which are shown the directions of men's souls') now seem rather dated.

4 Nancy Armstrong, *Desire and Domestic Fiction: A Political History of the Novel* (New York: Oxford University Press, 1987).

5 Nancy Armstrong and Leonard Tennenhouse, *The Imaginary Puritan: Literature, Intellectual Labor, and the Origins of Personal Life* (Berkeley: University of California Press, 1992).

6 Ioan Williams (ed.), *Novel and Romance, 1700–1800: A Documentary Record* (London: Routledge & Kegan Paul, 1970). Williams's excellent survey consists of approximately a hundred comments from the Preface of Congreve's *Incognita* (1691) to Richard Cumberland's novel, *Henry* (1795).

7 The vagueness over numbers only reflects the fact that the 101 attributions by Defoe's first biographer had swollen to 572 in the 1970s, to be almost halved by his most recent bibliographers. See J. R. Moore's *A Checklist of the Writings of Daniel Defoe*, 2nd edn (Hamden, Conn., 1971); and then P. N. Furbank and W. R. Owens, *The Canonisation of Daniel Defoe* (London, 1988) and *A Critical Bibliography of Daniel Defoe*.

8 Quoted by P. N. Furbank and W. R. Owens in *Defoe: Deattributions* (London: Hambledon Press, 1986), p. xvii.

9 Lillian Robinson, 'Treason Our Text: Feminist Challenges to the Literary Canon', in Elaine Showalter (ed.), *The New Feminist Criticism: Essays on Women, Literature and Theory* (New York, 1985).

10 Jane Spencer, *The Rise of the Woman Novelist: From Aphra Behn to Jane Austen* (Oxford: Basil Blackwell, 1986).

11 Dale Spender, *Mothers of the Novel: 100 Good Women Writers before Jane Austen* (London: Pandora Press, 1986).

12 Clive T. Probyn, *English Fiction of the Eighteenth Century, 1700–1789* (New York: Longman, 1987).

13 Janet Todd, *The Sign of Angellica: Women, Writing and Fiction, 1660–1800* (London: Virago, 1989).

14 Ros Ballaster, *Seductive Forms: Women's Amatory Fiction from 1684 to 1740* (Oxford: Clarendon Press, 1992).

15 April Alliston, *Virtue's Faults: Correspondences in Eighteenth-Century British and French Women's Fiction* (Stanford, Cal.: Stanford University Press, 1996).

16 Claudia L. Johnson, *Equivocal Beings* (Chicago: University of Chicago Press, 1997).

17 Mary Anne Schofield, *Masking and Unmasking the Female Mind* (Newark: University of Delaware Press, 1990).

18 Catherine Gallagher, *Nobody's Story: The Vanishing Acts of Women Writers in the Marketplace, 1670–1820* (Oxford: Clarendon Press, 1994).

19 Ian Watt, *The Rise of the Novel: Studies in Defoe, Richardson and Fielding* (London: Chatto and Windus, 1957).

20 See, for example, the findings of the Group discussed in J. Paul Hunter's *Before Novels: The Cultural Contexts of Eighteenth-Century English Fiction* (New York: W. W. Norton, 1990), pp. 63–4 and pp. 112–13. See also Percy G. Adams, *Travel Literature and the Evolution of the Novel* (Lexington: University Press of Kentucky, 1983).

21 See J. Paul Hunter's reference to Stone in his detailed discussion of literacy with reference to Watt's 'triple-rise theory' (*Before Novels*, pp. 65–9).

22 Michael McKeon, *The Origins of the English Novel, 1600–1740* (Baltimore, Md.: Johns Hopkins University Press, 1987).

23 See his *Anatomy of Criticism: Four Essays* (Princeton, NJ: Princeton University Press, 1957), and particularly 'The Theory of Genres', pp. 303–14.

24 Robert Scholes and Robert Kellogg, *The Nature of Narrative* (London: Oxford University Press, 1966).

25 Northrop Frye, *The Secular Scripture: A Study of the Structure of Romance* (Cambridge, Mass.: Harvard University Press, 1976).

26 See, above all, volume 1: *An Introduction*, trans. Robert Hurley (Harmondsworth: Penguin Books, 1990). Armstrong's thesis is summarized briefly in *Desire and Domestic Fiction*, p. 8.

27 Lennard J. Davis, *Factual Fictions: The Origins of the English Novel* (New York: Columbia University Press, 1983).

28 Terry Castle, *Masquerade and Civilization: The Carnivalesque in Eighteenth-Century English Culture and Fiction* (Stanford, Cal.: Stanford University Press, 1986). Bakhtin's *Rabelais and his World* (published in Russian in 1965) was translated by Helen Iswolsky (Bloomington: Indiana University Press, 1984).

29 Catherine Craft-Fairchild, *Masquerade and Gender: Disguise and Identity in Eighteenth-Century Fictions by Women* (University Park, Pa.: Pennsylvania State University Press, 1993).

30 John Bender, *Imagining the Penitentiary: Fiction and the Architecture of the Mind in Eighteenth-Century England* (Chicago: University of Chicago Press, 1987).

31 Bender draws on Michel Foucault's *Discipline and Punish: The Birth of the Prison*, trans. Alan Sheridan (London: Allen Lane, 1975).

32 James Thompson, *Models of Value: Eighteenth-Century Political Economy and the Novel* (London: Duke University Press, 1996).

33 Margaret Anne Doody, *The True Story of the Novel* (London: Fontana Press, 1998).

34 This is effectively a political (read feminist and multi-cultural) updating of Thomas Hägg's *The Novel in Antiquity* (Oxford: Basil Blackwell, 1983).

35 From the Preface to Behn's play *The Forced Marriage* (1670), quoted by Janet Todd in *The Secret Life of Aphra Behn* (London: Virago, 1996), p. 23.

36 Nicola J. Watson, *Revolution and the Form of the British Novel, 1790–1825* (Oxford: Clarendon Press, 1994).

37 Mary Poovey, *The Proper Lady and the Woman Writer: Ideology as Style in the Works of Mary Wollstonecraft, Mary Shelley and Jane Austen* (Chicago: University of Chicago Press, 1984). Discussion of the Gothic is obviously concentrated on Shelley.

38 See Gary Kelly, *The English Jacobin Novel, 1780–1805* (Oxford: Clarendon Press, 1976); Marilyn Butler, *Jane Austen and the War of Ideas* (Oxford: Clarendon Press, 1975; rev. with new introductory essay, 1987); Eleanor Ty, *Unsex'd Revolutionaries: Five Revolutionary Novelists of the 1790s* (Toronto: University of Toronto Press, 1993); Gary Kelly, *Women, Writing and Revolution, 1790–1827* (Oxford: Clarendon Press, 1993).

39 Ronald Paulson, *Don Quixote in England: The Aesthetics of Laughter* (Baltimore, Md.: Johns Hopkins University Press, 1998)

Chapter 2   Sounding the Canon

1 Among recent criticism, these issues are a recurrent concern of Homer Brown's *Institutions of the English Novel from Defoe to Scott* (Philadelphia: University of Pennsylvania Press, 1997). More specific are William Warner's essay, 'The Elevation of the Novel in England: Hegemony and Literary History', in Richard Kroll (ed.), *The English Novel: 1700 to Fielding* (London: Longman, 1998), pp. 49–69; and his monograph *Licensing Entertainment: The Elevation of Novel Reading in Britain, 1684–1750* (Berkeley, Cal.: University of California Press, 2000).

2 See, for example, J. Paul Hunter's discussion in *Before Novels*, pp. 65ff.

3 Many critics have emphasized the elitist and politically reactionary tendencies of Modernism. In contrast, Italian intellectual Umberto Eco – medieval scholar and founding father of modern semiotics, as well as bestselling author and popular journalist – is a striking example of the new eclecticism of postmodernism.

4 F. R. Leavis, *The Great Tradition* (London: Chatto and Windus, 1948).

5 Published as the last of the *Dissertations Moral and Critical* (1783). There is an interesting discussion of Beattie and other pioneer critics of the Scottish enlightenment in Robert Crawford's *Devolving English Literature* (Oxford: Clarendon Press, 1992), ch. 2, 'British Literature', pp. 45–110.

6 Under the title of *The Novels and Novelists of the Eighteenth Century in Illustration of the Manners and Morals of the Age* (1871).

7 The studies in question are Robert Adams Day, *Told in Letters: Epistolary Fiction before Richardson* (Ann Arbor, Mich.: University of Michigan Press, 1966); Ros Ballaster, *Seductive Forms: Women's Amatory Fiction*

from 1684–1740 (Oxford: Clarendon Press, 1992); and Ronald Paulson, *Satire and the Novel in Eighteenth-Century England* (New Haven, Conn.: Yale University Press, 1967).

8 The anecdote is recounted in Boswell's *Journal of a Tour to the Hebrides* and quoted in Fred W. Boege's *Smollett's Reputation as a Novelist* (Princeton, N.J.: Princeton University Press, pp. 40–1.

9 There is brief comment on Defoe's intellectual formation in Paula Backscheider's comprehensive *Daniel Defoe: A Life* (Baltimore, Md.: Johns Hopkins University Press, 1990), ch. 1, 'Fire and Plague'.

10 Of particular interest here is William Warner's argument that Fielding and Richardson aimed quite consciously at displacing the fiction of Behn, Manley and Haywood in public awareness. See 'The Elevation of the Novel in England: Hegemony and Literary History', in Richard Kroll's *The English Novel: 1700 to Fielding*.

11 Frank Kermode, *The Classic: Literary Images of Permanence and Change* (London: Harvard University Press, 1983).

12 Robert D. Mayo, *The English Novel in the Magazines, 1740–1815* (London: Oxford University Press, 1962).

13 *Greaves* was more accurately the first 'long piece of original fiction written expressly for publication in a British magazine' (Mayo, *The English Novel in the Magazines*, p. 277).

14 Hunt collected fifty-seven examples of what he regarded as 'classics', including *Rasselas* and Hawkesworth's *Almoran and Hamet*, entire, as well as extracts from Henry Brooke's *The Fool of Quality*, *Tristram Shandy* and *A Sentimental Journey* (two pieces).

15 The classic account of these early collections is Michael Sadleir's *XIX Century Fiction: A Bibliographical Record based on His Own Collection*, 2 vols (London: Constable, 1951).

16 See April Alliston's *Virtue's Faults*.

17 There are thus *Tales of the Genii* (by the pseudonymous 'Sir Charles Morrell'), *Chinese Tales* and *Tartarian Tales* (from Gueulette), *Persian Tales* and *Peruvian Tales*, besides the better known *Arabian Nights Entertainments* (after Galland) and the *Moral Tales* of Marmontel.

18 The full title of the collection is *The British Novelists with an Essay, and Prefaces Biographical and Critical*, 50 vols (1810); for reasons of availability, this study uses the second edition, of 1821.

19 It derives ultimately – like several of its English predecessors – from Pierre-Daniel Huet's *Traité de l'origine des romans* (1670).

20 It is unclear whether Mrs Barbauld has read the similarly sailor-less *Ferdinand Count Fathom*, or whether – like some of her critical successors – she is prepared to be economical with the truth for the sake of a good joke (or theory).

21 'As long as *Atalantis* shall be read . . .', an ironic comment in the light of Manley's subsequent reputation.

22 Barbauld, *The British Novelists*, vol. XXVIII, p. 56.

23 The original French *Gil Blas de Santillane* began appearing in 1715; *Le Diable boiteux* was published in 1707 and *Estévanille de Gonzalès* in 1734.

24 Scott is thinking of Eliza Haywood's late and highly respectable *The History of Jemmy and Jenny Jessamy* (1753).

25 George Cruikshank (1792–1878) illustrated Dickens's *Sketches by Boz* and *Oliver Twist*, as well as works by Thackeray and Harrison Ainsworth.

26 The series is probably most famous for the first Collected Edition of Austen, but it also contains three novels by Godwin, together with Brunton's *Self-Control* and *Discipline*, Inchbald's *A Simple Story* and *Nature and Art*, and one text each from Beckford, Walpole, Lewis, and the Lee sisters.

27 *British Novelists, 1660–1800*, 2 vols, ed. Martin C. Battestin, Volume 39 of the *Dictionary of Literary Biography* (Detroit: Gale Research Inc., 1985).

28 Barbauld, *The British Novelists*, vol. 19, p. xxv.

29 Brunton is thus too late for Barbauld's *British Novelists* and features in a later volume of the *DLB*.

30 Bunyan's *The Pilgrim's Progress* appeared in 1678, the more realistic *The Life and Death of Mr Badman* in 1680; both thus preceded Behn's fictional debut with *Love-Letters Between a Nobleman and His Sister* (1684).

Chapter 3   Genre and Gender

1 See Paul Hernadi's *Beyond Genre: New Directions in Literary Classification* (London: Cornell University Press, 1972); more comprehensive, if less lucid, is Alastair Fowler's *Kinds of Literature: An Introduction to the Theory of Genres and Modes* (Oxford: Clarendon Press, 1982). There is a helpful entry on *genre* in *The Princeton Handbook of Poetic Terms*, ed. Alex Preminger et al. (1986).

2 These comments, quoted by Hernadi (pp. 15ff), are taken from Burke's *Attitudes Towards History* (Berkeley, Cal.: University of California Press, 1984).

3 Samuel Wesley the Elder (1662–1735) produced his Christian epic *The Life of Our Blessed Lord* (1693); Sir Richard Blackmore (*c*.1655–1729) wrote 'epic verses' – religious and patriotic – including *The Creation* (1712) and *Redemption* (1722).

4 See Ronald Paulson's *Satire and the Novel in Eighteenth-Century England* (New Haven, Conn.: Yale University Press, 1967). Paulson deals at length with Fielding and Smollett, but also provides extensive treatment of continental picaresque and 'anti-romance', together with a pioneering discussion of Delarivier Manley.

5 There were several eighteenth-century English translations of *Don Quixote*, including one by Smollett himself (1755). Charles Sorel's *L'Anti-roman, ou Le Berger extravagant* (1627) and Paul Scarron's *Virgile travesti* (1648–53) were also well known in the original and in translation. *Lazarillo de Tormes* was still often read in an Elizabethan translation from the Spanish by David Rouland of Anglesey (1586); Lesage's *Gil Blas* was also translated by Smollett (1748).

6 *The Adventures of Eovaai, Princess of Ijaveo* (1736), reprinted as *The Unfortunate Princess* in 1741; *Jonathan Wild* appeared in 1743.

7 The baleful influence on Burney's writing of her father and a family friend ('Daddy Crisp') is discussed in detail by Margaret Doody in her *Frances Burney: The Life in the Works* (New Brunswick: Rutgers University Press, 1988).

8   Of Juvenal's sixteen satires, for example, Congreve translated number XI, Fielding modernized number VI, and Matthew Lewis imitated number XIII; Smollett virtually re-created Juvenal in his early poems *Advice* and *Reproof*, whilst Johnson's 'London' (number III) and 'The Vanity of Human Wishes' (number X) are the most famous adaptations of the Roman author.

9   The classical model is the *Metamorphoses* or *Golden Ass* of Apuleius (*fl.* AD 155), a fantastic romance in eleven books, and the only Latin novel to survive in its entirety.

10 From the *Monthly Review*, February 1751.

11 See the *Monthly Review*, December 1750.

12 Named after the Greek Cynic philosopher of the third century BC, whose works were lost, but imitated by the Roman satirist Varro, and the Greek author Lucian (*c.*AD 118–80).

13 All three narratives are incidentally letter fictions (supposedly a female form), underlining once again the pitfalls of genre–gender alignments.

14 Smollett edited a 39-volume edition of Voltaire, appearing in 1761 and 1765. Even if he only wrote the notes, as is widely believed, this clearly represented considerable labour.

15 John Shebbeare had a long-standing feud with Smollett, perhaps due to strong affinities – and thus potential rivalries – in the two men's respective literary and medical careers; John Moore, on the other hand, was a personal friend, and the two men were companions on the trip to France which provided much of the material for *Peregrine Pickle*. The uniformly evil protagonist of *Zeluco* (1786) appears to rely heavily on the mock-heroic model of *Ferdinand Count Fathom*. Another great enemy, the versatile hack 'Sir' John Hill, published his *History of a Woman of Quality* in 1751, thus pre-empting the lengthy memoirs of Lady V[ane] in Smollett's *Peregrine Pickle*.

16 Quoted by Miriam Allott in her anthology *Novelists on the Novel* (London: Routledge & Kegan Paul, 1959), pp. 258–9.

17 Quoted by Ioan Williams in the indispensable collection *Novel and Romance, 1700–1800: A Documentary Record* (London: Routledge & Kegan Paul, 1970), p. 406.

18 See the 'Chronological List of English Letter Fiction 1660–1740', compiled by Robert Adams Day and included in his *Told in Letters: Epistolary Fiction Before Richardson* (Ann Arbor; Mich.: University of Michigan Press, 1966). Day cites Manley's 'A Stage-Coach Journey to Exeter' in *Letters Written by Mrs Manley* (1696) and *The Lady's Pacquet of Letters* (1707). The *Works* of Mary Davys (1725) include the *Familiar Letters Betwixt a Gentleman and a Lady*, Haywood's *Irish Artifice; or, The History of Clarina* (1728) also used epistolary form.

19 The story of Abelard, the twelfth-century scholar who fell in love with his pupil, Héloïse, existed as an epistolary narrative in Latin from 1616. It was also well known in a translation from the French by John Hughes (1713), the basis for Pope's *Eloisa to Abelard*. The *Lettres portugaises* (1669; ten editions before 1740) were ostensibly written by a Portuguese nun, Marianna Alforcado, to her lover, a French officer. Jane Barker (in her *Lining of the Patchwork Screen*), Haywood and Behn all borrowed the relationship

between a nun and a cavalier. See Day, *Told in Letters*, ch. 3, 'The Importance of Translations'.

Marie-Catherine Le Jumel de Barneville, Comtesse d'Aulnoy (*c.*1650–1705) is equally known in France as an author of fairy-tales and a writer of travel narratives.

20 Day proposes Ovid himself (in the *Heroidum epistulae*) as the 'father of epistolary, sentimental, and psychological fiction'; whilst Elizabeth Rowe's *Friendship in Death, in Twenty Letters from the Dead to the Living* (1728) seems to borrow its form directly from another classical model, Lucian's *Dialogues of the Dead.*

21 Day's check-list of almost 200 examples rather surprisingly contains 72 volumes by men and only 54 by women (including 29 by Haywood alone). For 68 volumes there is no recorded author, although it may be safely assumed that *anon.* concealed many a respectable lady.

22 Samuel Pratt's *The Pupil of Pleasure* (1776) and *The Tutor of Truth* (1779) may thus be seen as reworkings of *Clarissa* and *Grandison*, respectively, whilst Henry Mackenzie's *Julia de Roubigné* (1777), a tale of passion in conflict with filial duty, also owes much to Richardson.

23 Cleland's little-known final novel, *The Woman of Honour* (1768), on the other hand, with its multi-focal account of the virtuous orphan Clara Maynwaring pursued by the dissipated Lord Lovell, seems to echo Richardson even as it anticipates Burney.

24 The real antecedent of this eighteenth-century genre is *L'Espion turc*, by the Genoese, Giovanni Paolo Marana (1642–93), letters supposed to be have been written by a Turkish spy from Paris. An English continuation, probably by Defoe, was published in 1718. *L'Espion turc* was also the inspiration for Montesquieu's more famous *Lettres persanes* (1721).

25 The learned Mackenzie (an Edinburgh graduate) is the sole exception here to a tendency embracing Richardson himself (a putative year at Merchant Taylors School), Cleland (just two years at Winchester), Pratt (curate turned actor after secondary school), and the autodidacts, Holcroft and Bage. One might even view this tendency as a retreat into subjectivity on the part of authors who quite literally lack the *authority* of a Swift or Graves.

26 The other two were the rather happier *Emily Montague* (1769), noted for its setting in Canada (where the novelists's husband was chaplain to the British army), and (of doubtful attribution) *All's Right at Last* (1774). Sarah Scott's final novel, *The Test of Filial Duty* (1772), was epistolary, as were two of Clara Reeve's, the highly didactic *The Two Mentors* (1783) and the tragically sentimental *The Exiles* (1788). The Lee sisters produced one letter fiction each: Harriet's *The Errors of Innocence* (1786) was a daring exploration of extra-marital love; Sophia's *The Life of a Lover* (1804) has strange premonitions of *Jane Eyre*. Charlotte Smith also wrote her revolutionary *Desmond* (1792) as letter fiction. Maria Edgeworth used the technique in her *Letters for Literary Ladies* (1795), and produced one complete epistolary novel with *Leonora* (1806).

27 This useful and self-explanatory distinction is made by Janet Altman in *Epistolarity* (Columbus, Ohio: Ohio State University Press, 1982), ch. 1, 'Epistolary Mediation', pp. 13ff.

28 Manley's *The Lost Lover; or, The Jealous Husband* (1696) combined
    Restoration intrigue with the new sentimental comedy; *The Royal Mischief*
    (1696) was a blank-verse tragedy, heroic after Dryden and erotic after
    Manley's own fashion; a second tragedy, *Almyna; or, The Arabian Vow*
    (1706), drew on the newly popular *Arabian Nights* stories, translated into
    English in 1704. There was also a historical drama entitled *Lucius, The
    First Christian King of Britain* (1717).
       With characteristic versatility, Haywood wrote *A Wife to Be Lett* (1723),
    a domestic comedy; *The Fair Captive*, a heroic drama of Spaniards and
    Turks; *Frederick, Duke of Brunswick-Lunenburgh* (1729), a historical
    tragedy; and the *Opera of Operas; or, Tom Thumb the Great*, a musical
    adaptation of Fielding. Mary Davys's *The Northern Heiress* and *The Self-
    Rival* are broad comedies. Penelope Aubin's *The Merry Masqueraders; or,
    The Humorous Cuckold* (1733) looks back to the freedoms of the Restora-
    tion stage.
       Among the other eight, Elizabeth Griffith (*The School for Rakes*, 1769)
    adapted the French dramatist Beaumarchais; Charlotte Lennox (*Old City
    Manners*, 1775) adapted Jacobean comedy; Frances Brooke produced
    both tragedies and comic operas; and the Lee sisters ranged from Gothic-
    inspired melodrama to sentimental comedy.
29 Other tragedies of the mid-century included Johnson's *Irene* (1749),
    Hawkesworth's *Amphitryon* (1756) and Cleland's *Titus Vespasian* (1755),
    based on Metastasio's *libretto* for Mozart's *La Clemenza di Tito*.
30 Goldsmith's second comedy was staged in the same year as *The Prince of
    Tunis*, one of three tragedies by Mackenzie.
31 *Antonio* was given once at the Haymarket in 1800, while *Faulkner* –
    adapted from his novel *Caleb Williams* – was rather more successful in
    1807, perhaps owing to help from Holcroft.
32 See Martin Battestin's *Henry Fielding: A Life* (London: Routledge,
    1989), particularly in the context of Fielding's play *The Modern Husband*,
    pp. 99–100.
33 See Richard Bevis's important revisionist study *The Laughing Tradition:
    Stage Comedy in Garrick's Day* (Athens, Ga.: University of Georgia Press,
    1980).
34 The former renounced a curacy for the Dublin stage (under the name of
    Courtney Melmoth), whilst the latter (without formal education and once
    a Newmarket stableboy) was a strolling player in England for six years.
35 On the 'new man', see Gerald Barker, *Grandison's Heirs: The Paragon's
    Progress in the Late Eighteenth-Century Novel* (Newark: University of
    Delaware Press, 1985); on the 'feminine plot', see Katherine Sobba
    Green's *The Courtship Novel, 1740–1820: A Feminized Genre* (Lexington:
    University Press of Kentucky, 1991).
36 This is argued by Robert L. Mack in the Introduction to his *Oxford
    World's Classics* collection, *Oriental Tales* (1992). His hypothesis may be
    partly conditioned by his own selection: Hawkesworth's *Almoran and
    Hamet*, Sheridan's *The History of Nourjahad*, Reeve's *The History of Char-
    oba, Queen of Aegypt*, and Edgeworth's *Murad the Unlucky*: three of the
    four pieces are by women. The oriental tale nevertheless introduced that
    archetypal *female* story-teller, Sheherazade.

37 Samuel Pratt made a dramatic adaptation of *Almoran and Hamet* as 'The Fair Circassian' (1781), and Holcroft translated *Vathek* from Mme de Genlis's *Theatre of Education* (1781).
38 Mack, *Oriental Tales*, p. xix.
39 Henry Weber's classic three-volume *Tales of the East* (1812) thus innocently gathers not only the English translation of the *Arabian Nights*, but also the *New Arabian Nights, Persian Tales, Tales of Inatulla of Delhi, Oriental Tales, Mogul Tales, Turkish Tales, Tartarian Tales, Chinese Tales, Tales of the Genii*, and *Tales of Abdallah, the Son of Hanif*.
40 Gillian Beer, *Romance* (London: Methuen, 1970), p. 4.
41 Elements of the French heroic romance resurface in such widely contrasting works as Jane Barker's *Galesia* trilogy, Eliza Haywood's best-selling *Love in Excess* (1719) and Penelope Aubin's *The Noble Slaves* (1722).
42 Erich Auerbach, *Mimesis: The Representation of Reality in Western Literature*, trans. Willard R. Trask (Princeton, N.J.: Princeton University Press, 1953).
43 The opening lines of St John's Gospel ('In the beginning was the word . . . ' etc.) are a spectacular example; the original language of the New Testament is known precisely as *demotic* Greek.

Chapter 4   Two Literary Parabolas (i): Richardson from the Familiar Letters to *Grandison*

1 See Gerald Barker's *Sir Charles Grandison: The Compleat Conduct Book* (Lewisburg, Pa.: University of Pennsylvania Press, 1986) and Nancy Armstrong's *Desire and Domestic Fiction: A Political History of the Novel*, respectively.
2 For Fielding, see my discussion in the following chapter. Carroll's Humpty Dumpty moves into the realm of semantics in *Alice Through the Looking Glass* (ch. 6): 'When *I* use a word . . . it means just what I choose it to mean – neither more nor less' (Puffin Books, 1973), p. 274.
3 As Alan McKillop noted long ago: 'It is the gentility of *Grandison*, rather than the crude portraiture of *Pamela* or the tragedy of *Clarissa*, that set the tone for the feminine novel of the second half of the century, and established the tradition in which Jane Austen triumphed.' *Samuel Richardson, Printer and Novelist* (Chapel Hill: University of North Carolina Press, 1960), p. 213.
4 See chapter 7, 'To *Grandison* and After', in Jocelyn Harris's *Samuel Richardson* (Cambridge: Cambridge University Press, 1987), pp. 136f.
5 *The Apprentice's Vade Mecum* has been published by the Augustan Reprint Society (Los Angeles: University of California, 1975). For remarks on the stage, see pp. 9f and p. 16. In the theatre, Richardson seems to make a sole exception of George Lillo's educative domestic tragedy, *The London Merchant* (1731), which he would have had apprentices see once a year! And as for the effect on men of classical mythology, 'It taught them to worship an Adulterer and Usurper of his Father's Throne, under the name of *Jupiter*: a Harlot under the Name of *Venus*: and a Thief under the Name of *Mercury*', ibid., pp. 65–6.

6   There is, for example, the memorable vignette of a city fop:

> And I have seen a prim young Fellow, with a *Cue* of *Adonis*, as they call the effeminate Wigs of the Present Vogue, *plaister'd* rather than *powder'd*, and appearing like the *Twigs* of a *Gooseberry Bush* in a *deep Snow*.   (pp. 34–5)

And so on for some forty lines, although such flashes are admittedly rare.

7   See T. C. Duncan Eaves and Ben Kimpel, *Samuel Richardson: A Biography* (Oxford: Clarendon Press, 1971), ch. 4, 'Successful Printer and Editor, 1733–1739'. Richardson's Preface to the *Complete English Tradesman* incidentally describes Defoe as being 'too verbose and circumlocutory', obliging the editor to 'pare away these luxuriencies' (Eaves and Kimpel, *Samuel Richardson*, p. 37).

8   The less than riveting full title of Richardson's epistolary guide is *Letters Written to and for Particular Friends, on the Most Important Occasions. Directing Not Only the Requisite Style and Forms to Be Observed in Writing Familiar Letters; but How to Think and Act Justly and Prudently, in the Common Concerns of Human Life*. A modern edition of the *Familiar Letters* was edited by Brian Downs (London: Routledge, 1928).

9   See William C. Slattery, (ed.), *The Richardson–Stinstra Correspondence and Stinstra's Prefaces to Clarissa* (London: Southern Illinois Press, 1969), p. 52.

10 See also John Carroll's *Selected Letters of Samuel Richardson* (Oxford: Clarendon Press, 1964), pp. 39–40. For a fuller account, see also Eaves and Kimpel, *Samuel Richardson*, ch. V, 'The Composition and Publication of *Pamela* and the *Familiar Letters*, 1739–1741', pp. 87–99. Richardson wrote of the *Familiar Letters* to Aaron Hill that he 'thought of giving one or two as cautions to young folks circumstanced as Pamela was' (quoted by Eaves and Kimpel, *Samuel Richardson*, p. 89).

11 See also Katherine Hornbeak's 'Richardson's "Familiar Letters" and the Domestic Conduct Books'; 'Richardson's "Aesop"', *Smith College Studies in Modern Languages*, no. 19, parts 1–2 (Northampton, Mass.: Smith College, 1938). Hornbeak describes the *Familiar Letters* as 'a *letter-writer* in *form* but a *domestic conduct book* in *content*', and suggests that, in *Pamela*, *Clarissa* and *Grandison*, Richardson had 'just draped with fictions the principles and ideas of these Puritan handbooks', p. 9.

12 See Ira Konigsberg, *Samuel Richardson and the Dramatic Novel* (Lexington: University of Kentucky Press, 1968). The most interesting part of Konigsberg's study may be his ploy of rewriting *verbatim* exchanges from *Clarissa* (*Pamela* might also have been suitable) in the form of theatrical dialogue interspersed with stage directions (pp. 112–14). Such an experiment also implicitly distinguishes between the marginal notion of theatrical *sources* in Richardson and the more central question of actual dramatic *technique*.

13 Gillian Beer argues that *Pamela* is a 'revisionary reading and rewriting of [Sir Philip Sidney's] *Arcadia*' in the more democratic code of Christian pastoral. See her '*Pamela*: rethinking *Arcadia*', in *Samuel Richardson: Tercentenary Essays*, ed. Peter Sabor and Margaret Anne Doody (Cambridge: Cambridge University Press, 1989), pp. 23–39.

14 Drawing on the version by Sir Roger L'Estrange (1692), Richardson's collection contained only 240 fables as opposed to L'Estrange's 500.

Richardson's use of Aesop is discussed at length in Margaret Anne Doody's *A Natural Passion: A Study of the Novels of Samuel Richardson* (Oxford: Clarendon Press, 1974), pp. 26ff. *Pamela*, for example, refers to 'The City Mouse and the Country Mouse', 'The Ant and the Grasshopper', 'The Wolf, Lamb and Vulture', 'The Oak and the Willow', and 'A Daw and Borrowed Feathers'. The latter tale also appears in *Clarissa*, together with 'The Sun and the Wind', 'The Lady and the Lion', 'Mercury and the Statuary', and 'Death and the Old Man', whilst *Grandison* includes 'The Ass and the Two Bundles of Hay'.

15 References to *Pamela* (hereafter incorporated in the text) are to the Penguin Classics edition (1980), ed. Peter Sabor, intro. Margaret Anne Doody.

16 The extent to which Pamela and Mr B. (as opposed to Clarissa and Lovelace) may be discussed as conventional novelistic characters is interestingly raised in Jocelyn Harris's *Samuel Richardson*, ch. 2, 'From *Pamela* to *Clarissa*', pp. 38–50.

17 The fact that the major English exponent of the epistolary novel is a *man* merely adds to the tensions and paradoxes surrounding the writer in question. In his own family, for example, Richardson seems to have been an unambiguously patriarchal figure. Nancy Miller's *The Heroine's Text: Readings in the French and English Novel, 1722–1782* (New York: Columbia University Press, 1980) includes a provocative study of Richardson's 'feminocentric' discourse.

18 There was, for instance, the *Anti-Pamela; or, Feign'd Innocence Detected* (1741), probably by Eliza Haywood, and James Parry's *True Anti-Pamela* (1741).

19 References to *Clarissa* (hereafter incorporated into the text by letter-number) are to the one-volume Penguin Classics edition (1985) edited by Angus Ross.

20 The genealogy of Lovelace's claims (Restoration drama and Augustan verse in the short term, classical tradition in a longer perspective) may be pursued indirectly, but no less effectively, in Katherine Rogers's *The Troublesome Helpmate: A History of Misogyny in Literature* (Seattle: University of Washington Press, 1966).

21 The reader is assured in the novel's 'Conclusion' that Anna actually married her long-suffering Hickman a mere six months after Clarissa's death; but such a detail may also be regarded as a mere residue of romance convention – Richardson's more traditional relation to 'writing beyond the ending'.

22 See *Grandison*, vol. I, Letters XI–XIII. With his own modest education, Richardson is unquestionably on the same side as the 'ladies' in this debate. The best discussion of the question occurs in Eaves and Kimpel's biography (ch. XXIII, 'Richardson's Reading and Criticism'). Although Richardson was deferential, for example, to his friend Dr Graham ('The very great Advantage of an Academical Education I have wanted'), he was sensitive to incompatibilities between classical humanism and Christianity: 'I always thought, that the Cause of the Christian Religion was sometimes far from being strengthened by that implicit Regard that is paid to the Antients' (quoted by Eaves and Kimpel, p. 569).

23 Texts cited include three heroic tragedies, Sir Robert Howard's *The Vestal Virgin*, Otway's *The History and Fall of Caius Marius*, and Dryden's *Tyrannic Love* (twice); two Shakespeare plays, *Othello* and *The Tempest*; and a poem from Cowley's *The Mistress*.

24 He thus quotes, in rough chronological order, Horace (L57), Aesop (L167), Dryden's *Don Sebastian* and Lee's *Tamerlane* (both in L160), *Aureng-Zebe* (L190), Waller ('Women are born to be controlled', L207), *Troilus and Cressida* (L209), Milton (gratuitously comparing himself to a devil in *Paradise Lost*, L233), 'my worthy friend Mandeville' (L246), Ariosto twice (L267 and L512), Heraclitus and Democritus (L277), Virgil (L370), and Nicholas Rowe (L371).

25 In over forty lines of quotation, he cites Shakespeare, Dryden, and Lee from the volumes in his friend Belton's library, before turning to the homiletic strains of Pomfret's *Prospect of Death* and Norris's *Miscellanies*.

26 Influential concepts here have been Roland Barthes's 'death of the author' (effectively, the death of the authoritative *A*uthor with a capital 'A'); Mikhail Bakhtin's polyphony (potraying the literary text as a virtual battle-ground of competing voices); and Julia Kristeva's 'intertextuality' (challenging the more traditional and woolly concept of 'literary influence').

27 Between Richardson and Fielding, it is unquestionably the former who has the capacity for self-effacement required for successful impersonation: in this respect, Lovelace's parody of the marriage certificate is still sensational. Broader textual paradoxes of the same kind include the prospect of the patriarchal Richardson producing the most profoundly 'feminocentric' of novels, or the relatively unlettered Richardson producing correspondence jam-packed with literary allusion. On the latter point, however, note that many of Richardson's references were second-hand and taken from a popular contemporary anthology. See Michael E. Connaughton's 'Richardson's Familiar Quotations: *Clarissa* and Bysshe's *Art of English Poetry*'. *Philological Quarterly*, 60 (1981), pp. 858–85.

28 From Richardson's letter to his Dutch translator, Johannes Stinstra, quoted in Alan McKillop's *Samuel Richardson, Printer and Novelist*. McKillop also discusses the novelist's earliest known attempts at letter-writing, pp. 5–7.

29 Tom Keymer gives a fascinating account of these in his essay 'Richardson's *Meditations*: Clarissa's *Clarissa*' (*Tercentenary Essays*, ed. Doody and Sabor). Clarissa's 'legacy' of five meditations was printed separately by Richardson, six months after the second edition of the novel (1749); the full title was *Meditations Collected from the Sacred Books; And Adapted to the Different Stages of a Deep Distress; Gloriously surmounted by Patience, Piety, and Resignation. Being those mentioned in the History of Clarissa as drawn up by her for her own Use*. An enlarged edition of the *Meditations* from 1750 had five additional pages by the 'editor' of *Clarissa*, a three-page preface signed 'Clarissa Harlowe' and seventy-six more pages of text: a total of thirty-six meditations in all. They are dated 18 June to 29 August, after which point – as Keymer suggests – Clarissa more or less ceases to narrate.

30 Quotations from *Sir Charles Grandison* (hereafter incorporated in the text) are from the Oxford *World's Classics* edition, ed. Jocelyn Harris (1972).

31 Other examples include Harriet's purely 'external' account of Grandison's youth in Italy (Vol. III, Letter XX), or an interpolation like the story of Danby (Vol. III, Letter XVIII).

32 The nature of 'free indirect discourse' (FID) should emerge from the following brief discussion. There is more detailed discussion of this topic, however, in the context of Jane Austen (Ch. 10), the first virtuoso practitioner of this technique in English fiction.

33 'The *Histories* may be considered as the LIVES of so many eminent persons, and this collection of *Maxims* as the MORALS.' The writer is Benjamin Kennicott, discussed by Tom Keymer, 'Richardson's *Meditations*' (see above, note 29).

34 Keymer, 'Richardson's *Meditations*', p. 207.

35 See John Carroll, *Selected Letters of Samuel Richardson* (1964), p. 455. The 'History of Mrs Beaumont' was published by Mrs Barbauld with her edition of Richardson's letters in 1804.

36 Tom Keymer makes an interesting case for regarding this collection as a potential *fifth* epistolary history beside *Pamela I* and *II*, *Clarissa*, and *Grandison*.

37 Jocelyn Harris, *Samuel Richardson* (Cambridge: Cambridge University Press, 1987), p. 81.

Chapter 5 Two Literary Parabolas (ii): Fielding from *Jonathan Wild* to *Amelia*

1 It is notable how Fielding has interested contemporary scholars far less than Richardson. The most significant monographs on him are generally, therefore, from earlier decades and include Robert Alter, *Fielding and the Nature of the Novel* (Cambridge: Harvard University Press, 1968); J. Paul Hunter, *Occasional Form: Henry Fielding and the Chains of Circumstance* (Baltimore, Md.: Johns Hopkins University Press, 1975); Claude Rawson, *Henry Fielding and the Augustan Ideal under Stress* (London: Routledge, 1972). More recent and particularly relevant to this study are Jill Campbell, *Natural Masques: Gender and Identity in Fielding's Plays and Novels* (Stanford: Stanford University Press, 1995); and Angela J. Smallwood, *Fielding and the Woman Question: The Novels of Henry Fielding and the Feminist Debate, 1700–1750* (Hemel Hempstead: Harvester Wheatsheaf, 1989). Apart from Martin Battestin's definitive *Henry Fielding: A Life* (London: Routledge, 1989), some of the most useful recent work is in separate sections of comparative studies of eighteenth-century fiction; several of these were discussed in Chapter 2.

2 References (hereafter incorporated in the text) are to *Jonathan Wild* (with *Journal of a Voyage to Lisbon*), ed. A. R. Humphreys (London: J. M. Dent, 1973). For discussion of dates of composition, see Battestin's *Life*, pp. 280–2.

3 Another parallel which would have struck contemporary readers was the comic genealogy of Wild in the second chapter: William Musgrave had published a sycophantic *Brief and True History of Sir Robert Walpole and his Family* in 1736, of which just over half was dedicated to the statesman's ancestors.

4   For a thorough account of Fielding's earliest writing, see Part II of Battestin's *Life*, 'Playwright and Libertine (1727–1739)', pp. 53–254.

5   Coventry is widely assumed to have written the influential but anonymous 'Essay on the New Species of Writing founded by Mr Fielding' (1751).

6   He taught *Tom Thumb* strange victories to boast,
             Slew Heaps of Giants, and then – kill'd a Ghost!
                To Rules, or Reason, scorn'd the dull Pretence,
             And fought your *Champion*, 'gainst the Cause of Sense!

    And in a copy of the same play dispatched to his cousin, Lady Mary Montagu, he notes the gulf between farce and heroic comedy, begging comprehension for his attempts to write the latter:

    > I hope your Ladyship will honour the Scenes which I presume to lay before you with your Perusal. As they are written on a Model I never yet attempted, I am exceedingly anxious least they should find less Mercy from you than my lighter Productions.
    >   Quoted in Battestin (*Henry Fielding: A Life*), p. 99.

7   Paul Scarron (1610–60), *Virgile travesti* (1648–52); Nicolas Boileau (1636–1711), *Le Lutrin*, a parochial dispute about the placement of a lectern in the Sainte-Chapelle (1774/1683).

8   Of the four figures mentioned: Aristides (presumably the Athenian states-man, Aristeides the Just) and Lysander (the Spartan naval commander in the Peloponnesian War) are featured in lives by the Roman biographers Nepos and Plutarch; Brutus, Julius Caesar's prime assassin, and the Emperor Nero are described by Suetonius.

9   This is presumably the 'Grammaticae Rudimenta' of William Lilly (1468?–1520), contributed to John Colet's *Aeditio* (1527). It is mentioned more than once in Shakespeare's *Twelfth Night* and remained a standard text into the nineteenth century.

10 The misogynistic tradition may be easily traced to the invective of another canonic text doubtlessly familiar to every 'fine gentleman', Juvenal's *Sixth Satire*. Fielding's version of this piece has already been noted.

11 From the occasional poem 'To a Friend on the Choice of a Wife', quoted in Battestin's *Life*, p. 187.

12 Battestin defends Fielding for his generous Preface to Sarah Fielding's *Familiar Letters between the Principal Characters in David Simple and Some Others* (1747), although this is to ignore the crudely patronizing Preface to *David Simple* itself, three years earlier.

13 The story of the 'Man of the Hill' in *Tom Jones* (Book VIII, chs 11–14) is marginally longer, but it is interrupted in turn by a kind of sub-digression. This, after Fielding's narrator suggests that a 'short breathing time' (p. 423) may be necessary.

14 The latter element is suggested most clearly by the detail of the Schach Pimpach, or chief magistrate, the kind of cryptic nomenclature familiar from *Gulliver's Travels*.

15 Cf. the 'dialogue matrimonial' between Wild and Laetitia (Book III, ch. 8) and the conversation between Wild and a gaoler (Book IV, ch. 13), both

set out as stage exchanges. On other occasions, characters deliver dramatic monologues, like that of Wild when set adrift in a small boat (p. 77), or Heartfree arrested for debt.

16　See the detailed account of the passing of Walpole's Licensing Act in Battestin, pp. 225–31. The immediate pretext was a particularly scurrilous farce, called *The Golden Rump*, which Fielding and others immediately assumed Walpole to have commissioned for his own ends.

17　On the reception of *Pamela* and Fielding's comments, see, for example, Margaret Ann Doody's essay on Richardson for the *DLB*, pp. 391ff.

18　References to *Shamela* and *Joseph Andrews* (hereafter incorporated into the body of the text) are to the joint edition in the Oxford World's Classics series, ed. Douglas Brooks-Davies (1980).

19　The references in this unlikely collection are to a theological dispute, a widely read devotional work, part of Delarivier Manley's scandalous novel, the translation of a French pornographic work, musings by the famous Methodist preacher and an opera-pantomime. See Douglas Brook-Davies's note, pp. 390–1.

20　The way in which Fielding (and Richardson) also consciously belittled and displaced another fictional tradition, namely the amatory fiction of Behn, Manley and Haywood, is convincingly argued by William Warner in his essay 'The Elevation of the Novel in England: Hegemony and Literary History', in *The English Novel, 1700 to Fielding*, ed. Richard Kroll (Harlow, Essex: Longman, 1998), pp. 49–69.

21　'Yo soy el primero que ha novelado en lengua castellana' (I am the first to have written *novelas* in Spanish). It is also interesting to note that several interpolations in *Don Quixote* (e.g. 'The Tale of Foolish Curiosity') are also effectively 'Exemplary Novels'; they have similar kinds of thematic and structural relations to the complete novel as, for example, 'The History of *Leonora*, or the Unfortunate Jilt' (Book II, ch. 4) to *Joseph Andrews* or 'The Man of the Hill' to *Tom Jones*.

22　From the Preface to *Don Quixote*, trans. J. M. Cohen (Harmondsworth: Penguin Books, 1950), p. 30 (further page references in text).

23　Cf. *Hamlet* II.2: 'The best actors in the world, either for tragedy, comedy, history, pastoral, pastoral-comical, historical-pastoral, tragical-historical, tragical-comical-historical-pastoral, scene individable, or poem unlimited...'

24　This widespread assumption of social hierarchy is traced throughout European literature in Erich Auerbach's epoch-making *Mimesis*, where it is related to classical tradition and contrasted with the more egalitarian implications of pure Christianity.

25　See the extended discussion in E. M. Forster's *Aspects of the Novel* (1927; Pelican Books, 1962), pp. 75–85.

26　Ideas first formulated in Martin Battestin, *The Moral Basis of Fielding's Art: A Study of Joseph Andrews* (Middletown, Conn.: Wesleyan University Press, 1959).

27　See Rawson's essay on Fielding in *The Cambridge Companion to the Eighteenth-Century Novel*, ed. John Richetti (Cambridge: Cambridge University Press, 1996), pp. 120–52.

28　*Shamela*, p. 329; also quoted by Rawson in Richetti (ed.), *The Cambridge Companion*, p. 128.

29 'Cits' are the lower ranks of the citizens of London. Rawson's whole discussion of irony in Fielding and his Augustan predecessors is particularly suggestive.

30 In England, the controversy goes back to an essay on the relative merits of 'Ancient and Modern Learning' by Swift's employer, Sir William Temple, inspiring Swift's satire 'The Battle of the Books' (1704). This only echoes an earlier dispute at the court of Louis XIV, however, in which the best-known contestants were the neo-classical theorist Boileau and the famous collector of fairy-tales Charles Perrault.

31 The references to *Don Quixote* are Part I, ch. 35 ('The battle with the wineskins'), Part I, ch. 16 ('The inn which he took for a castle') and Part I, ch. 18 ('A second conversation with Sancho, etc.').

32 Alain-René Lesage (1668–1747) produced the classic picaresque novel (translated by Smollett) in 1715. Pierre Carlet de Chamblain Marivaux (1688–1763), supporter of the moderns, was author of a burlesque *Iliade travestie* in 1717. His two unfinished novels, *La Vie de Marianne* (1731–41) and *Le Paysan parvenu* (1735–6) probably influenced *Joseph Andrews*.

33 These were first noted by R. S. Crane in his essay 'The Concept of Plot and the Plot of *Tom Jones*', in *Critics and Criticism: Ancient and Modern*, ed. R. S. Crane (Chicago: University of Chicago Press, 1952).

34 Also quoted by Battestin in his essay on Fielding in the *DLB*, p. 187.

35 This passage is quoted appositely by several Fielding scholars, see Battestin (ibid.), p. 186. There is a fuller discussion of the topic in John Preston's '*Tom Jones*: Irony and Judgment', in *The Created Self: The Reader's Role in Eighteenth-Century Fiction* (New York: Barnes and Noble, 1970), pp. 94–132, a chapter also collected in Leopold Damrosch, Jr. (ed.), *Modern Essays on Eighteenth-Century Literature* (New York: Oxford University Press, 1988).

36 *The History of Tom Jones*, ed. R. P. C. Mutter (Harmondsworth: Penguin Books, 1966), p. 88; further references are incorporated into the text.

37 Parallels between legitimizing a new fictional form and establishing a new monetary stability are the subject of James Thompson's fascinating study, *Models of Value: Eighteenth-Century Political Economy and the Novel* (London: Duke University Press, 1996).

38 For Fielding in the role of literary censor, for example, see his efforts to repress early eighteenth-century women's writing, discussed in William Warner's essay in *The English Novel, 1700 to Fielding*, ed. Richard Kroll (Harlow: Longman, 1998).

39 Quoted by Battestin, *Henry Fielding: A Life*, p. 538.

40 Such parallels are fairly common in the critico-biographical approach employed in Battestin's *Life*.

41 Quoted in Battestin, *Henry Fielding: A Life*, p. 540.

42 References to *Amelia* (hereafter incorporated in the text) are to the Everyman Library edition, ed. A. R. Humphreys (London: J. M. Dent, 1962).

43 Sarch Fielding, *The Adventures of David Simple*, ed. Malcolm Kelsall (Oxford: Oxford University Press, 1987), p. 6.

44 Anne Dacier (Lefebvre) (*c.* 1654–1720); French editor and translator of the classics, including the *Iliad* (1711) and the *Odyssey* (1717).

45 Quoted in Battestin, *Henry Fielding: A Life*, p. 381.

46 See Battestin, *Life*, p. 381, and *David Simple*, Preface, p. 3.

Chapter 6 Aphra Behn's *Oroonoko* and Daniel Defoe's *Moll Flanders*

1 Two earlier critical biographies of Behn, necessarily speculative in view of the scant information available, are Maureen Duffy's *The Passionate Shepherdess: Aphra Behn, 1640–1689* (Atlantic Highlands, N.J.: Humanities Press, 1977), and Angeline Goreau's *Reconstructing Aphra: A Social Biography of Aphra Behn* (New York: Dial Press, 1980). Both are superseded by Judith Todd's exhaustive *The Secret Life of Aphra Behn* (London: Routledge, 1996). Invaluable for the critical fortunes of Behn are *Reading Aphra Behn: History, Theory and Criticism*, ed. Heidi Hunter (London: University Press of Virginia, 1993), and Todd's own *The Critical Fortunes of Aphra Behn* (London: Camden House, 1988). The key work on Behn in the context of slavery is Moira Ferguson's *Subject to Others: British Women Writers and Colonial Slavery, 1670–1834* (London: Routledge, 1992), see especially ch. 2, '*Oroonoko*: Birth of a Paradigm', pp. 27–50.

2 Most of the details surrounding Behn's life are obscure. Leading Behn scholar Judith Todd candidly admits that 'What is securely known about Aphra Behn outside her works could be summed up in a page' (*The Secret Life of Aphra Behn*, p. 1), before going on to produce a five-hundred-page biography.

3 The passage is widely quoted by modern critics; cf. Clive T. Probyn, *English Fiction of the Eighteenth Century: 1700–1789* (London: Longman, 1987), p. 2. A complete version of *Incognita* may be found in the Oxford World's Classics *Anthology of Seventeenth-Century Fiction*, ed. Paul Salzman (1991).

4 For a full exposition of this concept, see 'The Violence of the Letter: From Lévi-Strauss to Rousseau', in Jacques Derrida, *Grammatology*, trans. Gayatri Chakravorty Spivak (Baltimore, Md.: Johns Hopkins University Press, 1976), pp. 101ff.

5 Quoted in *Novel and Romance 1700–1800: A Documentary Record*, ed. Ioan Williams (London: Routledge & Kegan Paul, 1970), pp. 100–1. Williams's collection is the indispensable guide to eighteenth-century concepts of fiction.

6 The unpromising full title is *The Progress of Romance, through Times, Countries and Manners; with Remarks on the Good and Bad Effects of It, on Them Respectively; in a Course of Evening Conversations*, 2 vols (Colchester, 1785). There is a modern Garland imprint (New York, 1974).

7 Laura Brown refers to some of these in her *Ends of Empire: Women and Ideology in Early Eighteenth-Century English Literature* (London: Cornell University Press), ch. 2, 'The Romance of Empire: *Oroonoko* and the Trade in Slaves', pp. 23–63. The quotation from Yearworth is on p. 45.

8 References to *Oroonoko* (hereafter incorporated in the text) are to Aphra Behn, *Oroonoko, The Rover and Other Works*, ed. Janet Todd (Harmondsworth: Penguin Books, 1992).

9 This is the kind of 'naive empiricism' theorized by McKeon and satirized by Swift.

10 The requisite (male!) *authority* for her detailed knowledge of the colony was long assumed to be George Warren's *Impartial Descriptions of*

Surinam, (1667); see Ernest Bernbaum's 'Mrs Behn's Biography, a Fiction', *PMLA* 28 (1913), pp. 432–53. The suggestions that Behn had never even been in Surinam have long been refuted.

11 See Gillian Beer, *The Romance* (London: Methuen, 1970); Thomas McDermott, *Epic and Romance: From the Odyssey to Tom Jones.*

12 The two writers of this name were brother and sister. Georges (1601–67) was principally a dramatist, although he seems to have had some hand in the long sentimental romances of his sister, Madeleine (1607–1701). The paradigmatic examples of the latter were *Le Grand Cyrus* (1649–53) and *Clélie* (1654–60), the chief objects of Lennox's satire in *The Female Quixote* (see Chapter 8).

13 The 'Parallel Lives' of Plutarch (*fl. AD* 65) comprised biographies of 23 Greeks and 23 Romans; the *Lettres portugaises* (1669), now generally thought to be the work of the Vicomte de Guilleragues (d. 1685), were ostensibly the five letters of Marianna Alcaforado, a Portuguese nun, to her lover, a French army officer.

14 The author of the vast prose romance *L'Astrée* (1607–27; concluded in 1628 by another hand) was Honoré D'Urfée (1567–1625).

15 Aphra Behn, *Oroonoko, The Rover and Other Works*, ed. Janet Todd (Harmondsworth: Penguin Books, 1992), p. 35.

16 The popular dramatization of her *novella* was in fact made by Thomas Southerne in 1695.

17 As in the case of Fielding, some of the most interesting writing on Defoe is found in the relevant sections of comparative studies of eighteenth-century fiction. There is nevertheless wide consensus on a select group of critical monographs over the last five decades; some of these are noted below. The most comprehensive biography is now Paula Backscheider's *Daniel Defoe: a Life* (Baltimore, Md.: Johns Hopkins University Press, 1990). Earlier studies stressing religious traditions behind Defoe are George Starr's *Defoe and Spiritual Biography* (Princeton, N.J.: Princeton University Press, 1965), and J. Paul Hunter's *The Reluctant Pilgrim: Defoe's Emblematic Method and Quest for Form in Robinson Crusoe* (Baltimore, Md.: Johns Hopkins University Press, 1966). Broader concerns are addressed in Maximillian E. Novak's *Defoe and the Nature of Man* (Oxford: Oxford University Press, 1965) and *Realism, Myth and History in Defoe's Fiction* (Lincoln: University of Nebraska Press, 1983); two equally useful monographs are John Richetti's *Defoe's Narratives: Situation and Structures* (Oxford: Oxford University Press, 1975) and the introductory *Daniel Defoe* (Boston: G. K. Hall, 1987). An important new dimension to Defoe criticism is offered by Lincoln Faller's *Crime and Defoe: A New Kind of Writing* (Cambridge: Cambridge University Press, 1993).

18 *The Life and Adventures of Robinson Crusoe* (London: Dent, 1966), pp. 149–50.

19 See J. Paul Hunter, *Before Novels: The Cultural Contexts of Eighteenth-Century English Fiction* (New York: Norton, 1990).

20 Page references to *Moll Flanders* (hereafter incorporated in the text) are to the Everyman edition (London: J. M. Dent, 1972).

21 P. N. Furbank and W. R. Owens, in their *Critical Bibliography of Daniel Defoe* (Oxford: Oxford University Press, 1998), make a convincing case for

dropping almost half of the 570 items in J. R. Moore's long standard *Checklist of the Writings of Daniel Defoe* (Bloomington: Indiana University Press, 1960).

22 John Sutherland, *The Best Seller* (London: Routledge & Kegan Paul, 1981).

23 The suggestion is slightly fanciful, of course, since – for Defoe's novel to qualify literally as ghost-writing – it would be necessary to prove both that Moll actually existed *and* that she supplied some version of her own story. Defoe nevertheless roused critical interest for his anticipation of techniques associated with Norman Mailer, Truman Capote and the American 'New Journalism' of the 1960s. See Mas'ud Zavarzadeh, *Mythopeic Reality: The Postwar American Nonfiction Novel* (Chicago: University of Illinois Press, 1976).

24 When Dryden edited a collection of Ovid's heroic epistles in translation, Behn insisted it be pointed out – with reference to her own contribution – that she knew no Latin. Quoted by Goreau, *Reconstructing Aphra*, p. 254.

25 This was founded by Charles Morton in 1672, since Oxford and Cambridge Universities were barred to those who did not belong to the Church of England.

26 On Defoe's education, see Paula Backscheider's *Daniel Defoe*, ch. 1: 'Fire and Plague', especially pp. 13–21.

27 Attempts to project Defoe as a pioneer of the classic realist novel tend to overlook the writer's satirical talents. Among his contemporaries, however, he was often best-known as author of the long satirical poem *The True-Born Englishman* (1701), and the even longer *Jure Divino: A Satyr in Twelve Books* (1706).

28 See the structure of Richetti's *Popular Fiction before Richardson: Narrative Patterns, 1700–1739* (Oxford: Oxford University Press, 1969/1992).

29 See the references to Starr and Hunter in note 17.

30 In addition to Zavarzadeh (note 23), see also John Hollowell's *Fact and Fiction: The New Journalism and the Nonfiction Novel* (Chapel Hill: University of North Carolina Press, 1977), and John Hellmann's *Fables of Fact: The New Journalism as New Fiction* (Chicago: University of Illinois Press, 1981).

31 The writings of Behn, Manley and Haywood are the particular subject of Ros Ballaster's *Seductive Forms: Women's Amatory Fiction from 1684 to 1740* (Oxford: Clarendon Press, 1992).

32 There are no indispensable monographs on Manley. The most helpful discussion is probably that in Ballaster's *Seductive Forms*, which considers her together with Haywood in ch. 4, 'As Long as Atalantis Shall be Read', pp. 119–67.

33 See the previous note. Mary Anne Schofield's *Masking and Unmasking the Female Mind* (Newark: University of Delaware Press, 1990) has interesting chapters on the early and late Haywood, respectively.

34 William McBurney's 'Mrs Penelope Aubin and the Early Eighteenth-Century English Novel', *Huntingdon Library Quarterly*, 20 (May 1957), pp. 245–67, was the pioneering essay on Aubin. Outside brief discussion by Richetti, there is a separate chapter in Mary Anne Schofield's *Masking and Unmasking the Female Mind*.

35   Barker has aroused additional critical interest because of the autobiograph-
     ical dimension of her fiction (e.g. Patricia Meyer Spacks's *Imagining a Self:
     Autobiography and Novel in Eighteenth-Century England*, 1976).

**Chapter 7   Laurence Sterne's *Tristram Shandy* and Tobias Smollett's
*Humphry Clinker***

1   The standard biography of Sterne is the two-volume study by Arthur H.
     Cash, *Laurence Sterne: The Early and Middle Years* (London: Methuen,
     1975) and *Laurence Sterne: The Later Years* (London: Methuen, 1986). As
     a study of philosophical undercurrents in Sterne, John Traugott's *Tristram
     Shandy's World: Sterne's Philosophical Rhetoric* (Berkeley, Cal.: University
     of California Press) is still useful. Melvyn New, general editor of the
     definitive Florida edition of Sterne's works, emphasizes the novelist's
     satirical dimension in *Laurence Sterne as Satirist: A Reading of Tristram
     Shandy* (Gainesville: University Presses of Florida, 1975). The most
     important more recent monograph is Jonathan Lamb's *Sterne's Fiction and
     the Double Principle* (Cambridge: Cambridge University Press, 1989).
     Lamb's emphasis on Sterne's ambivalent attitudes towards various
     eighteenth-century discourses also informs his essays in the *Cambridge
     Companion to the Eighteenth-Century Novel*, ed. John Richetti (1996) and
     The English Novel, Smollett to Austen, ed. Richard Kroll (Longman, 1998).
2   Sterne's *Political Romance, Addressed to* —— *Esq. of York* (York, 1759)
     was immediately repressed, although not before shaming the parties in a
     clerical dispute into agreement. Of *Tristram Shandy*, Volumes III and IV
     date from January 1761; V and VI from December 1761; VII and VIII
     from January 1765; the solitary Volume IX from January 1767. Although
     it is widely regarded as a completed work, there is little reason to doubt
     that – health and popularity permitting – Sterne could have continued
     Tristram Shandy indefinitely. See Wayne Booth. 'Did Sterne Complete
     Tristram Shandy?', *Modern Philology*, 48 (1951), pp. 163–85.
3   This was already noted by eighteenth-century readers and demonstrated at
     length by the antiquarian John Ferriar in his *Illustrations of Sterne* (1789).
4   A shrewd publisher actually reissued Dunton's *Voyage* in 1762 as *The Life,
     Travels, and Adventures of Christopher Wagstaff, Grandfather to Tristram
     Shandy*; Dunton is discussed at length in J. Paul Hunter's *Before Novels*,
     pp. 99–106.
5   Ephraim Chambers, *Cyclopaedia; or, An Universal Dictionary of Arts and
     Sciences*; Sterne used the second edition of 1738.
6   Quotations from *The Anatomy of Melancholy* are from the edition of Floyd
     Dell and Paul Jordan-Smith (New York: Tudor Publishing Company, n.d.).
7   Quotations from *Tristram Shandy* (by volume and chapter) are from the
     Oxford World's Classics edition, ed. Ian Campbell Ross (1983).
8   References to Dulcinea and the Enchanters are recurrent in *Don Quixote*.
     The Yanguesans appear in Part I, ch. 15; the ass is stolen in Part I, ch. 23,
     although a few pages later – in a famous Cervantean oversight – Sancho is
     riding it again.

9   The classic study of an English literary type with antecedents in *Don Quixote* is Stuart M. Tave's *The Amiable Humorist* (Chicago: University of Chicago Press, 1960).

10 See Ronald Paulson's *Don Quixote in England: The Aesthetics of Laughter* (Baltimore, Md.: Johns Hopkins University Press, 1998).

11 Northrop Frye, *Anatomy of Criticism: Four Essays* (Princeton, N.J.: Princeton University Press, 1957). 'Menippean satire' is discussed in the fourth essay, 'Rhetorical Criticism: Theory of Genres', pp. 309–12. See also George Sherbert's *Menippean Satire and the Poetics of Wit* (New York: Peter Lang, 1996). Menippus, a third-century BC Cynic philosopher from Syria, satirized (in Greek) the follies of mankind. His writings are lost, but are a major inspiration to the Greek writer Lucian (*c.* AD 115–80), invoked by Sterne.

12 See Felicity Nussbaum's essay 'Heteroclites: The Gender of Character in the Scandalous Memoirs', in *The New 18th Century*, ed. Felicity Nussbaum and Laura Brown (London: Methuen, 1987).

13 See Melvyn New's substantial essay on Sterne in the *DLB*, Vol. 39, Part II, pp. 471–99. This particular idea is developed at pp. 480ff.

14 Of the many excellent studies of sensibility, see e.g., Janet Todd, *Sensibility: An Introduction* (London: Methuen, 1986); and John Mullan, *Sentiment and Sociability: The Language of Feeling in the Eighteenth Century* (Oxford: Clarendon Press, 1988).

15 See Clive T. Probyn's *English Fiction of the Eighteenth Century* (Harlow, Essex: Longman, 1987), p. 134.

16 See Roy Porter's *English Society in the Eighteenth Century* (Harmondsworth: Penguin Books, 1990), especially ch. 7, 'Changing Experiences', pp. 276f.

17 For the story of Smollett's waning literary reputation, see Fred Boege's *Smollett's Reputation as a Novelist* (Princeton, N.J.: Princeton University Press, 1947). Smollett also suffers from a lack of informative critical monographs, although Paul-Gabriel Boucé's comprehensive *The Novels of Tobias Smollett* (New York: Longman, 1976) is still helpful; in the absence of full-length studies, G. S. Rousseau and P.-G. Boucé (eds), *Tobias Smollett: Bicentennial Essays* (New York: Oxford University Press, 1971) is useful. The following section also draws on my own *Constructions of Smollett: A Study of Genre and Gender* (Newark: University of Delaware Press, 1996).

18 The definitive biography is still Lewis M. Knapp's *Tobias Smollett: Doctor of Men and Manners* (Princeton, N.J.: Princeton University Press, 1949).

19 This is a classic issue of Smollett biography, discussed at length by Boucé and hotly contested by G. S. Rousseau in his *Tobias Smollett: Essays of Two Decades* (Edinburgh: T. & T. Clark, 1982).

20 The quotations from Smollett's works are taken from the Oxford World's Classics editions, except in the case of *Sir Launcelot Greaves* and *Ferdinand Count Fathom*, which rely on the Penguin Classics texts.

21 There is a short but helpful discussion of eighteenth-century travel guides to France and Italy in Frank Felsenstein's edition of the *Travels through France and Italy* (Oxford World's Classics, 1979).

22 See Philip Thicknesse's *Useful Hints to Those Who Make the Tour of France* (1768), p. 4; quoted by Felsenstein (see previous note), p. xii.

23 *Travels through France and Italy*, ed. Frank Felsenstein, p. 327.

24 *The Adventures of Ferdinand Count Fathom*, ed. Paul-Gabriel Boucé (Harmondsworth: Penguin Books, 1990), pp. 179–80.

25 The nineteenth letter actually includes 'Dr Smollett's' *Ode to Leven-Water*. In the course of his final exile in Italy, Smollett was to miss the inheritance of the family estate by a mere three years when he predeceased his cousin, the then incumbent, in September 1771.

26 Barbauld, *The British Novelists*, vol. xxx, p. 5.

27 See Sandra M. Gilbert and Susan Gubar, *The Madwoman in the Attic* (New Haven, Conn.: Yale University Press, 1979), p. 31.

28 Quoted by Katherine Rogers in *The Troublesome Helpmate: A History of Misogyny in Literature*, p. 39.

29 See Clara Whitmore's *Women's Work in English Fiction from the Restoration to the Mid-Victorian Period* (London: G. P. Putnam's, 1910), pp. 24–5.

30 See Felicity Nussbaum's essay 'Heteroclites: The Gender of Character in the Scandalous Memoirs', in *The New 18th Century*, ed. Felicity Nussbaum and Laura Brown (1987). The 'Memoirs of a Lady of Quality' in *Peregrine Pickle*, based on the historical Lady Vane (1715–88), were pre-empted by the lightly disguised fictional account of 'Sir' John Hill's *The Adventures of Lady Frail* (1751).

31 In this context, it is interesting to compare it with some of the comments assigned to Catherine Morland in *Northanger Abbey* (see Chapter 10).

32 The *Monthly Review* of December 1750 made this comment on *Peter Wilkins*; *John Buncle*, whose protagonist successfully courts a sequence of seven beautiful, rich, Unitarian women (who each die shortly after marriage), is – in many ways – an even stranger performance.

33 See note 11 above on Sterne, and Frye's *Anatomy of Criticism*.

34 Anthony Ashley Cooper, third Earl of Shaftesbury (1671–1713); Jean-Jacques Rousseau (1712–78). Shaftesbury's most influential work in this context was the 'Essay on Virtue', written in 1699 and published in his 'Characteristics of Men, Manners, Opinions, Times' (1711; revised 1713); Rousseau's voluminous treatise on education, *Émile*, was published in 1762.

35 In addition, the three volumes of the *Juvenilia* are virtually a satirical anatomy of sensibility.

36 Viktor Shklovsky's essay is collected in Lee T. Lemon and Marion J. Reis's *Russian Formalist Criticism: Four Essays* (Lincoln: Nebraska University Press, 1965).

37 See Robert Alter's *Partial Magic: The Novel as a Self-Conscious Genre* (Berkeley, Cal.: University of California Press, 1975).

38 The latter can be divided into the traditional soliloquy, the direct internal monologue, the indirect internal monologue and the 'omniscient' author's monologue; as Sterne's narrative *persona*, Tristram effectively represents the last of these variants.

39 Salman Rushdie, *Midnight's Children* (London: Jonathan Cape, 1981), p. 465.

40 I have discussed the question of Smollett and picaresque at length with particular reference to *Ferdinand Count Fathom* in *Constructions of Smollett*, pp. 119–24. In his *Literature and the Delinquent: The Picaresque Novel in*

Spain and Europe (Edinburgh: Edinburgh University Press, 1967), the noted Hispanist A. A. Parker cites *Fathom* as the classic example of English picaresque. There is a lively debate on the whole issue of definitions and terminology between the two Smollett scholars G. S. Rousseau and Paul-Gabriel Boucé, included in *Tobias Smollett: Essays of Two Decades* (1982).

41   There is a seminal essay by Claudio Guillén entitled 'Towards a Definition of the Picaresque', in his *Literature as System: Essays Towards the Theory of Literary History* (Princeton, N.J.: Princeton University Press, 1971).

42   For a broader discussion, see Adams's *Travel Literature and the Evolution of the Novel* (Lexington: University Press of Kentucky, 1983).

43   This was a widely understood division in eighteenth-century letters. Smollett, as successfully as anyone, reproduced the *'saeva indignatio'* [fierce indignation] of Juvenal, although *Humphry Clinker* also has more benign touches, worthy of Horace.

44   Quoted by Clive Probyn in *English Fiction of the Eighteenth Century, 1700–1789* (New York: Longman, 1987), p. 147.

45   Jeremy Hawthorne, in his *Concise Glossary of Literary Theory* (London: Edward Arnold, 1992), explains *skaz* as 'a mode or technique of narration that mirrors oral narrative', also quoting Ann Banfield's definition that it is 'the only type of literary first person narrative which clearly has a second person' (p. 166). As an example of the form, he cites Marlow's narrative in Joseph Conrad's *Heart of Darkness*.

Chapter 8   Charlotte Lennox's *The Female Quixote* and Frances Burney's *Evelina*

1   See *The Journals and Letters of Fanny Burney (Madame d'Arblay)*, ed. Joyce Hemlow and others, 12 vols (Oxford: Clarendon Press, 1972–84). English imitations of *Don Quixote*, on the other hand, are extensively discussed in Ronald Paulson's *Don Quixote in England: The Aesthetics of Laughter*.

2   Two older critical biographies of Lennox are Miriam Rosseter Small's *Charlotte Ramsay Lennox: An Eighteenth-Century Lady of Letters* (New Haven, Conn.: Yale University Press, 1935) and Gustavus Howard Maynadier's *The First American Novelist?* (Cambridge, Mass.: Harvard University Press, 1940). Newer criticism tends to be found in sections of longer works. Briefly discussed by Spencer (*The Rise of the Woman Novelist*), Spender (*Mothers of the Novel*) and Todd (*The Sign of Angellica*), *The Female Quixote* gets more extensive treatment in the first chapter of Patricia Meyer Spacks's *Desire and Truth: Functions of Plot in Eighteenth-Century Novels* (Chicago: University of Chicago Press, 1990), pp. 12–33. Other recent discussions appear in Catherine Gallagher's *Nobody's Story* (1990) and Mary Anne Schofield's *Masking and Unmasking the Female Mind* (1994).

3   On eighteenth-century readings, see Ronald Paulson's *Don Quixote in England* (1998) and Stuart Tave's far earlier *The Amiable Humorist* (1960).

4 Quotations from *The Female Quixote* (subsequently indicated in the text) are taken from the Oxford World's Classics edition, ed. Margaret Dalziel (1989).

5 Cervantes's digressions include an exemplary *novella*, 'The Tale of Foolish Curiosity' (Part I, chs 33–4), and a possibly autobiographical 'Captive's tale' (Part I, chs 39–41). Part I, ch. 6 ('The inquisition in the library'), on the other hand, is a parody *auto da fé*, from which a number of romances are pointedly spared. Chapter headings are taken from J. M. Cohen's translation (Penguin Books, 1950).

6 '...Three thousand Lines of an Epic Poem; half a Dozen Epitaphs; a few Acrostics; and a long String of Puns, that would serve to embellish a Daily Paper, if I was supposed to write one' (p. 252).

7 It was Johnson and his drinking companions of the Ivy Lane Club who arranged 'a whole night spent in festivity' to celebrate the completion of Lennox's first novel, *The Life of Harriot Stuart* (1750).

8 See the Appendix to the World's Classics edition, 'Johnson, Richardson and the *Female Quixote*', by Duncan Isles, p. 424.

9 In the World's Classics edition, Margaret Dalziel supplies a long note on the controversy over this chapter (Book VIII, ch. 11), admitting that the widely made attribution to Johnson 'remains a plausible theory' (p. 415); Duncan Isles, in his Appendix to the same edition, suggests more sceptically that the claim is 'by no means adequately supported' (p. 422).

10 *The Rambler*, no. 37 (24 July 1750).

11 The English prose translation of Baretti's twenty-six-line stanzas or *settinari* cannot quite do justice to the original:

> Alas what fatal powers, envious of the glories of British soil, suggest these thoughts to you, make you rebel against Phoebus and Love?
>
> . . .
>
> What? But I already divine the secret cause of all this waywardness. I know who it is would dissuade you from the beautiful road. I know, I know, who is opposed to me.
>
> Johnson, inflexible Englishman, who thinks a graceful nothing a sin and vice; who weighs for a month in the balance of his judgment every one of his own lines.
>
> Johnson, whose heart is full of austerities, whose head is filled with serious philosophy; who fears that an innocent feeling can only be the key to the temple of Priapus;
>
> Johnson, Johnson, it is he who has been at you with his terrible words, and I myself feel his austere voice lording it over my own mind and senses.
>
> Quoted by Miriam Rosseter Small in *Charlotte Lennox: An Eighteenth-Century Lady of Letters*, pp. 158–9

12 See, for example, the Introduction to Eagleton's *The Rape of Clarissa* (Oxford: Basil Blackwell, 1982), pp. 13f.

13 See the discussion of the new 'companionate marriage' running through Lawrence Stone, *The Family, Sex and Marriage in England, 1500–1800* (Harmondsworth: Penguin Books, 1979).

14 Jane Austen, *Mansfield Park*, ed. Tony Tanner (Harmondsworth: Penguin Books, 1966), p. 349.

15 On hearing that the seventeenth-century writer Scudéry is French, he dismisses him outright: 'I read no Authors, but the Ancients, Madam, added he, with a Look of Self-applause; I cannot relish the Moderns at all; I have no Taste for their Way of Writing' (p. 267). He had nevertheless just claimed to have found Scudéry (here, George, the brother of the more famous Madeleine) frequently quoted by ancient historians.

16 Of *Measure for Measure*, for example, she wished that Shakespeare 'had left the Fable simple and entire as it was without loading it with useless Incidents, unnecessary Characters, and absurd and improbable Intrigue' (quoted by Small, *Charlotte Ramsay Lennox*, p. 191).

17 The Burney bibliography is substantial. Major monographs include Margaret Anne Doody, *Frances Burney: The Life in the Works* (New Brunswick, N.J.: Rutgers University Press, 1988); Julia Epstein, *The Iron Pen: Francis Burney and the Politics of Women's Writing* (Madison: University of Wisconsin Press, 1989); Katherine Rogers, *Frances Burney: The World of Female Difficulties* (Hemel Hempstead: Harvester Wheatsheaf, 1990); Joanne Cutting-Grey, *Woman as 'Nobody' and the Novels of Fanny Burney* (Gainesville: University Presses of Florida, 1992). There are good chapters on Burney in Catherine Gallagher's *Nobody's Story* and Terry Castle's *Masquerade and Civilization*. Julia Epstein has contributed useful essays on Burney to both Richetti's *Cambridge Companion to the Eighteenth-Century Novel* and Richard Kroll's *The English Novel: Smollett to Austen*.

18 See note 1 to this chapter.

19 References (incorporated in the text) are to the Oxford World's Classics edition (1982), ed. Edward A. Bloom.

20 Walter Allen, *The English Novel: A Short Critical History* (Harmondsworth: Penguin Books, 1958), p. 94.

21 To escape religious persecution, Rousseau actually spent a year in England (1766–7), the year before Burney began her diary.

22 '. . . if you happen to have any learning, keep it a profound secret, especially from the men, who generally look with a jealous and malignant eye on a woman of great parts, and a cultivated understanding' (from Dr John Gregory's 'A Father's Legacy to his Daughters', 1774); quoted with other such gems by Vivien Jones (ed.), *Women in the Eighteenth Century: Constructions of Femininity* (London: Routledge, 1990), p. 46.

23 See, for example, Nancy Armstrong's *Desire and Domestic Fiction*, especially Section 2, 'The Rise of the Domestic Woman', pp. 59–95.

24 Manley ran the satirical *Female Tatler* in 1709, and briefly took over Swift's editorial post on the *Examiner* in 1711.

25 Eugenia Tyrold in *Camilla*, when given the opportunity to study the classics, easily outstrips her male cousin, Clermont Lynmere, in an interesting anticipation of Tom and Maggie Tulliver in George Eliot's *The Mill on the Floss*.

26 The story is told by Margaret Doody in *Frances Burney: The Life in the Works*, p. 241.

27 Margaret Doody describes the rejection of the play by the novelist's father and a family friend, Samuel 'Daddy' Crisp ('the two cooks who spoiled her

broth', *Frances Burney*, p. 71): their negative reactions were grounded in fears that the play's satire could give offence to luminaries of London's literary world.

28 Doody, *Frances Burney*, p. 73.

29 Quoted by Doody, *Frances Burney*, p. vii and p. viii, respectively.

30 Allen, *The English Novel*, p. 94.

31 The following passage is fairly representative:

> We are to go this evening to a private ball, given by Mrs. Stanley, a very fashionable lady of Mrs. Mirvan's acquaintance.
> We have been *a shopping*, as Mrs. Mirvan calls it, all this morning, to buy silks, caps, gauzes, and so forth.   (p. 27)

32 See Ronald Paulson's *Don Quixote in England: The Aesthetics of Laughter* (1998) for some account of this family. Austen's comments on Lennox and Eaton Stannard Barrett are discussed in Chapter 10.

33 See Vivien Jones's invaluable anthology, *Women in the Eighteenth Century: Constructions of Femininity*, collecting contemporary views under the four headings of 'Conduct', 'Sexuality', 'Education' and 'Writing'. The pieces in the third section are particularly suggestive here.

34 See note 12 to this chapter.

35 See Katherine Sobba Green's *The Courtship Novel, 1740–1820* (Lexington: University Press of Kentucky, 1991).

36 Green, ibid., p. 5; Mikhail Bakhtin, *The Dialogic Imagination*, trans. Caryl Emerson and Michael Holquist (Austin: University of Texas Press, 1981).

37 Collyer is also interesting for her translation of Marivaux's influential *Vie de Marianne* – a possible stimulus for both Fielding and Richardson – as *The Virtuous Orphan* (1742).

38 An epistolary novel, like its predecessor *The History of Julia Mandeville* (1763), *Emily Montague* is nevertheless as interesting for its Quebec setting as for its young heroine: Brooke spent five years in Canada with her army-chaplain husband and her second novel is often heralded as Canada's first.

Chapter 9   Ann Radcliffe's *The Mysteries of Udolpho* and William Godwin's *Caleb Williams*

1 There are relatively few monographs on Radcliffe, but note David Durant's *Ann Radcliffe's Novels: Experiments in Setting* (New York: Arno, 1980), and Robert Miles's *Ann Radcliffe: The Great Enchantress* (Manchester: Manchester University Press, 1995). The author is obviously central, on the other hand, in more general studies of the Gothic, some of which are discussed at the end of this chapter. Other seminal essays in collections include Terry Castle's 'The Spectralization of the Other in *The Mysteries of Udolpho*', in Felicity Nussbaum and Laura Brown (eds), *The New Eighteenth Century: Theory, Politics, English Literature* (London: Methuen, 1987) and Margaret Doody's 'Deserts, Ruins and Troubled Waters: Female Dreams in Fiction and the Development of the Gothic Novel', in

Richard Kroll (ed.), *The English Novel: Smollett to Austen* (Harlow, Essex: Longman, 1998).

2 Walpole, together with the Lee sisters and Clara Reeve (the latter as both critic and practitioner), is discussed further at the end of this chapter.

3 The action moves from Roussillon and the French Mediterranean coast to the Alps at Mont Cenis and Italy beyond: Piedmont (Novalesa and Sousa to Turin), Lombardy (Milan with its 'vast cathedral . . . then building'), to Venice (with subsequent descriptions of Palladian villas on the Brenta).

4 This journey moves through Tuscany (Florence, Pisa) to Livorno (Leghorn), over the Gulf of Lyons to Marseilles, and later Narbonne, before returning to Château-le-Blanc on the banks of the Aude.

5 These are the countries described in Radcliffe's one, more explicit, contribution to travel literature: *A Journey made in the Summer of 1794 through Holland and the Western Frontier of Germany* (1795). Due to a bureaucratic tangle, the journey ended at the Swiss border.

6 The sublime landscapes of Rosa (1615–73) are probably Radcliffe's greatest visual inspiration, although the novelist also alludes to the 'dark pencil' (p. 30) of Rosa's countryman and compatriot, Domenichino (1581–1641).

7 Piozzi's *Observations and Reflections made in the Course of a Journey through France, Italy and Germany* are demonstrably the source for Radcliffe's descriptions of Venice.

8 Shakespeare has a clear ascendancy, with twenty-one quotations, followed at some distance by the eighteenth-century poet Thomson, with nine, and Milton with five. Lesser eighteenth-century figures such as Collins, Beattie and Mason (with two or three quotations each) confirm a conventional eighteenth-century literary sensibility.

9 The concept of intertextuality is particularly associated with the Bulgarian-born French theorist Julia Kristeva. Jeremy Hawthorne (*A Concise Glossary of Contemporary Literary Theory*, 1992) helpfully quotes Kristeva's definition from *Desire in Language* (Oxford: Blackwell, 1980): 'a permutation of texts, an intertextuality: in the space of a given text, several utterances taken from other texts, intersect and neutralize each other'.

10 What Radliffe describes as the 'latent powers of her fortitude' (p. 379) seem to be secular – a belief in the law and the 'justice of her cause' – rather than emphatically Christian, as in the case of Clarissa.

11 This important insight is developed by Canadian critic and theorist Linda Hutcheon in *A Theory of Parody: The Teachings of Twentieth-Century Art Forms* (London: Methuen, 1984). See, in particular, Ch. 2, 'Defining Parody', p. 32.

12 Beginning with a remarkable unaided flight to the polar regions, this novel is effectively a precursor of twentieth-century 'magical realism'.

13 Quotations from *The Mysteries of Udolpho* are from the Oxford World's Classics edition (Oxford, 1966), ed. Bonamy Dobrée.

14 This is the supernatural tale of *Sir Bevys* in Vol. IV, ch. 6.

15 It was not until the Married Women's Property Act of 1857 that a married woman had any control over her own fortune. If Radcliffe's novel is an indirect critique of women's position, then Godwin – at the other end of the political spectrum – questions the concept of private property for either sex.

16 A seminal study exemplifying this approach is Peter Brooks's *Reading for the Plot: Design and Intention in Narrative* (New York: Random House, 1985).

17 The quotation is the main title of D. A. Miller's *Narrative and its Discontents: Problems of Closure in the Traditional Novel* (Princeton, N.J.: Princeton University Press, 1981).

18 Although all three authors wrote in French, the materialist and atheist Baron d'Holbach (1723–89), author of the *Système de la Nature* (1770), was German, while philosopher and novelist Jean-Jacques Rousseau (1712–78) was Swiss. Only the thinker Claude-Adrien Helvetius (1715–71) was, despite his name, originally French.

19 The most comprehensive biography is Peter H. Marshall's *William Godwin* (New Haven: Yale University Press, 1984). As with Radcliffe, monographs on the fiction are few, although B. J. Tysdahl's *William Godwin as Novelist* (London: Athlone Press, 1981) is helpful. All the more important, however, are the separate chapters or essays in more general studies, including: Robert Kiely, *The Romantic Novel in England* (Cambridge, Mass.: Harvard University Press, 1972); Gary Kelly, *The English Jacobin Novel, 1780–1805* (New York: Oxford University Press, 1976); Marilyn Butler, *Romantics, Rebels and Reactionaries: English Literature and its Background, 1760–1830* (London: Oxford University Press, 1981/1995).

20 References to *Caleb Williams* (hereafter incorporated into the text) are to the Penguin Classics edition, ed. Maurice Hindle, with its particularly helpful appendices on the original ending of the novel, Godwin's account of its composition (in the Preface to *Fleetwood*) and the author's previously unpublished essay 'Of History and Romance' (discussed below).

21 These include the 'Adventures of Mademoiselle de St Phale' (the story of a persecuted French Huguenot) and J. Reynolds's *God's Revenge against Murder* (an account of divine retribution for the guilty).

22 Godwin had regularly visited the same prison to see his friend Joseph Gerrald, awaiting transportation for political activism.

23 In addition, the early rivalry between Falkland and Tyrrel may owe something to that between the hero and Sir Hargrave Pollexfen in *Grandison*.

24 See Gerald A. Barker's *Grandison's Heirs: The Paragon's Progress in the Late Eighteenth-Century Novel* (Newark: University of Delaware Press, 1985).

25 Justice Underwood thus indignantly opposes the idea of tenants voting of their own free will, which would 'deprive [landlords] for ever of the power of managing any election' (p. 71); whilst the anonymous magistrate in Volume III foresees an end to all order and good government, 'if fellows that trample upon ranks and distinctions . . . were upon any consideration suffered to get off' (p. 286). The passages might have come from Fielding.

26 This classicizing tendency clearly correlates with the gendering of eighteenth-century literary forms attempted in Chapter 3, reflecting the wide educational gulf normally found between male authors and female novelists. And even on the unlikely assumption that a female novelist might possess a classical education, she would be unlikely to dismiss an elderly housekeeper as a 'swarthy sybil' – a conventional enough male epithet for a woman fallen both socially and sexually beneath consideration.

27 Louis-Dominique Bourguignon (1693–1721), the son of a Paris wine-merchant and known popularly as *Cartouche*, was the leader of a famous

band of robbers. *Guzmán de Alfarache* (1603) was a long picaresque novel by the Spanish writer Mateo Alemán (1547–1613?).

28 'Mirror-text' is sometimes used to translate the French expression, *mise-en-abîme*, referring to the kind of 'interior duplication' found in heraldry, where a complete design is reproduced in miniature on one particular section of a coat-of-arms.

29 For example, 'That catastrophe I shall shortly have occasion to relate' (p. 82), or 'I shall come soon enough to the story of my own misery' (p. 129).

30 Emily St Aubert had incidentally mastered what, in the 1590s, must have been one of the less 'polite' European languages: English!

31 From the preface to the 1832 edition of *Fleetwood* (Appendix to Penguin Classics edition of *Caleb Williams*), p. 351.

32 He says: 'To avoid confusion in my narrative, I shall drop the person of Collins, and assume to be myself the historian of our patron' (p. 11).

33 A number of details in the novel, such as the unexpressed thoughts of Falkland's footman, Thomas (p. 210), or the intimate history of Gines (*passim*), are in fact difficult to reconcile with the *a priori* limited knowledge of Godwin's first-person intradiegetic narrator.

34 The comparison draws on a traditional formal division (fabula *vs.* suzhet, histoire *vs.* discours, story *vs.* discourse), which contrasts a presumed objective narrative core with all the rhetorical devices used in its presentation.

35 Published in the *New Monthly Magazine and Literary Journal*, n.s., 16 (1826).

36 The reference is to the influential essay by the Irish political philosopher Edmund Burke (1729–97), entitled *A Philosophical Enquiry into the Origin of our Ideas of the Sublime and the Beautiful* (1757).

37 See Maurice Hindle's Penguin Classics edition of *Caleb Williams* for the full text.

38 David Punter, *The Literature of Terror: The Gothic Tradition*, 2nd edition, 2 vols (London: Longman, 1980). See also Robert Miles, *Gothic Writing, 1750–1820* (London: Routledge, 1993); Maggie Kilgour, *The Rise of the Gothic Novel* (London: Methuen, 1995); and Fred Botting, *Gothic* (London: Edward Arnold, 1996).

39 See *Ferdinand Count Fathom*, chs 20–1, a section leaning decidedly closer to 'horror' than to 'terror'.

40 Even on a purely economic level, Radcliffe received due recognition for her writing. The copyright fees for *The Mysteries of Udolpho* and *The Italian* were £500 and £800, respectively. See, for example, Cheryl Turner, *Living by the Pen: Women Writers in the Eighteenth Century* (London: Routledge, 1992).

41 See Anne Williams, *Art of Darkness: A Poetics of Gothic* (Chicago: Chicago University Press, 1995), p. xiii.

Chapter 10 Jane Austen's *Northanger Abbey* and *Mansfield Park*

1 Biographical issues regarding Austen can usually be resolved with reference to R. W. Chapman's frequently reprinted *Jane Austen: Facts and Problems*

(Oxford: Clarendon Press, 1970). Two reliable modern biographies are John Halperin's *The Life of Jane Austen* (Brighton, Sussex: Harvester Press, 1984), and Park Honan's *Jane Austen: Her Life* (London: Oxford University Press, 1988).

2 All of the comments on Austen may be found in the two Jane Austen volumes (ed. B. C. Southam) of the Critical Heritage series (London: Routledge and Kegan Paul, 1968–87). The Scott quotation is from the writer's *Journal* (ed. J. G. Tait), p. 135.

3 George Steiner, *After Babel* (London: Oxford University Press, 1975), pp. 8–9.

4 Walton Litz's comments occur in his essay on the *Juvenilia* (pp. 1–6) in *Jane Austen's Beginnings: The Juvenilia and Lady Susan*, ed. J. David Grey (Ann Arbor: University of Michigan Research, 1989).

5 The twenty-nine pieces forming the *Juvenilia* survived in the Austen family in manuscripts labelled *Volume the First*, *Volume the Second* and *Volume the Third*. They are now most readily available in the Oxford World's Classics edition (1993), ed. Margaret Anne Doody and Douglas Murray.

6 Page references are to the Oxford World's Classics edition of *Northanger Abbey* (1998; together with *Lady Susan*, *The Watsons* and *Sanditon*), ed. John Davies.

7 The case for Jane Austen as conservative, if not reactionary, is well made in Marilyn Butler's *Jane Austen and the War of Ideas* (Oxford: Clarendon Press, 1975; rev. edn 1987). The most convincing of the countless presentations of Austen as a proto-feminist radical is Claudia L. Johnson's *Jane Austen: Women, Politics and the Novel* (London: University of Chicago Press, 1988). Ideologically between the two – and perhaps the single most accessible critical monograph on Austen – is Tony Tanner's *Jane Austen* (Cambridge, Mass.: Harvard University Press, 1986).

8 The quotation is from the introduction to the revised edition of *Jane Austen and the War of Ideas*, p. xxxi. On the older tradition of Tory women's writing, see Janet Todd's *The Sign of Angellica* (London: Virago Press, 1989), pp. 16–19 and 85–6.

9 See *Jane Austen: Selected Letters, 1796–1817*, ed. R. W. Chapman, intro. Marilyn Butler (Oxford: Oxford University Press, 1955/1985). For *The Female Quixote*, see p. 48; for *The Heroine*, see p. 155.

10 See Watt's assessment of Austen in *The Rise of the Novel*, pp. 337–40; this particular comment is at p. 338.

11 See Watt's extended discussion in *The Rise of the Novel*, pp. 298–305.

12 Quotations from the Oxford World's Classics edition of *Persuasion*, ed. John Davie (1998), pp. 29–30.

13 Henry Fielding, *Shamela* (Oxford World's Classics edition), p. 331.

14 Particularly suggestive in this context is the opening chapter ('The Comfort of Civilization') in Franco Moretti's *The Way of the World: The Bildungsroman in European Culture* (London: Verso, 1988).

15 See Booth's 'Control of Distance in Jane Austen's "Emma"', Part II, ch. 9 of *The Rhetoric of Fiction*, 2nd edn (Chicago: University of Chicago Press, 1983).

16 This theme is developed in Tanner's *Jane Austen*, ch. 5, 'The Quiet Thing: *Mansfield Park*', pp. 142–75.

17 See note 28, on this device in *Caleb Williams*, in Chapter 9. See also Bruce Morrissette's essay 'Interior Duplication', in *Novel and Film: Essays in Two Genres* (Chicago: University of Chicago Press, 1985).

18 Three modern studies are invaluable here: Roy Pascall's *The Dual Voice* (Manchester: Manchester University Press, 1977) actually quotes passages of free indirect discourse in *Sense and Sensibility* and *Mansfield Park*. A more detailed treatment of the device appears in Dorrit Cohn's *Transparent Minds. Narrative Modes for Presenting Consciousness in Fiction* (Princeton: Princeton University Press, 1978), where FID is concerned with the representation of *thoughts* as much as *speech*, hence Cohn's useful term, 'psycho-narration'. The most theoretically demanding discussion of FID, finally, is Ann Banfield's *Unspeakable Sentences: Narration and Representation in the Language of Fiction* (London: Routledge and Kegan Paul, 1982). Banfield also refers to Bally's original suggestion (1912) that *free indirect discourse* 'derives from an increasingly marked tendency of literary language to approximate the processes of the spoken language'.

19 See Shlomith Rimmon-Kenan's *Narrative Fiction: Contemporary Poetics* (London: Methuen, 1983), pp. 110–16. Jeremy Hawthorn's one-page entry on FID in his *Concise Glossary of Contemporary Literary Theory* (1992) is also exemplary in its clarity.

20 Margaret Anne Doody notes the significance of FID in Burney, both in her *DLB* essay on the writer and in her full-length study, *Frances Burney: The Life in the Works* (New Brunswick: Rutges University Press, 1988).

21 This example is also discussed by Pascall. Fielding claimed in a footnote to the second edition that he had been criticized here for imputing to Adams's host learning he had never demonstrated, but he nevertheless refused to amend the passage. It is no oversight, however, but an early example of free indirect speech, together with some characteristic gentle ribbing on the author's part.

22 See note 45, on *skaz*, in Chapter 7.

23 For the analysis of *Mansfield Park*, see Pascall, *The Dual Voice*, pp. 49ff.

Select Bibliography

The following list is arranged for the sake of convenience into five self-explanatory categories. There are further reading suggestions in the notes for each of the writers discussed more fully in Part II, together with references to other secondary sources. The number of scholars represented in this bibliography has been pointedly limited to fifty, i.e. one less than the pool of novelists provided by Mrs Barbauld and the *DLB*.

1 Collections and Anthologies of Primary Material

Backscheider, Paula R., and John J. Richetti (1996), *Popular Fiction by Women, 1660–1830: An Anthology* (Oxford: Oxford University Press).
Jones, Vivien (ed.) (1990), *Women in the Eighteenth Century: Constructions of Femininity* (London: Routledge).
Williams, Ioan (ed.) (1970), *Novel and Romance, 1700–1800: A Documentary Record* (London: Routledge and Kegan Paul).

2 Collections of Critical Essays

Damrosch, Leopold, Jr (1988), *Modern Essays on Eighteenth-Century Literature* (Oxford: Oxford University Press).
Kroll, Richard (ed.) (1998), *The English Novel*, vol. 1: *1700 to Fielding* (Harlow, England: Longman).
—— (ed.) (1998), *The English Novel*, vol. 2: *Smollett to Austen* (Harlow, England: Longman).
Richetti, John (ed.) (1994), *The Columbia History of the Novel* (New York: Columbia University Press).
—— (ed.) (1996), *The Cambridge Companion to the Eighteenth-Century Novel* (Cambridge: Cambridge University Press).
Schofield, Mary Anne and Cecilia Macheski (eds) (1986), *Fetter'd or Free? British Women Novelists* (Athens: Ohio University Press).

3 Theoretical and Comparative Studies of the Novel

Alliston, April (1996), *Virtue's Faults: Correspondences in Eighteenth-Century British and French Women's Fiction* (Stanford: Stanford University Press).

Armstrong, Nancy (1987), *Desire and Domestic Fiction: A Political History of the Novel* (Oxford: Oxford University Press).

Ballaster, Ros (1992), *Seductive Forms: Women's Amatory Fiction from 1684 to 1740* (Oxford: Clarendon Press).

Bender, John (1987), *Imagining the Penitentiary: Fiction and the Architecture of the Mind in Eighteenth-Century England* (Chicago: University of Chicago Press).

Castle, Terry (1986), *Masquerade and Civilization: The Carnivalesque in Eighteenth-Century English Culture and Fiction* (Stanford: Stanford University Press).

Davis, Lennard J. (1983), *Factual Fictions: The Origins of the English Novel* (New York: Columbia University Press).

Day, Robert Adams (1966), *Told in Letters: Epistolary Fiction Before Richardson* (Ann Arbor: University of Michigan Press).

Doody, Margaret Anne (1998), *The True Story of the Novel* (London: Fontana Press).

Gallagher, Catherine (1994), *Nobody's Story: The Vanishing Acts of Women Writers in the Market Place, 1670–1820* (Oxford: Clarendon Press).

Hunter, J. Paul (1990), *Before Novels: The Cultural Contexts of Eighteenth-Century English Fiction* (New York: W. W. Norton).

Johnson, Claudia L. (1995), *Equivocal Beings: Politics, Gender, and Sentimentality in the 1790s: Wollstonecraft, Radcliffe, Burney, Austen* (Chicago: University of Chicago Press).

Kelly, Gary (1976), *The English Jacobin Novel, 1780–1805* (Oxford: Clarendon Press).

—— (1993), *Women, Writing and Revolution, 1790–1827* (Oxford: Clarendon Press).

McKeon, Michael (1987), *The Origins of the English Novel, 1600–1740* (Baltimore: Johns Hopkins University Press).

Paulson, Ronald (1967), *Satire and the Novel in Eighteenth-Century England* (New Haven: Yale University Press).

—— (1998), *Don Quixote in England: The Aesthetics of Laughter* (Baltimore: Johns Hopkins University Press).

Poovey, Mary (1984), *The Proper Lady and the Woman Writer: Ideology as Style in the Works of Mary Wollstonecraft, Mary Shelley and Jane Austen* (Chicago: University of Chicago Press).

Punter, David (1988), *The Literature of Terror: The Gothic Tradition*, 2nd edn, 2 vols (London: Routledge).

Rawson, Claude (1994), *Satire and Sentiment, 1660–1830* (Cambridge: Cambridge University Press).

Richetti, John J. (1969), *Popular Fiction Before Richardson: Narrative Patterns, 1700–1739* (Oxford: Clarendon Press).

Schofield, Mary Anne (1990), *Masking and Unmasking the Female Mind* (Newark: University of Delaware Press).

Spacks, Patricia Meyer (1976), *Imagining a Self: Autobiography and the Novel in Eighteenth-Century England* (Cambridge, Mass: Harvard University Press).

—— (1990), *Desire and Truth: Functions of Plot in Eighteenth-Century Novels* (Chicago: University of Chicago Press).

Spencer, Jane (1986), *The Rise of the Woman Novelist* (Oxford: Basil Blackwell).

Thompson, James (1996), *Models of Value: Eighteenth-Century Political Value and the Novel* (London: Duke University Press).

Todd, Janet (1986), *Sensibility, An Introduction* (London: Methuen).

—— (1989), *The Sign of Angellica: Women, Writing and Fiction, 1660–1800* (London: Virago, 1989).

Turner, Cheryl (1992), *Living by the Pen: Women Writers in the Eighteenth Century* (London: Routledge).

Warner, William (2000), *Licensing Entertainment: The Elevation of Novel-Reading in Britain, 1684–1750* (Berkeley: University of California Press).

Watt, Ian (1957), *The Rise of the Novel: Studies in Defoe, Richardson and Fielding* (London: Chatto and Windus).

Williams, Anne (1995), *Art of Darkness: A Poetics of Gothic* (Chicago: University of Chicago Press).

4   Studies of Single Authors

Battestin, Martin (1959), *The Moral Basis of Fielding's Art: A Study of* Joseph Andrews (Middleton, Conn.: Wesleyan University Press).

Butler, Marilyn (1975; rev. 1987), *Jane Austen and the War of Ideas* (Oxford: Clarendon Press).

Campbell, Jill (1995), *Natural Masques: Gender and Identity in Fielding's Plays and Novels* (Stanford: Stanford University Press).

Castle, Terry (1982), *Clarissa's Cyphers: Meaning and Disruption in Richardson's* Clarissa (Ithaca: Cornell University Press).

Doody, Margaret Anne (1974), *A Natural Passion: A Study of the Novels of Samuel Richardson* (Oxford: Clarendon Press).

Eagleton, Terry (1982), *The Rape of Clarissa: Writing, Sexuality and Class Struggle in Samuel Richardson* (Oxford: Basil Blackwell).

Epstein, Julia (1989), *The Iron Pen: Francis Burney and the Politics of Women's Writing* (Madison: University of Wisconsin Press).

Faller, Lincoln D. (1993), *Crime and Defoe: A New Kind of Writing* (Cambridge: Cambridge University Press).

Hunter, J. Paul (1966), *The Reluctant Pilgrim: Defoe's Emblematic Method and Quest for Form in* Robinson Crusoe (Baltimore: Johns Hopkins University Press).

Hunter, J. Paul (1975), *Occasional Form: Henry Fielding and the Chains of Circumstance* (Baltimore: Johns Hopkins University Press).

Johnson, Claudia L. (1988), *Jane Austen: Women, Politics and the Novel* (London: University of Chicago Press).

Lamb, Jonathan (1989), *Sterne's Fiction and the Double Principle* (Cambridge: Cambridge University Press).

Rawson, Claude (1972), *Henry Fielding and the Augustan Ideal under Stress* (London: Routledge).

Richetti, John (1975), *Defoe's Narratives: Situations and Structures* (Oxford: Oxford University Press).

Skinner, John (1996), *Constructions of Smollett: A Study in Genre and Gender* (Newark: University of Delaware Press).

Tanner, Tony (1986), *Jane Austen* (Cambridge: Harvard University Press).

Todd, Janet (1988), *The Critical Fortunes of Aphra Behn* (London: Camden House).

Tysdahl, B. J. (1981), *William Godwin as Novelist* (London: Athlone Press).

Warner, William (1979), *Reading* Clarissa: *The Struggles of Interpretation* (New Haven: Yale University Press).

5 Major Critical Biographies

Backscheider, Paula (1990), *Daniel Defoe: A Life* (Baltimore: Johns Hopkins University Press).

Battestin, Martin and Ruth Battestin (1989), *Henry Fielding: A Life* (London: Routledge).

Cash, Arthur H. (1975), *Laurence Sterne: The Early and Middle Years* (London: Methuen).

Cash, Arthur H. (1986), *Laurence Sterne: The Later Years* (London: Methuen).

Doody, Margaret Anne (1988), *Frances Burney: The Life in the Works* (New Brunswick: Rutgers University Press).

Eaves, T., C. Duncan, and Ben Kimpel (1971), *Samuel Richardson: A Biography* (Oxford: Clarendon Press, 1971).

Honan, Park (1988), *Jane Austen: Her Life* (London: Oxford University Press).

Knapp, Lewis M. (1949), *Tobias Smollett: Doctor of Men and Manners* (Princeton: Princeton University Press, 1949).

Marshall, Peter. H. (1984), *William Godwin* (New Haven: Yale University Press).

Miles, Robert (1995), *Ann Radcliffe: The Great Enchantress* (Manchester: Manchester University Press).

Rosseter, Miriam (1935), *Charlotte Ramsay Lennox: An Eighteenth-Century Lady of Letters* (New Haven: Yale University Press).

Todd, Judith (1996), *The Secret Life of Aphra Behn* (London: Virago).

Index